ON PERFECTION

First published in the UK in 2013 by
Intellect, The Mill, Parnall Road, Fishponds, Bristol, BS16 3JG, UK

First published in the USA in 2013 by
Intellect, The University of Chicago Press, 1427 E. 60th Street, Chicago, IL 60637, USA

A catalogue record for this book is available from the
British Library.

Cover designer: Holly Rose
Production Manager: Bethan Ball
Copy-editor: Michael Eckhardt
Typesetting: Stephanie Sarlos
Series Editor: Alfredo Cramerotti

ISBN 978-1-84150-710-1
Critical Photography Series ISSN 2041-8345

Printed & bound by Gwasg Gomer Cyf / Gomer Press Ltd, UK

ON PERFECTION

AN ARTISTS' SYMPOSIUM

EDITED BY JO LONGHURST

intellect Bristol, UK / Chicago, USA

CONTENTS

INTRODUCTION

This publication celebrates a two-day symposium, 'On Perfection', which took place at the Whitechapel Gallery, London on 2nd–3rd February 2012. Staged as a cultural response to the Olympics, the event provided a timely opportunity to question how an idea of perfection informs both historical and contemporary practices in photography and film; and how these in turn shape our experience of being in the world.

When I originally conceived this project, I was keen to explore how we engage with ideas of perfection, and also to identify what those ideas might be – the term perfection having many connotations: physical, moral, practical and aesthetic. To this end, I invited a group of artists and writers whose eclectic lens-based practices engage or disrupt ideas of perfection to question how these ideas shape our personal identities and our social and political systems.

During programming, numerous other questions surfaced, including a central conundrum around the relation of the notion of perfection to a work of art. Indeed, is there such a thing as a perfect work of art? And, if such a thing exists, how might we recognize it? Might it involve immaculate construction, perfect technique, a capturing of the decisive moment? Or is a perfect artwork something more elusive, intangible, sublime? Are perfectionist tendencies in the maker a necessary prerequisite for a perfect artwork? Or, conversely, is the idea of perfection sterile? Do contemporary artists prefer to embrace chance happenings, accidents, imperfections in form or technique to grasp the essence of an idea, or to open up new ways of thinking?

Attempts to grapple with such fundamental questions on ideas of perfection in contemporary practice, and in the context of our cultural and political heritage, provided a starting point for the magnificently diverse contributions to this volume.

Although there was a sporting thread to the symposium – original footage of Riefenstahl's Olympia and her discussion with director Ray Müller of both her innovative filming techniques, and her relationship with the Nazi elite; Douglas Gordon and Philippe Parreno's sublime anti-heroic portrait of Zidane, 'the total footballer';

Jane and Louise Wilson's study of the legacy of a eugenic fitness regime; and my own work with elite gymnasts in training and competition – the programme embraced a much broader variety of subject matter and interpretation, which encouraged lively debate around key issues of relevance to contemporary lens-based practices.

The symposium included papers, screenings, artist talks, performances, conversation, new works by emerging artists, and presentations from international guests. Unlike many events of this kind, the emphasis was on contributions which foregrounded the voice of the artist, rather than that of the theorist or art historian. Observations and ideas provoked by the presentations were skilfully opened up to debate by specially invited chairs, who made their own connections between the presentations and initiated discussion with our lively audience – some of which is reproduced here. The contributions in this volume are presented in the same order as the original programme, with each pairing crafted to bring out a particular aspect of this multifaceted and complex concept. The rich variety of original imagery is complimented by both formal and informal texts to best reflect the eclectic mix of the live event. The symposium concluded with a panel discussion with all participants led by Charlotte Cotton, to whom I am most grateful for helping us to draw out new thinking, and for imbuing the event with such emotionally intelligent humour, spirit and energy.

It is almost impossible to replicate such a rich experience in a book. The event had an invigorating atmosphere of openness and of genuine enquiry, a particular energy which is inevitably diluted as words and images are committed to a page. However, this volume offers a taster of the ideas and discussions initiated at the symposium 'On Perfection', which I hope will continue to resonate through future artworks, writing and debate.

Jo Longhurst, editor

THE SPACE IN THE MIDDLE

THE (SERIES) EDITOR TO THE READER

A somersault is obviously not the end of a process. It's not even the beginning of the end. It's a spatial-temporal state in between. Much like a film, lecture, or artwork, it's the beginning of an experiment in continuous jumps between past, present and future, connecting different spaces at the same time. Abstracting it further, it may be considered a physical and visual metaphor for a non-linear concept of history.

As cultural producers, athletes as well as artists (and those working along with them) have to think of a way to produce a collective experience that allows for different histories. An idea of history that doesn't command me to follow the line, and that allows me to start from the middle, like in a perfect, virtual somersault. It's not uncommon for athletes and artists to construct space-time 'realities' in that undefined realm where spectators, and participants can experience the dialogue with different 'systems' (of sport or cultural disciplines), time structures (when time seems *really* to slow down to a standstill) and mechanisms of representation (like the Olympics, or a biennial).

It is as if they work to keep humanity in a state of permanent reformulation.

Alfredo Cramerotti, editor, 'Critical Photography' series

A NOTE FROM OUR SPONSOR

Hiscox enjoys an ongoing commitment to the arts. Art covers almost every wall in our offices and is an integral part of the culture of our company. We are not only major insurers of art, but, for over fifty years, we have been collectors and enablers of it as well. It gives us enormous pleasure to be able to support a project from its inception and to be a part of its realisation.

Jo Longhurst approached us in 2011 with the idea of 'perfection' as a subject for a symposium and book. We were already familiar with her work from her time at the Royal College of Art, where we bought an edition of her striking photographs of champion whippets. The purebred whippets perhaps represented an ideal of physical perfection. Having had this introduction to Longhurst's work, we were intrigued by her tackling the complex notion of perfection in a broader sense.

As an insurance company we are very much in the business of imperfection, covering damage from natural catastrophes, and disasters, and from the imperfections and mistakes of humans. As an imperfect human being, I have always been wary of perishing on the shrine of perfection as the perfect can be the enemy of the good. As Dr Johnson said, nothing will ever be attempted if all possible objections must first be overcome.

Let's see what Jo Longhurst finds.

Robert Hiscox, June 2013

DESPOILING THE IDEAL

EVA STENRAM

This is a transcript of Eva's talk.

The title, 'Despoiling the Ideal', has for me a double pull, containing two contrary meanings: despoiling – as in ruining or vandalizing – the ideal; but also *de*-spoiling, as in undoing the spoiling of, the ideal.

1

Absent Fairies (Figure 1) is based on one of the famous 'Cottingley Fairy' photographs – *Frances and the Fairies* (1917) – taken by Elsie Wright, of her 10-year-old sister Frances posing with what appears to be a number of fairies. The girls' parents didn't believe Frances when she told them about fairies she had seen in their garden. Elsie, in response, borrowed her father's camera and took a number of photographs of fairies, of which *Frances and the Fairies* is the first. The photographs eventually made it to publication in *The Strand*, and helped provide a generation of spiritualists with 'proof' that their belief in a spirit world was well-founded.

In 1983, Frances and Elsie confessed that the fairies were actually drawings made by Elsie that were stuck in the ground with hatpins. Frances died in 1986 but always maintained that she had seen fairies. *Frances and the Fairies* is displayed on her tombstone.

The original photograph was not, strictly speaking, 'incorrect'. Everything in the photograph was indeed in front of the camera, captured without double exposures, combination printing, retouching or other tricks. The fairies were simply props.

In *Absent Fairies*, I have removed these props, which in one way makes the picture more 'real', and in another not. The spirits, the fairies, are in fact very material (drawn on and made from card). The fantasy needed to be removed using image manipulation, which is the reverse of what often happens when an image is digitally altered: usually the symbolic or idealized aspects become more important, and the link to what we might call 'the real' is broken. What we are left with when the cardboard fairies are removed is simply a photograph of a girl day-dreaming; her imagination remains

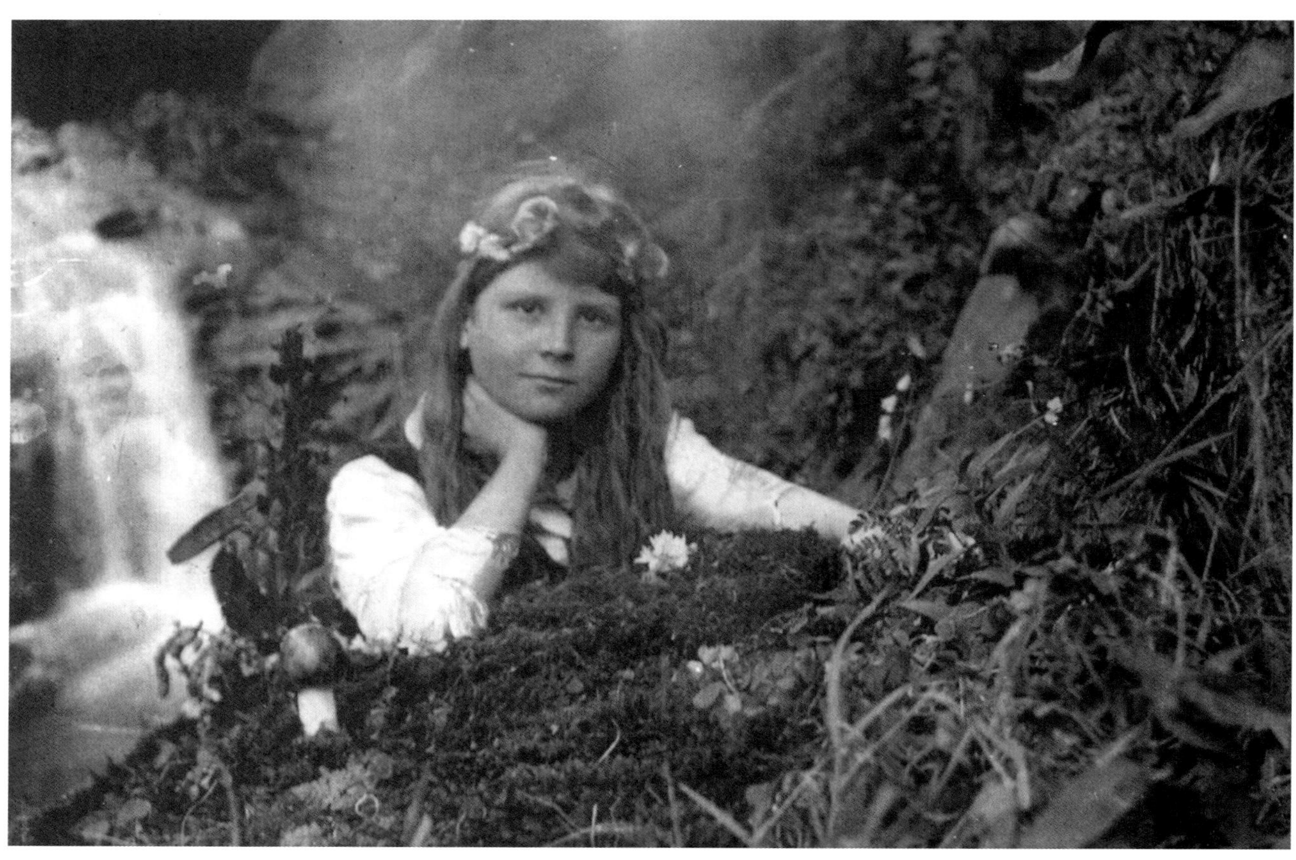

Figure 1: Eva Stenram, *Absent Fairies*, 2004; lambda print. Based on *Frances and the Fairies* (1917) by Elsie Wright.

invisible even though it's the thematic content of the photo. This is still a picture of a young girl seeing fairies.

2

'pornography/forest-pics' is a series of images based on hardcore pornographic images that are set within or around forests (Figures 2–4). The pictures were found on the Internet and downloaded, after which the human bodies were digitally removed.

Like all pornography, these source images are staged scenes constructed to fuel viewers' fantasies, not straightforward documents of people having sex – yet they are, of course, 'real'. The pornographic ideal, or what Susan Sontag calls 'the pornographic imagination', inhabits a universe in which 'all action is conceived of as a set of sexual exchanges [...]. It has the power to ingest and metamorphose and translate all concerns that are fed into it, reducing everything to the one negotiable currency of the erotic imperative.'[1] The world proposed by pornography is a total universe – a kind of ideal universe that Sontag compares to certain religious belief systems.[2]

Just as in *Absent Fairies*, the fantasy has been removed, but in this series a number of visual scars or cuts have been left within the image, emphasizing the deletion. The digital manipulation has deliberately been made quickly so that the picture's imperfections are visible. The viewer can see that the image has been tampered with (the bodies were obscured by repeating other sections of the photograph). By taking away the constructed fantasy, the pornographic ideal has on the one hand been spoiled, and on the other the pastoral ideal of the forest landscape (which the porn was sort of profaning) has been restored to its pristine condition, unspoiled. In either case, the viewers are left to project their own ideal or fantasy onto the image, to complete the scene imaginatively.

The photographs, once denuded of their 'action', also (for me) bring to mind police forensic photography, as though these were the sites of forbidding, if unnamed, events. The forest setting complements this ambiguity: at once a place of beauty and danger, of obscuring and clearing, a public as well as a private space. The human bodies in many cases gets replaced by the ground, become earth, dust and debris.

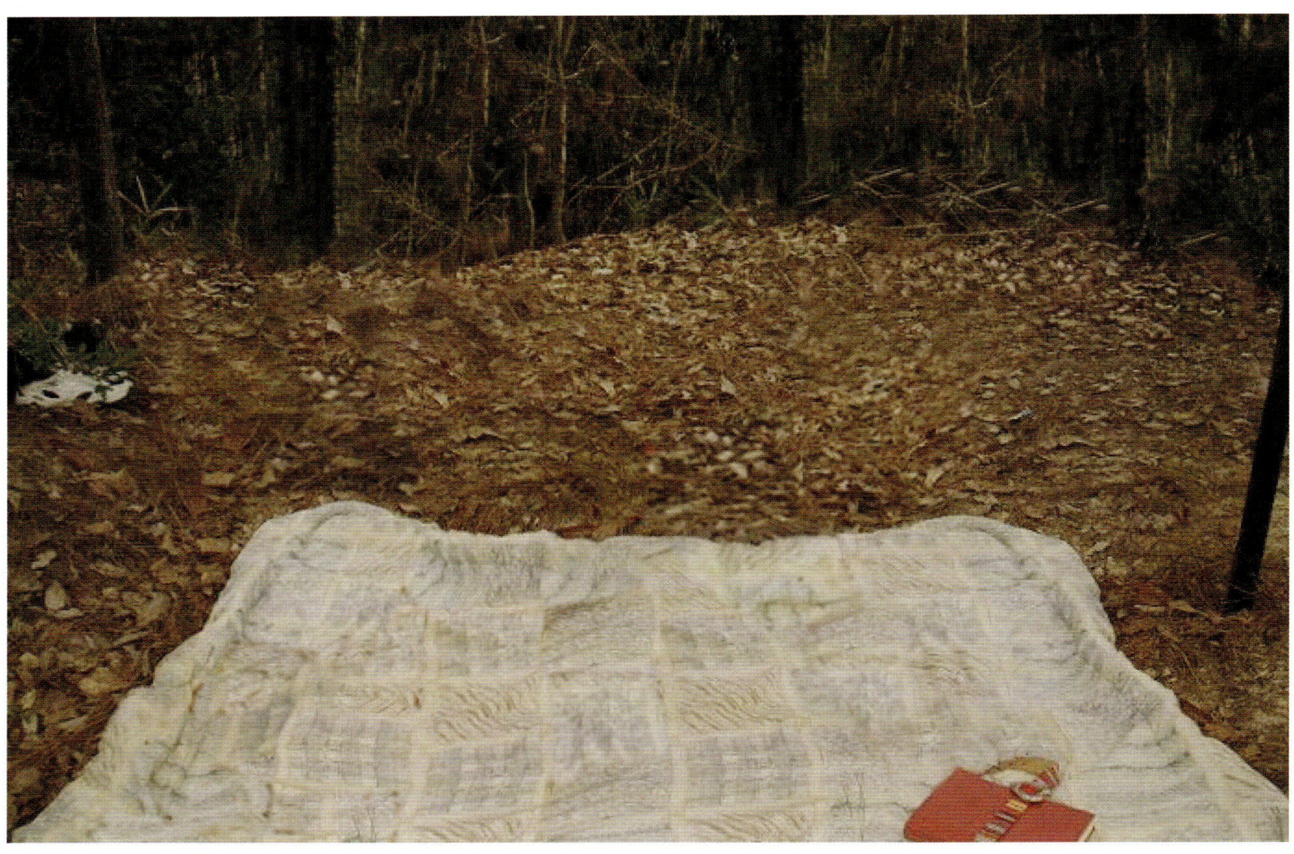

Figure 2: Eva Stenram, *pornography/forest_pic_1*; lambda print. From the series 'pornography/forest_pics' (2004–12).

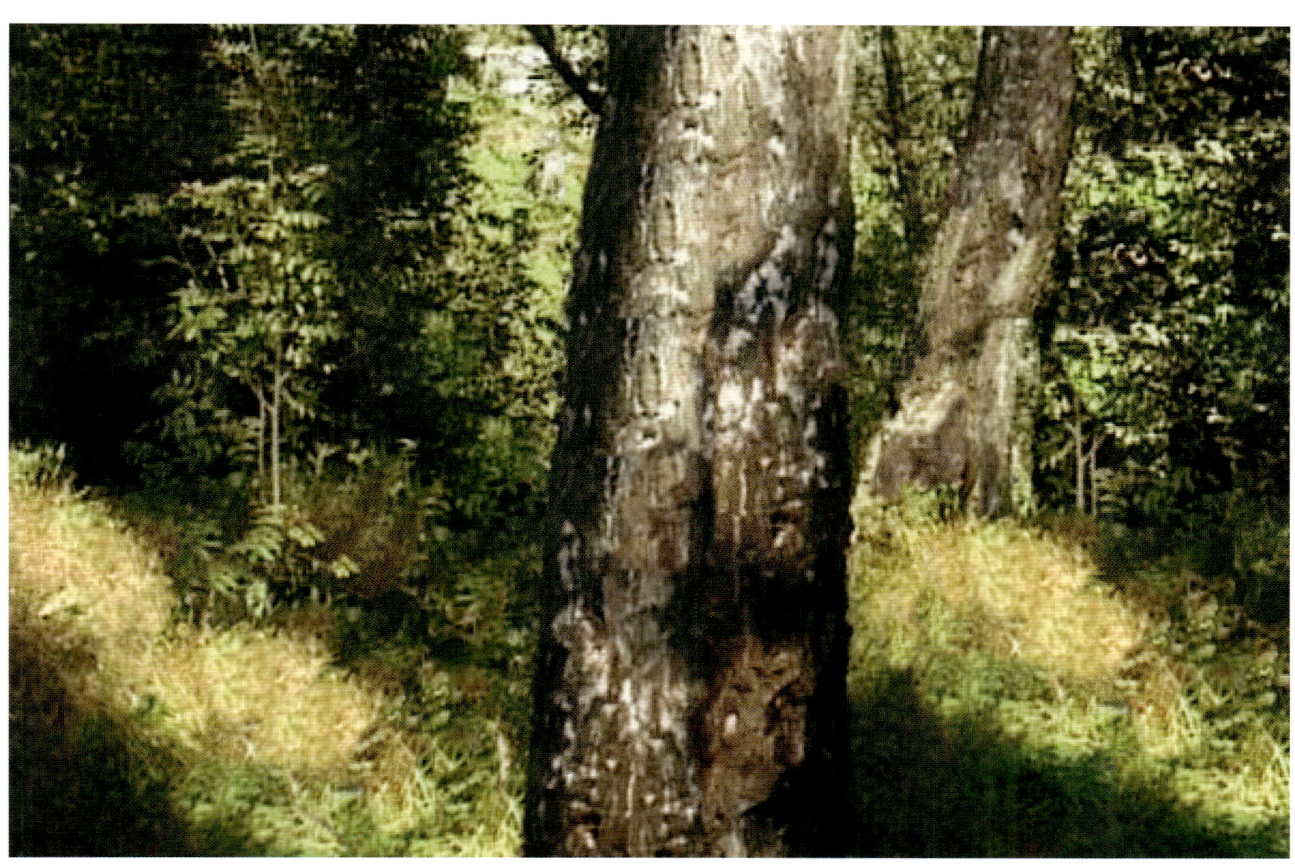

Figure 3: Eva Stenram, *pornography/forest_pic_2*; lambda print. From the series ‘pornography/forest_pics’ (2004–12).

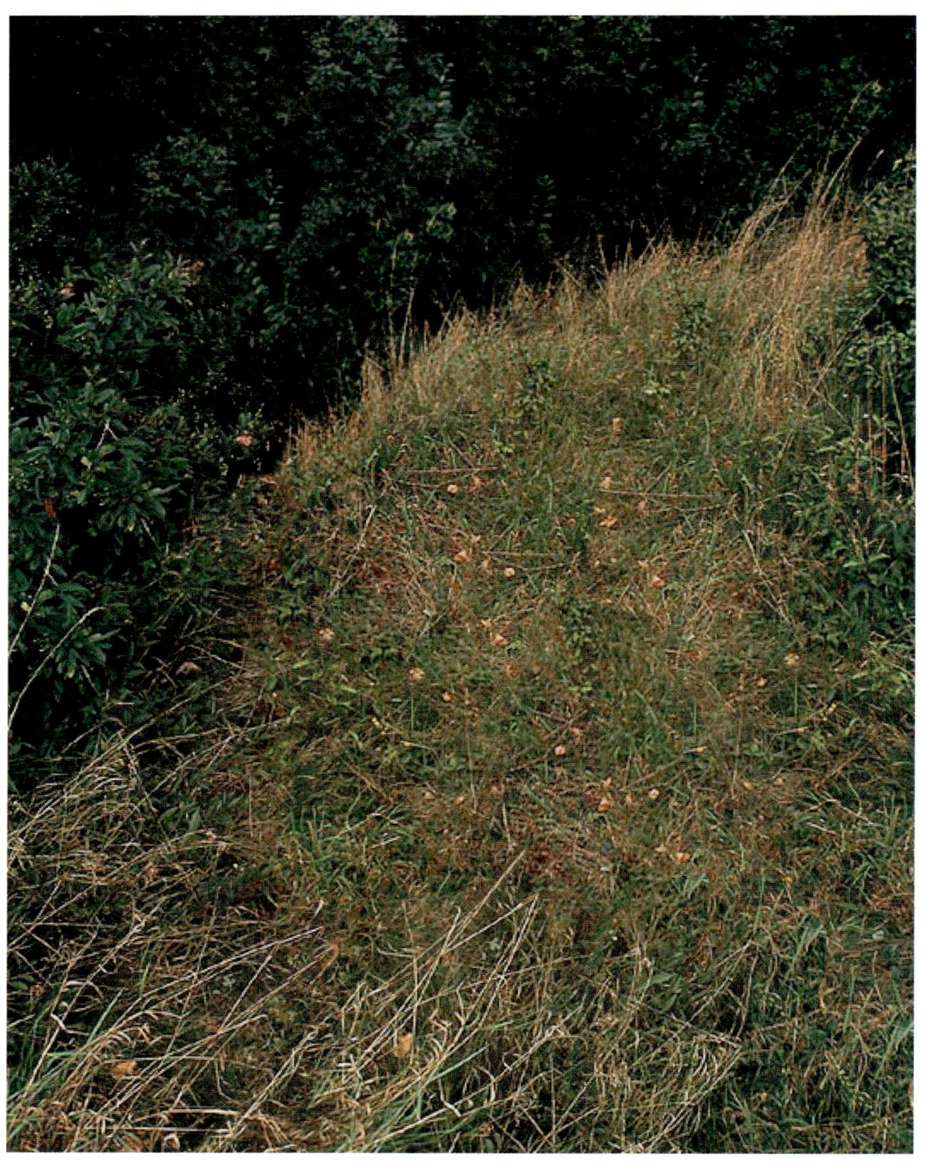

Figure 4: Eva Stenram, *pornography/forest_pic_7*; lambda print. From the series 'pornography/forest_pics' (2004–12).

3

In 'Per Pulverem Ad Astra' (Latin: 'Through Dust to the Stars'), the starting point was a series of images of the planet Mars, downloaded from NASA's website. These photographs are at first glance a perfect example of objective visual representations: photographic images taken by robotic machines on a landscape no person has ever been to. There is seemingly no subjective author and no contrasting opinions: the ultimate in technical seeing. They thus represent a certain photographic as well as conceptual ideal.

However, there are a number of oddities and imperfections within the images: they are stitched together from many photographs into one panorama, and the Martian landscape seems to change colour a lot. They are in fact mostly shown in what NASA calls 'approximately true-color' – a human estimate of what the scene might look like if we were there and able to see it with our own eyes. This is a nice reminder of how photography is always constructed – and how this often is done to provide a photographic image that corroborates with our idealized conception of what the subject image *should* look like. Even in the nineteenth century, landscape photographers took two different exposures of a landscape – one for the sky and one for the landscape – and combined them.

After downloading the images, I cropped and outputted them as 35mm analogue negatives. This step brought them away from the domain of the 'poor image'[3]: the virtual, immaterial, widely circulated and downloadable; instead they become a strip of unique, one-off, material negatives. These small negatives were then left around my flat, underneath furniture, in order to gather dust. After a couple of weeks I took them to the darkroom where I made prints from these, with the dust still on the negatives (Figures 5–8).

The white marks left are the result of this dust. Dust is dirt, waste and excess material, and is usually something to be swept away, hidden and discarded. Dust on a negative is usually a photographic mistake, an imperfection. Here, by contrast, it becomes the main feature of the image. The marks begin to interact with the Martian landscape, resembling smoke, clouds, flight patterns, electrical storms or as yet unlabelled light phenomena.

The project is inspired by Man Ray's photography – in particular his series 'Electricité' – which innovatively combines the normal printing of a negative with the making of a photogram. In one print, an electrical coil is placed on the photographic paper while printing the negative of a cooked chicken; in another a light switch is combined with the moon. Man Ray, of course, also made *Dust Breeding* together with Marcel Duchamp, which brilliantly confuses scale.

I wanted to achieve a sense of dizziness when looking at the images: a pull upwards into space, away from the ground underneath our feet, towards the gravitational field of Mars, as well as a gravitational pull downwards towards the Earth and the dust around us. For me, this dizziness is echoed in Paul Virilio's *Open Sky*, in which, offering a new way of thinking about perspective, he suggests that we have now become prone to 'reverse vertigo', a sense of falling *up*wards.[4] Not only does he posit a vanishing point above us, a vertical vanishing point, but he also postulates a new horizon opened up by instant telecommunication: the screen (which is of course where I got these images from).[5]

The NASA images of Mars represent people's fantasies and faith about the future, and by extension a wish for eternal life through a continuation of human habitation beyond our planet. Meanwhile dust, which is largely made up of dead skin and hair, denotes death, impermanence and the past. The dust in these photos acts as a non-figurative *vanitas*, like the skull in Holbein's *The Ambassadors* once it has undergone full anamorphosis.

When making 'Per Pulverem Ad Astra', George Bataille's text *The Big Toe* was also on my mind:

> Although within the body blood flows in equal quantities from high to low and from low to high, there is a preference for that which elevates itself, and human life is erroneously seen as an elevation. The division of the universe into subterranean hell and a perfectly pure heaven is an indelible conception, mud and darkness being the *principles* of evil as light and celestial space are the *principles* of good: with their feet in the mud but with their heads somewhat approaching the light, men obstinately imagine a tide that will elevate them, never to return, into pure space. Human life requires, in fact, this rage of seeing oneself as a back and forth movement from ordure to ideal, and from the ideal to ordure, a rage that is easily directed against an organ as *base* as the foot.[6]

For Bataille, the task is to bring things down in the world: to refocus our attention on the filth at our feet. In 'Per Pulverem Ad Astra', I wanted to achieve a kind of collapsing of space, in which the near and far, the imperfect and the ideal, can coexist.

This conflating of different spaces into one, and this interpretation of abstract shapes, can also be seen in nineteenth-century spirit photography. In a set of spirit photographs by John Beatie, the spirits appear as abstract forms, as if there were something blocking the light from coming through the negatives. In some photographs by the Crewe Circle, the spirits seem to appear within a cloud of dust. Parallel to this is 'thoughtography', or the photography of thought: the belief that photographic emulsion was sensitive to the radiation of thought. Louis Darget, a major proponent of thoughtography, made images by placing a hand on the photographic plate, pressing the plate against his forehead, or simply staring at it while thinking very hard. Often the content of thought was identified after the plate was developed. For example, a dream was identified through what appeared on a photographic plate that had been placed above the forehead of a person asleep. In this way, photographic imperfections were interpreted as pure thought.

In another photograph of Darget himself, *La Lune au Front/ The Moon on my Forehead*, Darget claimed that the moon had appeared on his forehead in the photograph because that is what he was thinking about at the time of the photographic exposure. It looks like some smudge on either the photograph or negative. Conversely, in 'Per Pulverem Ad Astra', rather than an interplanetary body appearing on my own image, dust from my body and belongings have appeared on Mars: the human body is introduced into the Martian landscape. 'Per Pulverem Ad Astra' can be thought of as a self-portrait; an alternative title for the series could (after, or rather against, Darget) have been 'My Forehead on Mars', bringing a subjective and more intimate quality to these otherwise technological images.

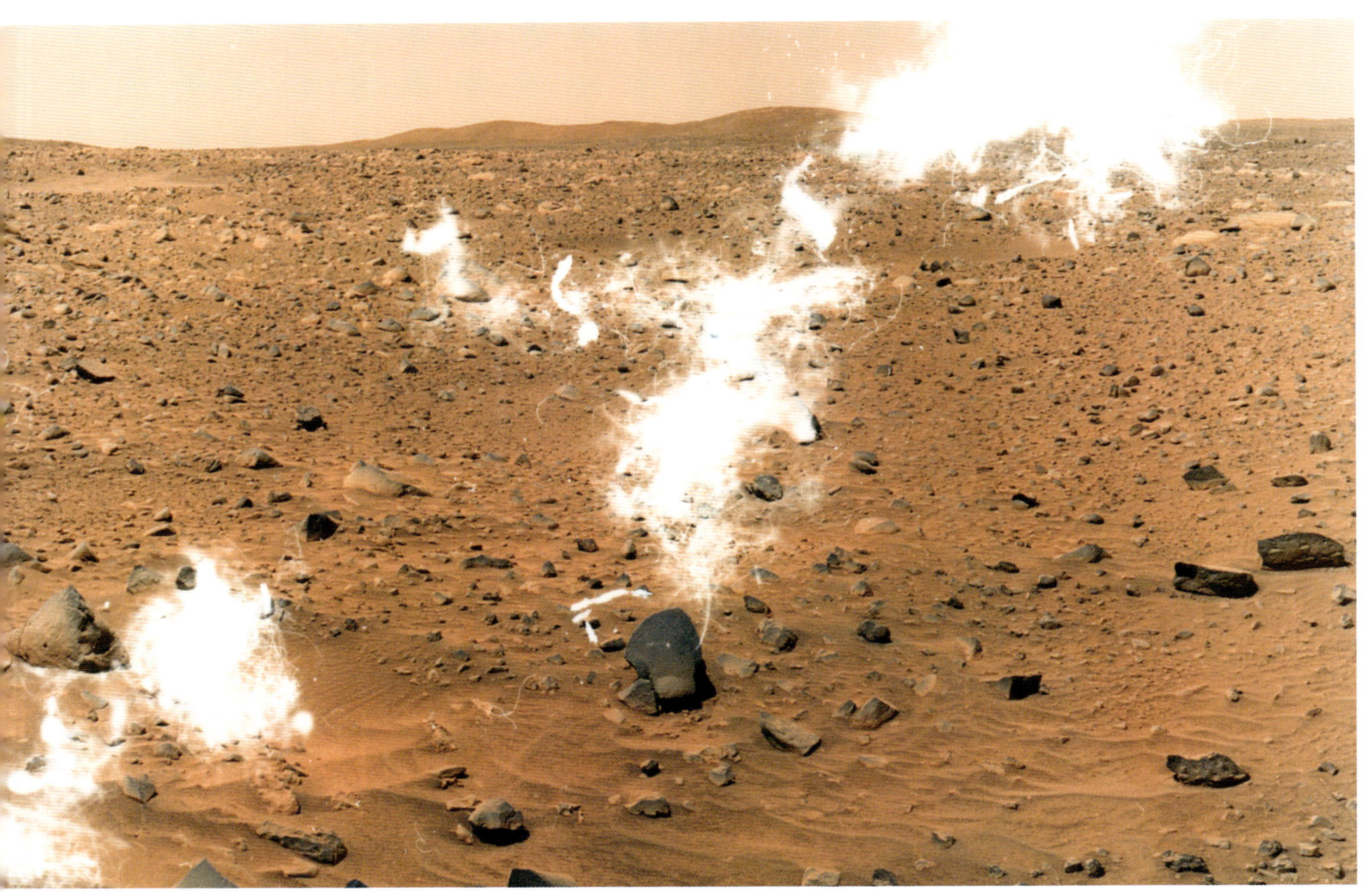

Figure 5: Eva Stenram, *Per Pulverem Ad Astra 2.AP1*, 2007; C-type print.

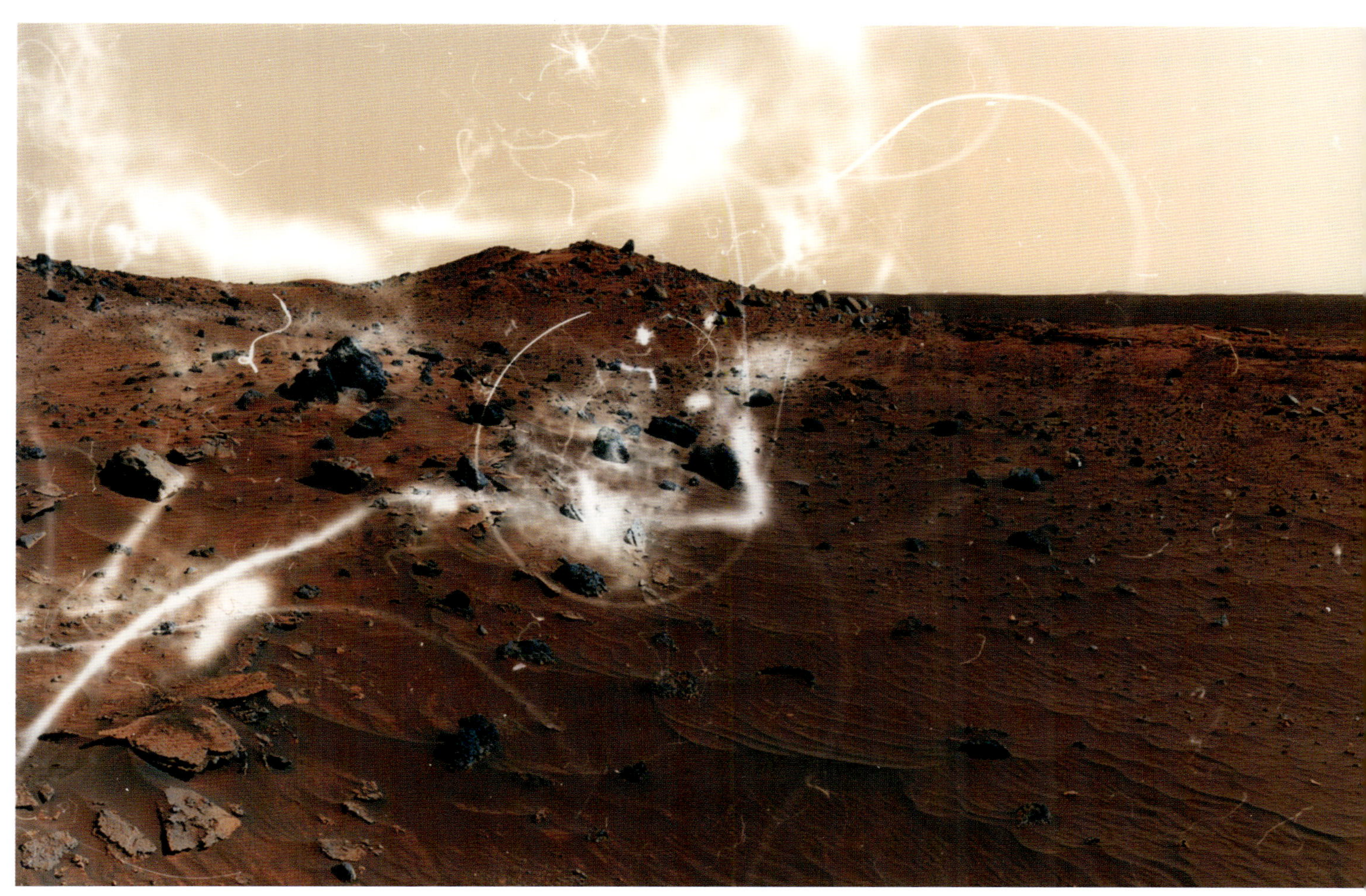

Figure 6: Eva Stenram, *Per Pulverem Ad Astra 8.1*, 2007; C-type print.

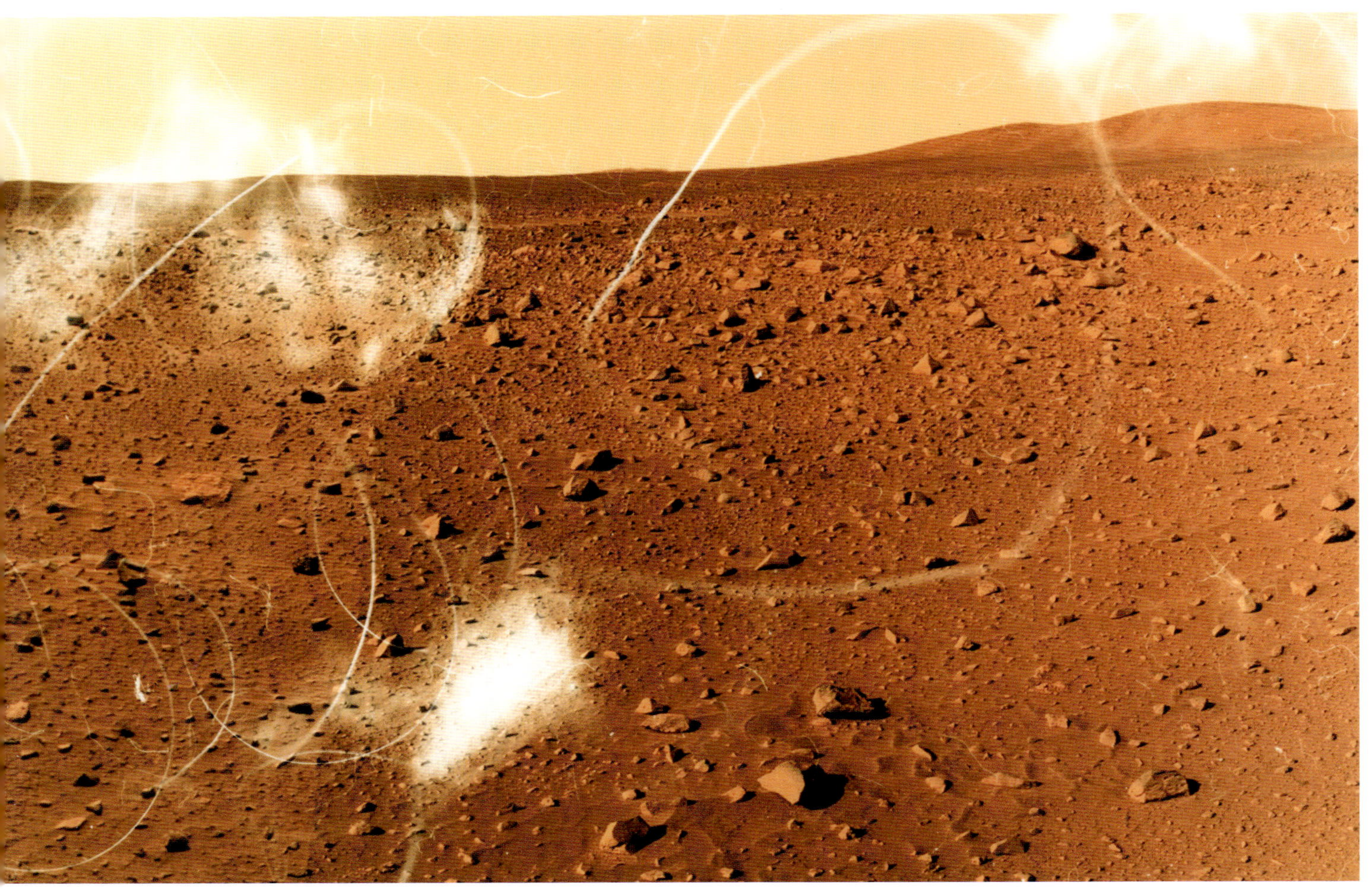

Figure 7: Eva Stenram, *Per Pulverem Ad Astra 1.4*, 2007; C-type print.

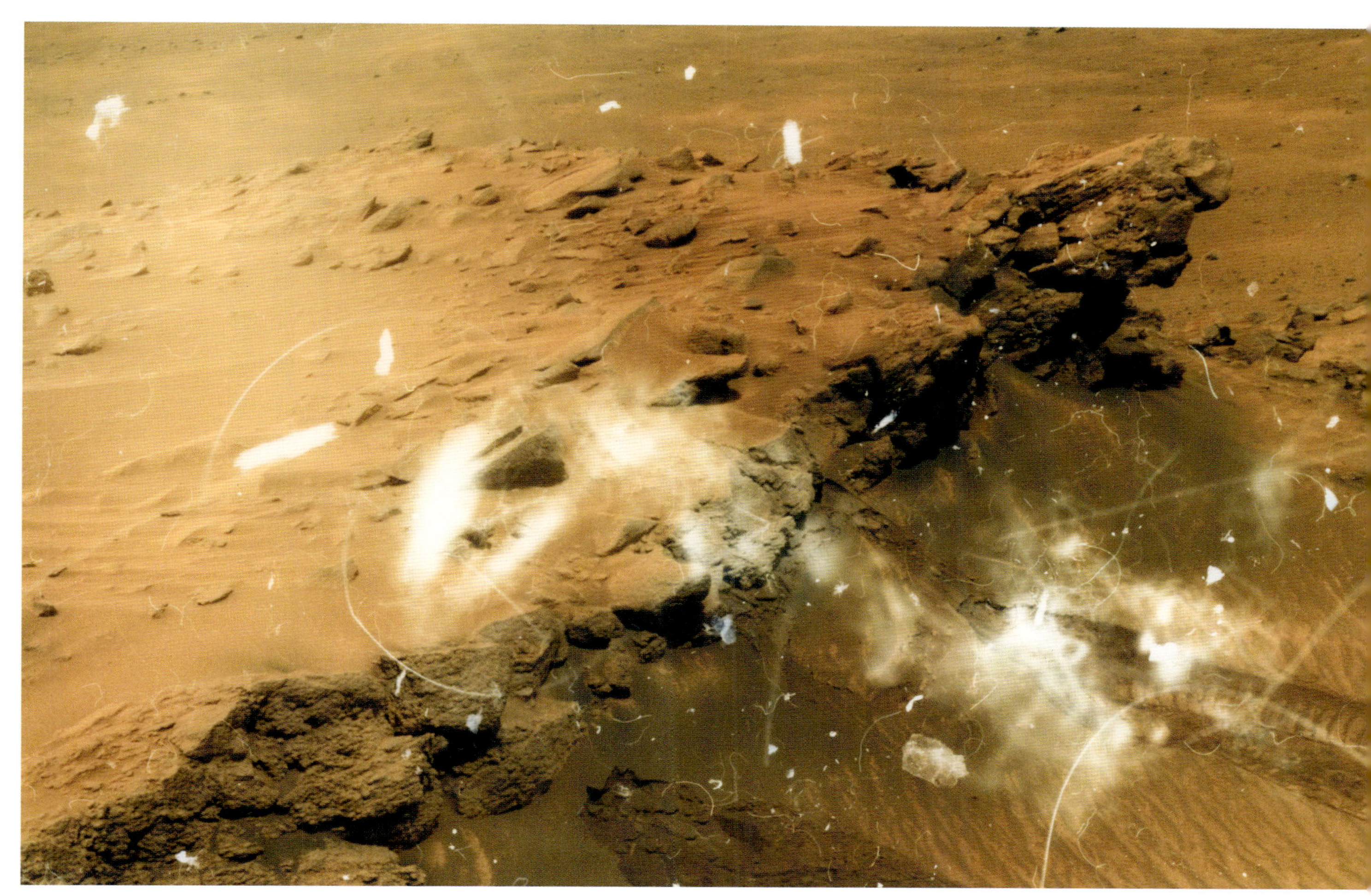

Figure 8: Eva Stenram, *Per Pulverem Ad Astra A.AP1*, 2007; C-type print.

NOTES

1 Susan Sontag, 'The Pornographic Imagination', in *Styles of Radical Will*, New York: Picador, 2002, p. 66.
2 Ibid. pp. 66–67.
3 Hito Steyerl, 'In Defense of the Poor Image', *e-flux Journal*, #10, November 2009, http://www.e-flux.com/journal/in-defense-of-the-poor-image/ (accessed 15th January 2013).
4 Paul Virilio, *Open Sky*, London & New York: Verso, 1997, p. 2.
5 Ibid. p. 25.
6 George Bataille, 'The Big Toe', in *Visions of Excess: Selected Writings 1927–39*, trans. Allan Stoekl, Minneapolis: University of Minnesota Press, 1985, pp. 20–21.

ON PERFECTION & AFFIRMATION IN STREET PHOTOGRAPHY

MARK DURDEN

I will be responding here to photographs before which one might use or at least suggest the word 'perfect'. This paper concerns street photography. I will make some initial commentaries on a few classic images: one by Henri Cartier-Bresson, a few of Joel Meyerowitz's colour European and New York photographs, one photograph by Garry Winogrand, and then concentrate on some recent photographs by Tom Wood, pictures that continue the tradition, but at the same time offer his own very distinctive and personal variation.[1]

According to Colin Westerbeck and Joel Meyerowitz, street photography tells us 'something crucial about the nature of the medium as a whole, about what is unique to the images that it produces.'[2] It explores and exploits the properties of instantaneity and multiplicity: taking many, multiple shots, the street photographer can either strive for the singular image, a perfect composition that condenses and trumps all other possibilities or present us with pictures that are more 'open-ended', pictures that are less autonomous and 'can't stand alone and need to be played off one another in groups or runs in books.' The choice is presented as one between the 'decisive moment' of Henri Cartier-Bresson's photography, or Robert Frank's more happenstance and formally less coherent pictures, a photography that, one might argue, is closer to the flux of public life. The opposition between a coherent formal picture versus the chancy and more disordered and formless picture is a useful one, but at the same time, the two tendencies are not always so clear to separate. With Meyerowitz, Winogrand and most certainly Wood, it's not a question of either/or as they move between the two tendencies – their aesthetic is informed by elements from both Frank and Cartier-Bresson.

Cartier-Bresson's decisive moment was caught up with a lyrical and transcendent form, his famous credo exemplified by his 1932 picture of the shadowy silhouette of a male figure caught as he jumps across and into a pool of water, *Behind the Gare Saint-Lazare*. It is an unprepossessing and non-pictorial spot, cluttered with objects from the repair work that is taking place behind the station: the rubble of stones, the makeshift wooden ladder that has been used as a springboard for the jumping man, the wheelbarrow and planks of wood. To take the picture, Cartier-Bresson said he pushed his Leica between the gaps in a plank fence put up around the repair work.[3] The central event and incident that is pictured affects everything around it in the photograph: details within the everyday quotidian banality of this site start to interplay with the form of the animate jumper – the counterpoint of the stationary man in the corner, a labourer perhaps, looking towards us or maybe through the railings; then the railings and the ladder, giving structure to the picture; and then the rhyming and doubling of the Railowsky posters, times two, times four, the posters with the ballet dancers, those circular bits of metal in the water – all are miraculously echoing and amplifying that formal doubling of the central figure, caught in not quite balletic mid-flight. Even the clock face of the station in the background seems to add meaning and significance, a civic measure of time, an order and normality distinct from this incredible moment.

Joel Meyerowitz's colour street photography has both a debt to and desire to break from Cartier-Bresson's lyrical form. His later pictures were no longer structured around one event, but attuned to many figures, objects, details, and events occurring at the same time; the chaos and flux of life brought in a disordering formlessness.

Street photography's insistence on an epiphanic and transcendent moment – often formally beautiful but also sometimes comic and even cruel – lifted out from a succession of moments, is a unique characteristic of the medium. Figurative painting used the pregnant moment, but this often was legible, an instant that carried meaning in terms of the historical events being narrated. Photography does not signal a continuity from this.[4] Nothing matches photography's temporal insistence on a decisive moment – a moment often resisting and beyond interpretation. There is, therefore, at the heart of classic street photography a certain magic and mystique. Forms, gestures and details come together to make the picture, as in Meyerowitz's 1967 Parisian street scene, *Fallen Man*, showing a labourer carrying a hammer as he sidles around a man lying convulsed on the road. The pictorial joke is, of course, that it looks as though he might have just hit him. But the event ultimately remains a mystery: we do not really know what is going on and maybe that is part of the pleasure and wonder of such pictures.

Longchamps Racetrack, Paris, France (1967) describes a comic but extraordinary moment, as a sudden gust of wind blows the straw hat off one of three ladies all dressed up for the races. But what makes this scene so amazing is the way the hat has landed and been fixed in the picture in an upright position, its brim just caught against the top step. One of the ladies has burst out laughing, while another in a yellow dress has turned towards her and is holding her hat down, her face covered. The other woman, in white, runs to return the hat. The whole event is witnessed by an array of people looking, often smiling and laughing: spectators that serve to reiterate the kind of fascination and joy Meyerowitz's photography brings us. But of course none are likely witnesses to the miraculous moment that Meyerowitz's photograph fixes, a fleeting moment integral to the speed of photographic vision rather than our more sluggish, all too human perception.

There is this extraordinary sense of wonder and utter amazement before such lyrical pictures. Consider, for example, the remarkable coincidences of dress, colour and light in his 1975 New York City street picture of a couple, both wearing similar yellow camel coats and walking away from camera. A patch of sunlight and a white cloud of steam lift them out of the shadowy crowds. This beautiful moment becomes even more extraordinary as the picture also manages to capture the backs of two other people wearing similar coats, each bearing the clearly defined shadow of a person behind them, the two shadows appearing like a cut out negative of the central couple.

It was about this time, the mid-1970s, Meyerowitz said how he was trying to make pictures on the street about what he refers to as the 'all of it', that is, pictures without a central subject, as in his kaleidoscopic street scene *New York City, West 46th St* (1976), which is teeming with signs and people competing for attention. Meyerowitz 'wanted all the information, near and far to hold our interest equally', and importantly, was 'trying to unlock photography from the aesthetic of the decisive moment.'[5] Stepping back allowed more depth of field and greater clarity in the picture. Meyerowitz is trying to bring the photograph closer to the 'inchoate and unresolved' experience of being on the street. There is no central point of focus in this picture, despite its organization around classical perspectival recession. What appears to be a dodgy monetary transaction by the two guys in the lower centre of the picture maintains a fragile connection with the decisive moment, a moment soon offset by other distractions in the picture: the static portrait of the cigar-smoking and sunglass-wearing short, elderly male figure staring straight to camera, for example.

In his most extensive and informative interview, made just a few years before his death in 1984, Garry Winogrand gave an especially clarifying account of his photography. Defining his practice as concerned with 'the photograph', that is 'how the fact of putting four edges around a collection of information or facts transforms it', he immediately distinguished any evidentiary use of photography from ideas of simple transparency.[6] For him, the act of photographing changes things to such an extent that '[a] new world is created'. Thus, much as his pictures can be seen to fix events and particular moments in time, they are also very much about the still photograph's alteration of those events. There is no such thing as a photograph which functions as a window on the world. What we see are things transformed: transformed in Winogrand's case by the speed of the camera's record of street life, of human gestures and situations caught on the fly. In this respect, his seemingly simple statement, 'I photograph to find out what something will look like photographed', is actually quite complex and precise in terms of Winogrand's particular relation to and interest in the photographic; the photographic as not only distinct from, but transformative of the event or thing in the world it represents.

From 1969 until 1976, Winogrand photographed the effects of the media on events. He used up 700 rolls of film at public and semi-public events, edited for the book and exhibition *Public Relations* by Tod Papageorge.[7] The photographs are about the way scheduled events were designed to be reported – his many years working as a photojournalist meant he knew such events were not spontaneous, so he would show their construction and theatre. At the same time, what so many pictures do so well is to show us moments that don't go to script: the over self-satisfied grin of the seated mayor surrounded by press and adulators in *Mayor John Lindsay, Central Park, New York* (1969). Winogrand does not judge when he depicts rallies and protestors. Amidst all the petitioning and emotionalism, he does not petition the viewer with his ideological convictions. He is there as witness, but not part of the rallies and protests. This again distinguishes these pictures from the rhetoric of message-driven press reportage: this of course was integral to John Szarkowski's credo in *New Documents* (1967).

The contemporary artist Tom Wood photographs from life constantly. Born in Ireland, he lived in north-west England and now lives in north Wales. He is a great photographer of people: strangers, friends and family, people pictured individually, in pairs or in small groups, posed and unposed. And he photographs people of all ages. His photography is especially informed and influenced by family photographs, and pictures from his own family album are occasionally shown and published together with his own. While many of his photographs are taken with a handheld 35mm Leica, Wood also uses medium and large formats, as well as the more experimental and novel panoramic camera. He photographs in both colour and black-and-white. The photographs are intimate, but not too intimate. They are not prying or intrusive. His photography is not project-bound as so much photography can be, neither driven by an editorial mandate nor a commission. When exhibited or published, his photographs often span decades and are arranged non-chronologically, as pictures not documents.

Much as his photography is drawn from the world, Wood is very much concerned, like Winogrand, with how the camera transforms the real into still pictures, and how they formally work as pictures. Wood reminds us of his photograph's identity and difference as pictures through the recurrence of other images in his photographs, as I will show you. It is also there in his earlier *All Zones Off Peak* work – photographs taken from his bus journeys in Merseyside – with the bus as a corollary of the camera: the glass of the windows and the cutting edges of the frames producing picture within picture, and then the competing interplay of signage from outside, and from advertisements especially.[8]

In Wood's photograph of a group of young men beside a pub and on their way to a football match (there is also a woman among them, but she is occluded by the men and only partly visible), the picture is made through the rhythm of their gesturing hands – pointing, touching mouths, holding tickets, counting – and the way each is caught at a moment when they are looking elsewhere, away from each other. Above them there is the picture of an advert showing football shirts, photographed just as its image is about to change over into another – a subtle reiteration of the photograph's fixing of a moment, as well as a reminder of the ever-changing commercial images that now also fill the street. The break-up of the advertising image into lines as it changes formally echoes those of the railings beneath it – a fortuitous link that nevertheless adds to the beauty of this as a picture.

There is a certain pathos and comedy in Wood's portrayal of three elderly women, walking in line and set amidst the littered grounds of an outdoor market, and the bustling activity of buying and selling that fills the background. The woman in the middle has her head down and appears to be looking into the bin she carries at something one assumes she has just bought. We don't know what is in the bin and the joke seems to rest on the fact that we assume there is nothing inside it, and that in this existential moment of reflection she might well be contemplating her lot in life.

Images and pictures recur in Wood's photography as backdrop or in relation to the lives of the people he pictures. In his photograph looking through a barber's glass door, there is the interplay between the profiles of two men waiting to have their hair cut and a poster of Steve McQueen facing out and looking back at us. In his picture of men during a work break at Cammell Laird's shipyard in Birkenhead, they are all lying down horizontally on benches, beneath a fleshy display of topless girls on the walls around them. It is a space of both rest and fantasy in which all the men are shown engrossed in newspapers or magazines, with some of their reading matter's content clearing echoing the images above them. In another picture of the shipyard, Wood picks out the details of cut-out erotic pictures of women, vivid remnants of the place's former working life. They decorate screens from the work places, themselves also pictorially arresting, with their surfaces stained with paint and scratched with messages. Wood's photography stems from life and real situations, but nevertheless acknowledges a visual landscape of other photographic pictures also vying for attention, competing with and colouring our way of seeing.

One day-lit interior picture shows two men watching what looks like a porn video. We view them from behind so do not see their faces. Wood does not pass judgment through such pictures, but the scene, like those of the workers amidst their erotica, nevertheless reflects upon the domination of certain kinds of image of women in our culture and with it a certain idea of masculinity. It is there too in the picture at the barbers: the dominance of a certain ideal of masculine cool through the McQueen portrait and the detail of one of the men reading a soft porn magazine.

In a photograph of a pub interior, Wood plays with pictures of landscapes. The photograph opens out on to an exterior view of a landscape through its back windows, overexposed this view appears separate from the interior and becomes like a picture. It also formally corresponds to a painted landscape on the wall inside as it catches the early evening light. The pub is empty but for a woman with long hair at the far end of the bar and to the edge of the picture. The light makes the otherwise bland décor beautiful, and illuminates the amber of the beer in the glass held aloft by the woman, a small but significant gesture that animates the otherwise still scene, just as a small stone ripples a pond.

Light is integral to this picture as in so much of Wood's work. Many say photography lacks touch, that it lacks the animated surface we find in painting. But photography is nevertheless animated by the touch of light. Light makes photography into a sensuous medium.

Light is key to Wood's extraordinary portrait of a naked life model in an art studio setting; one in which the young woman adopts a formal position, standing upright against a blank wall, like a specimen. On the wall behind her, in line with her head, are pinned different-sized sheets of paper, while behind her feet are a series of dark blank sheets or boards, reiterating the context of the life room, and the relationship between her body and the discipline of drawing, picturing and framing. The band of daylight that runs over part of her body also produces a silhouette image of her lower right arm and hand on the wall behind her, as well as the curvaceous line of her lower body. The detail of the hand in shadow offsets the formality of the pose and, since the picture is in black-and-white, makes us think of a drawing.

The face-on portraits that run through his work introduce a different temporality to the fixing of an evanescent gesture; introduce something of the monumental, meditative and reflective in his photography. Such qualities characterize the portrait of the naked life model, or the old woman in a café with her green pinafore, striking red lipstick and green eyes, her stare to camera charged by the intensity of her being. There is a unitary presence and force to such portraits, a concentration on one person looking. In contrast, the group portraits invite a comparative looking, seeking likenesses and resemblances between features or inviting us to gauge the social dynamic among the sitters. Looking also becomes the subject in a number of pictures: the older woman in a shop store looking at herself in a handheld mirror as she tries on a new hat or the exchange between two girls on the Mersey ferry, both bathed in golden light, as one holds up a fragment of a picture – or is it a mirror? – to the other.

Wood's pictures go beyond the economic circle and context within which he makes them. He nevertheless describes a predominant working-class group, a people who seem to be more free and open, less uptight and constrained than the middle-classes. His pictures are historical, but they are not driven by the assumption of interpreting those events. One can sense his political allegiance, but that identification is to do with his overall affirmative way of picturing people, the respectful and open way in which he views others.

Panoramic photographs allow Wood to extend the field of vision and give us more than one scenario. His widescreen fairground picture rests upon the dynamic set up between its portrayal of two groups, with one side of the picture taken up with a portrait of young boys on the edge and outside of one of the rides, while the other shows girls occupying its interior – a division underscored by the play of lights, the overexposure of the irradiated exterior and the lush orange-reds inside. Outside the boys are idling, doing nothing, one seems to be whispering in the ear of the other, while another holds a big phallic-shaped pink balloon, a comic flag for their show of manliness. It is hot; two boys have no tops, and another has his shirt open. The girls remain contained inside, smoking. There is a sense of expectancy to do with this pairing of the sexes. The red hearts on the railings of one of the rides fits the slightly kitschy sentiment attached to such places, while the light and colour is suggestive of the heat and passions at play at the fairground, a world already lifted out of the ordinary and everyday.

Wood's photography responds to the sense of a world always brimming over and full. It is the sense of an infinite potentiality and possibility for beauty from life that we come across again and again in these remarkable and unforgettable pictures. Perfect pictures which keep on surprising us by creating occasions for wonderment from out of the day-to-day, and at the same time always appearing so disarmingly natural, simple and direct.

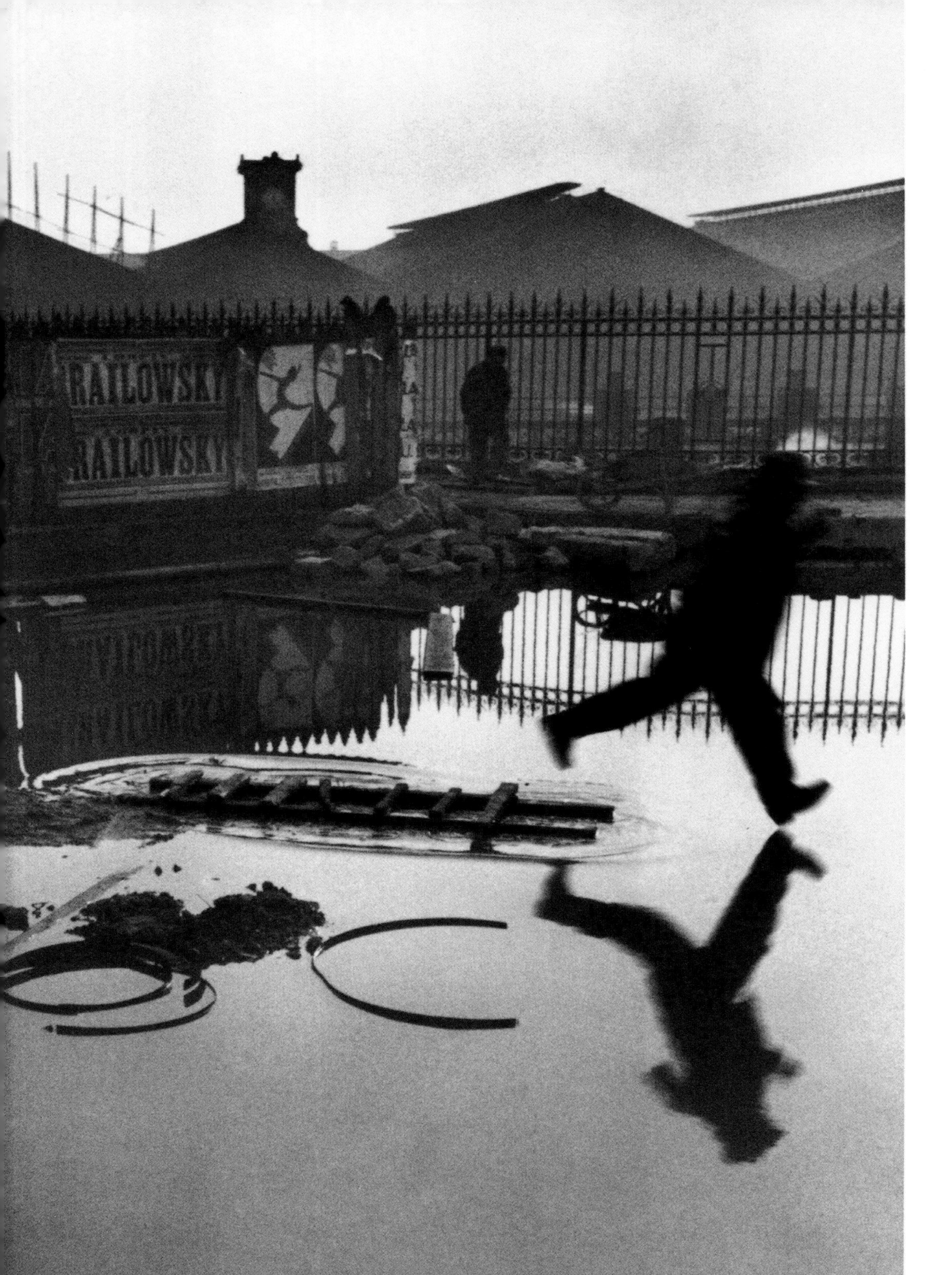
RAILOWSKY
RAILOWSKY

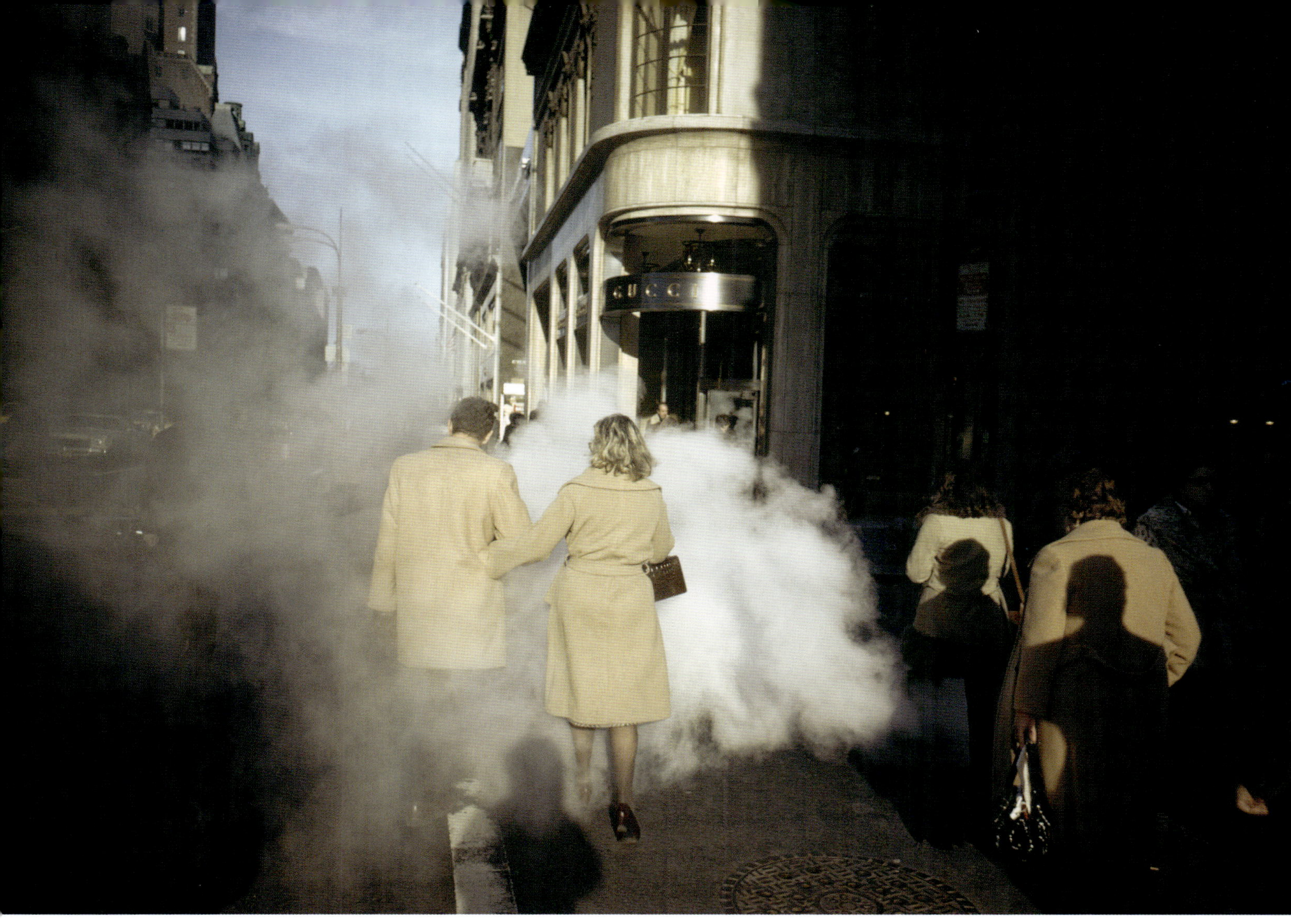

This page: Joel Meyerowitz, *Camel Coats, New York City*, 1975 (©Joel Meyerowitz; Courtesy Howard Greenberg Gallery).

Opposite page: Henri Cartier-Bresson, *Behind the Gare Saint-Lazare*, 1932 (©Henri Cartier-Bresson/ Magnum Photos).

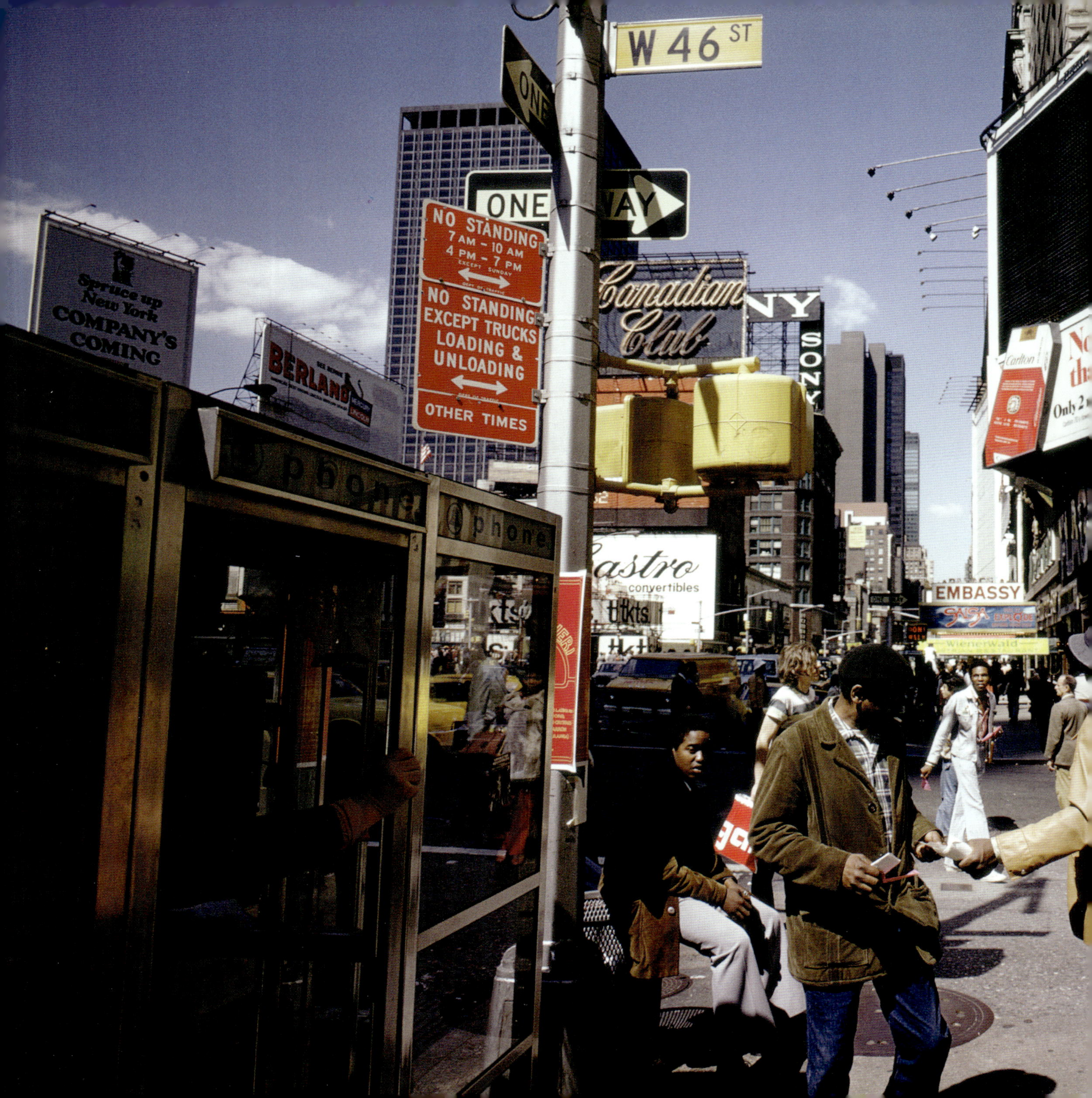
W 46 ST
ONE WAY
NO STANDING
7 AM - 10 AM
4 PM - 7 PM
EXCEPT SUNDAY
NO STANDING
EXCEPT TRUCKS
LOADING &
UNLOADING
OTHER TIMES
Canadian Club
SONY
Spruce up
New York
COMPANY'S
COMING
BERLAND
phone
phone
Castro
convertibles
tkts
EMBASSY
Wienerwald
Carlton

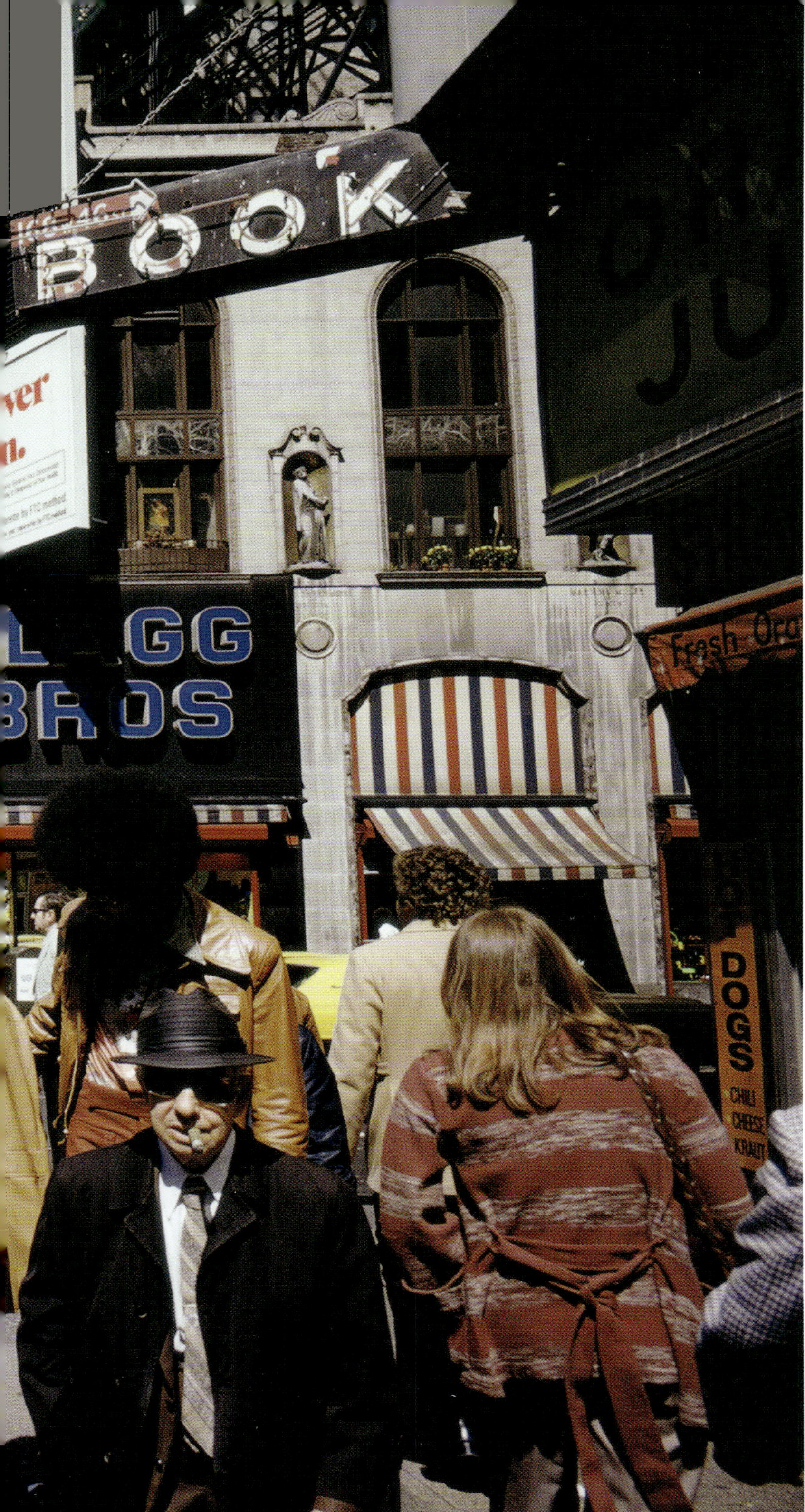

Joel Meyerowitz, *New York City, West 46th St*, 1976
(©Joel Meyerowitz; Courtesy Howard Greenberg Gallery).

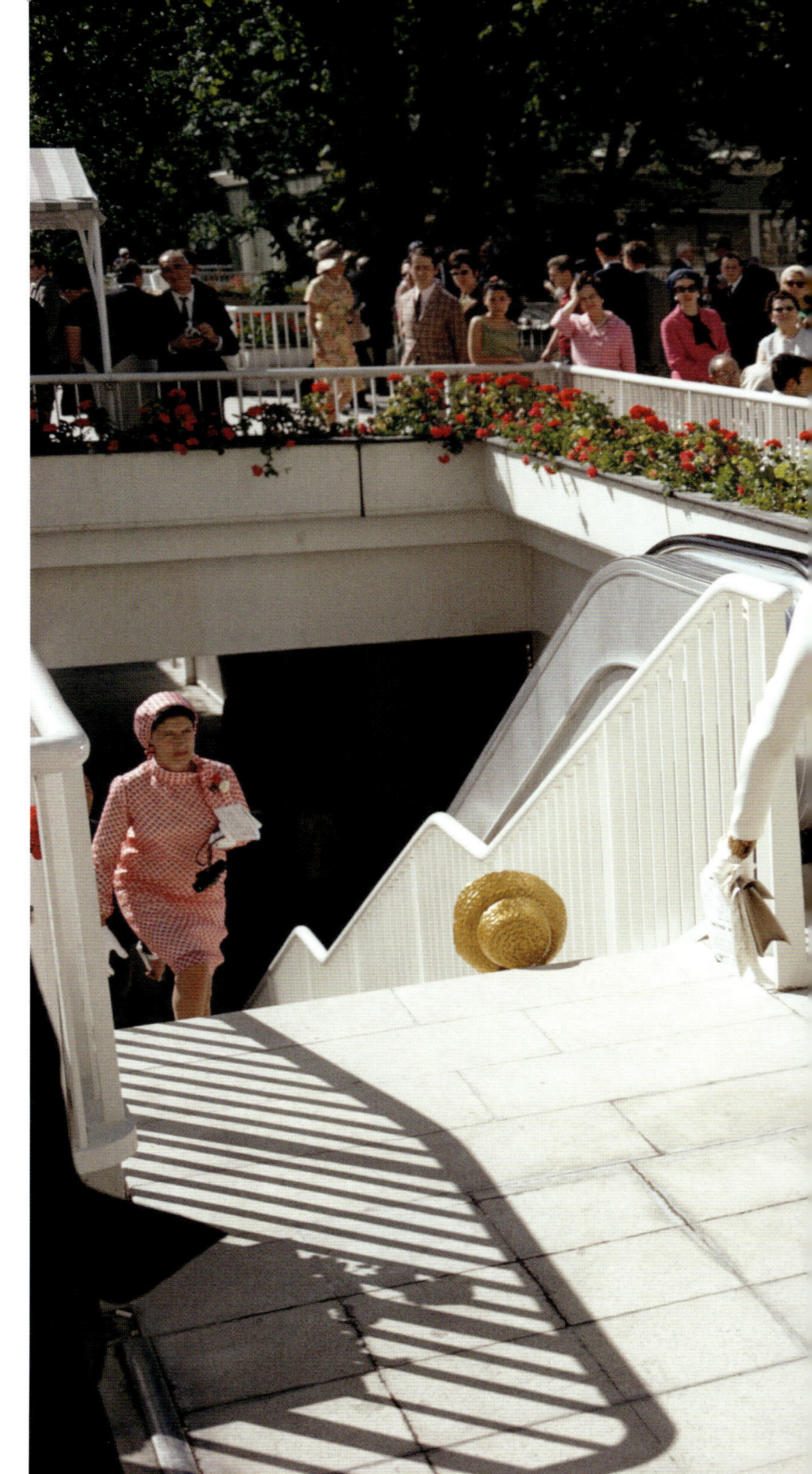

Joel Meyerowitz, *Longchamps Racetrack, Paris, France*, 1967 (©Joel Meyerowitz; Courtesy Howard Greenberg Gallery).

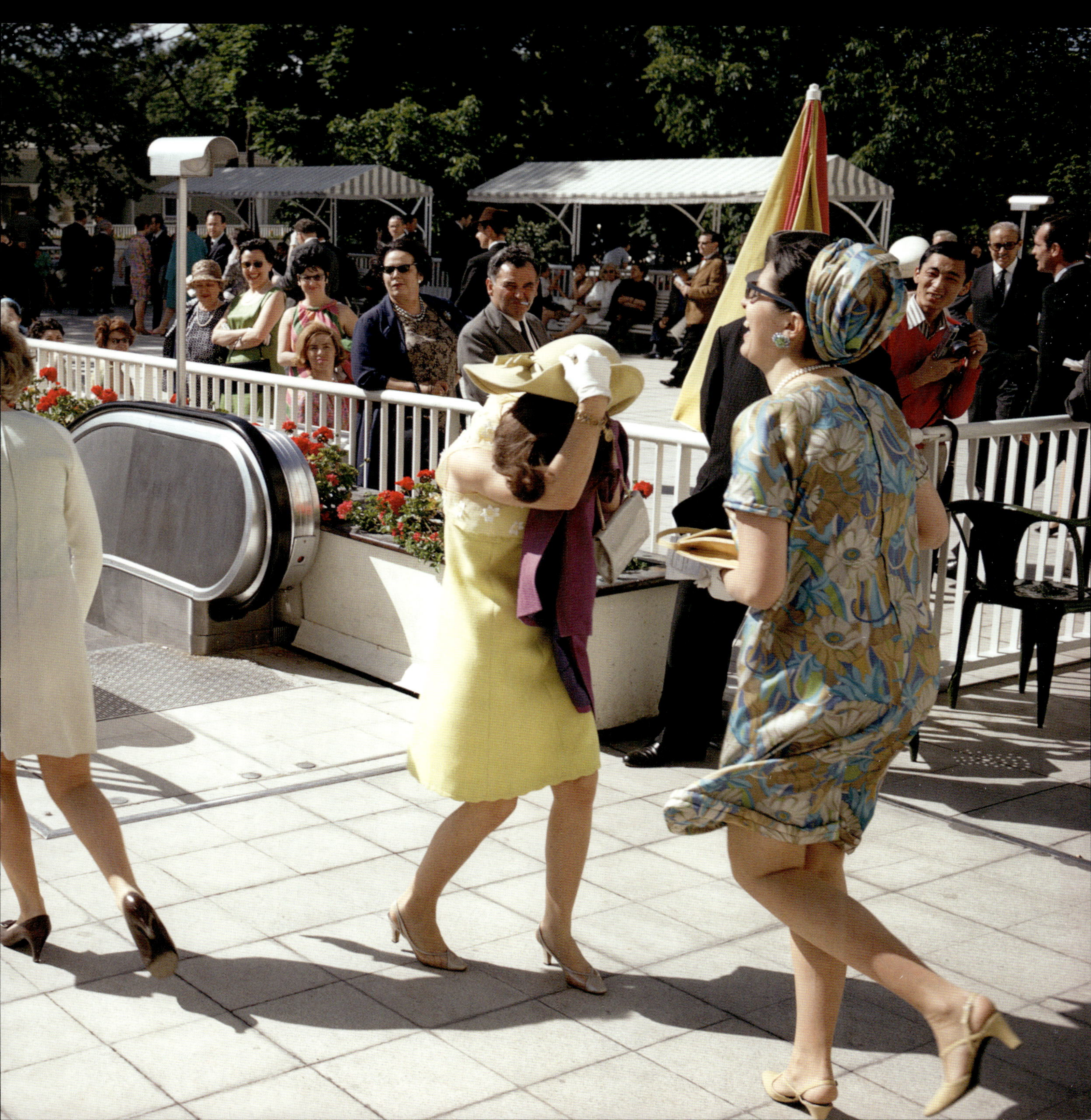

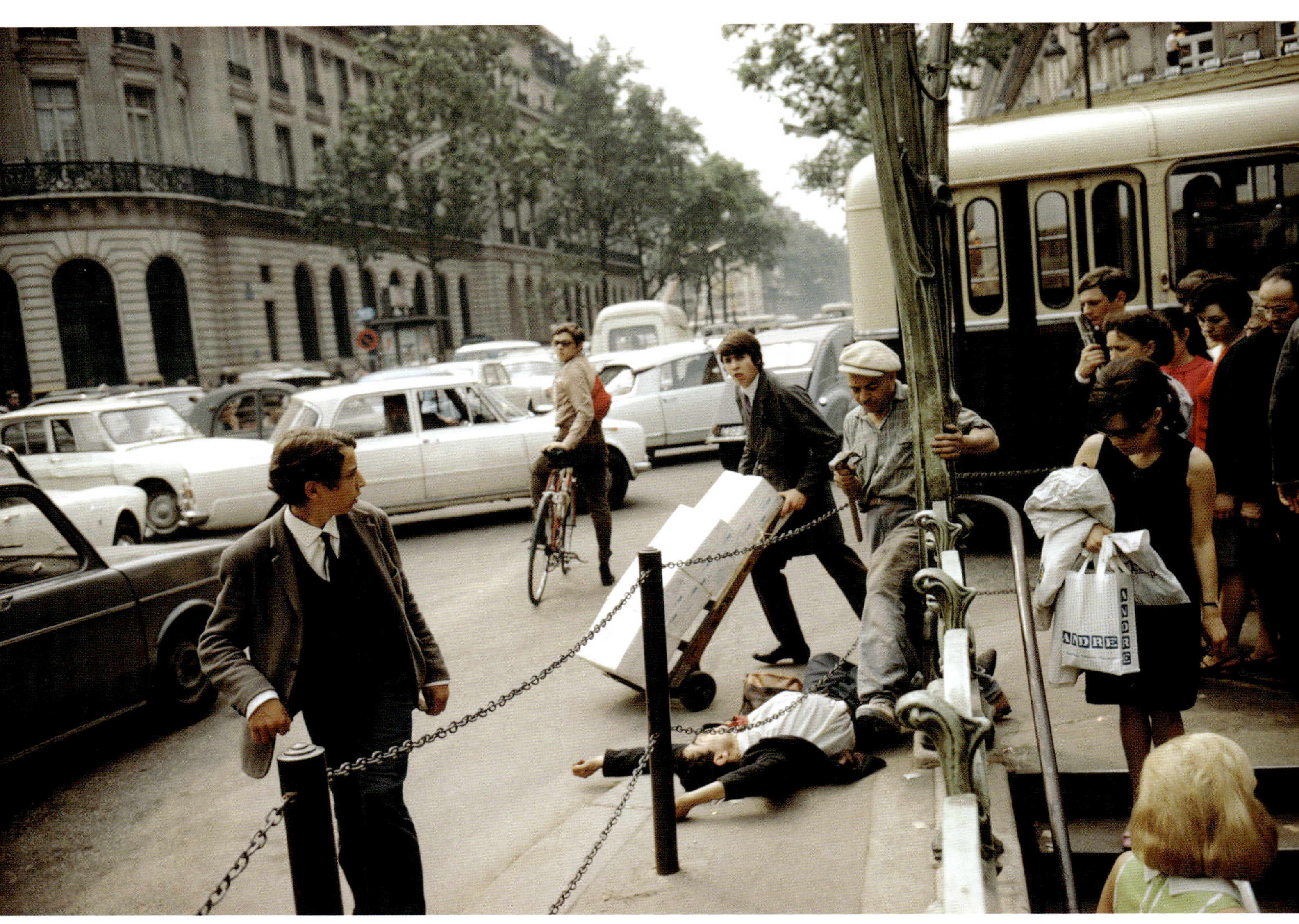

Joel Meyerowitz, *Fallen Man, Paris, France*, 1967 (©Joel Meyerowitz; Courtesy Howard Greenberg Gallery).

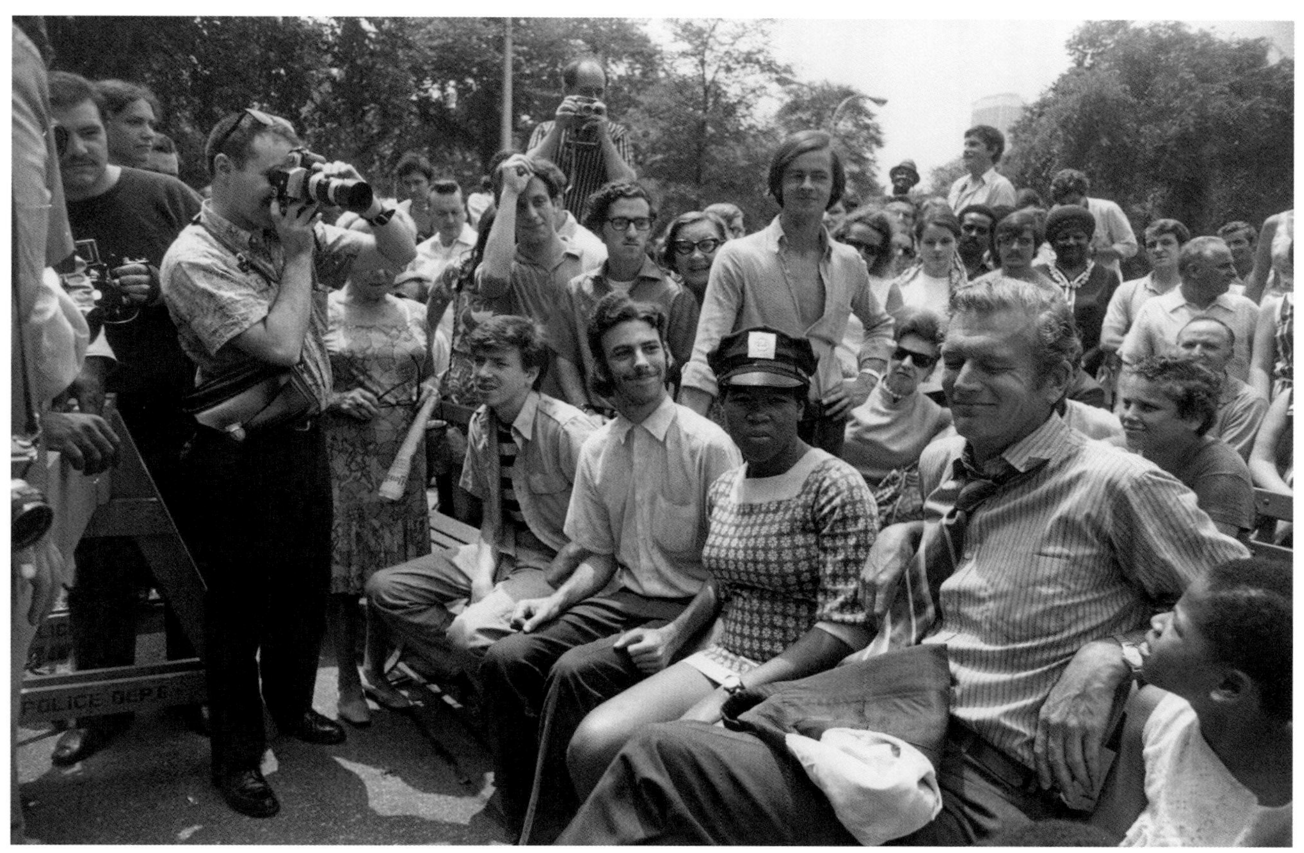

Garry Winogrand, *Mayor John Lindsay, Central Park, New York*, 1969 (©The Estate of Garry Winogrand; Courtesy Fraenkel Gallery, San Francisco).

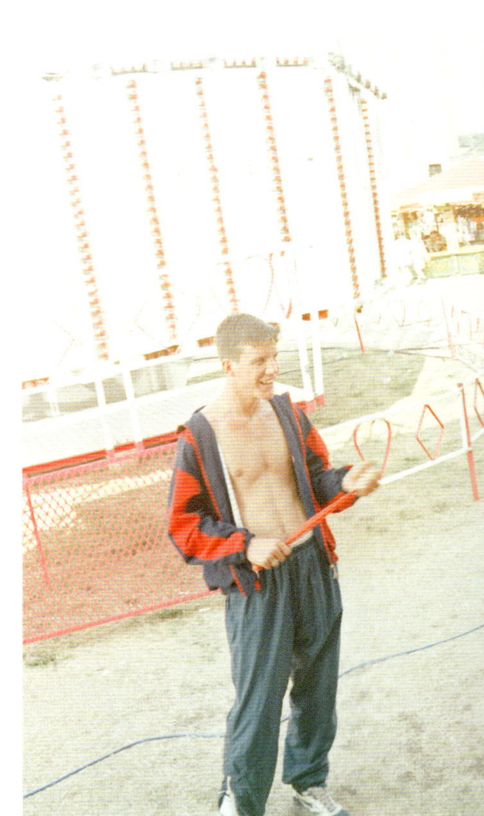

Tom Wood, *Inside and Out*, 1995 (©Tom Wood).

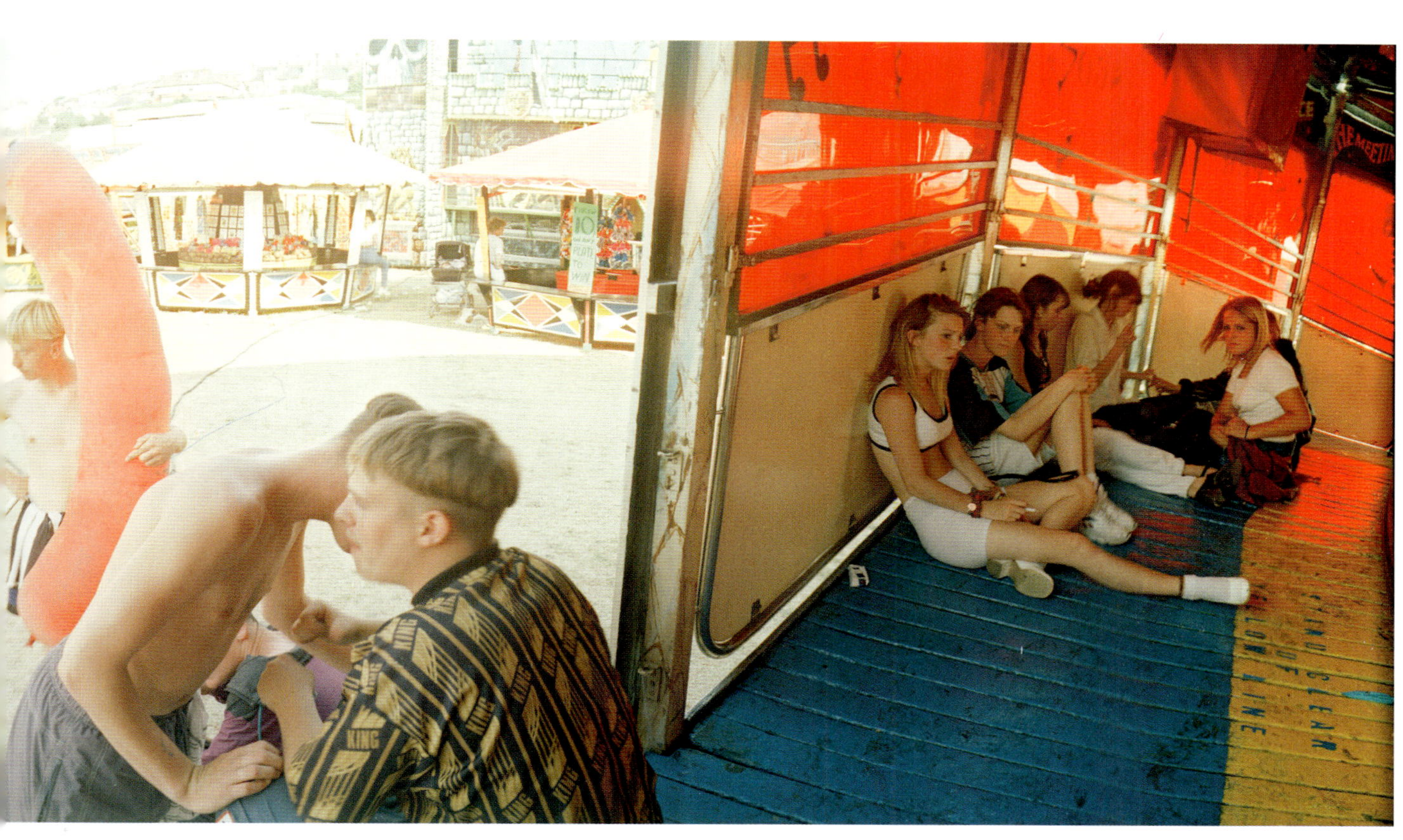
KING

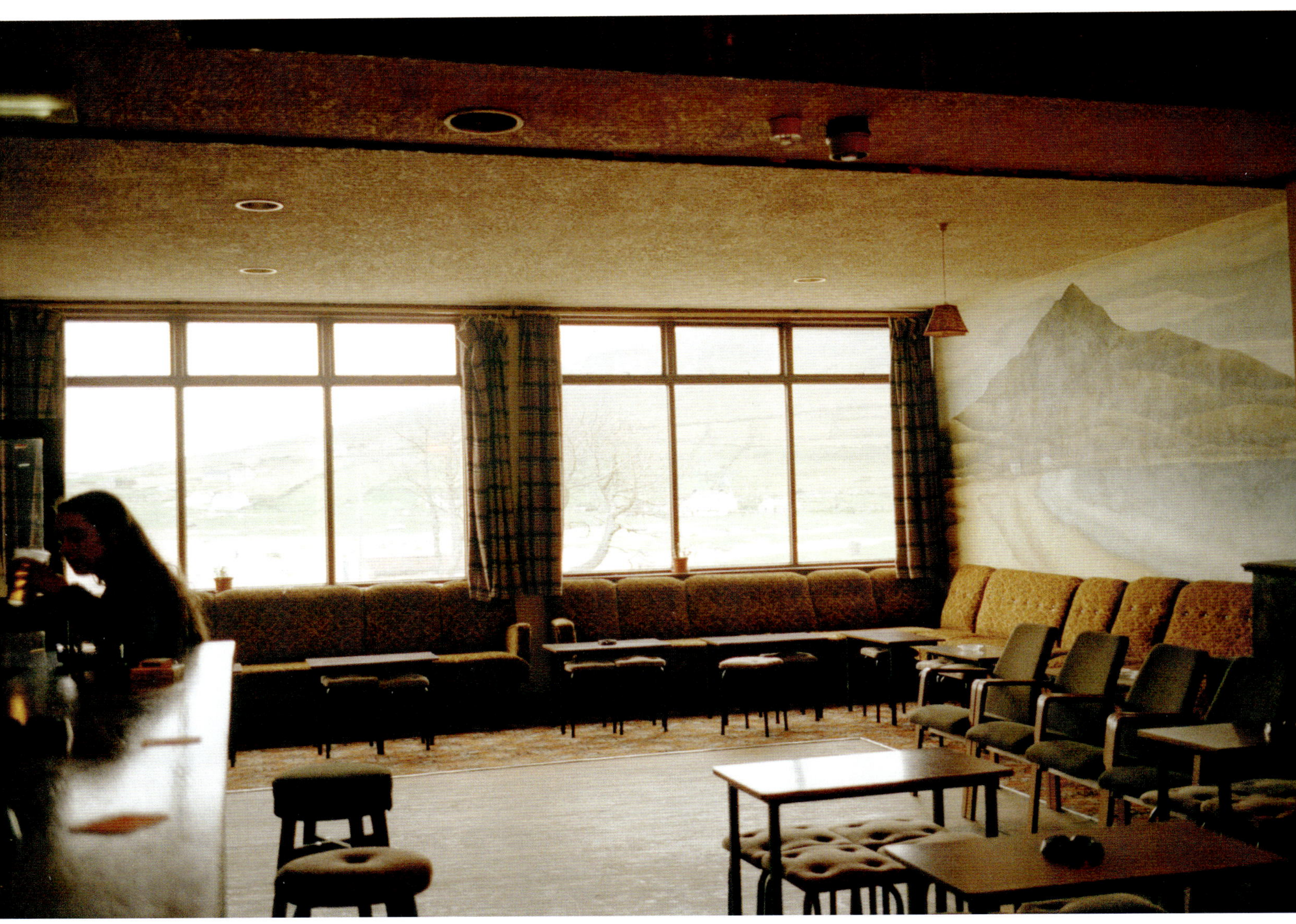

Tom Wood, *Slievemore (You're never alone at The Strand)*, 1986 (©Tom Wood).

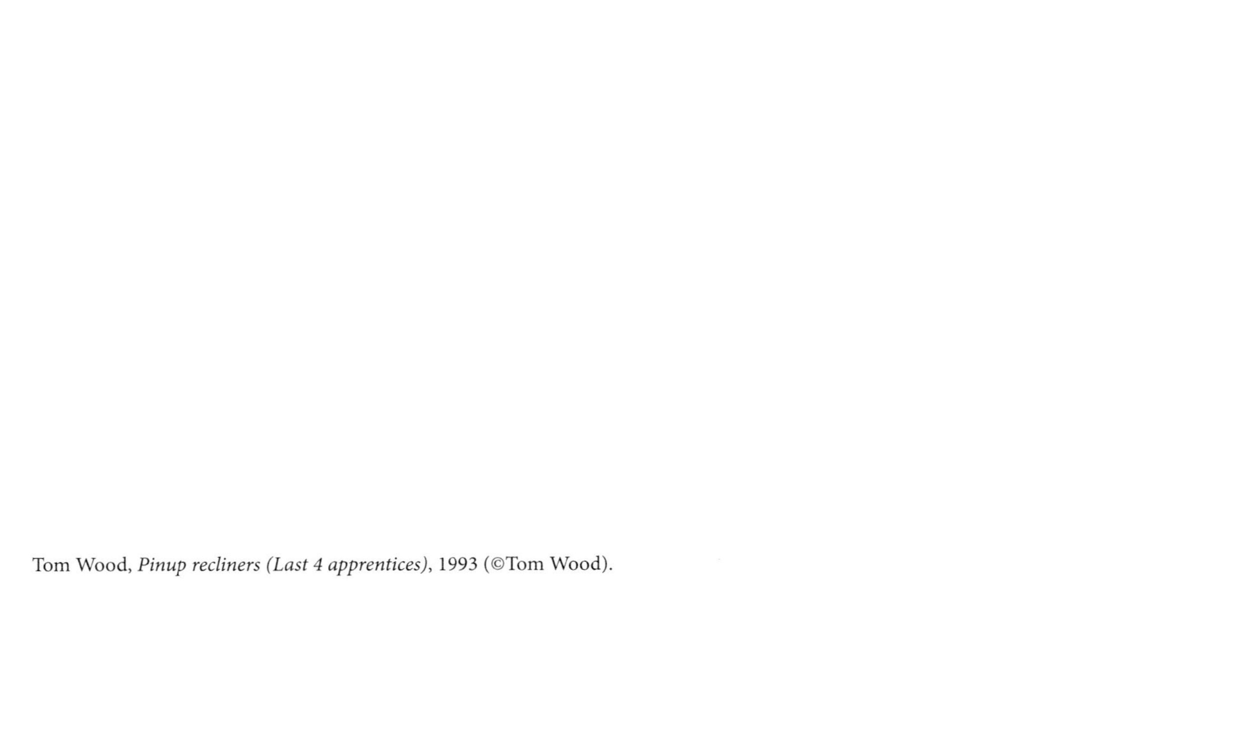

Tom Wood, *Pinup recliners (Last 4 apprentices)*, 1993 (©Tom Wood).

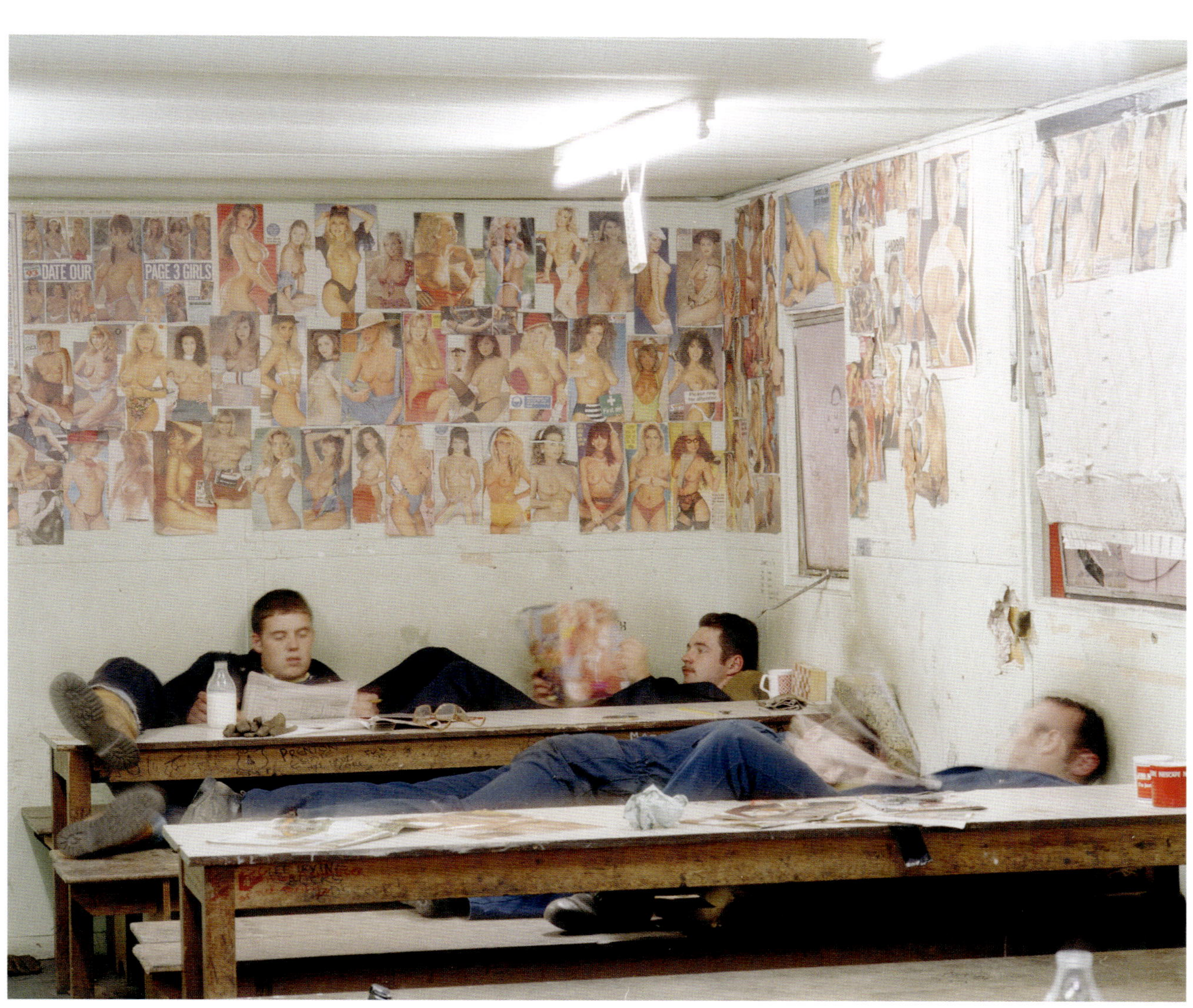
DATE OUR
PAGE 3 GIRLS

Tom Wood, *Life Room*, 1975 (©Tom Wood).

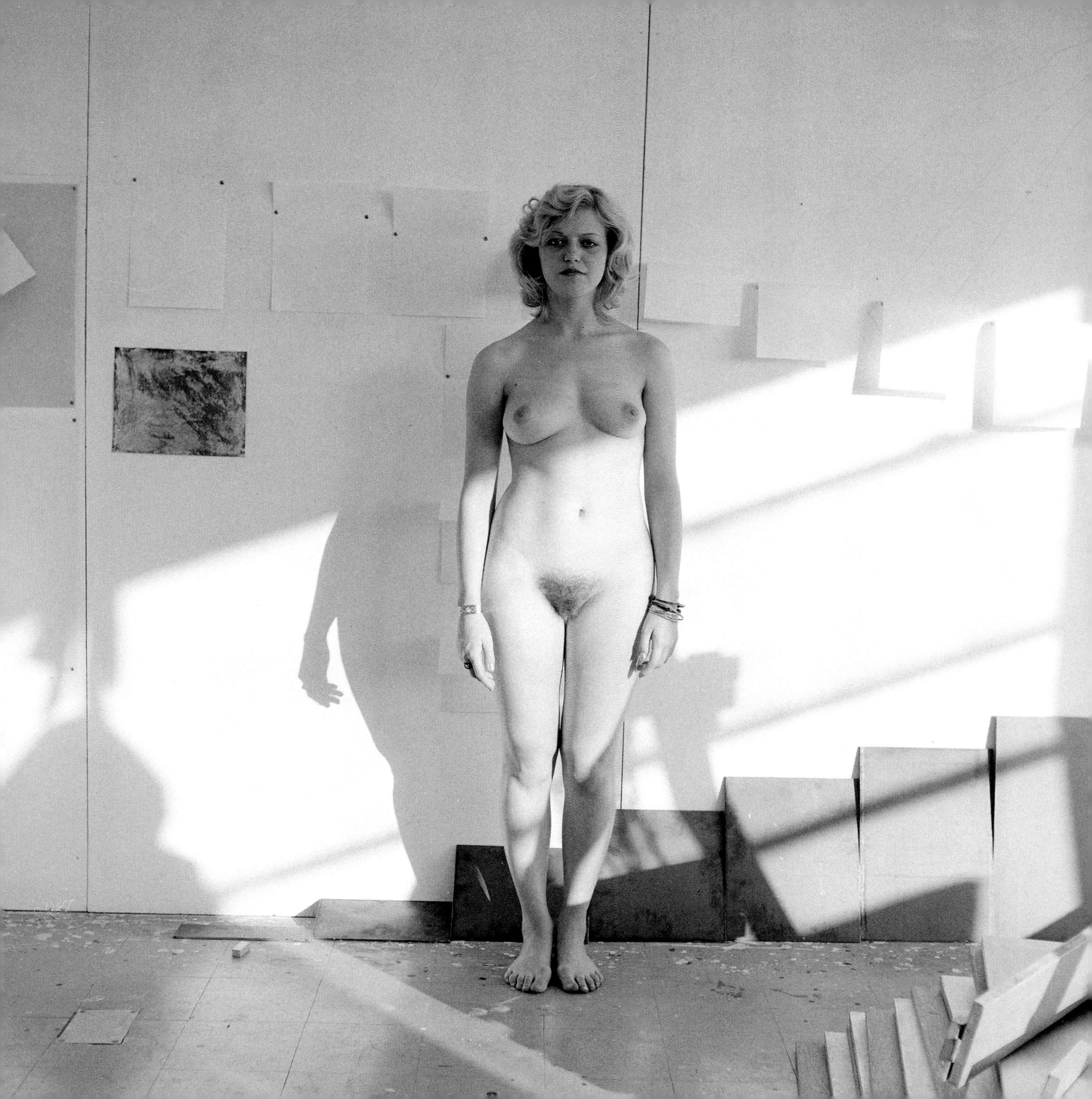

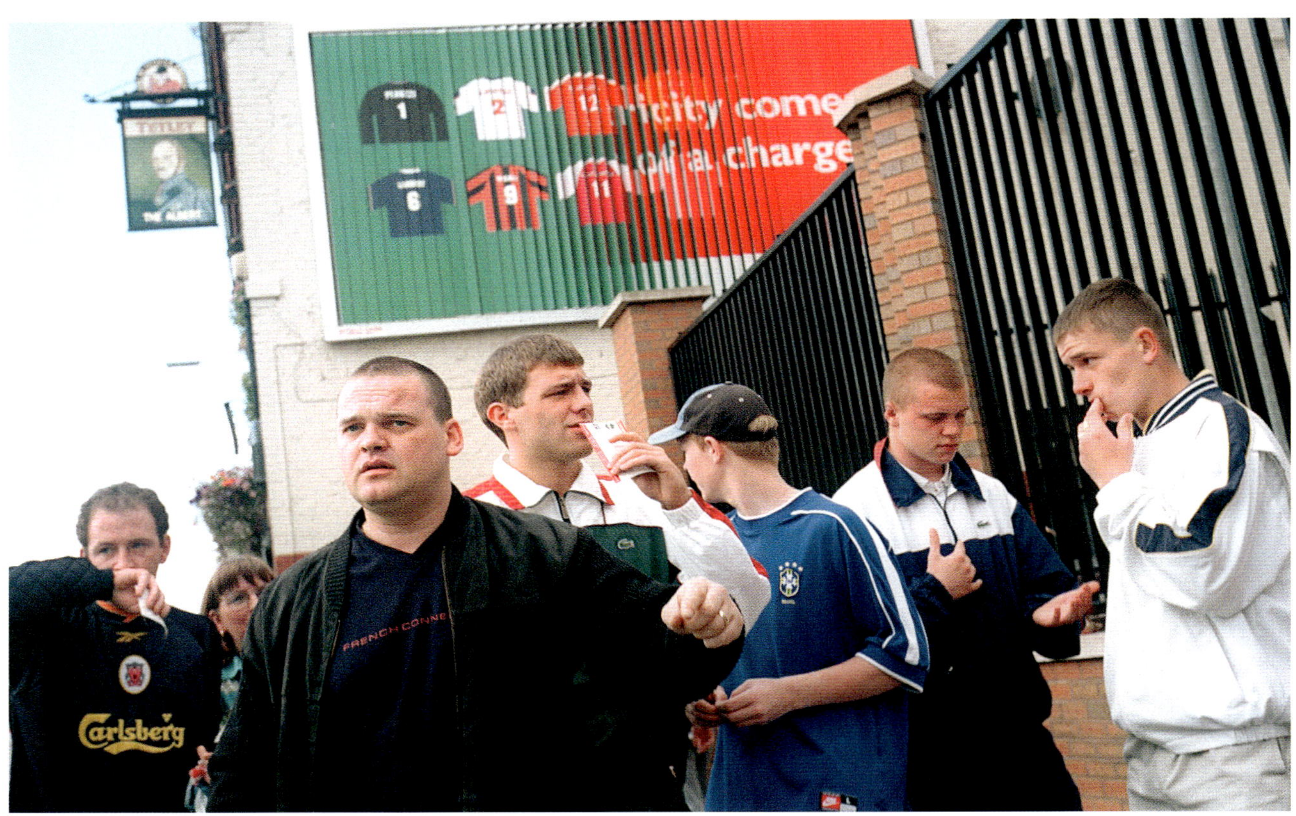

Tom Wood, *Calculating*, 1998 (©Tom Wood).

NOTES

1 My discussion of Tom Wood's work stems from an essay, 'From Life', originally published for his book, *F/M*, Villeurbanne: Editions deux-cent-cinq, 2011.
2 This and following quotes taken from Colin Westerbeck and Joel Meyerowitz, *Bystander: A History of Street Photography*, London: Thames and Hudson, 1994, p.34.
3 See http://iconicphotos.wordpress.com/2009/04/23/behind-the-gare-st-lazare/ (accessed 1st May 2012).
4 For more on this, see my essay 'Defining the Moment', in ed. David Brittain, *Creative Camera: Thirty Years of Writing*, Manchester: Manchester University Press, 2000, pp. 290–95. (Originally published in *Creative Camera*, February/ March 1998).
5 This and subsequent quotes from Meyerowitz taken from Colin Westerbeck's *Joel Meyerowitz*, London: Phaidon 2005.
6 Ed. Barbaralee Diamonstein, *Visions and Images: Photographers on Photography*, London: Travelling Light, 1982, p.181.
7 Garry Winogrand, *Public Relations*, New York: Museum of Modern Art, 1974.
8 Tom Wood, *All Zones Off Peak*, Stockport: Dewi Lewis, 1998.

LEADING PLATO INTO THE DARKROOM

CLIVE CAZEAUX

Perfection lies at the heart of Plato's metaphysics, his theory of the fundamental nature of being. He argues for the existence of a higher realm occupied by the Forms. Every kind of thing we experience in our world – physical or abstract – obtains its origin and shape from its higher, singular, perfect Form, much as if our world were made of dough cut into shapes by stencils. However, we ordinary mortals are not aware of this higher realm because we are tantalized by the senses, and representational art only makes things worse by glorifying appearances. Plato likens our situation to being prisoners in a cave, mistaking shadows on the walls for reality, and not realizing that ultimate existence lies outside in the light. The best we can do, he argues, is to lead a moral life, to excel, to approach the perfection of our Form. But then the Form of photography appeared, and led Plato back deeper into the cave, into the darkest space possible. This chapter considers the impact of photography on Plato's metaphysics and, in so doing, demonstrates the capacity of technology to challenge and generate philosophical thought.

To be perfect: the exemplary form of something; free from any blemish or flaw, and complete in the sense that you have all the required elements, properties or characteristics. Photography invites, points towards or demands perfection (I comment upon these relationships below) in a number of ways. Photographs of the human form, especially in advertising, are idealized (blemishes removed, height-to-width ratios made more pleasing) to denote beautiful people enjoying beautiful lives. In the countryside, if an object is present which upsets the (uncritical) sense of 'perfect nature' that is taken to pervade the scene, the photographer might have to move to the left a bit or down a bit so that the object is out of shot or, failing that, it can always be edited out later. In the case of documentary photography, have I 'done justice' to the scene? Do my photographs contain a complete record of the situation? Have they captured what was there? Did I capture the moment?

If these forms of perfection occupy photography's relationship with the world, then there are others which belong to the technology of photography, photography as a process in itself. The photograph should be speck-free. Areas of tone or colour which refer to continuous, blemish-free surfaces or expanses in reality – for example, a clear blue sky or reflections off glass – should not be interrupted by a dot or scratch. This tells us that a speck of dirt got in between the light and the photosensitive paper. Another element is the sharpness of lines, edges and borders between areas or objects.

This is vital since it determines the contrast between in-focus and out-of-focus, helping to create a figure-ground relationship and to instil a sense of depth. It used to tell us whether the camera was focused at the time the image was taken, but this can now be corrected digitally. Instead, sharpness can now be a matter of whether an image has been enlarged beyond the point where its pixels become visible. With digital photographic technology, cameras are caught within the drive to produce images made up of an ever-increasing number of megapixels. While this makes it possible to print and project photographs on an increasingly larger scale (the more pixels per square centimetre, the larger an image can be viewed before the pixels that make it up become visible), it is also wedded to the desire that, if the numbers were large enough, we would be able to record appearances with a precision which ensured that every visual aspect of the scene was recorded.

Conventions of composition, lighting, tone, contrast and depth of field set up the distinction between professional and amateur photography. These give professionals a set of criteria with which they can measure their professionalism, but also create problems of evaluation and classification for anyone wishing to challenge those conventions. Artistic departures from convention which might appear amateurish to a professional eye because they are blurred, poorly lit or 'uncomposed' invariably go under the name 'art photography'. Compositionally, once a frame has been placed around a series of objects, relationships – lines of connection or opposition – emerge, often demanding judgments as to the perfect state of balance or imbalance. Whether it happens consciously or unconsciously, there is a tussle over the extent to which one should work with or against arrangements governed by classical, numerical qualities such as rhythm, asymmetry and the golden section.[1]

Even though Plato's philosophy predates photography by over two millennia, there are at least four correspondences between it and photography, especially photography as something which invites or demands perfection:

- Perfection lies at the heart of Plato's metaphysics.
- His philosophy is organized by images of sunlight and dark chambers.
- According to his metaphysics, in order for the good life to prevail, visual representation must be banned.
- He also suggests that technology can assist human beings in pursuit of the good life.

Within Plato's philosophy as it can be applied to photography today, there are ideas, arguments and images that are thematically close to photography that argue vehemently against it, and that create intriguing collisions between photography and philosophies of technology. Ultimately, his philosophy is a metaphysics of perfection inclined against the value of photography, but which nevertheless offers concepts and claims that can be respectively worked with and challenged to arrive at a positive evaluation of the ontological value of photography; by which I mean the value of photography as a technological practice, which can upset the stable distinctions of reality. This helps to place photography within the wider, cultural project of demonstrating that things might be otherwise than they are, and calls attention to capacity of photography to be the creator of other worlds rather than the representation of the one we already have.[2]

Plato's philosophy is organized by images of sunlight and dark rooms or chambers. As ordinary mortals, we do not or cannot detect the existence of a higher realm beyond our sensory, physical reality. Plato likens our situation to being prisoners in a cave, mistaking shadows on the walls for reality, and not realizing that ultimate existence lies outside in the light. Because his entire metaphysics is structured by concepts of excellence and perfection, and about what we have to do in order to achieve excellence, goodness or 'the Good' plays a pivotal role. The Form of the Good, for Plato, 'gives the objects of knowledge their truth and the knower's mind the power of knowing.'[3] The Form of the Good is active within us in that it allows us to understand things clearly, where there is a triple-action in the sense that (1) the object, (2) the power to know the object for what it is, and (3) the Form of the Good as the enabling condition of both the object and knowledge of the object are present. Plato explains it by analogy again to the sun: 'The sun, I think you will agree, not only makes the things we see visible [1], but causes the processes of generation, growth and nourishment [2], *without itself being such a process* [3]'.[4] Thus the Form of the Good enables knowledge of the essence of things i.e. the Forms, without it (the Good) being the essence of things. Because the Good allows perception of the perfect state of being to which we aspire, it serves as a bridge between knowledge, morality and politics in Plato's metaphysics, a condition of 'knowing well' that is essential for leadership and the conferral of order in the interests of greater acquaintance with the Forms.

It does not take much interpretive work to read Plato's philosophy as an attack on photography in as much as it denies that visual representation is a form of knowing well. The visual representation of reality, Plato avows, is a 'at a third remove from the truth' because it is the product of imperfect knowledge about the physical world.[5] Empirical knowledge, that is, knowledge via the senses, of our everyday, physical reality is at one remove from the truth because, as far as Plato is concerned, it is indirect (via the senses) acquaintance of a secondary level of existence. To create representations of this secondary reality, as the photographer does, is not only at a second remove from the truth, but at a third (1) because it is a copy of a physical object (a copy of a copy of a Form), and (2) because photographic reproduction of an object will have been produced without proper knowledge of the object in question. Plato makes the point most forcefully through the dialogue between Socrates and Glaucon. What is it, Socrates asks, that a painter represents when they produce an image of a bed: is it the bed-in-itself as it is in nature, i.e. the Form of the bed, or the mere appearance of a physical bed?

SOCRATES: If you look at a bed, or anything else, sideways or endways or from some other angle, does it make any difference to the bed? Isn't it merely that it *looks* different, without *being* different? And similarly with other things.

GLAUCON: Yes, it's the same bed, but it looks different.

SOCRATES: Then consider – when the painter makes his representation, does he do so by reference to the object as it actually is or to its superficial appearance? Is his representation one of an apparition or of the truth?

GLAUCON: Of an apparition.

SOCRATES: The art of representation is therefore a long way removed from the truth, and it is able to reproduce everything because it has little grasp of anything, and that little is of a mere phenomenal appearance.[6]

As well as being the result of a lack of knowledge, of knowing well, visual representation can also be done quite quickly. As if to anticipate the portable and instantaneous properties of photography, Plato declares that the quickest way to create representations 'is to take a mirror and turn it around in all directions; before long you will create sun and stars and earth, yourself and all other animals and plants.'[7] The art of representation is therefore 'a long way removed from the truth' because, rather than attempting to know its objects well, it produces another reality, moving away from the reality of the Forms. This prompts Plato to judge the work of artists as morally reprehensible, and to declare that all artists should be banished from the state.[8]

So far, it would seem that Plato is against photography because of the wedge his philosophy places between representation and perfection. But he should in fact be congratulated for anticipating some of the ethical doubts surrounding photographic representation. If we recall the perfections I listed above regarding photography's relationship with the world – for example, idealized images of beautiful people, the perfect landscape, a moment captured – these are all questionable ethically to a greater or lesser degree. One of Plato's concerns with visual representation is that it may trick people into mistaking the image for reality. 'If [a painter] is skilful enough', he writes, 'his portrait of a carpenter may, at a distance, deceive children or simple people into thinking it is a real carpenter.'[9] This is arguably what happens when people experience feelings of inadequacy in the face of depictions of beautiful people leading perfect lives. My life should be like theirs, and I cannot be happy and fulfilled until I attain the state depicted in the photograph. A similar principle is central to censorship (Plato's declaration that artists should be banished from the state is the first step towards censorship in the history of western thought): a film, a censor might argue, should be banned if it depicts actions that, when enacted in real life, are illegal, harmful, degrading, etc.; in other words, if viewers mistake the material in the film for reality or actions which may be performed in reality. Although Plato reasoned that it is only the very young or 'simple' who might be prone to such deception, the media-saturatedness of our culture makes it difficult for any individual not to assign reality or importance to the vast number of visual representations which fill pages, screens, windows and billboards.[10] At the other end of the scale arguably in terms of ethical importance is the cost to the moment created by the attempt to capture it photographically. Preoccupation with what is required technologically to take a good photograph of a situation, it could be claimed, removes you from the situation, prevents you contributing to it. The ethical consequence, in Platonic terms, is that trying to capture the moment photographically could be construed as a period of time away from a practice or activity that is cultivating you as a human being; a period wasted on wrestling with the technology whose end product will be a distraction from life.

Another perspective is introduced by the concept of *technē*. The concept is ambiguous in Plato's writings. It does not receive a systematic treatment, but is rather given a number of overlapping meanings across his dialogues, and achieves some consistency as a result.[11] What is consistent is the definition of *technē* as knowledge of how to use an instrument well; it is more often than not translated as 'craft' or 'skill'.[12] There is a duality here: knowledge, something we possess as human beings, of how to use an instrument well. Two points follow from this. First, *technē* is a form of what we might today think of as the integration of theory and practice: the doing and knowledge about doing.[13] Second, the duality introduces the idea that technology has ontological significance: that is to say, it requires us to consider the kinds of being or process at work in any technological activity, and the broader metaphysics or theory of existence which these beings or processes serve. For Plato, *technē* involves the excellence or well-being of two entities: ours, as human beings who are trying to live in accordance with our essence, by expanding our knowledge; and that of the instrument. Any instrument or anything with a function, Plato argues, has an 'excellence' or a 'virtue', what we might call a 'perfect operation', that which it does best:

SOCRATES:	Could you cut off a vine-shoot with a carving-knife or a chisel or other tool?
THRASYMACHUS:	You could.
SOCRATES:	But you would do the job best if you used a pruning-knife.
THRASYMACHUS:	True.
SOCRATES:	Shall we then call this its 'function'?
THRASYMACHUS:	Yes, let us.
SOCRATES:	And I think you may see now what I meant by asking if the 'function' of a thing was not that which only it can do or that which it does best.
THRASYMACHUS:	Yes, I understand, and I think that is what we mean by a thing's function.

SOCRATES: Good. And has not everything which has a function its own particular excellence? Let me take the same examples again. The eyes have a function, have they not?[14]

The 'excellence' or 'virtue' is the essential property which allows any instrument to perform its function well, which allows a pruning knife to be better at cutting a vine shoot than a carving knife or a chisel.[15] The split between knowledge and instrumental excellence occurs in Plato because he is primarily concerned with the life of the mind, and the good life or living well (what he refers to as 'statecraft'), in the interests of gaining knowledge of the Forms. The good life is ultimately a life of the mind for Plato since he takes justice to be the excellence which drives the mind's ability to deal with life.

For our purposes, if we apply Plato's concept of *technē* to photography, we get a division between the knowledge of the photographer on the one hand, and the excellence of the photographic equipment, be it the camera, enlarger, printing technology or associated software, on the other. But what is the function of photography, and the excellence which powers it? One might be tempted to say its function is representation, in which case we would remain with the idea that Plato's philosophy is opposed to photography. But I don't think we can straightforwardly say that photography's function is representation. As I demonstrated at the start of the chapter, looking at the perfections of photography, photography opens onto two sets of properties: those connected with representation and others tied to its own operation. The distinction continues even with a broader consideration of photographic practice, one not immediately focused on the perfections of photography. Which camera should I take with me? Which format or film or lenses should I use, and where should I settle on the trade-off between the size and the portability of the camera? The 'should' in all three cases will be a matter of either what kind of technology I think is appropriate to the setting or situation in which I shall find myself, or the determination of what is possible photographically during the project; the manipulations, settings and the kind of handling which the camera will permit. Notice the opposition at work: my photographic equipment is selected either because I think it is the right kind of kit for the situation (but what determines rightness here?) or because *it* is calling the shots: that is to say, I want the properties introduced by the technology to determine or influence the work or be prominent within it.

The contrast between representation and photography's own operation suggests a number of functions are possible. To give just four (others may be conceivable): on the side of representation, (1) capturing or reproducing an appearance or event; and on the side of photography's own operation, (2) determining the range of technological settings, sensitivities and effects that are possible; (3) introducing properties into photographs which display its own operation, such as the selection and arrangement of objects, lighting, the grain of the image, contrast, colour density, sharpness or blur; and (4) promoting the creation of meanings through the combination of elements within a frame. The split between knower and instrument occurs within Plato's concept of *technē* because he is preoccupied with the life of the mind. The ambition is for the knower to become acquainted with the excellence behind the function of the instrument. But with photography, we have at least four functions. This suggests that photography poses a challenge to Plato's philosophy. The function of an instrument as far as Plato is concerned has to be singular, driven by an excellence which is a manifestation in this world of the instrument's perfect Form. The easiest way to enable Plato's thought to accommodate photography (which is not necessarily my intention) is to divide photography into four (or more) sub-practices, along the lines of the functions described above – we might call them 'representation', 'photographic self-determination', 'the display of technically-generated properties' and 'frame-based meaning generation' – so that each function has its own excellence.

But the more important issue, I think, is the fact that photography, considered in the light of Plato's thought, creates these splits. Photography brings complexity and manifoldness to a metaphysics which is predicated on simplicity and singularity. This is not considered by Plato because he does not get this far. Visual representation, as he understands it, does not have a *technē* because, even though it is something that can be done well, as in producing a lifelike portrait, it works against the greater metaphysical imperative of promoting knowledge of the Forms. Prior to the camera, visual representation was the mind (misguided, as Plato saw it) directing the hand which held a paintbrush, but the function of a paintbrush is to distribute paint, not to create likenesses. Rather than being a process in its own right, representation for Plato was simply movement in the wrong metaphysical direction. The only kind of representation that Plato valued was the literary form of epic poetry. It tells stories of individuals behaving courageously and ethically in the face of adversity, and therefore offers exemplars of how to live. But even epic poetry does not possess a *technē*. Rather, epic poets are able to speak well of heroic figures, Plato declares in the *Ion*, because they are men possessed by a divine power, much in the same way that a magnet is invested with the power to attract iron.[16]

The arrival of photography is not the arrival of just another instrument with a function, but the emergence of a complex of operations which resists reduction to a single aim or thing. It might sound as if this would be news only for philosophers, especially Platonic ones, keen to establish the perfect photograph or the essence of photography. But what is novel is the result that by approaching photography through Plato, by pressing it to see if it has an excellence, we find it fracturing into a number of different essences, different drives towards perfection. As we saw at the start, photography invites, points towards or demands perfection. Maybe the senses of 'invitation', 'pointing towards' and 'demand' are manifestations of photography's propensity for fracturing into individual operations. Anything can be done well, but with photography we have a technology that demands excellence in a number of different directions, where that sense of demand is the quantity of operations manifest as a felt quality. We think, when we pick up a camera, we are embarking on one activity, when in fact we are opening ourselves to many, where each makes very different demands upon us.

What are we to make of the splits in photography? If we work on Plato's terms for a moment to see what the implications of his metaphysics might be, they entail that we, as knowers, know each thing as one thing, and we know it well. These things are not different aspects of one thing, not splinters from a larger whole, but entirely different things. This is photography multiplied. For some, this might be an accurate description of how they think about photography: of the several photographies available, there is one which dominates and drives the practice, and which, for that photographer, is photography, such as trying to capture the moment. But are these multiple photographies truly different things? Could it not be the case that what we are here obliged to refer to as 'photographies' are in fact aspects of a larger whole, that photography possesses an integrity of its own which works against any philosophical ambition to identify and enumerate essences? I say this because it is by no means certain that the different photographies identified above – capturing the moment, technical settings, the display of technical properties, and meanings within a frame – can be separated out from one another as discrete objects or processes. There will be some arrangements of technical settings that are more amenable to capturing the moment than others. What those settings are, for example, whether a comparatively long or short exposure is set, will depend on the situation and the moment 'captured' from it; the moment may lend itself to a blurred image or a crisp, frozen one. Similarly, determining the range of technological settings, sensitivities and effects that are possible (point 2 above) cannot be easily separated from an interest in how these internal operations are displayed or become visible in the resulting photographs (point 3). The composition of a photograph, deciding which elements are included within the frame ostensibly as a record of 'what was there at the time' (point 1), may be influenced by the meanings generated when these elements when placed side-by-side one another in a frame (point 4). In other words, signification can precede or determine representation.[17] This suggests that photography challenges the metaphysical structure of Plato's philosophy by being a technology that resists singularity. It can do this, I propose, because its various functions do not operate purely within their own boundaries, but are always in a state of requiring or enabling other functions, as in the case of the correct settings required for representation or the generation of meaning from elements arranged within a pictorial frame. Instead of a single path towards an essence, we have a series of criss-crossing operations.

The splitting action exercised by *technē* is present in the sunlight metaphor that underpins Plato's philosophy of the Forms: (1) the sun is the power by which we know; (2) the sun generates the things we know; but (3) the sun is not itself a process of generation, but an entirely different object, therefore allowing it to play the role of the independently existing Form of the Good. These divisions affect how technology is conceptualized, how it is understood to operate in the world with us; in more philosophical terms, they cut up technology according to a specific, Platonic ontology. The three-way division serves a metaphysics which explains reality by illustrating how lots of different, earthly beings and objects, e.g. humans, cats, trees, knives, can know or be known at an earthly level (we might picture the knower and known as defining the base of a triangle), while simultaneously illustrating how they are all shadows of higher Forms, with some (humans) working towards knowledge of their original Form (with the sides of the triangle serving as lines of descent and ascent).

There are two ways in which this carving up of technology could be challenged:

contest the metaphysics of the Forms, especially the Form of the Good (since it is the Form of all Forms), and question the division between the knower and the known. I intend to pursue the latter because: (1) there is no shortage of accounts attacking the Forms – all the commentaries on Plato consulted so far include criticisms; (2) the division between the knower and the known fails to acknowledge an important aspect of the creative relationship we can have with technology; and (3) there is an alternative theory of technology which not only does justice to this creative aspect of technology, but also does so in terms of an organic, sunlight-related metaphor, except that 'the processes of generation, growth and nourishment' are put to different use. The alternative theory in question is provided by the twentieth-century German phenomenologist Martin Heidegger. Heidegger's phenomenology is very different from, and arguably opposed to, Plato's idealism. Whereas Plato presents the universe as organized by a set of singular essences, Heidegger's phenomenology is rooted in a tradition which rejects the idea that reality divided into objects is a valid basis for metaphysics. For Heidegger, neither an object, an objective essence, nor human subjectivity serves as the foundation for a theory of existence. Neither is knowledge or the acquisition of knowledge in pursuit of an end assumed to be the basis of human life. Although it is not readily associated with him, a shorthand term for Heidegger's philosophy might be 'ecological': he makes our condition as beings rooted in and engaged with the world the foundation for his thought, and asks what is possible in a situation given the potentialities that lie within it.

Heidegger's philosophy of technology is largely a negative one in that he thinks that technology puts us in the position of being manipulators of nature. While we might generally talk of technology being a means for us to organize and cope with the world, Heidegger finds greater significance in these activities. Technology, he writes, is 'no mere means'.[18] The essence of modern, instrumental technology, he declares, 'lies in enframing': 'the energy concealed in nature is unlocked', 'transformed', 'stored up', 'distributed', and 'switched about' according to human needs.[19] An aeroplane waiting on a runway is the result of enframing in as much 'as it is ordered to ensure the possibility of transportation. For this it must be in its whole structure and in every one of its constituent parts itself on call for duty, i.e., ready for takeoff'.[20] Human technological action is significant here: we with our tools (in fact, this could be hyphenated as 'we-with-our-tools' to emphasize the sense of rootedness and engagement underpinning

Heidegger's thought) are involved in the unlocking, transforming, storing, etc. Humans as technological beings are 'revealers' of nature; we-with-our-tools engage with nature in such a way as to allow it to present itself in different forms. For example, modern physics, Heidegger claims, is dependent upon technical apparatus for the disclosure or 'bringing-forth' of a realm of representation beyond human visualizability; 'the bursting of a blossom into bloom', as he describes it.[21] His warning to us is that unless we are aware of the fundamentally disclosive nature of technology, we stand to lose sight of the fact that for each realm which is revealed to us, other potential realms remain undisclosed. The danger is that technology is viewed as that which serves us as manipulators or 'master locksmiths' of nature, when Heidegger's ambition is that recognition of the revelatory, disclosive relation will promote a culture of working with nature.

The idea that technology is disclosive gives it a very different metaphysical status. Rather than technology being a means to a singular, predetermined end exercised by a knowing individual, it is instead a state of interaction in which there is awareness and examination of what might be possible given the items which are to hand in the situation. Heidegger intends this not to have the quality of a 'subject meets object' encounter, since this relies on a metaphysics of discrete, individual entities, but instead to acknowledge (and even promote) the difficulty involved in describing an experience in non-dualistic terms, and to present experience as something generative, an occasion where new things or aspects become possible through the attention that is paid to a situation. We can plot the change in the metaphysical status of technology through Heidegger's use of the sunlight-related 'generation and growth' metaphor. Whereas it serves a dualistic, if not trilogistic, system in Plato – illumination is divided to become the light with which the knower beholds the light-sustained object, with the sun all the while abiding as the origin of both – with Heidegger, the idea is that new things arise, possibilities emerge, hitherto unimagined actions are invited like 'the bursting of a blossom into bloom' (although it has to be recognized that not all of them will necessarily be good). This is not a 'process of generation' emitted by an essential sunlight, but one that is an opening constitutive of experience conceived in non-subject-object terms. Think of all the things and actions that become possible when a favourite tool is to hand, and all the things or actions that are closed off when that tool is lost or broken. These are not simply new things laid before us to consider casually.

For Heidegger, their becoming possible is intimately tied to our being. 'Possibility' is the most appropriate (and very Heideggerian) word for them, in as much as they are prospects or potential lines of action that are open for us to explore, with each exploratory step revealing new aspects inviting further enquiry, and where the state of 'being open for us' defines our existence in relation to them. We are not reviewing them as a detached bystander but rather, in this moment, are consumed by questions: 'Do I try this?'; 'Do I try that?'; 'What happens if I push here?' To put the point more strongly still: *we* become the questioning.

The Platonic division between the knower and the known, I think, fails to acknowledge the creative relationship which we can have with technology, and it is this aspect which Heidegger makes central, not only to his philosophy of technology but also to his phenomenology.[22] Let us look at this in relation to photography. What I have in mind draws upon on the criss-crossing of the different photographies which we reached with Plato: capturing the moment, familiarity with all possible technical settings, the capacity for the camera's technical condition to be manifest in an image, and the meanings created within a frame. Plato's knower-known relationship works on the understanding that a knower can approach complete knowledge of the known; these are the two sides of the triangle moving upwards to come together at the summit, the sun. But working with a camera creatively, I am looking to see what it can do, what it reveals.[23] There are three parts to this: 'looking', 'to see', and 'what it can do'. In reverse order: 'what it can do': the camera is active. The settings it permits (point 2 above) affect what is displayed (point 3 above). 'I am looking *to see*…': I don't know in advance the results of what it can do in that situation, the images generated through the interlocking of its settings and my handling of it in the environment. I want *to see* the results because they are unexpected. All four photographies are active here: (2) intermingling with (3) as before, but I am also attentive to how they represent or transform the setting (1), and the new meanings which might arise (4). Thirdly, 'I am *looking* to see…' in that all of the above is an appetite. My attention, my being, is not just given to seeing what is possible; I do not just casually survey what might have been revealed. Rather, during the process of making photographs, my being is the seeing what is possible. This description, in terms which deliberately avoid a clear subject-object partition, is a manifestation of the rootedness in the environment that is the ground of human being (or *Dasein*, 'being-there') for Heidegger. When one is creatively exploring what a camera can do, as opposed to, say, practising with it in order to perfect its supposed singular function, one is working across all these different functions, experimenting with how they intersect, how one operation might bring a new possibility to another.

I have been exploring the network of themes created by photography, perfection and Plato. Perfection is the basis of Plato's metaphysics, and prompts him to reject visual representation as a form of knowledge. The drive to know something as one thing well, expressed by the concept *technē*, leads to a series of divisions: between knower and known, and between different aspects of photography or different photographies. The latter show that photography is not just one more function among others, but a technology which resists Plato's metaphysics on account of the fact that it is a complex of interacting functions. The key point here is that the functions are interacting, contributing to one another, rather than serving the Platonic ideal of working in a single direction upwards towards the perfect Form of each individual photography. It was unlikely that Plato was ever going to be made out to be the photographer's friend due to his dismissal of representation. What this study has done is give the photographer a reply to Plato: my practice challenges your metaphysics. Photography's different functions or identities, working across the division between 'being about the world' and 'being about itself', not only frustrates the desire for unity, but rejects the notion of representation as a mere copy of reality, since representation cannot be divorced from the other, 'internal' functions of photography.

Maybe photographers ought to give Plato some credit. His metaphysics has allowed us to recognize that different excellences are at work in photography. Technically, we should refer to 'photography' in the plural. As I have suggested, it is possibly the number of photographies at work in the practice we ordinarily call photography, each with its own requirements, that is responsible for its inviting, pointing towards or demanding perfection. The thrust of my argument though has been to assert that these photographies criss-cross one another and, in so doing, resist Plato's philosophy. This gives us an instance of technology (including our relationship with it) impinging upon the metaphysical distinctions with which we carve up reality. It also shows how the pieces into which photography is cut by Plato can be put to different work by another metaphysics. Just as Heidegger realigns the metaphor of sunlight and growth, so his emancipatory philosophy of technology lets us witness how the various photographies intersect with one another as part of a rooted, creative exploration of what photographic technology makes possible. The tension between the two philosophies might be summed up as the difference between endorsing (with Plato) and rejecting (with Heidegger) a sense of 'belonging', 'ownership' or 'oneness'. In making or looking at a photograph, a positive Platonic assessment (in contrast to a negative one which would dismiss it as representation) might look for whether one of the photographies was approaching perfection or oneness, whereas a Heideggerian one would be preoccupied with what the various photographies had revealed, had made possible, fully mindful of the impossibility of trying to ascribe the revelation to one photography or another. This will be a photography which rejects perfection and turns instead to see what is possible.

NOTES

1 I owe many of the points here to discussions I had with my photographer friends Mal Bennett and Chris Short on the theme of perfection in photography.

2 Susan Sontag considers photography in relation to Plato in her essay 'In Plato's Cave'. She explores photography's promotion of subjectivity, its power to stand in for experience, its multiplication of representations, its capacity for generating moral outrage, and its ability to become a thing in itself – all Platonic themes. But she does not pursue the concept of perfection at length. See Susan Sontag, *On Photography*, New York: Penguin Putnam, 1977, pp. 3–24.

3 Plato, *Republic*, trans. D. Lee, Harmondsworth: Penguin, 1987, p. 508e.

4 Ibid. p. 509b.

5 Ibid. p. 597e.

6 Ibid. p. 598a–b.

7 Ibid. p. 596d–e.

8 Ibid. p. 605a–c.

9 Ibid. p. 598c.

10 This is taken further by Baudrillard's hyperrealism thesis. See, for example, Jean Baudrillard, *Simulacra and Simulation*, trans. S.F. Glaser, Ann Arbor: University of Michigan Press, 1984; Rex Butler, *Jean Baudrillard: The Defence of the Real*, London: Sage, 1999; and Andreas Huyssen, 'In the shadow of McLuhan: Jean Baudrillard's theory of simulation', *Assemblage*, No. 10, 1989, pp. 6–17.

11 For accounts of the various meanings of *technē* in Plato's philosophy, see J.C.B. Gosling, *Plato: Arguments of the Philosophers*, Abingdon: Routledge, 1973; George Harvey, '*Technē* and the Good in Plato's *Statesman and Philebus*', *Inquiry*, No. 47, 2009, pp. 1–34; Christopher Janaway, *Images of Excellence: Plato's Critique of the Arts*, Oxford: Clarendon Press, 1995; Jeff Mitscherling, T*he Image of a Second Sun: Plato on Poetry, Rhetoric, and the Technē of Mimēsis*, New York: Humanity Books, 2009; and Pheroze Wadia, 'The notion of *technē* in Plato', *Philosophical Studies*, No. 31, 1986, pp. 148–58.

12 See, for example, Gosling, 1973; G.M.A. Grube, *Plato's Thought*, London: Methuen, 1935; and Harvey, 2009.

13 This aspect of *technē* is prominent in Plato's dialogue *Gorgias*, as Gosling observes: 'A *technē* will yield an account of the nature of its subject and an explanation of its

activities, and will consider what is best for its subject. This latter is a matter of finding the right order and arrangement. For each thing has its proper order that constitutes its excellence, and is investigated by the skill covering it' (Gosling, 1973, p. 56).

14 Plato, 1987, pp. 353a–b.

15 The dialogue goes on to affirm that anything which has a function has that function as a result of an essential virtue or excellence, including the examples of the eyes and ears (whose respective functions are seeing and hearing). It is a step towards the conclusion that the business of life, such as management, control, deliberation, is the function of the mind or soul, behind which lies the excellence of justice.

16 Plato, 'Ion', in *Early Socratic Dialogues*, eds and trans. T. Saunders et al., Harmondsworth: Penguin, 1987, p. 533d.

17 It could even be argued the other way: that signification cancels or prevents representation, on the understanding that a photograph offers not the moment as it happened, but an appearance determined heavily by a series of interpretive decisions. We never witness the event as it happened; we only get to see an arrangement of elements composed by the photographer. In terms of the larger discussion underway here regarding the relationship between the various photographies created by Plato's metaphysics, this would amount to the need for photography's supposed representational function being discarded in favour of a notion of constructed meaning, or world-construction.

18 Martin Heidegger, 'The question concerning technology', in *Basic Writings*, ed. D.F. Krell, London: Routledge, 1993, p. 318.

19 Ibid. p. 322; p. 329.

20 Ibid. p. 322.

21 Ibid. p. 317.

22 The importance of tools and technology to Heidegger's philosophy is signalled by Harman, who entitles his study of Heidegger's metaphysics *Tool-Being*. See Graham Harman, *Tool-Being: Heidegger and the Metaphysics of Objects*, Chicago: Open Court, 2002.

23 I am drawing on conversations with photographer friends and colleagues, and on a combination of reading Heidegger and my familiarity with photography from my fine art degree practice.

FAILURE & PERFECTION

FILM WORKS BY JULIAN ROSEFELDT

JULIAN ROSEFELDT

Rosefeldt presents a series of production stills from his 'Trilogy of Failure': *The Soundmaker* ('Trilogy of Failure' / Part I, 2004); *Stunned Man* ('Trilogy of Failure' / Part II, 2004); and *The Perfectionist* ('Trilogy of Failure' / Part III, 2005). In these immaculate, looped film installations, Rosefeldt's tragicomedic protagonists are depicted in the privacy of their own homes – albeit in reconstructed/deconstructed studio settings – methodically going about their daily rituals. His characters unwittingly reveal unfathomable personal obsessions, the pursuit of which serve to reveal the fragility and absurdity of the human condition.

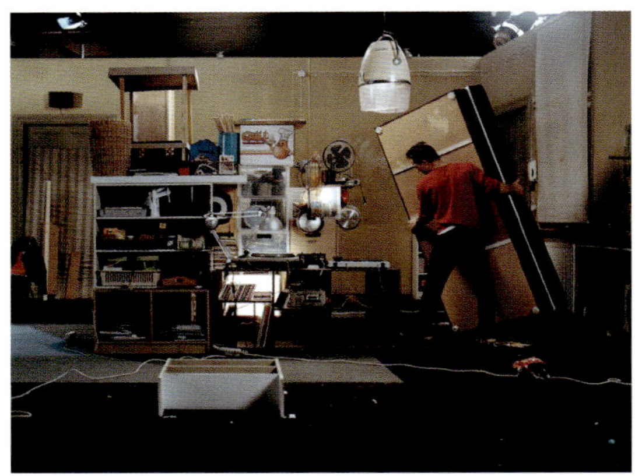

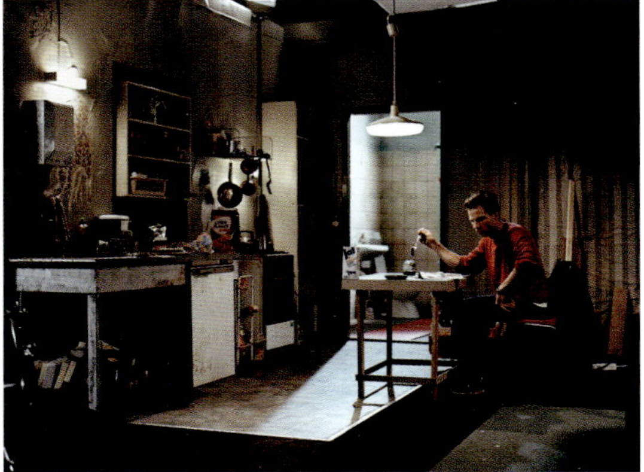

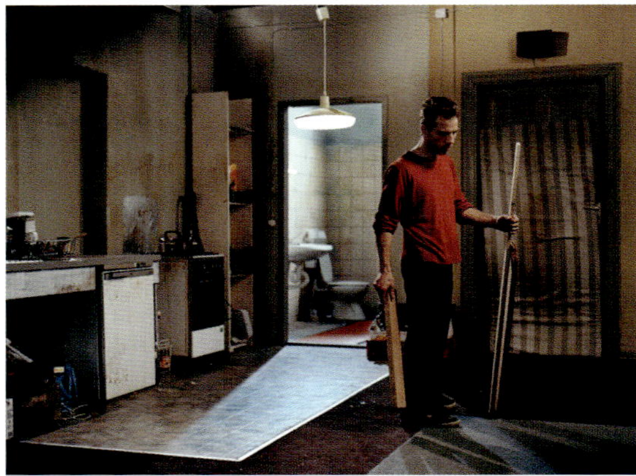

Above and opposite page: Julian Rosefeldt, *The Soundmaker* ('Trilogy of Failure' / Part I).

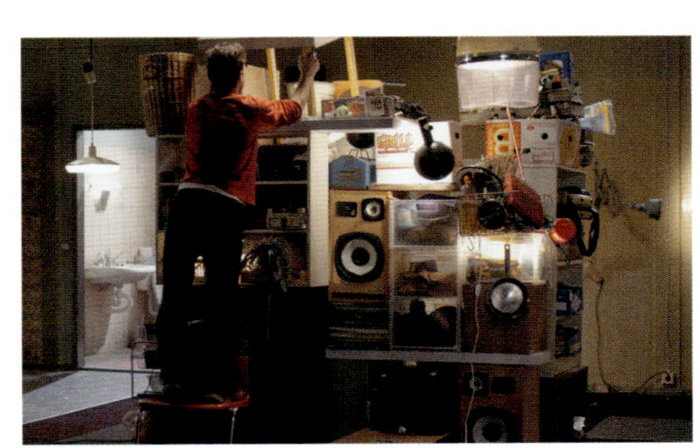

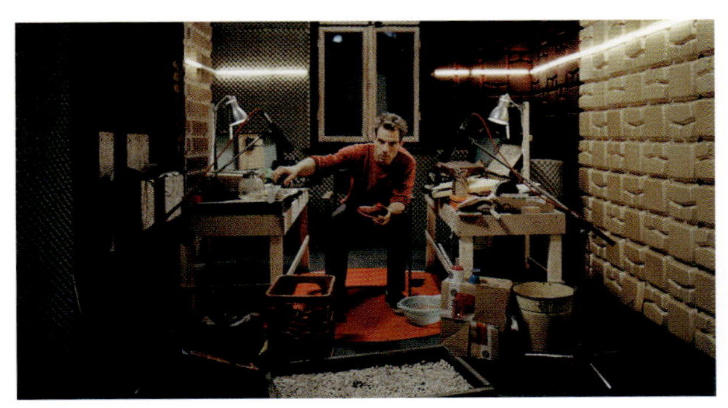

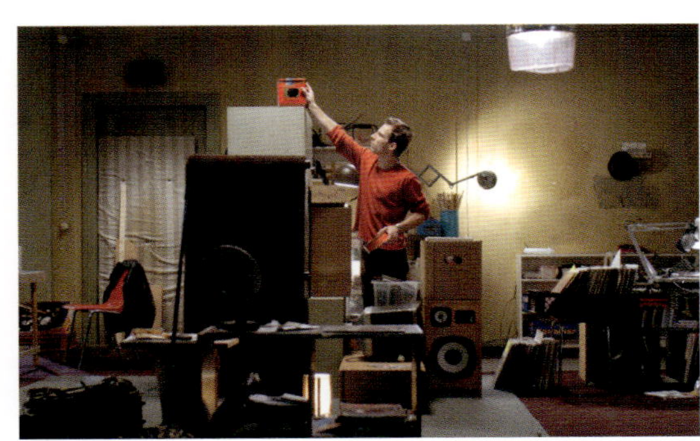

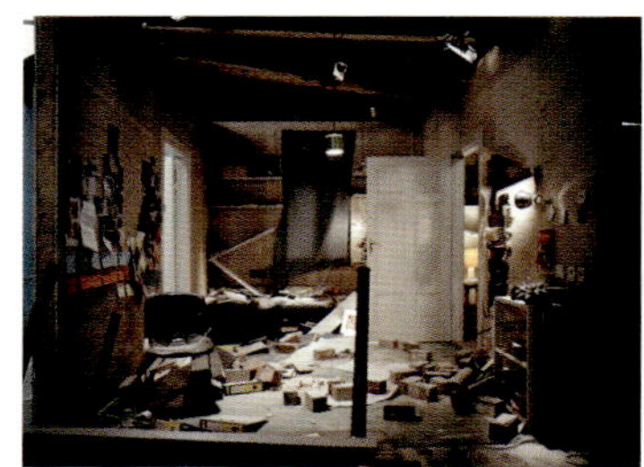

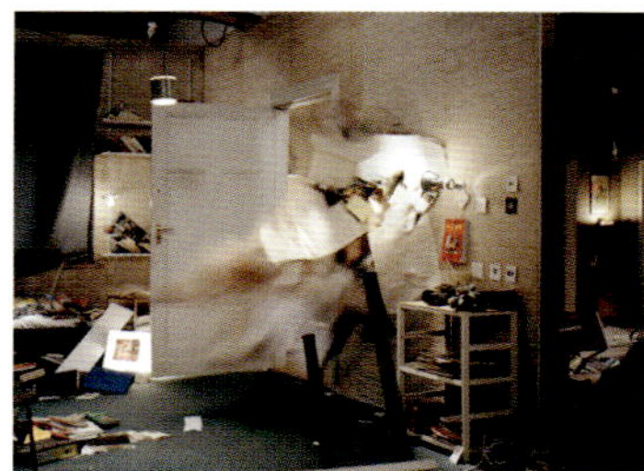

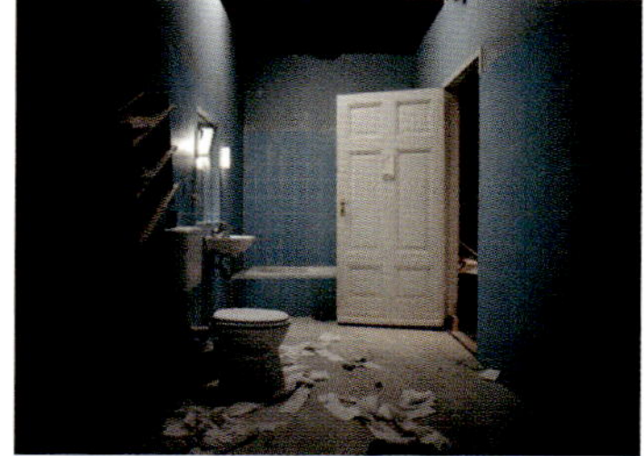

Above, opposite and following page: Julian Rosefeldt, *Stunned Man* ('Trilogy of Failure' / Part II).

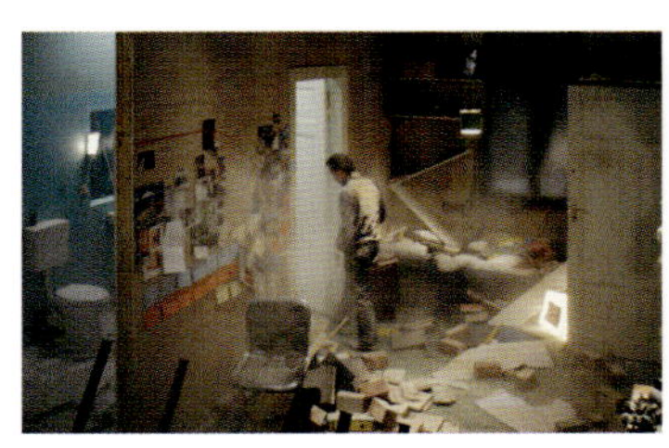

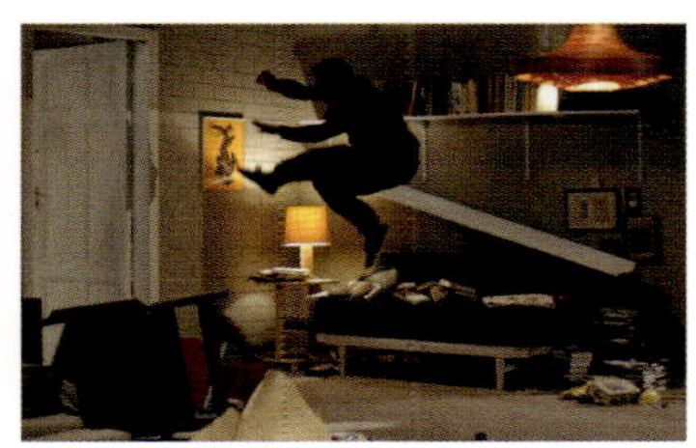

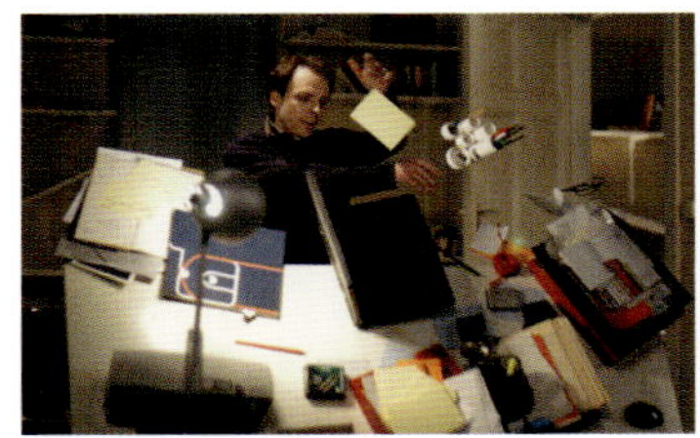

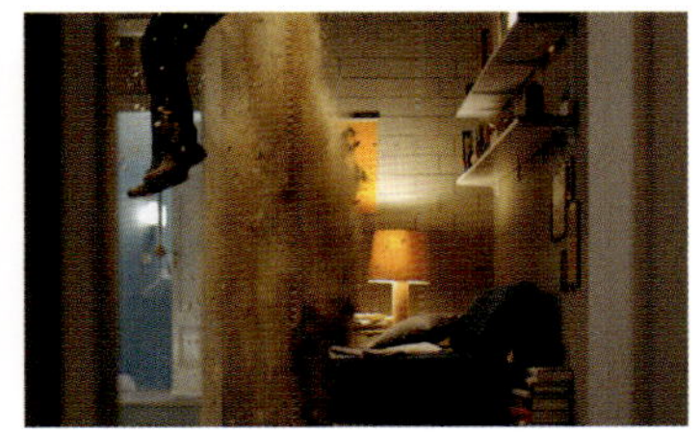

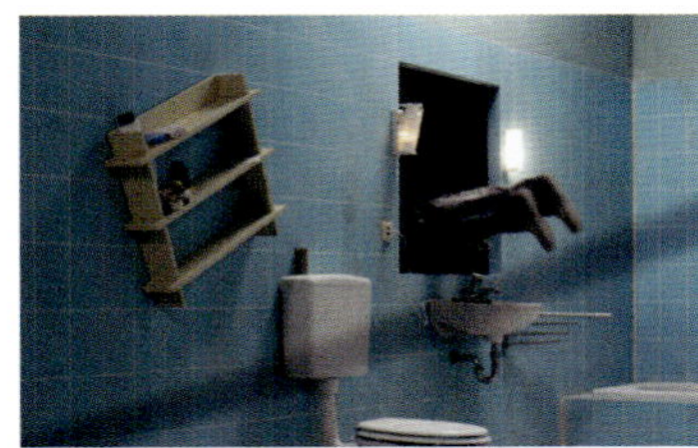

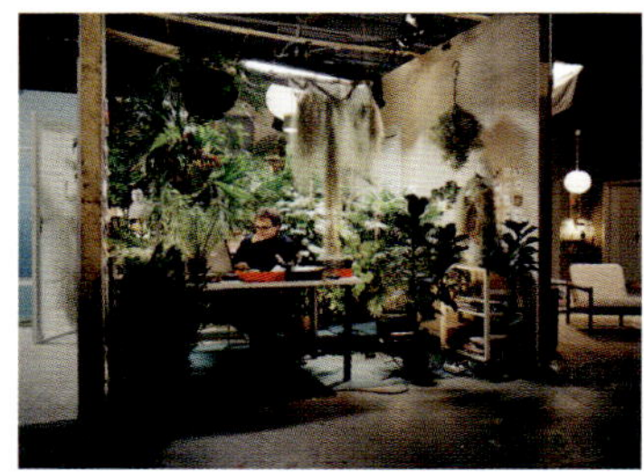

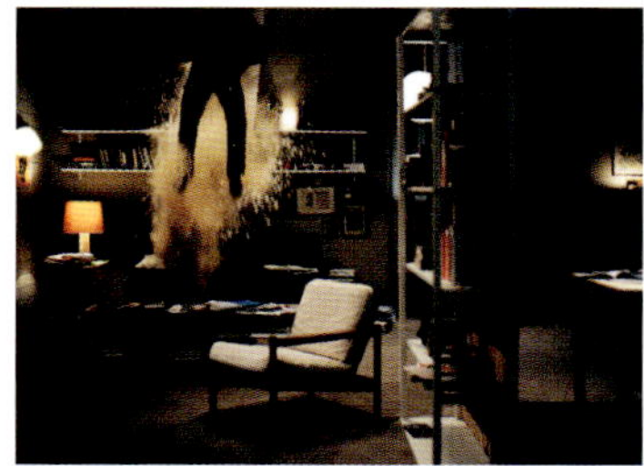

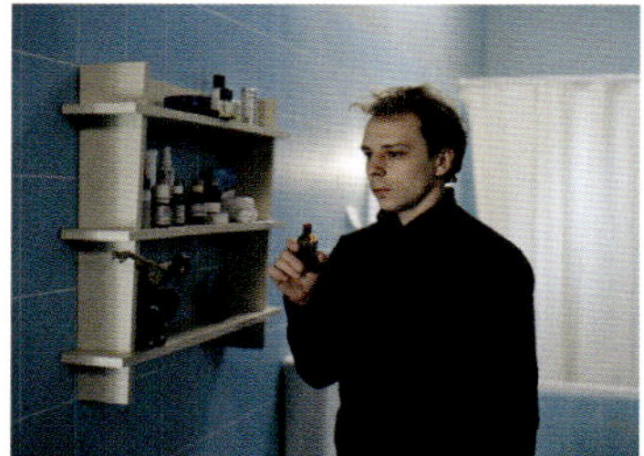

Opposite and following page: Julian Rosefeldt, *The Perfectionist* ('Trilogy of Failure' / Part III).

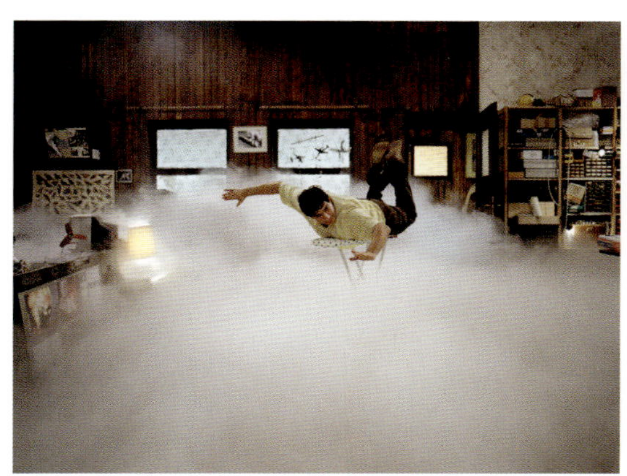
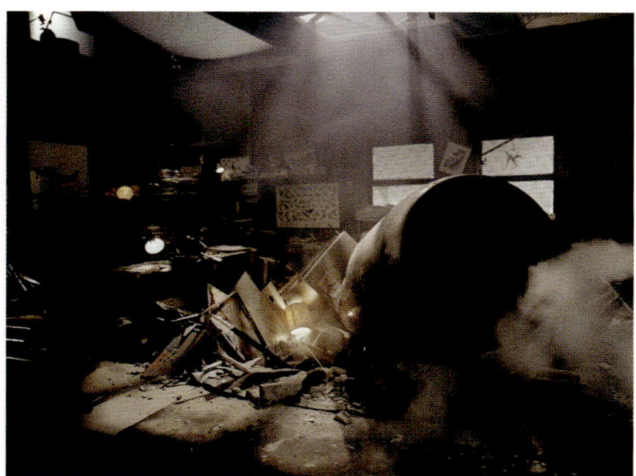
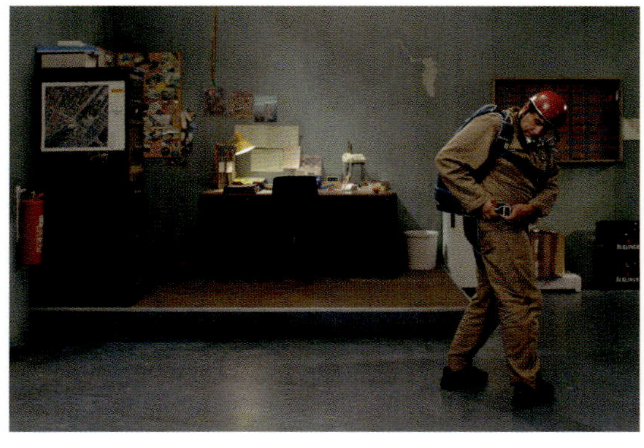
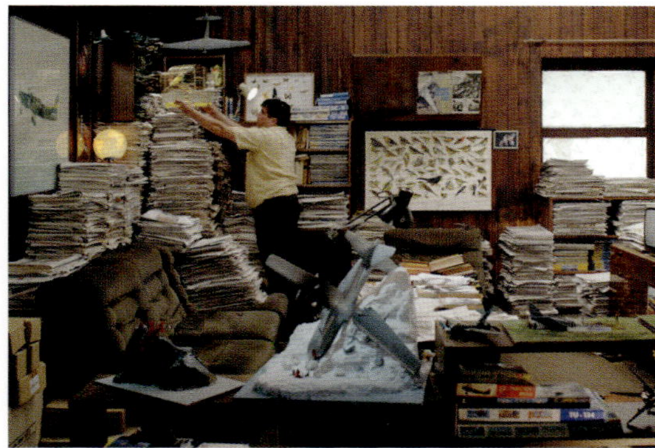

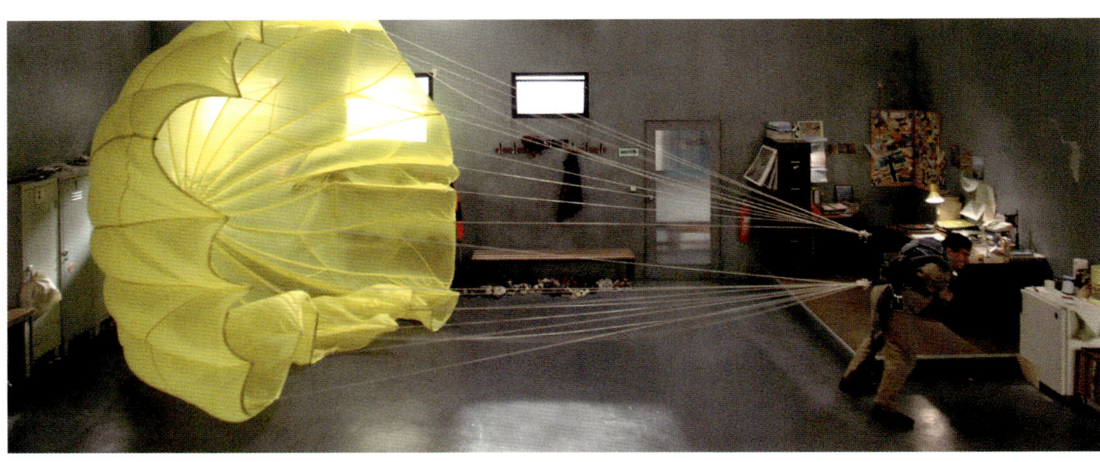

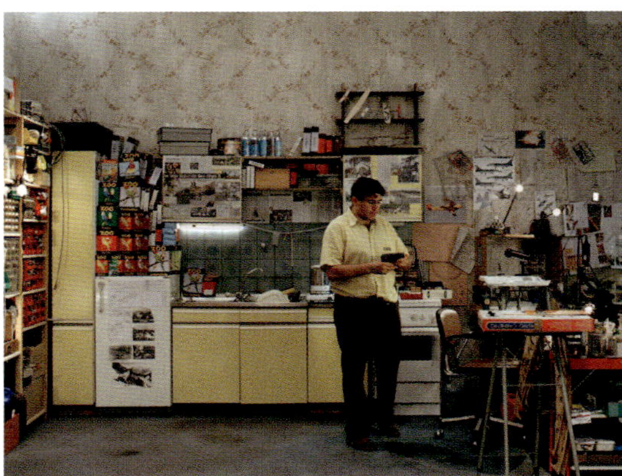

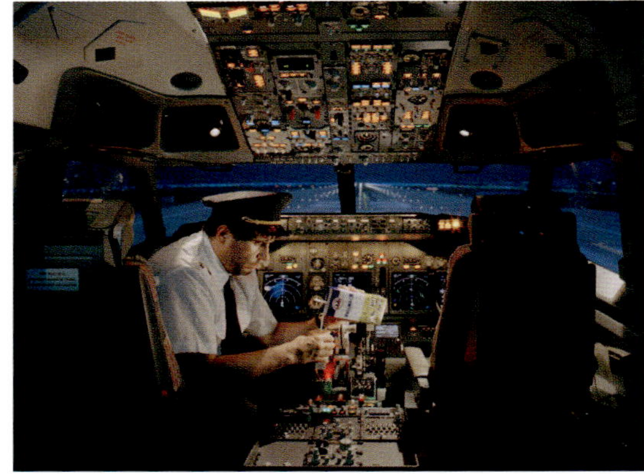

WORKS

The Soundmaker ('Trilogy of Failure' / Part I)
2004
3-channel film installation
Colour, sound
Filmed on Super-16mm
Converted to PAL SD and transferred onto DVD
Aspect ratio 16:9
35 min. 7 sec. loop

Stunned Man ('Trilogy of Failure' / Part II)
2004
2-channel film installation
Colour, sound
Filmed on Super-16mm
Converted to PAL SD and transferred onto DVD
Aspect ratio 16:9
32 min. 49 sec. loop

The Perfectionist ('Trilogy of Failure' / Part III)
2005
3-channel film installation
Colour, sound
Filmed on Super-16mm
Converted to PAL SD and transferred onto DVD
Aspect ratio 16:9 (left and right) and 4:3 (centre)
25 min. 18 sec. loop

CLIVE CAZEAUX
&
JULIAN ROSEFELDT

DISCUSSION, CHAIRED BY **LIAM DEVLIN**

Liam Devlin: First of all I would like to thank Clive and Julian for their very enjoyable talks. In relation to Clive's presentation, there is the idea that photography continues the trap of Plato's cave, by presenting us with appearances that we take to perfectly reflect reality. However, it always struck me that Plato's notion of perfect forms has a terrifying aspect. It works on almost a religious logic: the paradox within the idea of a perfect form that isn't possible, but it's desirable. There's a kind of energy within that aspiration, but the sense that everything's got its right place and everything its *technē* I find terrifying, deeply terrifying. Which brings me to art practice and your notion of failure, Clive. I just wanted to try and explore the position where – because art has no *technē* for Plato, no 'being done well', what potential does it have? How does it play a role in society, does it have a function?

Clive Cazeaux: Plato's metaphysics is set against art as representation. Art, for Plato, was something which worked against his theory of the Forms. There are lots of problems with the theory, as commentators on Plato have pointed out, not least how we might introduce the notion of a Form that corresponds with an artwork. That would be a very internal problem for Plato's system. Externally, as you quite rightly say, politically, the concept of a Form is very suspect, especially the idea that for every human being there's a perfect human form. The very fact that it's a philosophy opposed to difference means politically its consequences are dangerous, to say the least.

LD: I wanted to keep the image of Plato's cave as backdrop to the discussion. It encapsulates a lot of the potential issues: that we live in Plato's cave and we're distracted or entertained by these shadows that we think are reality. If we equate Plato's cave with the experience of cinema, we can think of Julian's work that breaks with the 'willing suspension of disbelief' through a disruption of cinematic language.

CC: Julian, you're referring to the idea of 'worlds' a lot; the idea that you wanted these things to be 'worlds in themselves', but then you have the beauty of the world that we can see as a construct, the film set you have built. You actually said one of these rooms went on view at the Royal Academy. So it's all about these two lives: the world we have *here*, i.e. the world of the film, and then the world that viewers or visitors to the Royal

Academy will actually see *there*, the set itself, but from a god's-eye or bird's-eye point of view.

Julian Rosefeldt: I want to talk a little bit about what you were saying before when you were talking about perfection in the digital image – that we are getting closer and closer to achieving reality, which is, of course, not true. I work in a very old-fashioned way, most of the work is shot on celluloid, on film, and I'm more and more often asked now, when are you using HD? And why aren't you projecting in a more crystal clear quality, and so on? And I think that's a very important and very actual discussion in the world of photographic-based media, because there seems to be an urge to be real, and the understanding of real is when we see something as we see it now. I can see you crystal clear, and you probably with your glasses too, you can see me crystal clear. But I believe it's something that we should entirely doubt. Isn't it more real when we translate something into another level; for example, painting may tell us more about reality than a photograph of the same situation. With the grain of the film, I refer much more to painting than I refer to video-making. Is that grain of the film containing the truth more than the crystal clear digital pixels?

CC: The view exists that some people believe that the more finely grained a photograph or film is, the truer it is, but I don't accept that, because it simply means there is an assumption that it's a one-way process: we are receiving reality in a purer and purer form. So you're trying to say you want to hold onto some notion of grain or granularity to draw attention to the fact that this is a highly constructed, highly pixelated version or form of view.

JR: Yes. And by getting closer and closer to a world where everything, every projected image, is absolutely crystal sharp and clear, these questions need to come up again.

CC: Well, you showed us the way the work is presented, and how much you are orchestrating, choreographing, to use that word again, that particular set-up, in terms of the size of the image. What if a person walked up to the wall and actually stood five centimetres away from the screen; what would they have, how much are those concerns paramount?

JR: Well, I plan the set-up of course, and I guess what happens all the time is that you automatically find your position because of your seeing customs, and you put yourself in the position that is comfortable. And normally people stay in the same position, so there must be some unwritten law about these things. That's what's interesting.

LD: Can I ask you a question about the installation of your work? Do you hope that people will sit the whole way through or is it something that you don't have control of?

JR: Surprisingly, they normally do, and I think that's because even in group exhibitions, where it's very difficult to hold the attention of somebody longer than five minutes in front of a piece of art, what I do is I break with all these rules of film-making. There's a narration, but it's also a loop so it doesn't really matter when you come inside the room to see that. So there's a curiosity of finding out what has happened before and where is it leading; but I think basically it's – first of all you see a person at home doing nothing important, nothing interesting, first of all. And that is highly interesting, because we never see that in a movie. We always see when somebody picks up the phone in a film it's to receive a very important message that brings him to somewhere else. So when he's opening a drawer, it's probably to take out a gun or something important for the plot of the film. And also, if you see the last forty years of film history, if you just calculate the pace of edit cuts, I think it's now approximately twelve times faster than it was for editing of the '50s. So we are of course used to that acceleration more. I remember when I saw my very first music clip when I was fifteen or something, I got sick from the quantity of cuts. My brain couldn't manage it. And I think, just by breaking with these laws you already attract the attention of the audience and they watch it through. Not always of course, but many people watch this through.

LD: It struck me that you use film language that we're quite familiar with, but you use it in a fantastic, perhaps even in a nonsensical sense. Going back to Plato's cave in a way, that your work is, if not telling us to get out of the cave, it's showing that, somebody's holding the puppets, whose shadows we can see.

It's time for some questions.

Kate Kotcheff: Julian, there's a comedic element to your work and I wanted to know if that was intentional, because you come across as very serious. The work has a lot of farce to it, and I'm interested to know what you think about that and the effect of your work.

JR: As I said before, the humour in Buster Keaton's films is that he's absolutely serious. And it's the most difficult thing to construct a joke in a movie. Because when you do a movie the joke is not just there happening, it's constructed of course, because there are many people at work on a film set, and it's not only the actor, everything has to be right in the place. And I wanted to keep the balance between this kind of tragic humour, because the protagonists, they're also like machines, like robots, because they have to follow the system that I constructed for them. And there's a moment of tragedy in it. There's Sisyphus in it of course, and there's the idea of Sisyphus as a happy person in it, not only as a tragic person. Of course, the humour is constructed by intention. If it is actually funny or not is totally up to you, and for me it's very hard to say. For me also, when I start to work on a project, I work on the character first, so I want to know that character by heart before I even start to think what he's doing. And not only how he looks and what his daily behaviours are, but also what his inner-world could be? I always try to give them certain secrets that they keep even from me. So they will do things that even I, although I invented them, would not understand. Like the stuntman is constantly going to the bathroom and having some drops there, and I don't know what's in that bottle, although I gave him the bottle. Or this guy is building his models of airplane catastrophes, but there's no explanation at all what's behind it. You see, it's very difficult to answer your question because it's a very serious thing. (Laughter)

Marie Brenneis: What theory do you look at in your practice? What theory do you read? Or you might not look at theory, I don't know.

JR: I do, but I do not directly translate what I read into a work. I couldn't say I'm following one theory. I'm reading the newspaper, I'm reading Borges, and I'm reading everything mixed up, so I couldn't give you a satisfactory answer. What do you think I read? That would be an interesting question. (Laughter)

Andrea Jespersen: I'm interested in duration. When you make a film how long do you actually work and plan, and how long are you actually shooting for? You talk about getting to know your character and it sounds like you're talking about quite a long period of preparation.

JR: Of course, when you see the production aspect of the work, it needs a lot of preparation, not only technically but also financially, so there's time passing by until I can finance the project. I do one project a year, and that's about the time I need to do it from the first sketch to the end of post-production. The shooting time is very short, but that's also due to financial reasons, because we have to account for time enormously. In film-making, you buy time, basically. If you have more money, you have more time. It's very simple. So we are trying to rehearse a lot before filming – for example when I work with one protagonist I would probably meet this person for a month or two and just rehearse with him in my studio and try to find out what the character is actually doing before I actually think about the set-up for it. But it normally starts with a long period of time where I'm alone in my studio, just writing and reading and shaping the idea a bit. Then there's pre-production, about three months. Shooting time – super short. Could be only a week. Could be two weeks. Maximum twenty days, but that's very seldom. Then there's the enormous process of post-production, especially in the projects where sound is very important. So it's about half a year of preparation, a short production time and then another few months of post-production.

THE EFFORT OF PERFECTION

PERFORMING ADOLESCENCE

CATHERINE GRANT

In this essay I want to think about perfection in relation to the female body, particularly the nude, and how it is depicted in photography.[1] My focus will be on photographs of girls by two contemporary artists – Rineke Dijkstra and Katy Grannan – and the ways in which their work converse with images of perfected femininity in popular culture. Whilst ideas of perfection change in relation to the female body, I want to consider the potent fantasy of the perfect female body that is increasingly figured through the adolescent in the twentieth and twenty-first centuries. The ways in which contemporary artists such as Dijkstra and Grannan have used this figure to reveal the 'effort of perfection' is my concern.

DEFINITIONS OF PERFECTION

I will begin with some definitions of perfection in relation to the perfect body and the perfect woman. Obviously the 'perfect body' and the 'perfect woman' will bring to mind different ideas, different examples. But when researching these terms, what struck me was the way in which the concept of the perfect woman in popular culture often focuses on the body, whereas the perfect man more often brings up issues of moral perfection or divinity rather than physical beauty. The commonplace of feminist theory, of the female body as an object of voyeuristic desire, finds it most extreme form in the perfect woman who has become completely *of* the body – with her will being suppressed or replaced. This perfect woman is a fantasy that can be found in popular culture through film, in particular. This perfect woman is a particularly twentieth-century invention, although she arises from much earlier precedents.[2]

In the 1975 film *The Stepford Wives*, directed by Bryan Forbes and based on the 1972 novel by Ira Levin, women are replaced by robots. Here their husbands' idea of perfection is a beautiful body and a completely controllable mind. This misogynist fantasy is one that is not as outlandish as it first seems, and can be seen as an extension of the patriarchal desire for women to be demure and subservient as the perfect accompaniment to good looks. In the film's climatic scene, the heroine's perfected body is revealed through her gauzy negligee, including pumped up, prosthetic breasts. In terms of today's normalization of breast augmentation, here science-fiction fantasy now reads as prescient representation of the increasing desire amongst women to perfect their bodies to attain an ideal that is not found in nature. In *The Stepford Wives*, the drive to perfect women is fuelled by the desires of men, but as I hope to show here, this increasingly has to be put alongside the desires of women to picture themselves perfectly.

In other films in which the perfect woman (or girl) is featured, she is nearly always created: by an evil genius, by some nerd boys, by a force of will that puts the character outside of the normal. Here the process of perfection is foregrounded, pointing to the difficulty of 'being perfect', and the understanding that the perfect woman is an erotic fantasy or, if enacted by the woman herself, a mask for evil intent. Here are just two more examples: John Hughes' 1986 teen comedy *Weird Science*, where two nerd boys are overwhelmed by their supernatural perfect girlfriend; or the 1956 melodrama *The Bad Seed*, in which a little girl appears to be perfect, but whose force of will allows her to perform perfection and mask the fact that she is a manipulative liar and murderer. In all three films – *The Stepford Wives*, *Weird Science* and *The Bad Seed* – the desire for perfection leads to monstrosity or excess. Rather than perfection being a state that can be attained and which then inspires contentment, the extremity of the process required to 'become perfect' results in a robot, a supernatural force of nature or a young murderess. In these filmic narratives, perfection is desire taken to an extreme, a desire that reveals the necessity of being imperfect in order to be able to live in the everyday. The shift in my last example to the girl being the creator of her own perfect image will become important as I look at the contemporary work of Dijkstra and Grannan.

Before turning to visual examples, I want to think further about perfection and its definitions. A question that comes up almost immediately in relation to the perfect body and the perfect woman is 'what is the difference between perfection and the ideal?' This is something that I've been preoccupied by in relation to photography and the nude, as it is generally understood that photography presents the particular, whereas painting or sculpture can present the ideal. In this way, formulations of the ideal body in art have come to contrast the ideal with the real, and the nude is contrasted with nakedness.[3] Thinking about perfection has given me some ways to shift the conversation that takes place between the ideal and the actual in the photographing of female bodies.

Turning to the *Oxford English Dictionary*, the ideal is defined as 'existing as an idea or archetype', whilst the various definitions of perfection reveal a different emphasis. Those that interest me are ones that foreground perfection as a process, with the first definition in the *OED* being: 'The action, process, or fact of making perfect or bringing to completion; completing, consummating, finishing, accomplishing.'[4] When turning to definitions of 'perfect', these are given as '[t]horoughly made, formed, done, performed, carried out, accomplished', as well as being '[i]n the state of complete excellence; free from any flaw or imperfection of quality; faultless.' With this second definition, a proviso is given: 'But often used of a near approach to such a state,' so that the state of complete perfection is rare, perhaps impossible to attain. It is here that the definitions of perfect and perfection are importantly different from those around the ideal: although one definition of perfection is 'a state of complete excellence' (as we might think about in relation to the ideal), to attain this state, perfection emphasizes the process needed on the path towards it.

In a book entitled *The Perfectibility of Man*, author John Passmore explains how:

> [...] the Greek word *teleio*, commonly translated as perfect, is etymologically related to *telos* (end) – the relationship between perfection and the achievement of an end is, as it were, written into it. The English word 'perfect', however, ultimately derives, by the way of Middle English, from the Latin word *perficere*, the roots of which, in turn, are *facere*, to make, and a prefix *per* suggesting 'thoroughly'. The perfect, that is, is etymologically definable as the 'thoroughly made', and the 'completed'.[5]

Rather than the static nature of an ideal – an idea to be embodied – perfection implies the outcome of a process, one which requires effort and does not always need to result in an ideal. This comes to the fore in yet another definition of perfect as something that is just right, typical, 'fully answering to what the name implies' (*OED*). In terms of a perfect body or a perfect woman, this can be just right for a particular circumstance, rather than an ideal, a way beyond the impossibility of inhabiting 'a state of complete excellence'.

PICTURING PERFECTION

As I've shown in relation to a number of films, this process of perfection in popular culture is often fantasized as the creation of a perfect woman, something that appears not to be possible to actually embody. This creation has been linked to technology: both the technology needed to create the perfect woman, and the technology used to represent her. In Laura Mulvey's essay on the technological uncanny, she discusses the automaton Olympia from E.T.A. Hoffmann's story 'The Sandman', a story that Freud uses in his essay on 'The Uncanny'.[6] Olympia is another example of the perfect woman being embodied by an inanimate object; with the hero of the story, Nathaniel, falling in love with her as if she was a real woman. Mulvey discusses how 'Olympia is the perfect fetish object. Her wooden, inanimate body is not "wounded"; and she acts as a screen for Nathaniel, reflecting directly back to him his unconscious fantasies, enabling the repression of his fears.'[7] One important element of Nathaniel 'seeing' Olympia as his perfect object of desire – rather than a pretty doll – is that he can only fall in love with her when he views her through magic eyeglasses. It is through these lenses supplied by the evil Coppelius that Olympia's perfection is animated. The links between this automated femininity and the gaze of cinema are key for Mulvey, as she considers how Freud could not see the uncanniness of Olympia because he was unable to engage with the new technologies of the cinema and 'the urban culture of the young modern woman.'[8] Rather than the maternal body – the site of the Freudian uncanny – Mulvey discusses the youthful modern woman as presenting a new version of the uncanny, one whose perfected body is equated with that of the automaton. Taking about the flapper she says: 'Just as the beautiful automaton has no "inside" apart from her mechanism, these bodies, artificially pre-pubescent, mechanised and modern, are eviscerated.'[9] For my discussion here, what is important about Mulvey's argument is that the representation of the perfect woman is integral: it is *how* she is represented that gives the appearance of perfection. Perfection is equated with uncanniness; an image that is not natural, but is created, mechanized, disavowed. This is something that can be dramatized in film, as we follow the process of the perfect woman being created, or her fiction being revealed. In photography, however, the fiction of perfection is harder to narrate.

To think about how photography creates images of perfect women, rather than simply documenting 'perfection', fashion photography gives us some clear examples. I want to look at two contrasting fashion ideals to think about how the perfect female body is presented. Mulvey's emphasis on the mechanized nature of modern woman brings to mind famous images of Helmut Newton's Amazonian models. Just as Nathaniel gazes at Olympia through magic eyeglasses, so Newton uses his camera to create uncanny images of female perfection. Rosetta Brooks' description of fashion photography in the 1970s echoes that of Mulvey's automatons:

> Models seemed to come straight off an assembly line representing a well-established physical norm. Most conspicuous was the repression of the model's distinctive individuality. She was wholly identified with her type, and seen not as an individual but as a model.[10]

Newton's models are an extreme version of this 'typical' body: 'The Helmut Newton model is one of a type, presented with the cold distance of a fleshy automaton, an extension of the technology which manipulates her and converts her into an object.'[11] This emphasis relates not only to perfection as an ideal, but also to the definition of perfection as being something that is just right, typical, 'fully answering to what the name implies'.

Many of Newton's shots from the '70s and '80s are photographic equivalents of *The Stepford Wives*, or Mulvey's mechanized fetish objects, as he foregrounds the voyeurism of his photography. In the famous *Self-portrait with June and Models* (1981), Newton dramatizes the act of creating his perfect Amazonian nudes, placing himself and his camera centrally on the roll of backdrop.[12] Here the perfected bodies of the models are contrasted with his wife June's gaze from the corner of the studio, who sits fully-clothed and coolly observant to the right of the mirror, Newton apparently enjoying the contrast between the women surrounding him. The process that the models themselves undertake in being photographed by Newton is described by Carol Squiers:

> [H]e induces his subjects to fantasise themselves as *images* seen through *his eyes*. At that double remove his sitters project themselves as a Newtonian idea and help tailor their mundane and idiosyncratic beings into flawless, daunting avatars of notoriety, triumph and style.[13]

In his self-portrait Newton dramatizes this process, showing how his act of creation is key in these perfect images.

PERFECT YOUTH

Whether this exchange actually takes place, this idea that Newton 'induces his subject to fantasise themselves' presents an important shift in focus for my discussion of works by Dijkstra and Grannan. Here the models' own internalization of their image takes centre stage – something that women are incited to do through fashion photography and advertising. This striving towards perfection is something that has been part of beauty regimes for centuries, but currently this striving has a particularly spectacular quality. With the advent of plastic surgery and more invasive ways of resculpting the body, perfecting the exterior self is an obsession that often leads to pain and grotesque results rather than anything approaching an ideal. This process of beautification is ironically presented in Annette Messager's compilation of images *Les Tortures Volontaires/ My Voluntary Punishments* (1972), which shows images of plastic surgery alongside more mundane beauty routines and images of women exercising (Figure 1). Messager's title presents the effort of perfection as being the work not of an evil genius, or the voyeuristic photographer in the studio, but of women themselves treating their bodies as objects to be perfected.

This punishing regime is supposedly put to one side in another set of images from recent fashion photography. If we think of Kate Moss in 1990, photographed by Corinne Day for *The Face*, here we have an image of the perfect female body in which the robotic has been replaced by the youthful (Figure 2). No less a fiction, the adolescent presents a perfect body that appears to require no effort to be so, but instead just *is*. The casual style of photography is linked with the casual beauty of the 15-year-old Kate, a model representing the return of 'natural' beauty which would first seem to be best considered under the rubric of imperfection. She is not a classical image of an ideal female body, but I think it is more accurate to think about Moss as representing a different version of the perfect female body. Rather than the timeless beauty of the mannequin or the automaton, here is the fleeting perfection of the youthful body, one which has paradoxically become the ideal for many women. It is precisely the supposed naturalness of the adolescent body that is used as its draw here: an accidental beauty, a perfection that is about nostalgia. Perfection here is about a captured moment rather than a stable body, a moment that will necessarily be gone and will have to be artificially recreated.

Across the twentieth century, the idea of the perfect woman has been caught up with youth. We can think of a recent name for a face cream, 'Youth Code', with the advertising slogan: 'Decode our secret to youthful looking skin... and reawaken skin's youthfulness, day after day.'[14] In the television, magazine and billboard adverts the women have preternaturally smooth skin, with the reference to science giving the validity to the cream's perfecting potential. Just as the effort of perfection is mostly effaced in fashion photography, here the effort of regaining younger looking skin is presented as a scientific fantasy of transformation. Ironically, the advertising images are digitally smoothed to the point of seeming plasticized, with the women's faces being used to sell this product not 'naturally' perfected enough without the aid of heavy digital retouching. Here the eviscerated body of the automaton is combined with the natural youth of the adolescent, again leaving us with an image that is uncanny in its artificiality, in its denial of the effort of perfection.

RINEKE DIJKSTRA

In opposition to this fantasy of instant perfection, a number of contemporary artists have used this temporality of adolescence to foreground the effort of perfection. An example from Rineke Dijkstra's 'Beaches' series (1992–2002) – *Hilton Head Island, S. C., USA, June 24, 1992* – should make this clear (Figure 3). In this photograph, the model stands carefully posed on the sand. For this series, Dijkstra took photographs of adolescents on beaches across Europe and then America, finding these subjects appealing because of the way they could not completely contain their self-image. One aspect that was remarkable for Dijkstra was the cultural differences found in the images. Talking about photographing in South Carolina she said: 'The Americans had very fancy bathing costumes and the poses were more self-conscious. One girl was really holding her belly in and her mother was behind her yelling "You're too fat". She was so unhappy.'[15] Here the effort of perfection is revealed through the mother's command. But equally this command comes from images around us all, as well as peers and a self-image that is constantly under scrutiny. Whilst Dijkstra says that the American adolescents reveal a more self-conscious self-presentation, this is not always evident in the photographs. In two images of girls from Poland and the States, I am unable to say categorically which is more westernized, although inferences can be made once the captions are read (Figures 4–5). What is more interesting for me is the tension in these images between the attempt to present a perfect body and the difficulty in doing so without the effort being revealed. However, this does not need to result in the final photograph being unappealing or shocking. Discussing the image of the girl in the orange bikini, Dijkstra commented how '[i]n this photograph it's the girl's attempt to be perfect, not perfection itself, that makes the image so beautiful.'[16]

Dijkstra has famously quoted Diane Arbus in discussing her approach to portraits:

> It's like what Diane Arbus said, you are looking for the 'gap between intention and effect'. People think that they present themselves one way, but they cannot help but show something else as well. It's impossible to have *everything* under control.[17]

This comment, with the phrase 'the gap between intention and effect', has been picked up by Michael Fried in his discussion of contemporary portraiture by artists such as Thomas Struth and Rineke Dijkstra.[18] This gap, for me, is one way to reveal the effort in perfection that a sitter undergoes when attempting to present themselves as an image of a perfect body; a gap that is denied in much fashion and advertising imagery. When Fried discusses the difference between Dijkstra's 'Beaches' photographs, and her various series that involve taking people's photograph after a particular event (childbirth and bullfighting being two examples), he says, 'in all these series the idea is that Dijkstra's subjects – unlike her kids on the beaches – have been at least temporarily marked by the experiences they have undergone [...].'[19] I would argue that the experience that marks Dijkstra's adolescents is the experience of coming into adulthood: the effort that is required to recreate the self from a child into a grown-up, drawing on the cultural fictions of femininity and masculinity to do so. It is in an image such as the American girl being exhorted by her mother that the effort of perfection is revealed: her self-consciousness before the camera makes us focus in on her experience of trying to embody a feminine ideal; her version of the constant stream of celebrities and fashion models parading their perfect bodies before us. This effort can be seen in other images from Dijkstra's series, with the boys also revealing their attempts to utilize the language of masculine self-presentation. However, it is the girls who most seem to concern themselves with taking up images of femininity in their portraits.

KATY GRANNAN

The western image of the perfected female body is a commonplace within fashion, advertising and film. What might be changing is the effort by which we attempt to match these images, as technologies allow us to shape our bodies more radically, as well as the representation of the Everyman and woman as celebrity now having become a cornerstone of television programming (the makeover effect on shows such as *The X Factor*, *Big Brother* or … *Next Top Model*). The perfect body is increasingly imagined as an avatar of the successful person – for both men and women. By thinking about the effort of perfection, rather than imperfection, the regulatory control of perfection comes into focus more precisely. I want to look at a number of works by the American artist Katy Grannan to see how this effort of perfection is performed by her adolescent models.

The American context for Katy Grannan's portraits is one that is important, and gives a cultural specificity to her models. Whereas I can't always tell which of Dijkstra's models are from westernized countries, the impact of spectacular femininity is presented in a particularly American context in Grannan's early photographs. The title for a series begun in 1998 – 'Poughkeepsie Journal' – takes the name of an upstate New York town's newspaper where she advertised for her models. What is interesting about Grannan's series is that she was initially open to who she would photograph, rather than selecting adolescents as her subjects. She put an advert in the *Poughkeepsie Journal* that read: 'Art models. Artist/photographer (female) seeks people for portraits. No experience necessary. Leave msg.' The majority of the sitters in this first series are young women, mostly photographed in their family home, when no one else is home. Like Dijkstra's 'Beaches' series, the photographs become a space in which the tension between what the sitter wants to present and what the photographer captures is the subject of the work. In one image, a young woman is photographed in a Venus-like pose, with the camera positioned low in relation to her body, making her appear at once statuesque and slightly absurd (Figure 6). If we compare this image to Dijkstra's *Hilton Head* portrait discussed above, we can see how the two photographers approach their subjects slightly differently.[20] Like Dijkstra, Grannan is interested in how to show something of the experience of being photographed, with the portraits often balancing between awkwardness and composure. However, in Grannan's portraits there is more variety of pose, and an emphasis on the scene in which her sitters are placed. Grannan's use of her sitters' homes as stage-sets increases the sense of private performance in her shots. Often the interiors are kitsch, but stripped down, with the photograph of the beach on the left hand side of her Venus-posed model ironically creating a seascape along with the swirling greens and blues of the carpet. Whilst Grannan does not pose her models to a great extent, she will choreograph the rooms in which they appear (Figures 7–8).

When I asked Grannan about the predominance of young women in this series, she linked their interest in being photographed to her own memories of trying to recreate images of perfect femininity. She recalls photographs of herself and friends when she was about 12, taken of them dressing up and posing like women in magazines. She describes the disconnect between her friends and herself thinking they looked exactly like the models and the actual images which she described as having a sadness and desperation.[21] What is obviously different in her portraits from childhood snapshots is the size and style of photography. Grannan uses a 4 x 5" camera to take large-scale colour portraits that demand the viewer's attention as sites of effort, not images to be glanced over. Grannan also undertakes editorial and fashion photography, and this informs her artistic practice. Many of these first portraits are taken from a low point of view, elevating her models to a position of monumentality in contrast with the gestures and remnants of awkwardness. What is remarkable is how many of her models wanted to be photographed in the nude, or semi-nude. Here it is their bodies that they want documented, as if they can find in a photograph the perfection that they fantasize attaining in everyday life. Like Newton 'induc[ing] his subject to fantasise themselves', or Nathaniel looking through the magic eyeglasses, here I would argue that the transformative potential of photography is being courted by Grannan's models. Grannan did not direct these young women in any great degree, instead allowing the difficulty of creating a perfect self-image to create the tension within the images.

In talking about setting up one portrait, she discusses how the girl knew exactly how she wanted to be seen, and wanted to be in control of the shot (Figure 9). For Grannan, the image only became interesting when the string of the girl's tampon fell down:

> [S]he was kneeling in her own little world and the string of her tampon fell down. Suddenly the picture became much more complex, through this one little indication of vulnerability [...]. [W]e believe we're presenting ourselves one way, but the camera always reveals something more vulnerable, despite our best efforts.[22]

Here we are back to the idea of the gap between intention and effect. In Grannan's images, all the details start to take on significance, particularly when the images are viewed one after another. The range of interior decoration, with the recurrence of wood panelling, stone cladding and garish carpets, provide a domestic context for these images; a repetitive suburban space from which the models are both attempting to define themselves against, but are as equally marked by them. In subsequent series, Grannan's models become more demographically various, but the recurrence of the young, white suburban girl wanting to be photographed in the nude remains a constant.[23] As the viewer looks across each image, the fantasy that is taking place for each of Grannan's models remains elusive, but for me is the central theme and intrigue of these portraits. Why did these girls want to be photographed like this? Why did they answer Grannan's advert? What did they think they would look like? Grannan reports how most of her models are pleased with their photographs, or are simply unconcerned with the final image. There seems to be a disinterest in the image after the photograph has been shot, as if the scene of being photographed is what is important, the fantasy image that the act of being photographed creates for Grannan's models. What the viewer is left with is the reality of the shot, presented not as a casual snapshot taken by friends, but as an encounter between strangers that elevates the everyday into a glimpse into the fantasy of perfection – that is what seems to have driven many of Grannan's models to pick up the phone and call her.

As part of an image culture in which the perfected body is becoming more and more ubiquitous, as digital photography allows even the most basic of shots to be 'retouched', Grannan refuses to overlay her sitter's performances with the smooth gloss of artificial perfection. Rather than the uncanny automaton of the perfect woman, here we are encouraged to imagine the interior life of these women, to imagine the effort of their self-presentation. If we recall the definition of perfect as being 'thoroughly made', these photographs are thoroughly made in the sitters' fantasies, but not in their final presentation. Sometimes it feels as awkward viewing these scenes as it appears they were to photograph. But still, they are reminders of the effort that is put upon us and we take upon ourselves in the creation of our image, and the way in which this is a particularly important aspect of the self during adolescence. By looking at these photographs as engaging with the effort of perfection, rather than portraits of imperfection, the emphasis on the models themselves and their conversation with images of perfected femininity comes into focus. To become adults, we are continually 'making' and imagining ourselves as part of an image world, to try and feel thoroughly made, perfected, although this is something rarely attained. Like Dijkstra's 'Beaches' portraits, Grannan's young women reveal themselves to the camera, but more importantly, reveal the fantasies of perfected femininity that we absorb every day. In these photographs, we can perhaps see some of the ways that the performance of these fantasises can start to remake them, to reduce them to playful roles, rather than insistent regulatory norms. Not quite feminist critique, but not assimilated to the image world they converse with, these portraits show us the effort of perfection, and make us think about what perfection means to our self-image. The definition of perfect as being 'thoroughly made' not only sums up the intensity of the fantasies presented here, but also the style in which the photographers have framed, shot and printed their large-scale images. These photographs emphasize the effort of becoming 'thoroughly made' to encourage us to take seriously the performances depicted in them, to give equal effort to viewing them, as to the effort of their making.

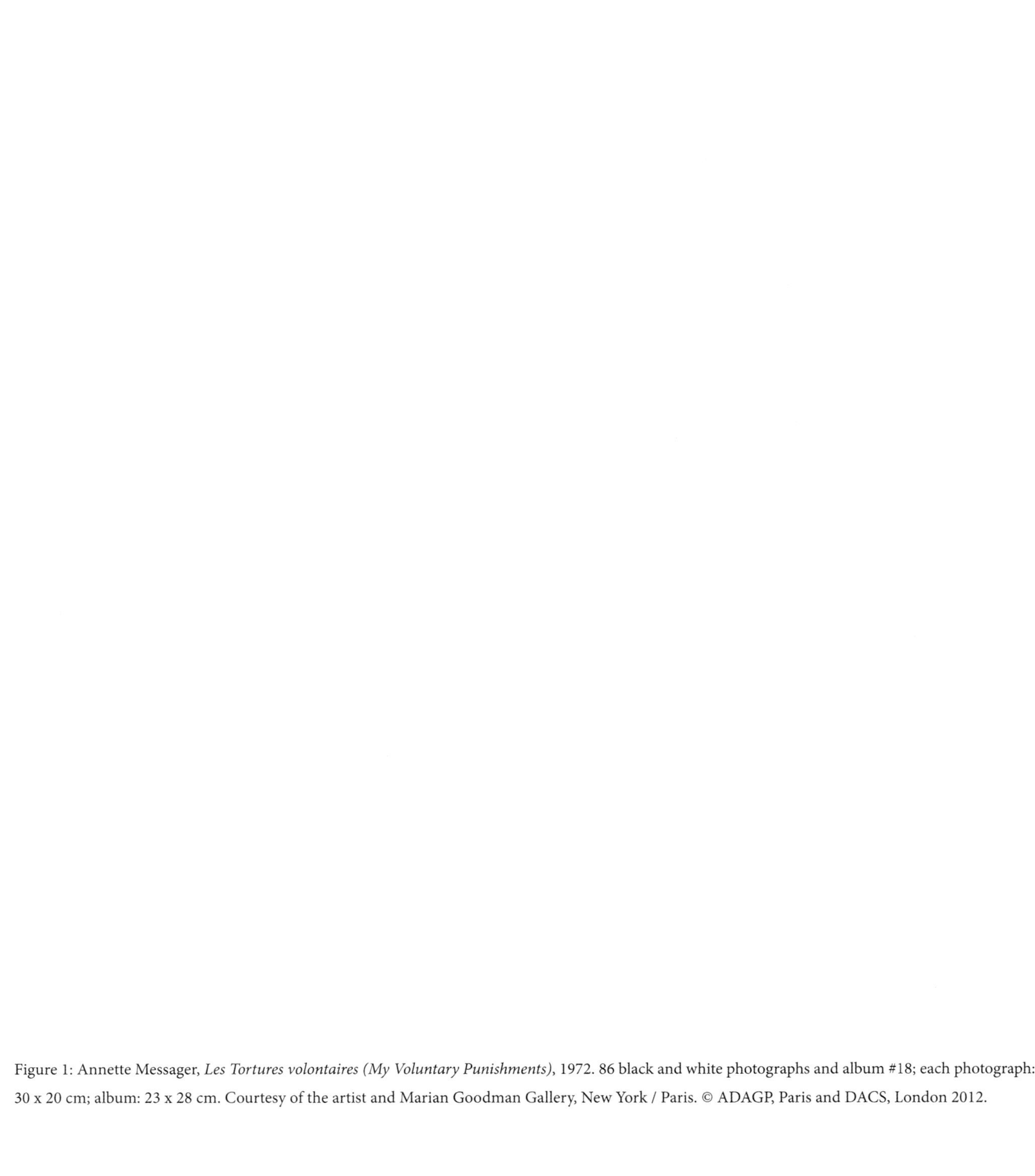

Figure 1: Annette Messager, *Les Tortures volontaires (My Voluntary Punishments)*, 1972. 86 black and white photographs and album #18; each photograph: 30 x 20 cm; album: 23 x 28 cm. Courtesy of the artist and Marian Goodman Gallery, New York / Paris. © ADAGP, Paris and DACS, London 2012.

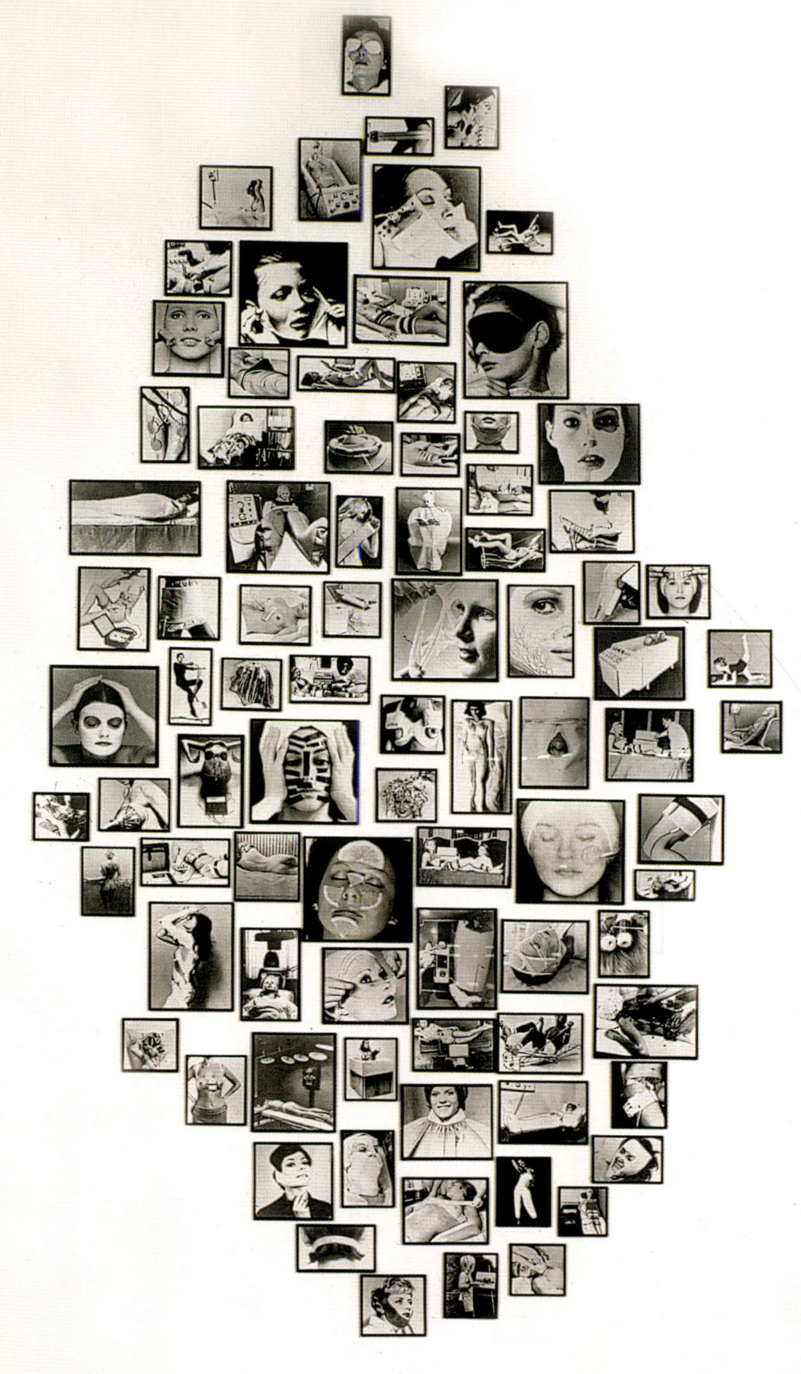

Figure 2: Corinne Day, Kate Moss photographed for *The Face*, 1990. Courtesy Corinne Day / Gimpel Fils Gallery / trunkarchive.com.

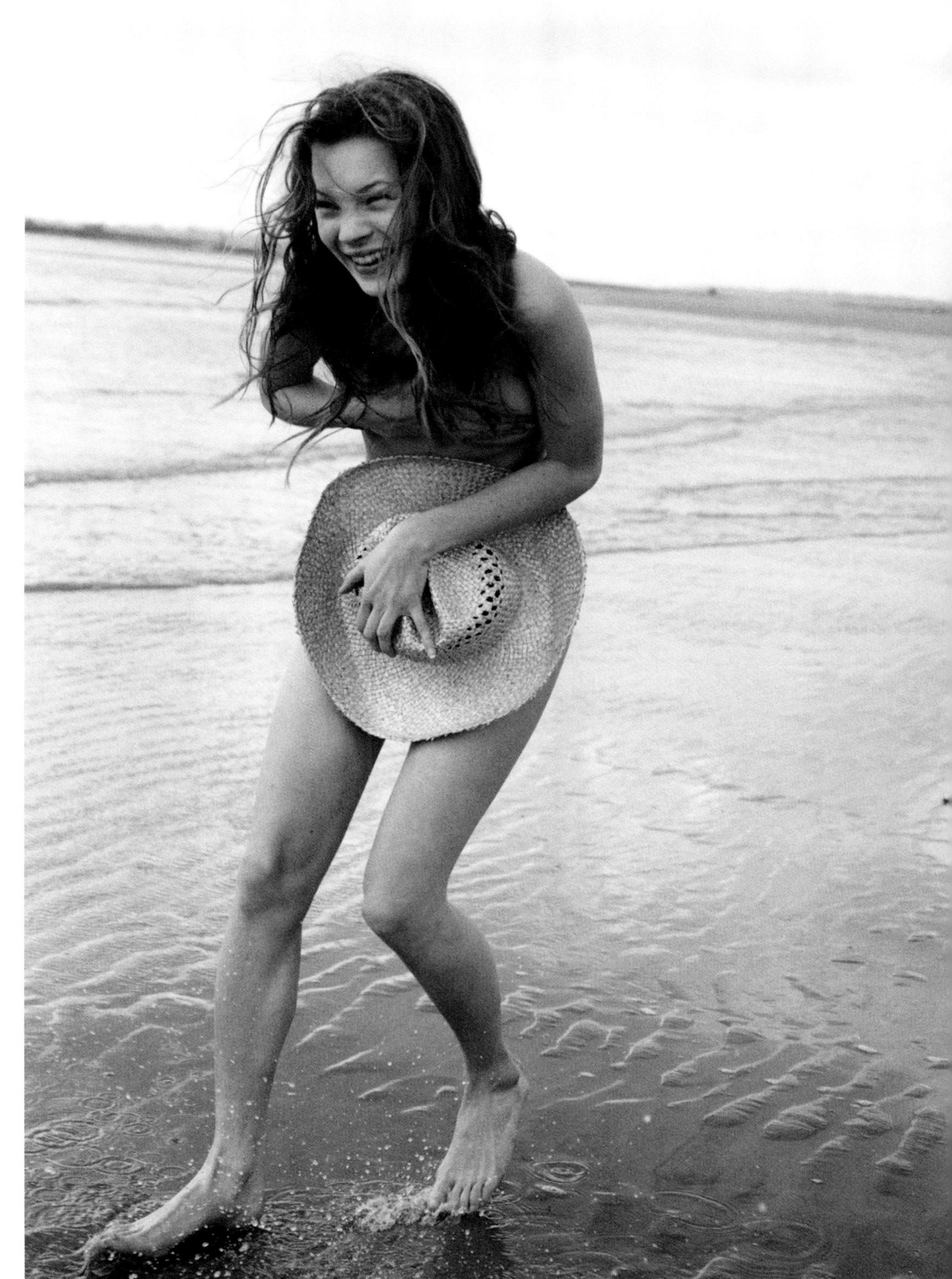

Figure 3: Rineke Dijkstra, *Hilton Head Island, S.C., USA, June 24, 1992*, 1992.

Chromogenic print, 153 x 129 cm. Courtesy of the artist and Marian Goodman Gallery, New York / Paris.

Following pages:

Figure 4: Rineke Dijkstra, *Hilton Head Island, S.C., USA, June 22, 1992*, 1992.

Chromogenic print, 153 x 129 cm. Courtesy of the artist and Marian Goodman Gallery, New York / Paris.

Figure 5: Rineke Dijkstra, *Hel, Poland, August 12, 1998*, 1998. Chromogenic print, 153 x 129 cm.

Courtesy of the artist and Marian Goodman Gallery, New York / Paris.

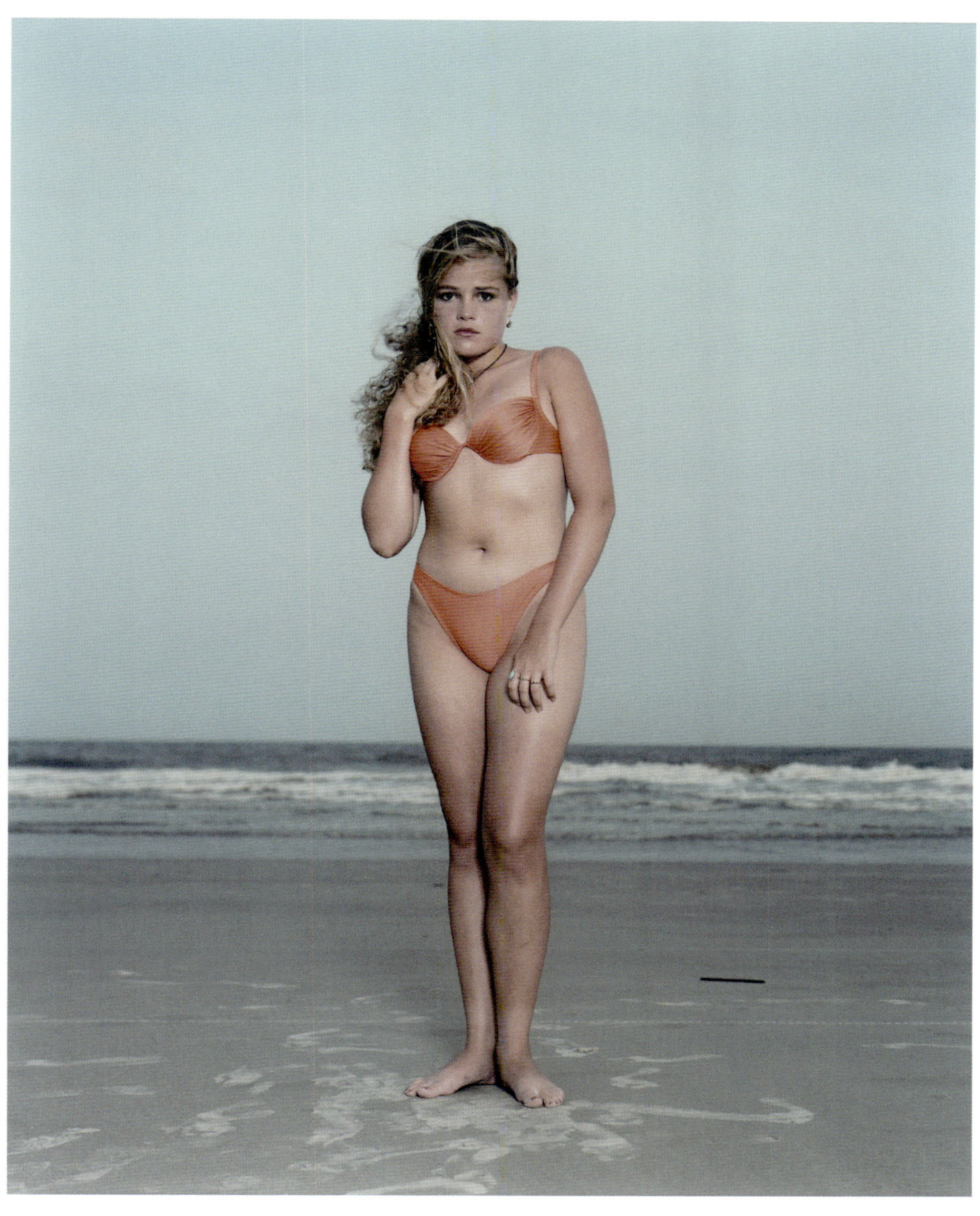

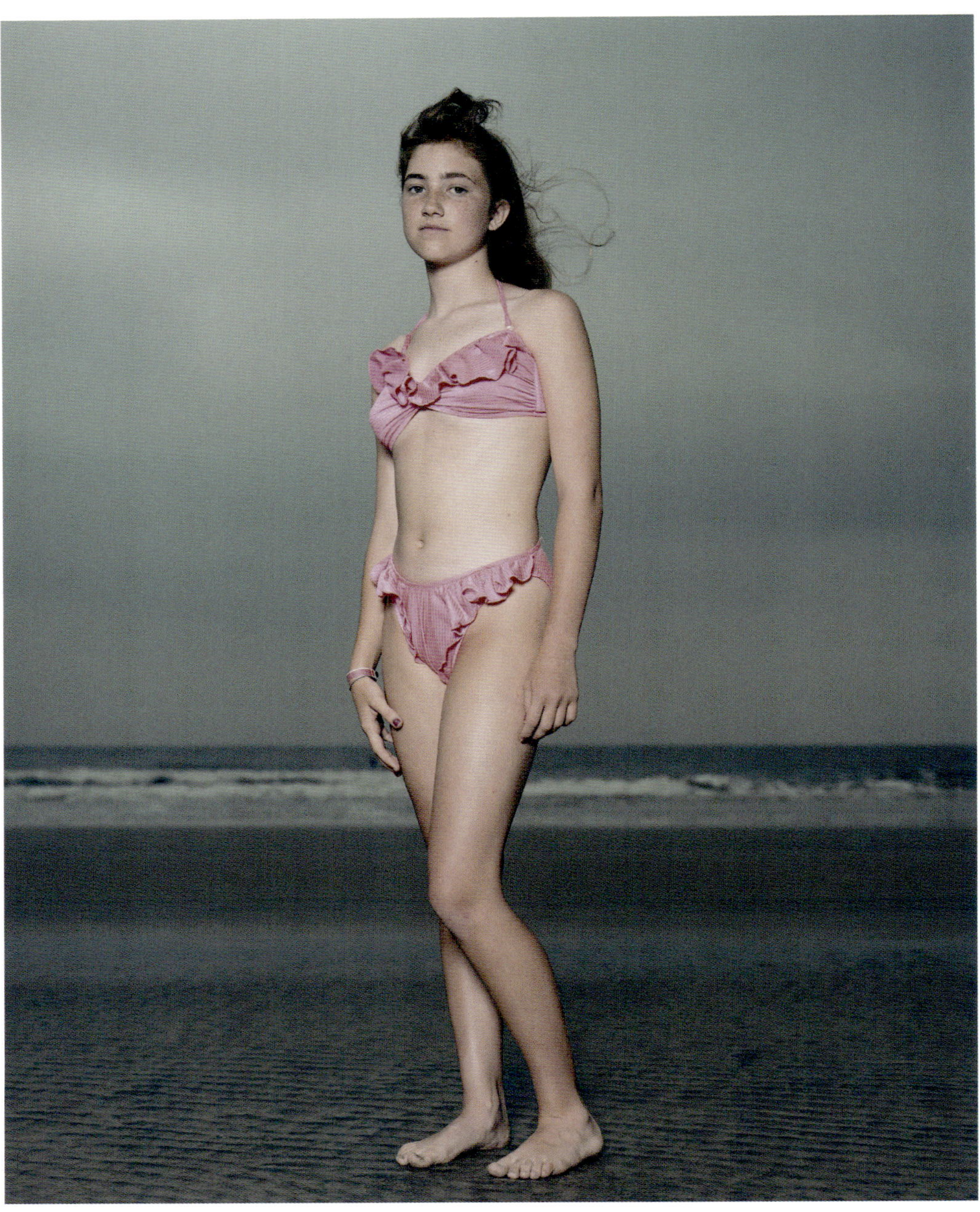

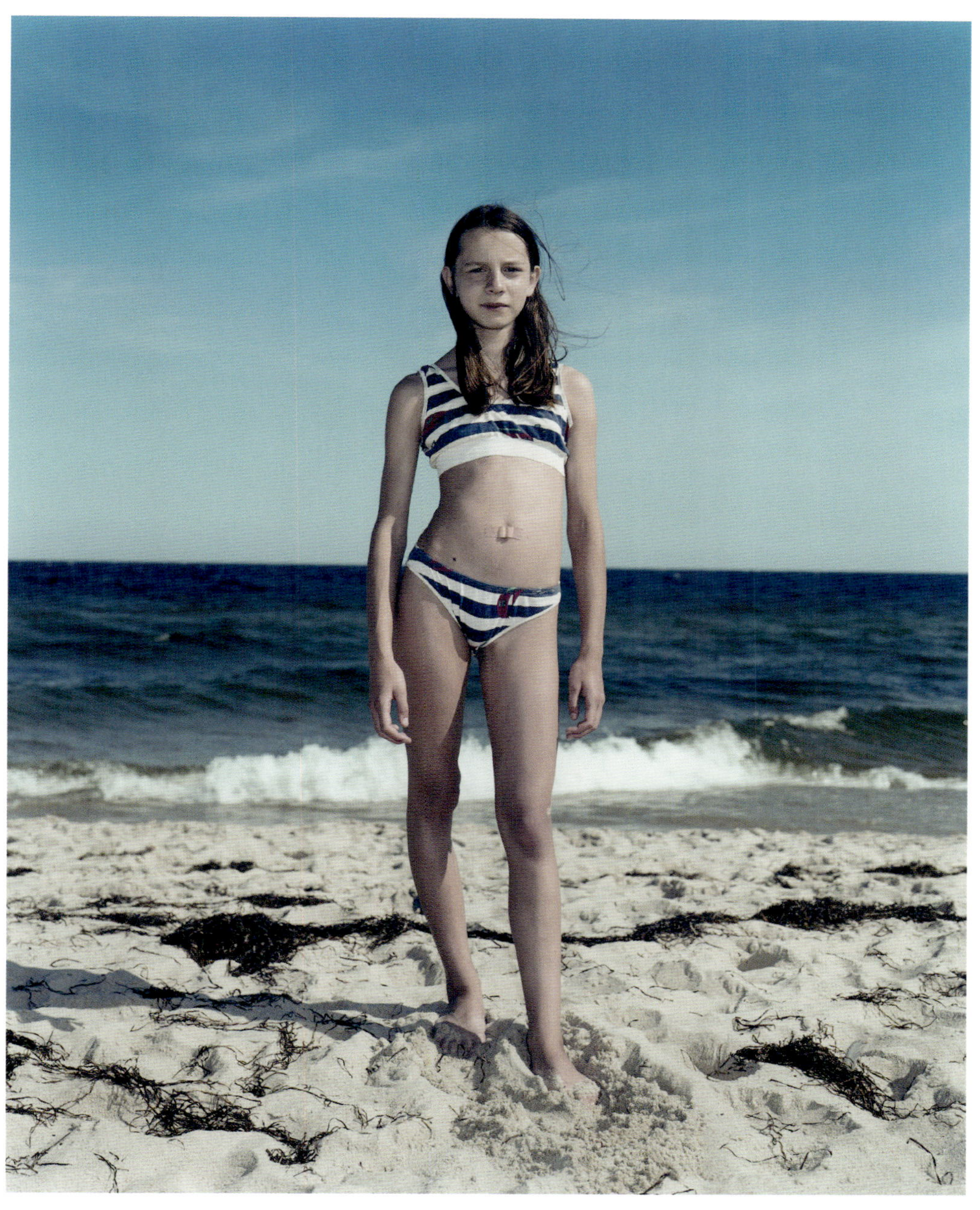

Figure 6: Katy Grannan, *Untitled* from *Poughkeepsie Journal*, 1998.

© Katy Grannan, courtesy Fraenkel Gallery, San Francisco and Salon 94, New York.

Following pages:

Figure 7: Katy Grannan, *Untitled* from *Poughkeepsie Journal*, 1998.

© Katy Grannan, courtesy Fraenkel Gallery, San Francisco and Salon 94, New York.

Figure 8: Katy Grannan, *Untitled* from *Poughkeepsie Journal*, 1999.

© Katy Grannan, courtesy Fraenkel Gallery, San Francisco and Salon 94, New York.

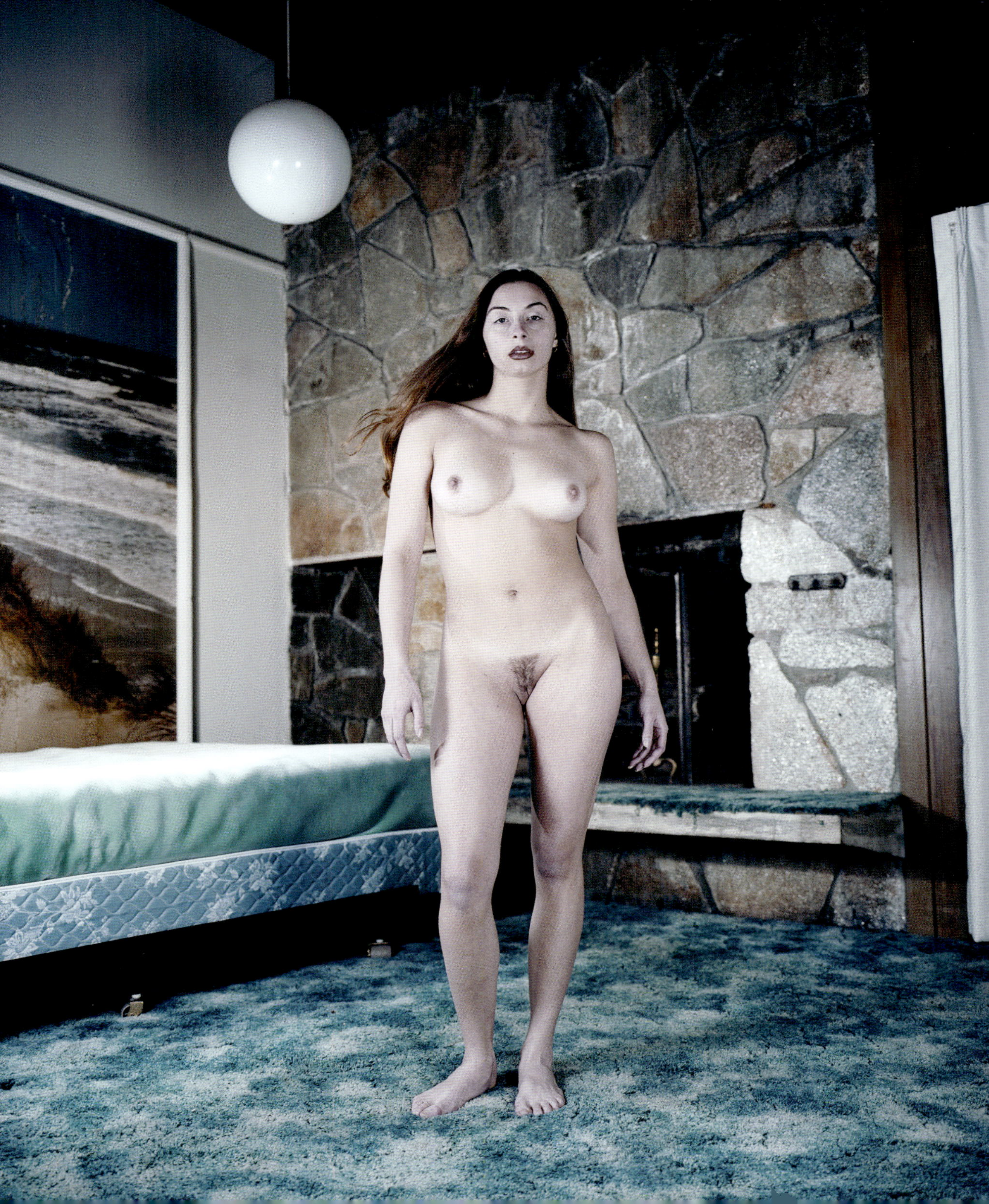

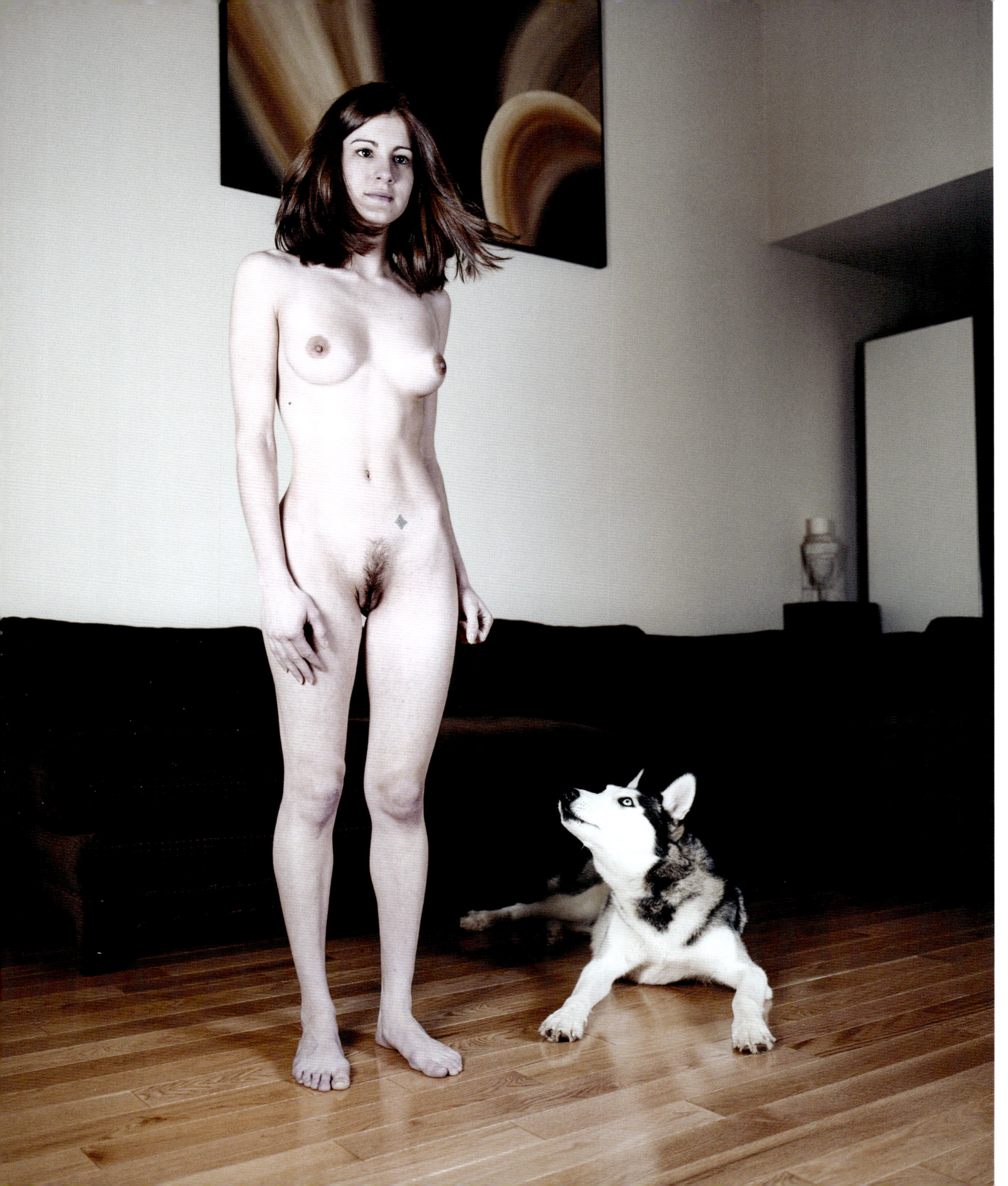

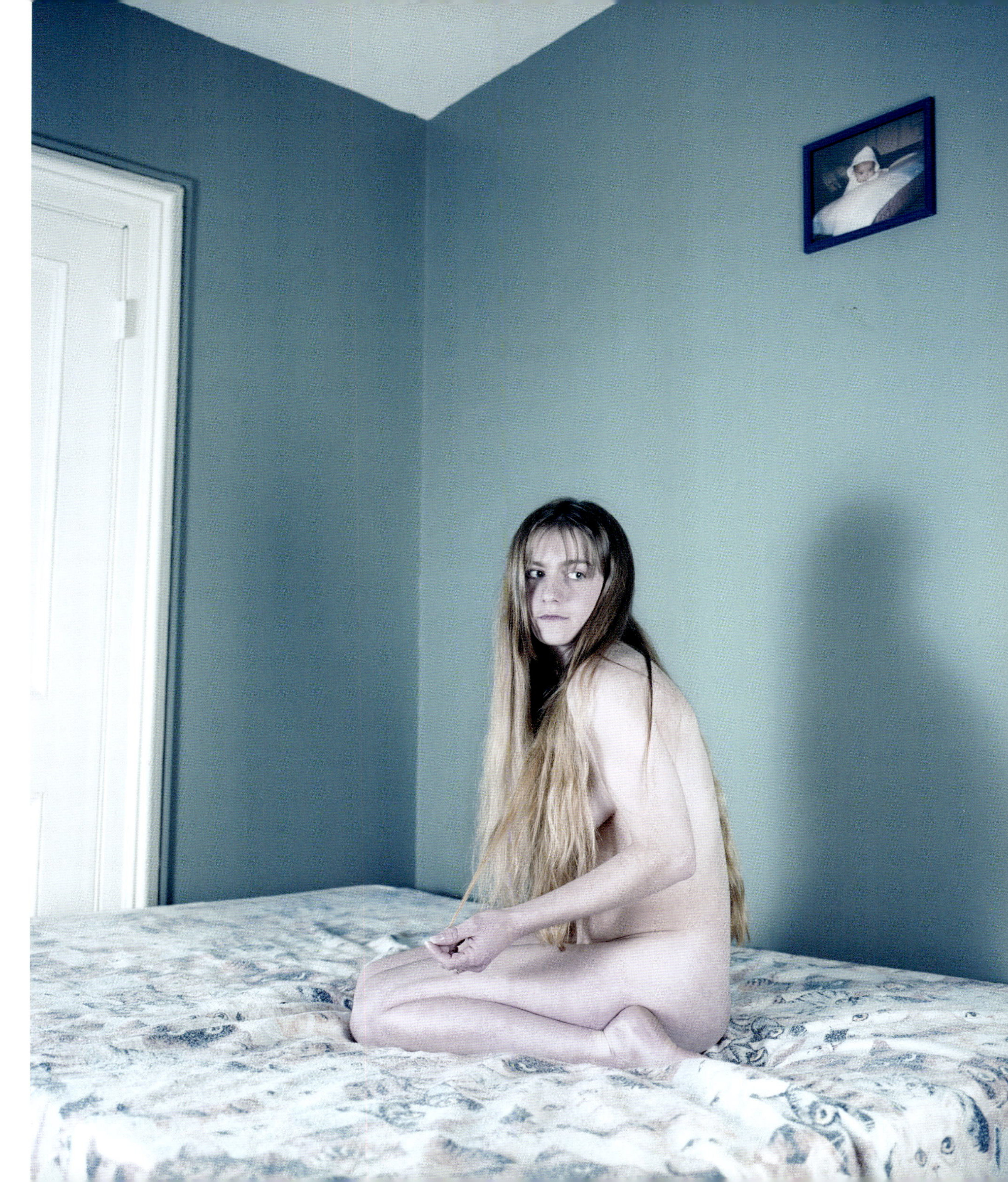

Figure 9: Katy Grannan, *Untitled* from *Poughkeepsie Journal*, 1998.

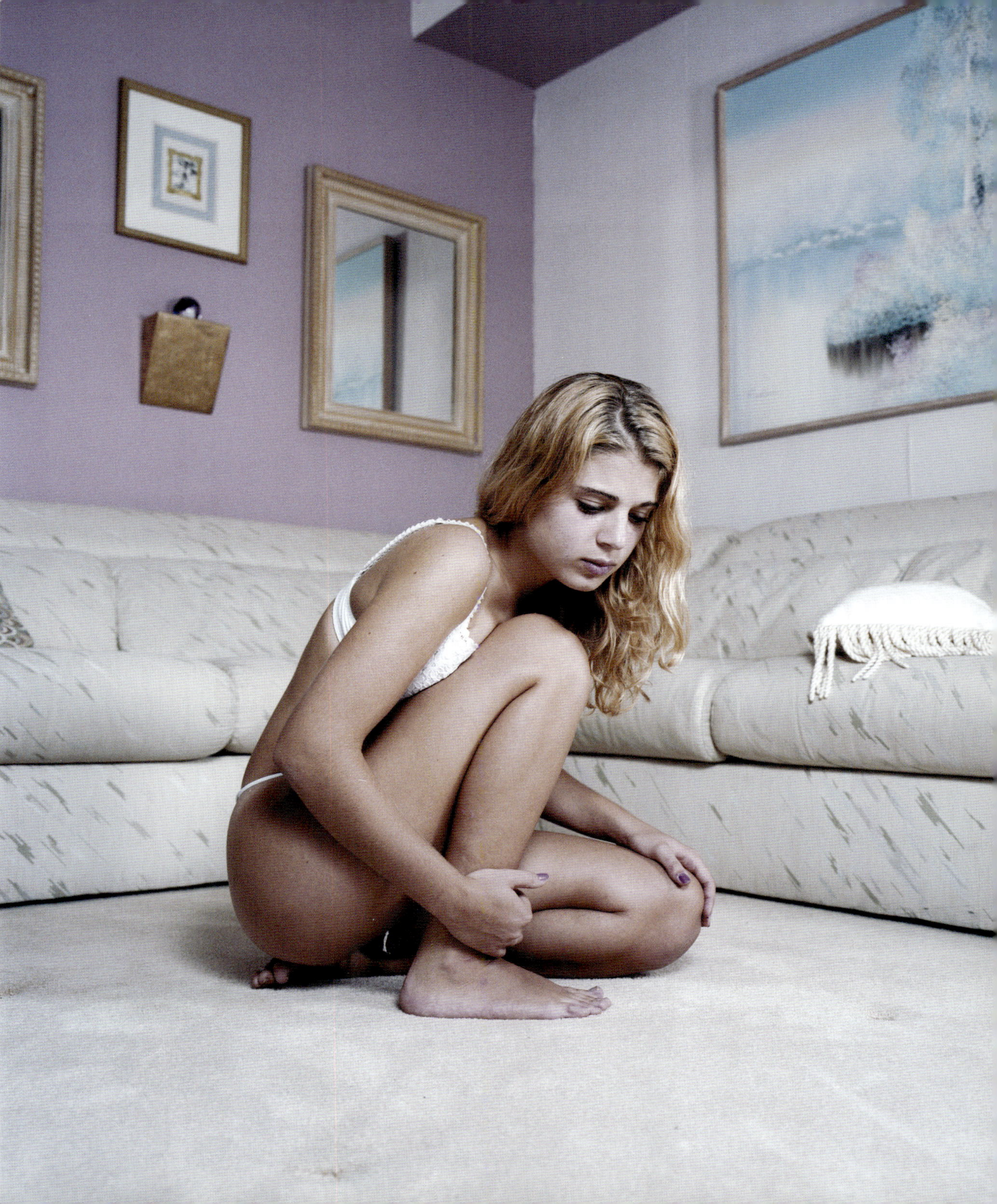

NOTES

1 I would like to thank the Association of Art Historians' Independent Members Group for a grant which has gone towards covering the cost of illustrations for this essay.

2 The perfect woman as a creation and fantasy of a male inventor can be traced back to the Pygmalion myth. I am interested in technological versions of this myth, beginning with E. T. A. Hoffmann's story, 'The Sandman' (1817), discussed below.

3 For a still influential and contentious discussion of these issues, see Kenneth Clark, *The Nude: A Study of Ideal Art*, London: J. Murray, 1956.

4 This definition, and those that follow are from the second edition of the *Oxford English Dictionary*, prepared by J.A. Simpson and E.S.C. Weiner, Oxford: Clarendon Press, 1989. It is only with the third and fourth definitions of perfection that a more ideal or otherworldly condition is defined: '3.The condition, state, or quality of being perfect or free from all defect; supreme excellence; flawlessness, faultlessness. But often treated as a matter of degree: Comparative excellence'; '4. The condition or state of being morally perfect; holiness.'

5 John Passmore, *The Perfectibility of Man*, London: Duckworth, 1970, p. 20.

6 E.T.A. Hoffmann, 'The Sandman' (1817), in *Tales from the German*, trans. John Oxenford and C. A. Feiling, London: Chapman and Hall, 1844, pp. 140–65. The story is discussed in Sigmund Freud, 'The Uncanny' (1919), in *The Standard Edition of the Complete Psychological Works of Sigmund Freud*, trans. James Strachey; ed. with Anna Freud, Vol. xvii, London: Vintage, 2001, pp. 217–56.

7 Laura Mulvey, 'Uncertainty: Natural Magic and the Art of Deception', in *Death 24x a Second: stillness and the moving image*, London: Reaktion, 2006, p. 49.

8 Mulvey, 2006, p. 50.

9 'An eviscerated, mechanised, femininity masks and marks disavowal of both the site of castration anxiety and the womb, the "first home". The element of uncertainty emanates not only from the blurred distinction between the inorganic and the organic but also from the uncertain nature of femininity itself': ibid. pp. 50–51.

10 Rosetta Brooks, 'Fashion Photography: The Double-Page Spread: Helmut Newton, Guy Bourdin and Deborah Turbeville', in *Chic Thrills: A Fashion Reader*, eds Juliet Ash and Elizabeth Wilson, London: Pandora Press, 1992, p. 18. This essay is a revised version of 'Fashion: Double-Page Spread', first published in *Cameraworks*, No. 17,

January/February 1980.

11 Brooks, 1992, p. 19. Brooks continues: 'Her veneer, which is at one with the gloss of the image, is to be flicked past and consumed in a moment' (ibid.).

12 The Helmut Newton Foundation refused permission to reproduce this image, saying that it was being requested for reproduction too often! This ubiquity means that it is easy to find, either by googling the title, or looking at one of the many monographs on his work.

13 Carol Squiers, 'Introduction', in *Helmut Newton Portraits: Photographs from Europe and America*, London: Quartet Books, 1987, p. 7.

14 Youth Code is the name of a L'Oreal range of beauty products. This slogan is taken from the 2011 advertising campaign, seen online at http://www.youtube.com/watch?v=uqgs1T6GUjs (accessed February 2012).

15 Rineke Dijkstra, in Jessica Morgan, 'Interview [with Rineke Dijkstra]', in *Rineke Dijkstra: Portraits*, Boston, MA: ICA, 2001, p. 80.

16 Rineke Dijkstra, interviewed by Jan van Adrichem, 'Realism in the Smallest Details', in *Rineke Dijkstra: A Retrospective*, New York: Guggenheim, 2012, p. 47. This is an expanded version of an interview first published in *Stedelijk Museum Bulletin*, No. 6, April 2005, pp. 51–54. See also the interview with Erin, the Hilton Head model in the orange bikini on page 48 of the Guggenheim catalogue. Erin talks about being photographed saying, 'I stumbled around, trying to give what I thought I was supposed to be giving.'

17 Dijkstra, in Morgan, 2001, p. 76. The quote is from Diane Arbus, *Diane Arbus*, New York: Aperture, 1972, p. 2.

18 Michael Fried, 'Portraits by Thomas Struth, Rineke Dijkstra, Patrick Faigenbaum, Luc Delahaye, and Roland Fischer; Douglas Gordon and Philippe Parreno's film *Zidane*', in *Why Photography Matters As Art As Never Before*, New Haven: Yale University Press, 2008, pp. 191–233.

19 Fried, 2008, p. 214.

20 However, the fact that there are similarities between the two photographer's works is not accidental. Grannan recalls seeing Dijkstra's work in the Museum of Modern Art in New York whilst studying at Yale, and that they were influential, alongside the portraits of Diane Arbus and August Sander. Katy Grannan, conversation with author, 2nd December 2008, The Photographer's Gallery, London.

21 Grannan in conversation with the author, 2008.

22 Katy Grannan, quoted in Melissa Denes, 'Our Little Secret', *Guardian Weekend* magazine, 5th November 2005, p. 37.

23 In subsequent series, Grannan has continued to photograph people she does not know, but has extended the range of the characters. One in particular stands out in relation to my theme. Mike is a man whose body is on show for Grannan's camera in a manner that demonstrates his pride in his physique, down to his shaped pubic hair. He appears in two portraits: *Mike, Private Property, New Paltz*, NY (2003) and *Mike, Hearthstone Motel, Upper Red Hook, NY* from 'Morning Call' (2004). Here, the perfected nude body is one which has increasingly become the focus of men as well as women.

OTHER SPACES
NEW WORKS WITH ELITE GYMNASTS

JO LONGHURST

I'm repeatedly drawn to human systems and structures, interested in our attempts to create order from disorder, and in the many ways we try to make sense of our place in the universe. I often return to the question of how we learn to be in the world: how we are judged, shaped or affected by our social and political environment, and how we are expected to 'fit in' or conform. Ideas of perfection have been central to much of my practice, yet while reading Michel Foucault's 1967 text *Des Espaces Autres*, which considers ideas of physical and psychological space in relation to location and time, I was drawn to the idea of the *heterotopia*. Foucault conceives the term *heterotopia* to describe real, but culturally-determined places of 'otherness' that have relationships to other places, or layers of meaning that are not immediately apparent.

Unlike Utopia – a fantastical place or idea that presents a perfected vision of society – Foucault proposes the *heterotopia* as a real place, or real site of activity, that offers many levels of engagement; a place where ideas about contemporary society might be explored. This proposition struck a chord with how I was thinking about the rigorous training regimes of elite gymnasts. Viewed through the selective lenses of the world's media, the performance and spectacle of international competition become a *heterotopian* stage on which broader ideas of excellence are played out.

Gymnastics has a long social and political history, and one often entwined with an idea of aesthetic perfection. My new hybrid works – inspired by Plato's perfect solids and Liubov Popova and Aleksandr Rodchenko's revolutionary experiments with aesthetic forms – reference earlier attempts to define and create perfect worlds.

Jo Longhurst, *Pinnacle*, 2012.

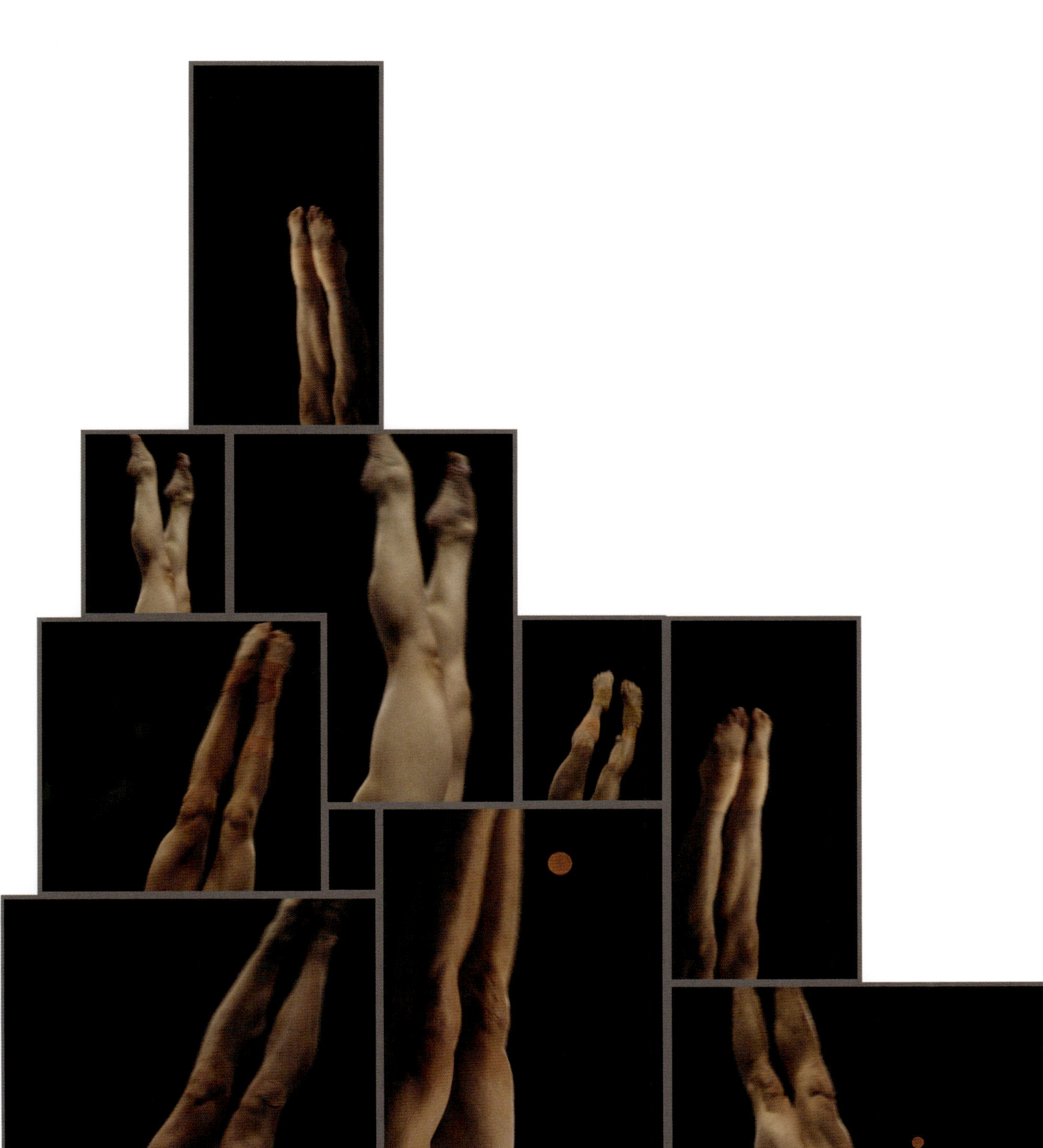

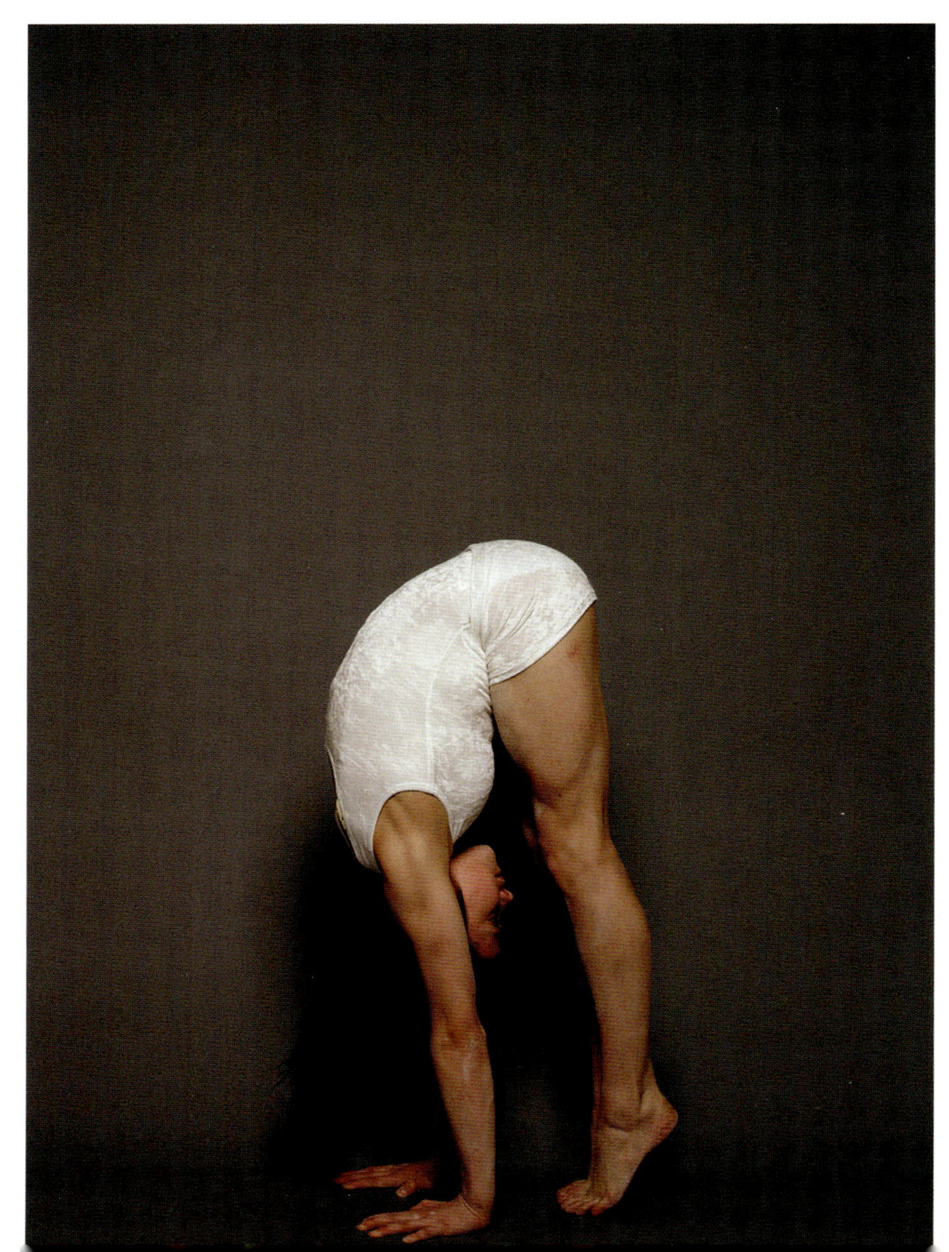

Opposite page: Jo Longhurst, *Peak*, 2012.

Following pages: *Peak and Pinnacle*; *Space-Force Constructions.*

All installation views: *Other Spaces*, Mostyn, Llandudno, 2012.

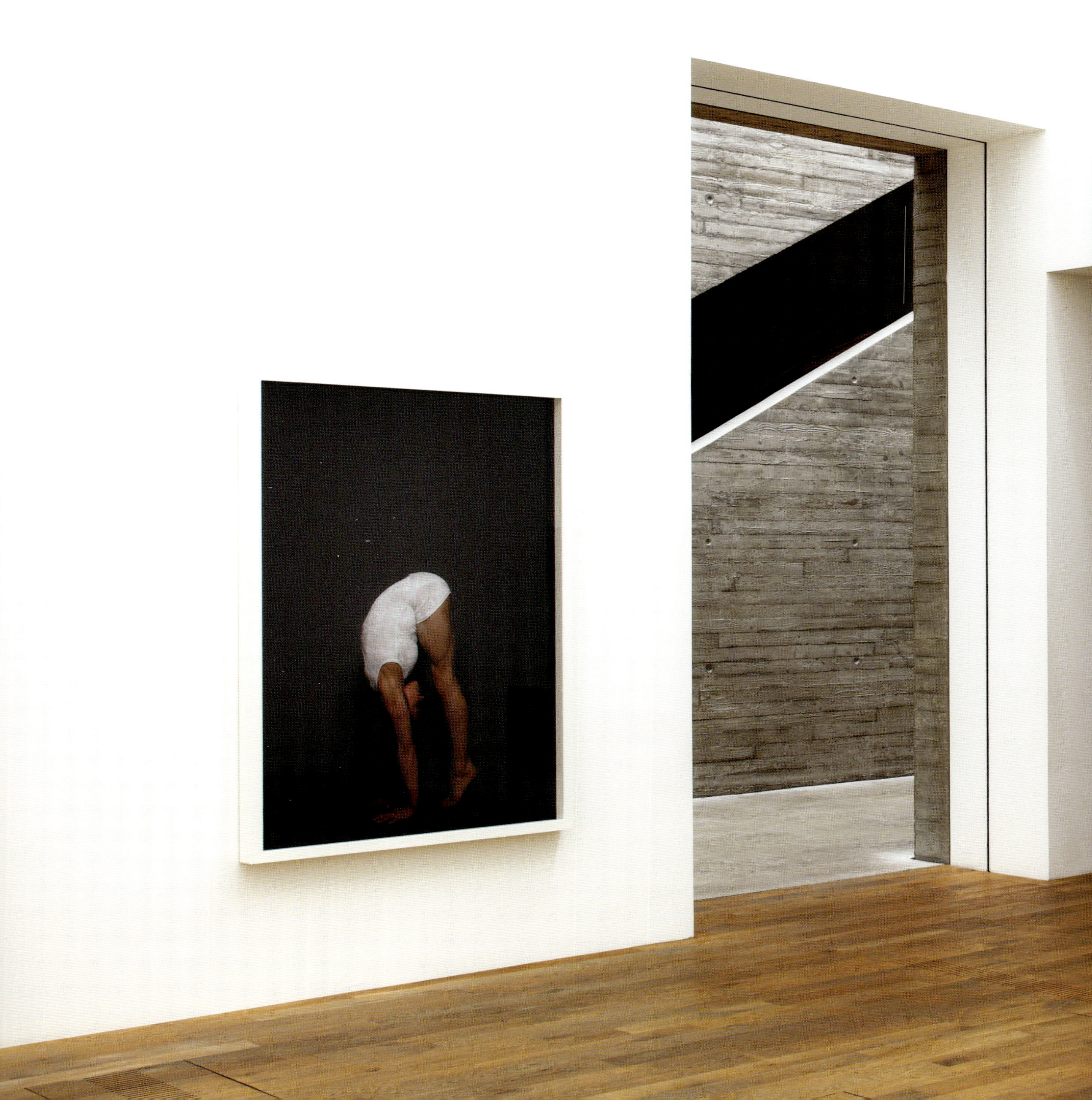

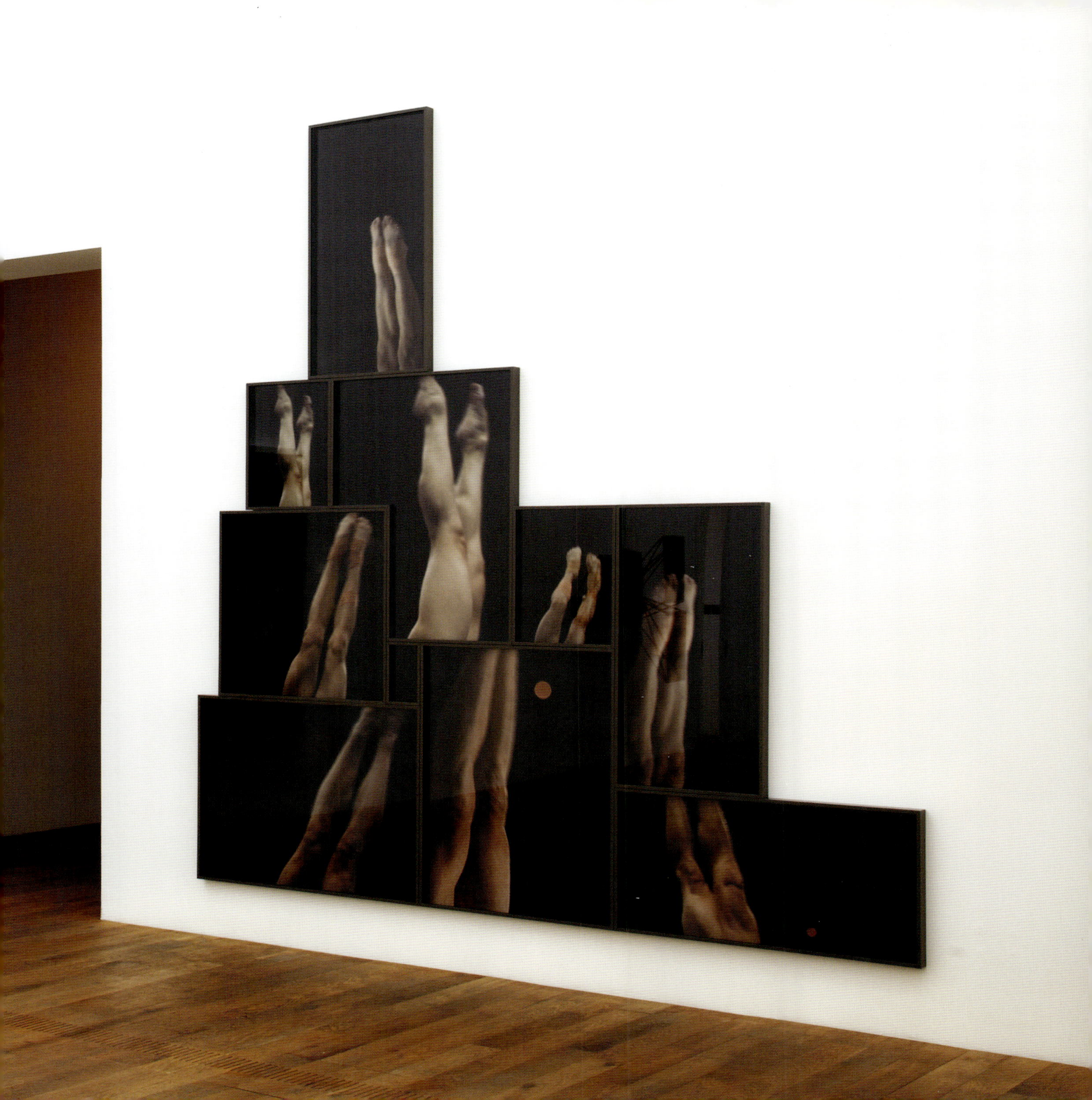

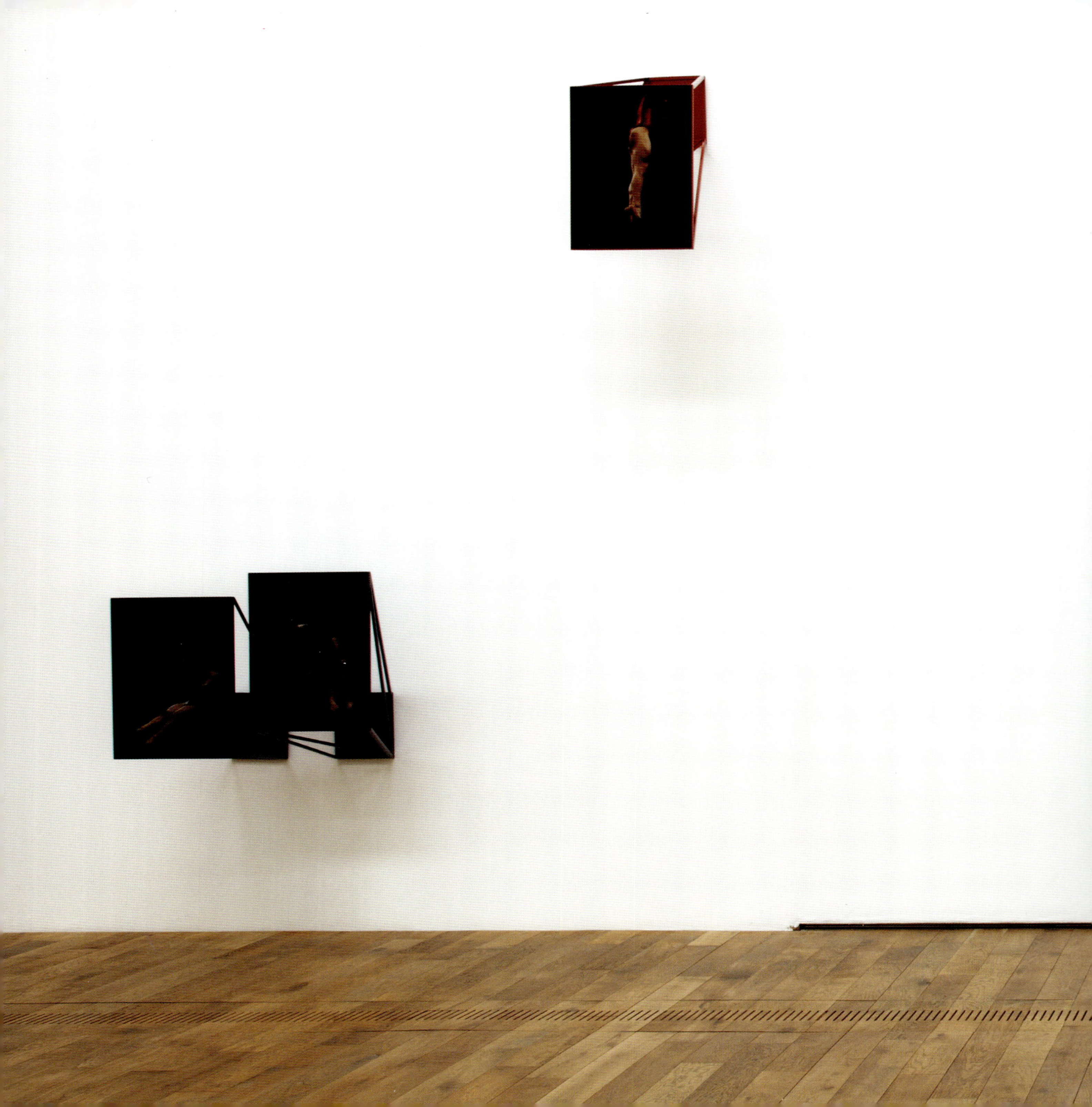

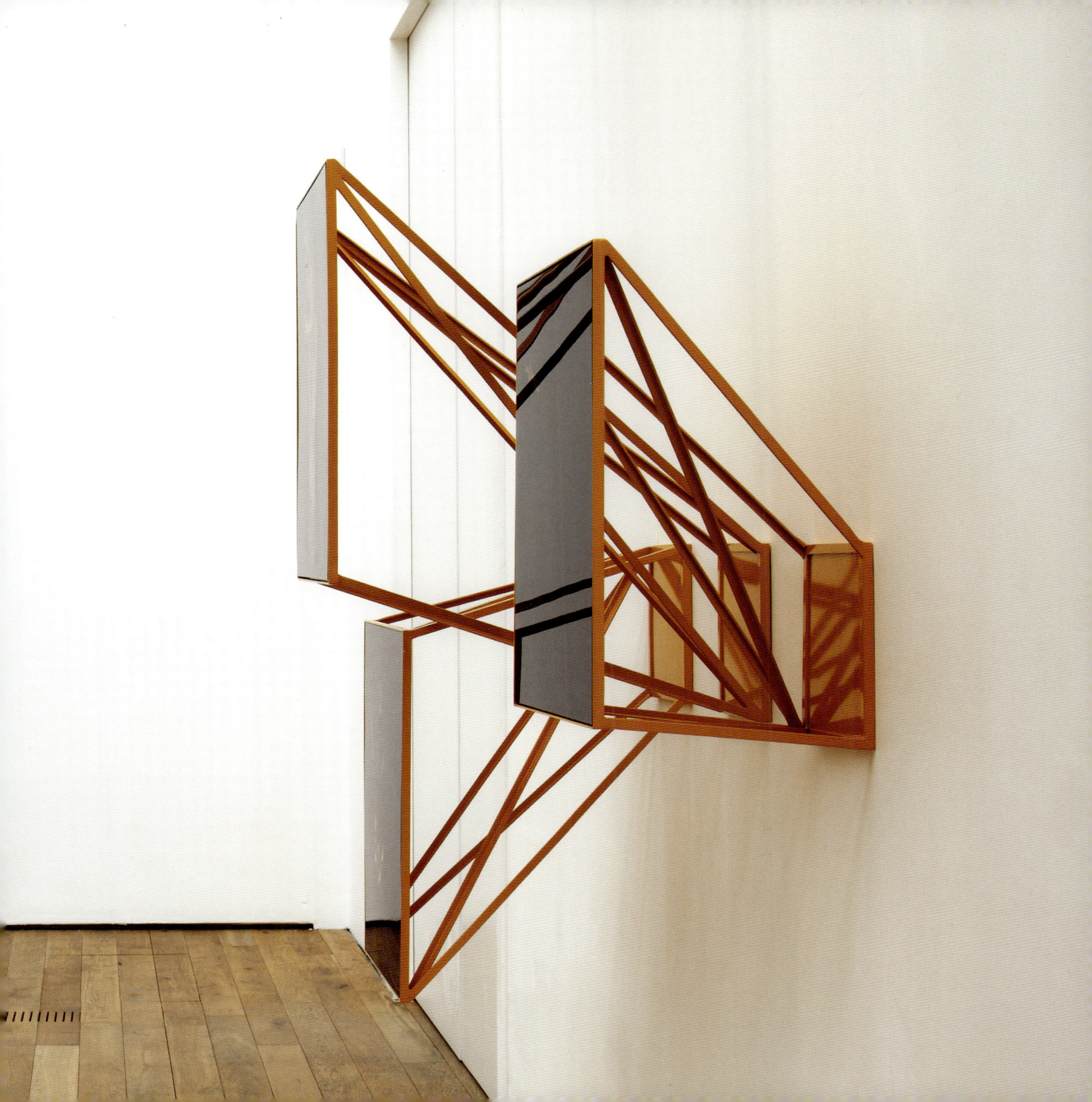

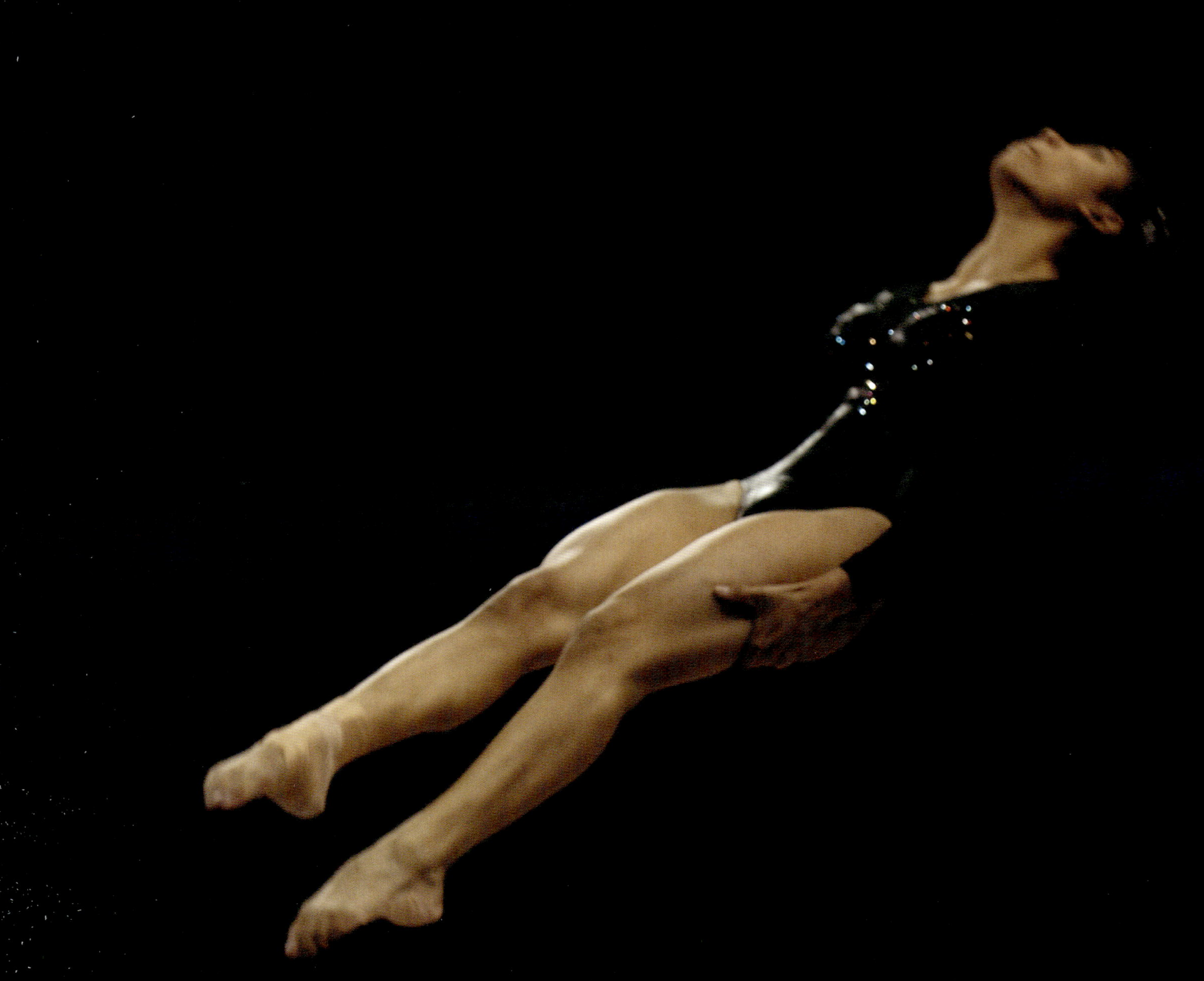

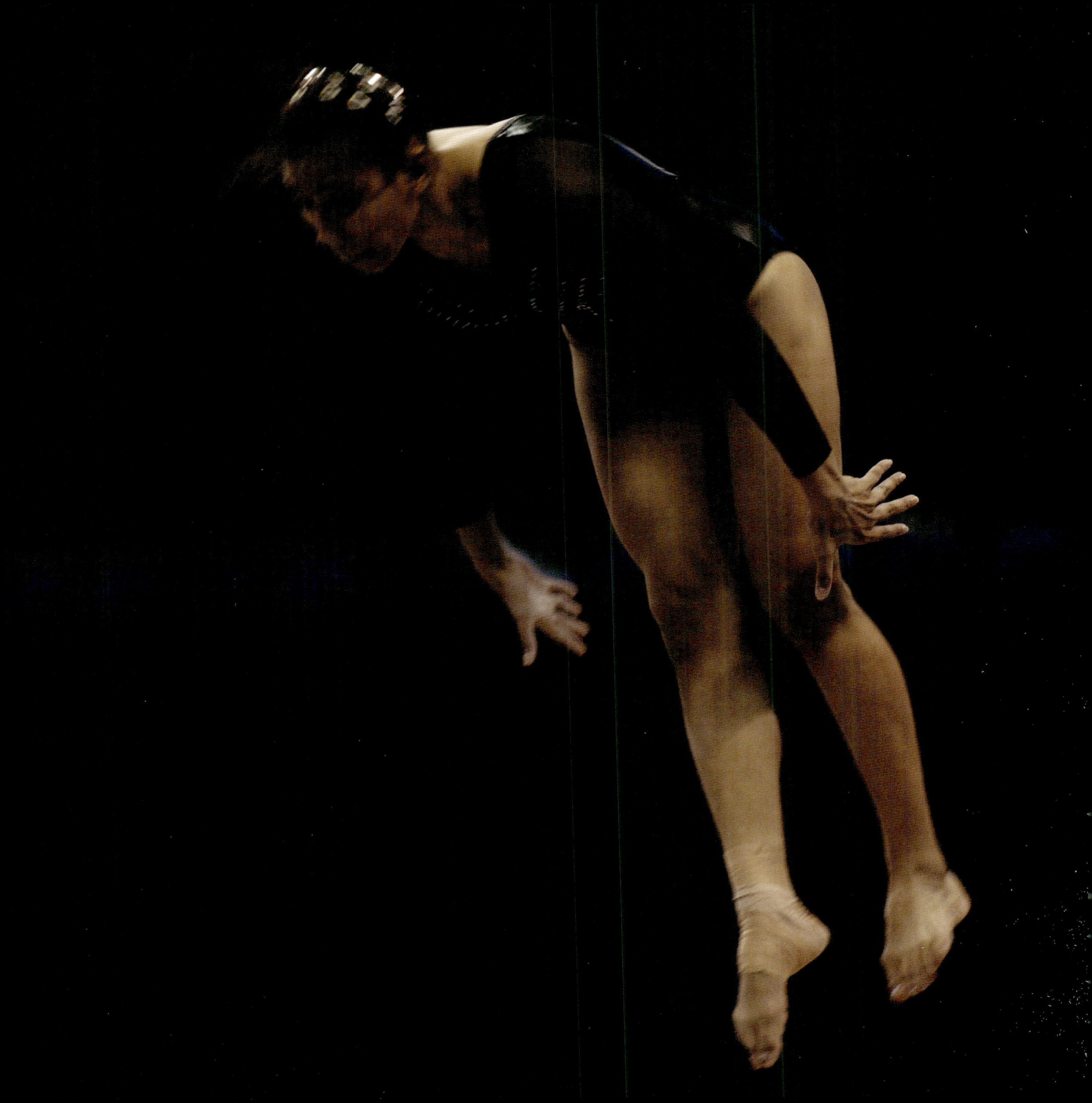

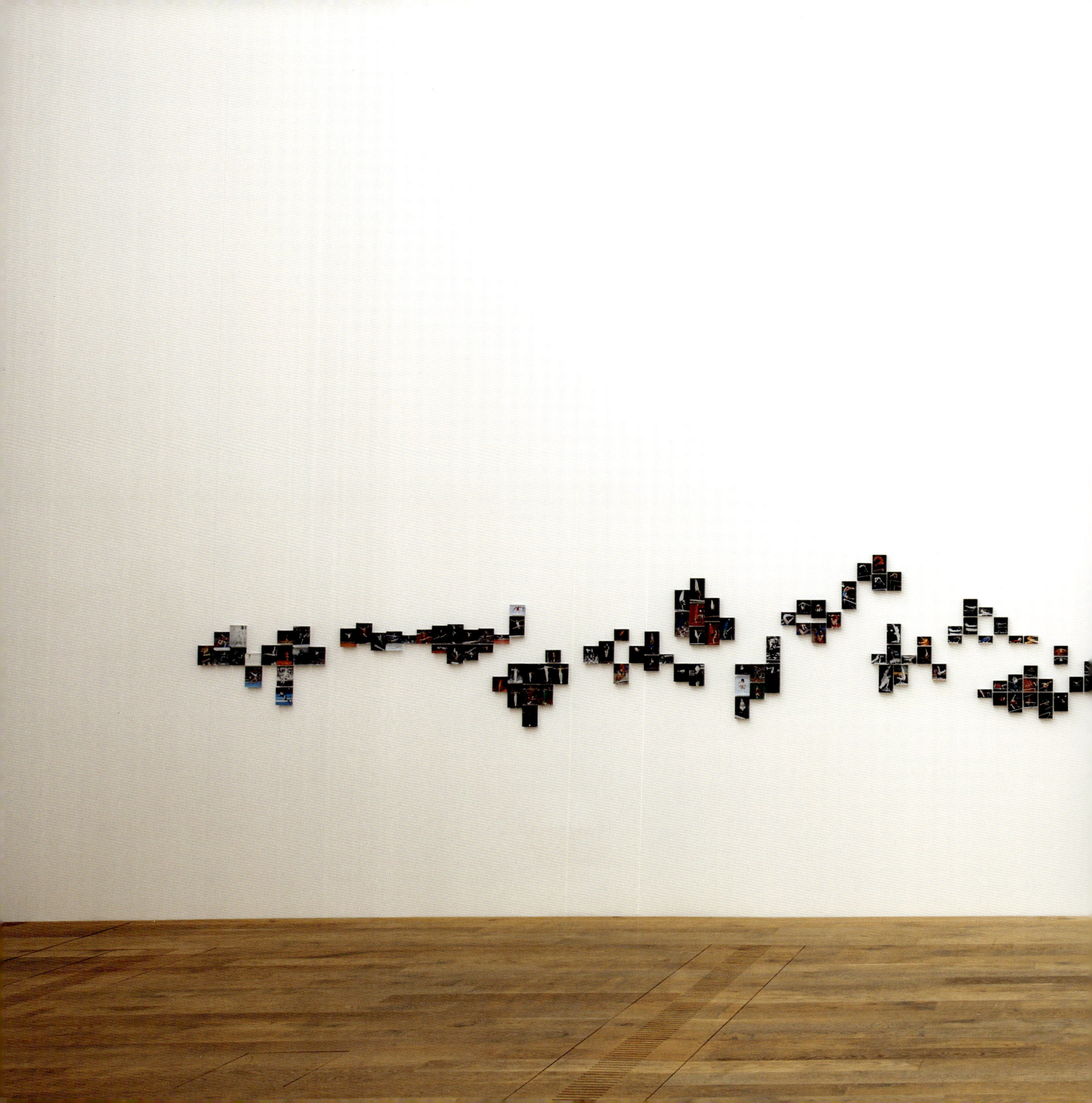

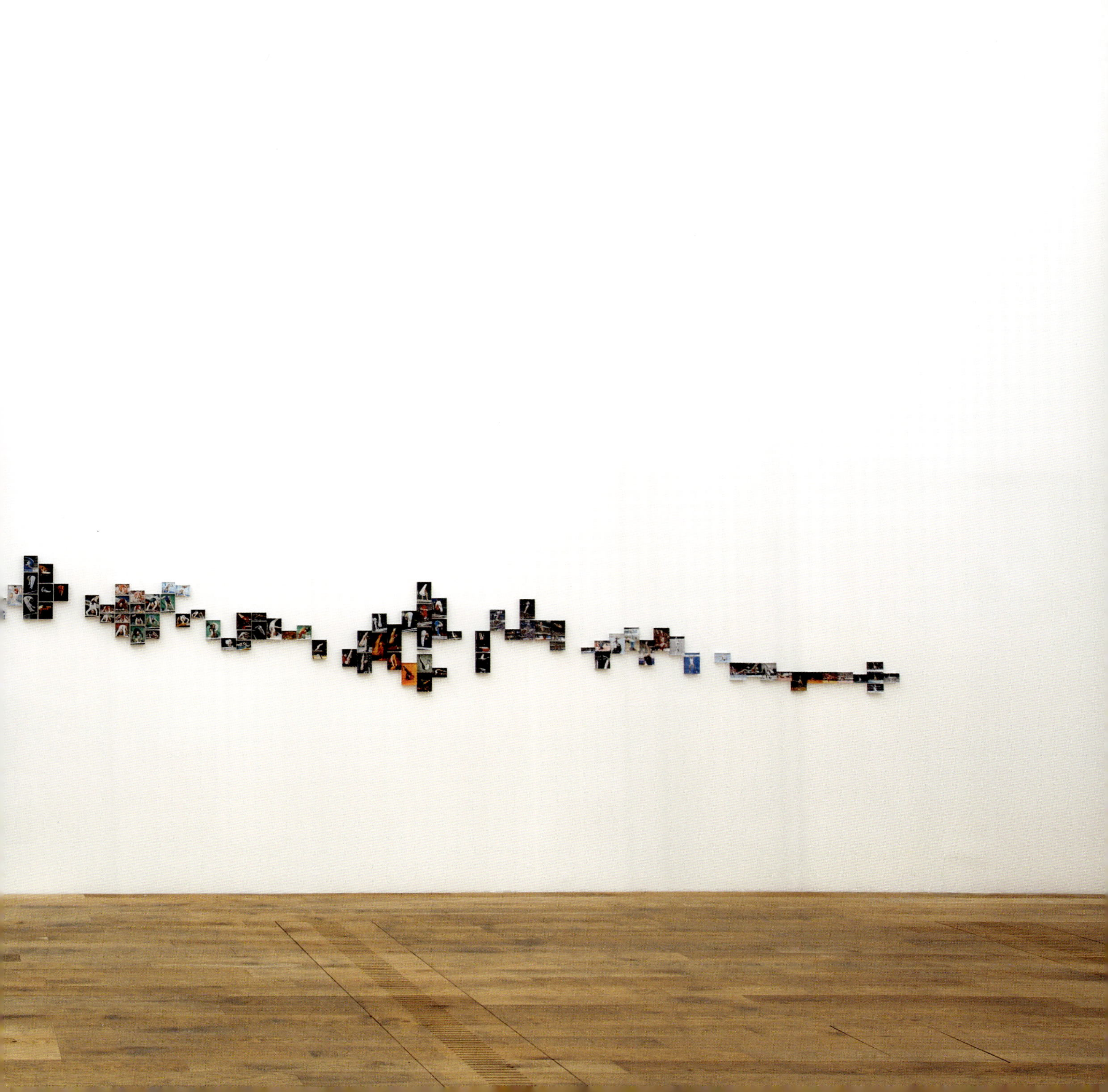

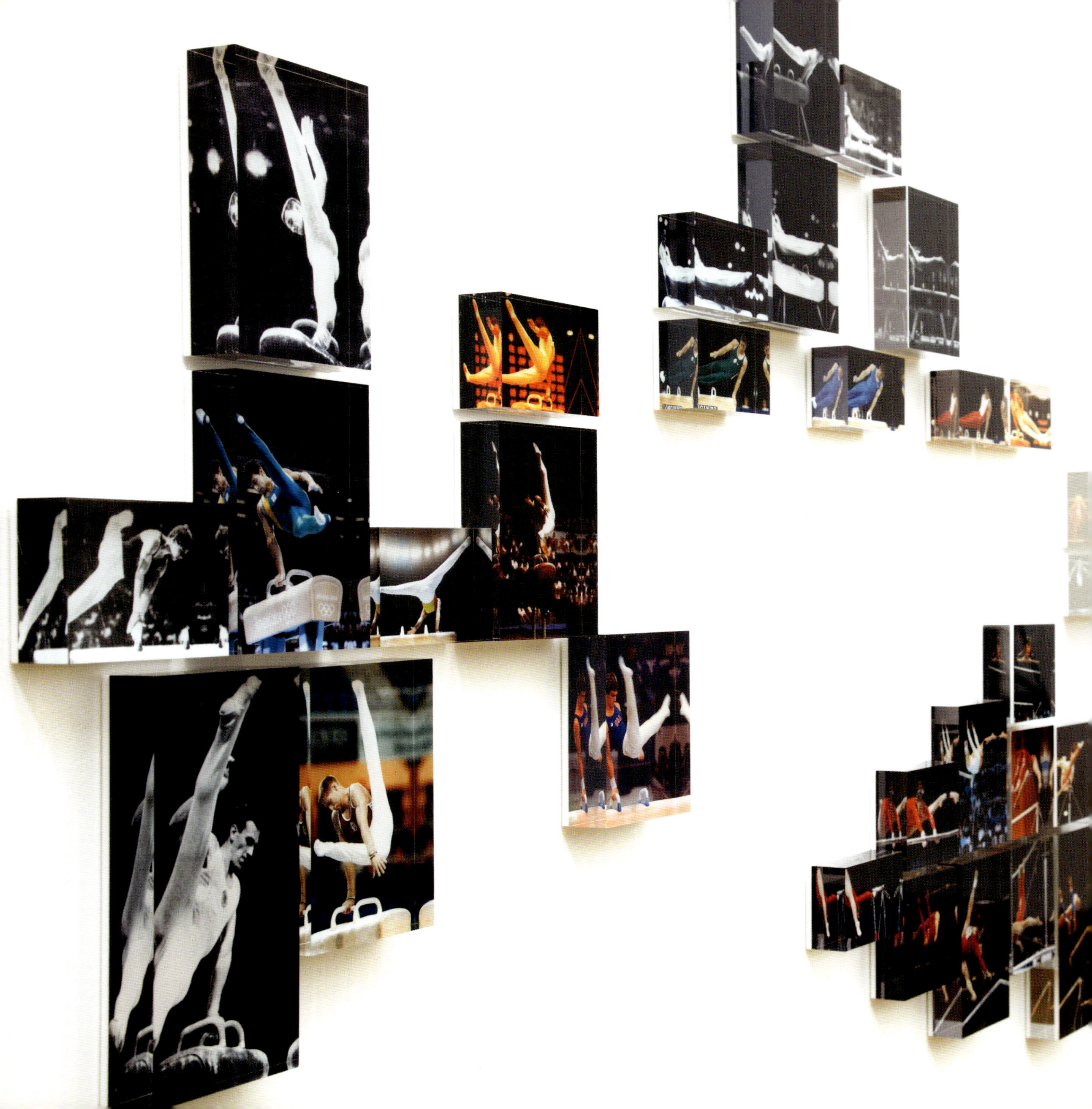

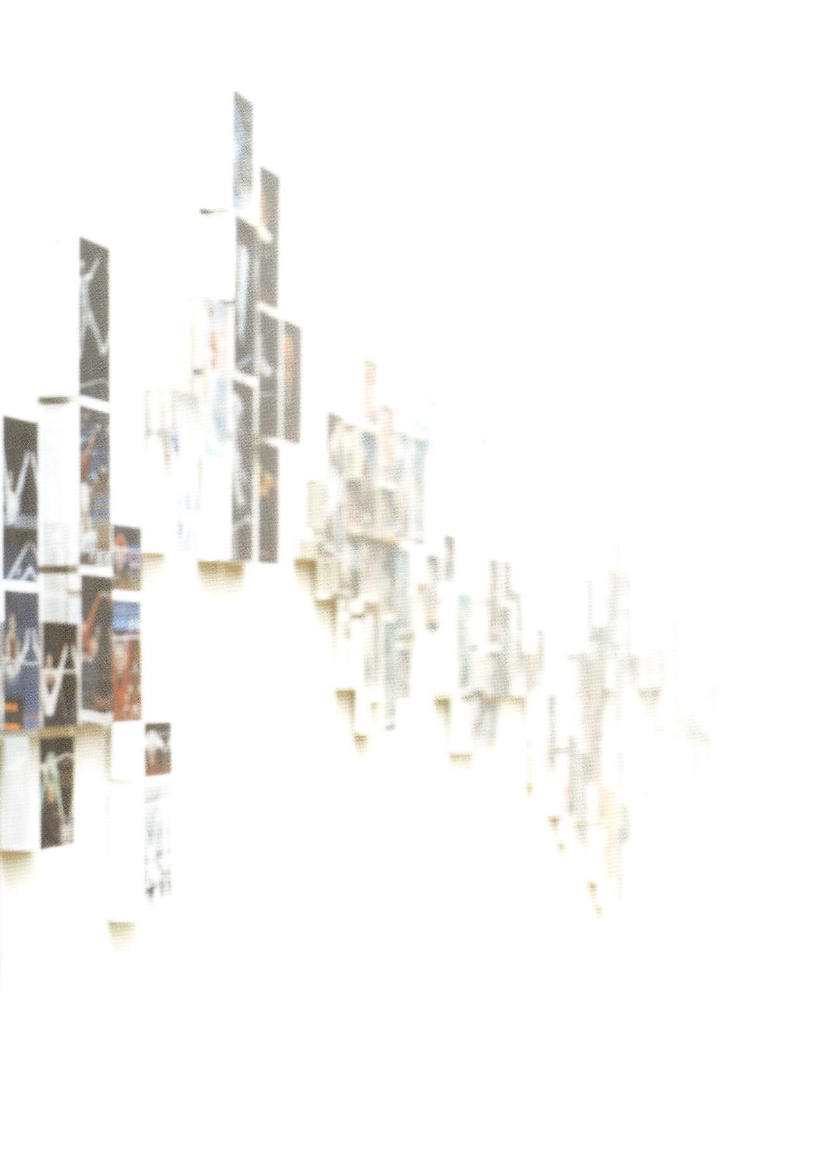

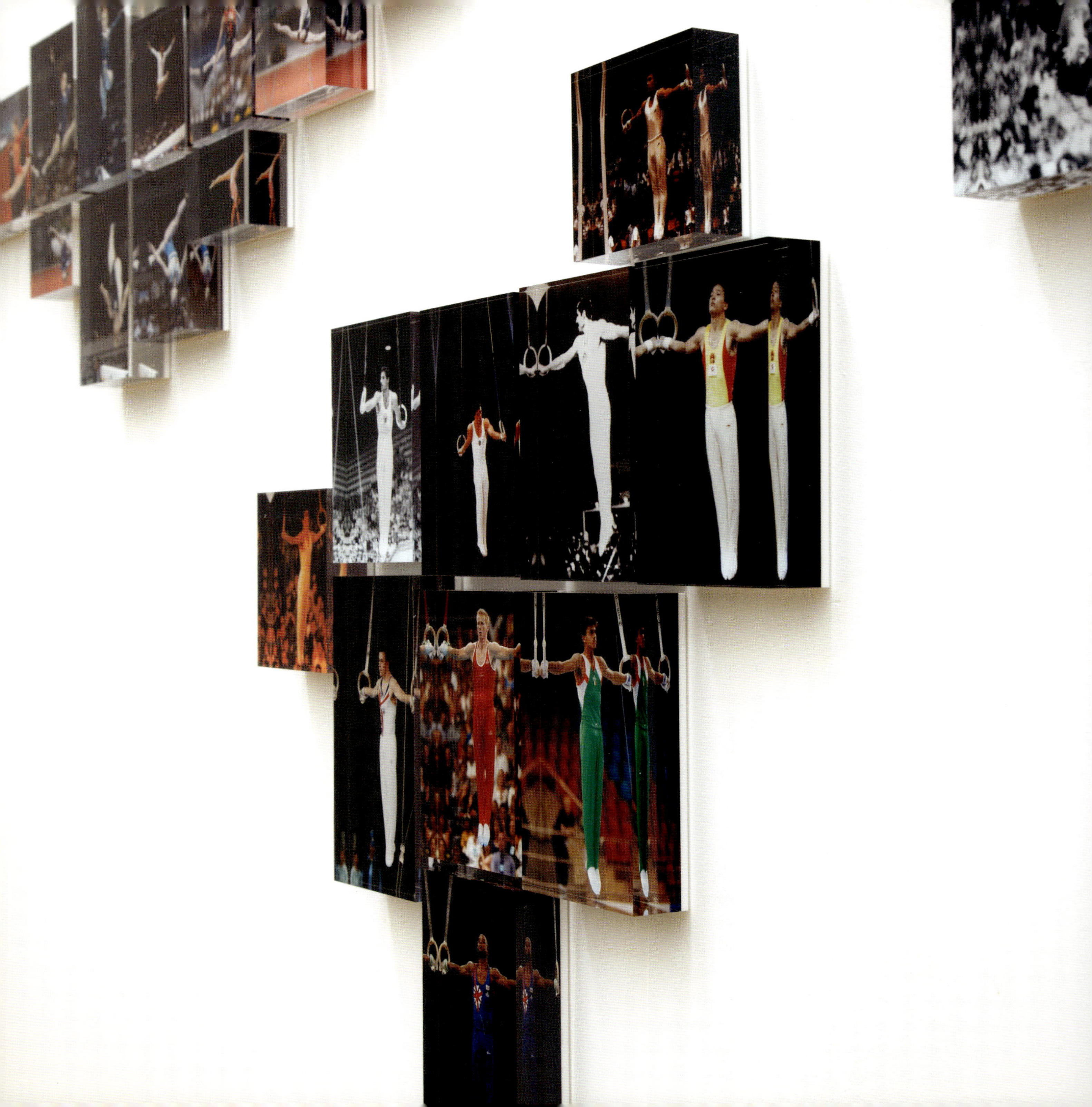

Opposite page and previous pages: Jo Longhurst, *A-Z*, 2012.

Pages 148-149: Jo Longhurst, *Space-Force Construction No. 3 (India)*, detail, 2012.

Jo Longhurst, *Cross*, 2013.

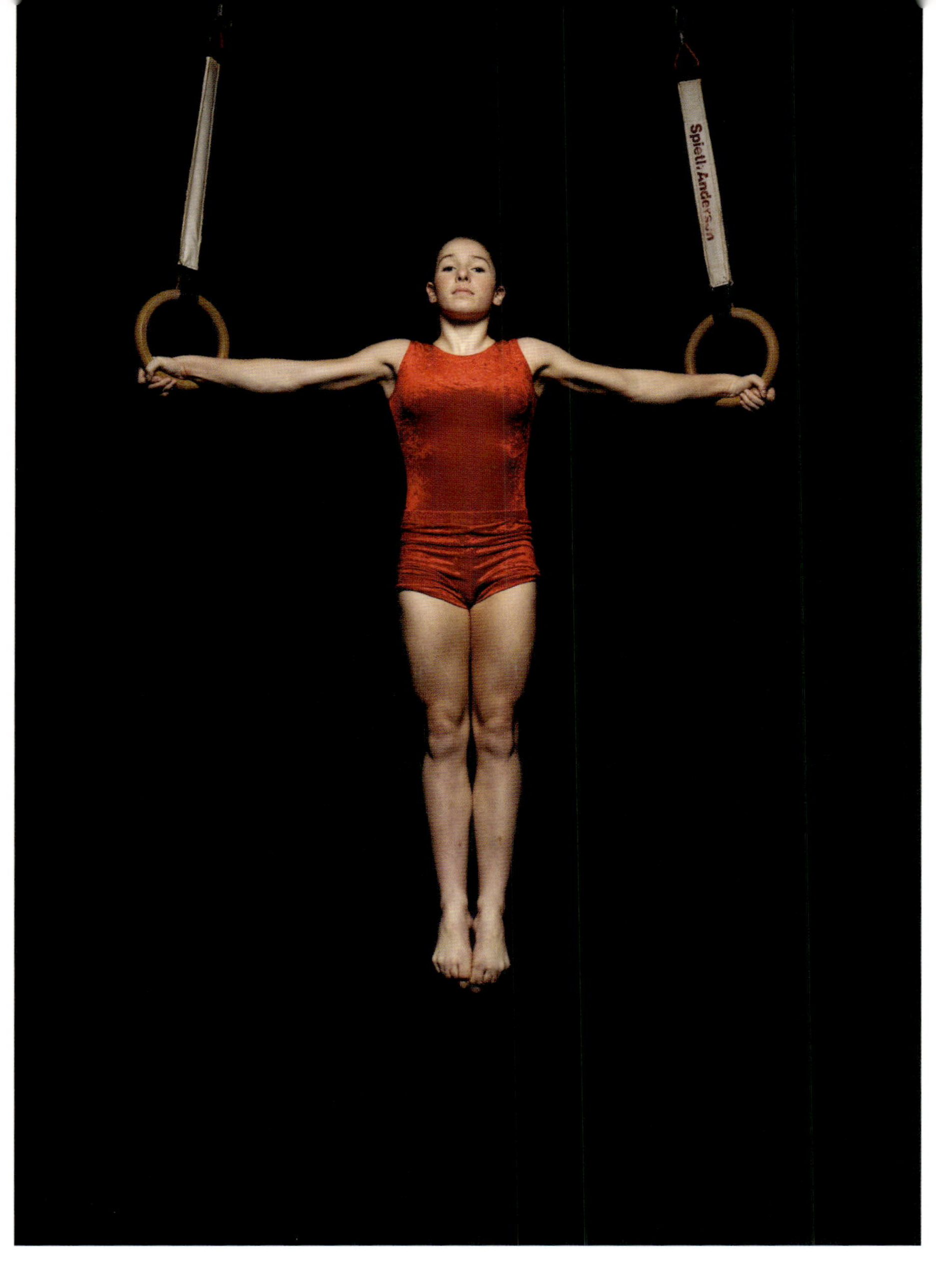

WORKS

Pinnacle
Shot 2009, first produced 2012
Eleven framed, tessellating photographs in grey powder coated metal frames
Installation 287cm x 315cm

Peak
Shot 2009, first produced 2012
Photograph in white box frame with perspex
168 x 117cm

Space-Force Construction No. 1 (United States of America), Space-Force Construction No. 2 (China), Space-Force Construction No. 3 (India)
Shot 2009, first produced 2012
Six photographs under perspex in powder-coated aluminium structures
Image plates each 40.6cm x 60.9cm, installation dimensions variable

A-Z
2008/ 2012
215 appropriated photographs under perspex
[Original MDF version commissioned by Pavilion, Leeds, 2008]
Each block 73mm x various heights; installation 1025cm x 95cm x 1.8cm
Photographs: Alan Baker, estate unknown; British Gymnastics Archive; Editura Sport-Turism, Spain; Alan Edwards; Girardet Archiv, Photographic Collection, Museum Folkwang; Hulton Getty Archive; Sing Lo; Volker Minkus [official photographer to the International Gymnastics Federation]; Press Commission of the Chinese Olympic Committee; and Vladimir Safronov, estate unknown

Cross
Shot 2012
Photograph in white box frame with perspex
183 x 264cm x 9cm

Jo Longhurst Other Spaces is published by Ffotogallery in partnership with Mostyn, 2012. Additional works from *Other Spaces* can be seen at www.jolonghurst.com

Other Spaces has financial support from Art Gallery of Ontario, Arts Council England, Arts Council Wales, John Kobal Foundation, Leverhulme Trust, Pavilion and the National Media Museum.

A PERFECT MYTH

RAY MÜLLER, DIRECTOR OF THE WONDERFUL HORRIBLE LIFE OF LENI RIEFENSTAHL, IN CONVERSATION WITH **CERI HIGGINS**

'The borderline between life and film is in constant flux with Leni Riefenstahl.'[1]

Ray Müller's 1993 film *Die Macht der Bilder* (literal translation: 'The Power of Images') was released in English with the rather more spectacular title of *The Wonderful Horrible Life of Leni Riefenstahl*. The two titles encapsulate the way in which the power of Riefenstahl's work has always been closely connected and studied in relation to her spectacular life, which presents a complicated negotiation for the scholar between intellect and emotion, fact and fiction. As a result, her films and the way in which she lived her 101 years have been a source of fascination since the 1930s.

With her status as the leading, creative force behind the cinematic iconography of the Third Reich and Hitler, Riefenstahl provokes extreme reactions. There are those who see 'the force of her work being precisely in the continuity of its political and aesthetic ideas'[2] and those, on the other hand, who in their attempts to rehabilitate her as an 'artist', fail to fully acknowledge, or indeed sideline, her deep engagement with National Socialist politics and the ideology her films served.

In his film, Müller states his aim is to go beyond these critiques of Riefenstahl and start from a point of 'no preconceptions': in other words, to examine Riefenstahl and her work from an objective viewpoint. Müller had unprecedented access to Riefenstahl and our discussion on the tempestuous and complex relationship he established with her opened up issues about Riefenstahl's obsession with perfection, its consequences for her responsibilities as a film-maker and whether any film on Riefenstahl could ever be objective. Gitta Sereny, who interviewed her during the production of Müller's film, says of Riefenstahl's memoirs: 'Like many people writing "imaginatively" about the past, Riefenstahl relies throughout her book on her reader's ignorance – which is how historical myths are made.'[3]

Riefenstahl's denial of historical facts and her retelling of the past in order to accommodate her personal myth of being the perfect film-maker in search of the perfect aesthetic style was central to our conversation. In contributing to the creation of Nazi mythology, Riefenstahl also created her own story, that of the misunderstood woman and artist, a 'witch' who was the object of a hunt, pursued by the ignorant. Indeed, Riefenstahl drew a parallel in Müller's film between herself and the character of the wild, magical woman, Junta, whom she played, in *Das Blaue Licht/The Blue Light* (Leni Riefenstahl, 1932), and to whom Hitler was so drawn.[4] In a compelling analysis and discussion of the *The Blue Light*, Eric Rentschler concludes:

> The film played a key role in Riefenstahl's revisionist fiction; the personal myth of an unknowing and innocent artist was configured as a multimedia event and a mass-market recollection. In this melodramatic spectacle, promulgated by Riefenstahl, supported by prominent artists and film directors, sustained by influential journalists and critics and followed by audiences throughout the world, Hitler's most prominent image maker metamorphosed into a preeminent victim of the past.[5]

Eighteen other directors had turned down the documentary before the producers offered the job to Müller. He was very aware of how contentious the subject matter was. His previous work had been in cultural and historical documentaries, yet this was to be the most political subject he had directed to date. He knew it would be a momentous undertaking, and for that reason he took the job. Indeed, when he accepted, some colleagues in Germany called him a Nazi. To make a film which did not become complicit with Riefenstahl's myth-making agenda and in which she was to be the star would be a difficult and complex task for any director. Müller's film has received acclaim, but has also been criticized for ultimately succumbing to the 'melodramatic spectacle' Riefenstahl actively encouraged.[6]

Consequently, our conversation highlighted the challenge of how contemporary film-makers, artists and audiences engage with a personality such as Riefenstahl; how we understand her notion of 'perfection' and how we might enter the space between the 'wonderful' and 'horrible' in her films to examine issues of purpose, responsibility and meaning, which have repercussions for all creative practitioners.

Ceri Higgins: How did your relationship with Riefenstahl develop, had you met her before?

Ray Müller: Only once, for a very brief interview, in another context. She wouldn't remember that. I hardly remembered it myself.

CH: So, how did the relationship develop? Did you talk to her before, or did you go straight to filming?

RM: A little bit, but not a lot. I did my research, but apart from that we didn't have a lot of pre-production meetings. We just agreed on the places we would go to and then the rest we developed from there. I had a concept of course – the subject I would have to talk about the places we would shoot – but what and how we would shoot at those locations was open. Because that's my style – to improvise.

CH: You make it apparent in the film there is a contentious relationship with her, where she often wants to take over the directing…

RM: The thing is, I found out, of course, she tried to influence me in all kinds of ways and she was very good at that. I read stories that when she shot *Olympia* and there was a 'No, don't dig here', she always got her way by either threatening with Hitler, being charming. In the end, she cried… whatever… she was an actress, she had all kinds of tools and she tried all the tools on me, too! Obviously! I thought the only way to survive is to become like a Zen monk, like a stone. Whatever happens I don't move. Don't move and when she has an outburst and we cut and she disappears and then after three hours she returns, we continue with the same question again. So I was totally uninfluenceable [sic] and that got her even madder, of course. But then, in the end, later on, she respected that. But it took a long time. It came into her head that she hardly came across somebody that was not to be influenced, as stubborn as she was in her job, but only with different tools. And that she appreciated. When the film was over, she actually – I wouldn't say admired the job I did – but almost… but this was much later.

She is an extremely dominant character. I always say she is not a woman, but she is a general in disguise as a beautiful woman. So she is giving orders all the time – she has been giving orders all her life. Later on I realized – since she was an actress, very famous before she met Hitler, a director herself and a producer – it was the first time in her life that she was being pushed around by somebody else, especially at such an age. So psychologically it must have been very difficult for her. Being told not to look here, but look at this and walk here… If she saw the point, you could do anything with Riefenstahl if it was for a good picture, a good shot. She would stand naked in the pouring rain on the roof if it is for a good image, but if it may have been for another purpose, she gets very distrustful, of course. So we developed a good relationship on the artistic point of view.

CH: How did you work with her concern about the way she was shot and what you asked?

RM: Well, of course, I know myself that at noon with the sun from above it doesn't work very well with a lady with a thousand wrinkles on her face, but for several reasons we could not always take this into account. If you started late, if it was raining, you know. There is this production pressure and you say, 'OK this is not the most important thing in this film,' the lighting on her face. But she saw that differently of course. I mean the funny thing… the first quarrel we had was at the first take, but it wasn't directed against me. She was sitting at her desk with a couple of photographs around her, and the camera is moving on rails around her and she was looking up at it, and we shot this two times and all of a sudden she looks at the camera, 'You cannot shoot me with a 50mm lens! Come on!' Then she shouted at the cameraman. I was out of focus for once, and they had a long discussion about what kind of lens you had to use on an elderly lady at a distance. It was quite interesting. But the cameraman was totally flabbergasted!

CH: So in the filming of her, she wanted perfection?

RM: She always wanted perfection in almost anything. Even in her house. When I went to see her first to say hello, I had a sweater around my neck and I'm a very negligent person, so I just threw it next to me on the sofa. She immediately picked it up and put it on the wall, nicely in order. When I looked around, the whole house looked as if it was not inhabited. I've never seen such a clean house; not only clean, there was nothing lying around. She is the most orderly person I have ever seen in my life. If you ask her, for example, I think there was an interview with you in 1922, in two minutes she would have the article.

The archives are amazing. Otherwise she could never have done the *Olympia* film because it's 400km of film, and just to organize the material – it took her four months just to screen it, so if you don't have an outstanding logistic system, you will get lost.

CH: So, how would you relate her need for perfection and control over the image to the politics in her films?

RM: She could be very charming when you were talking about art or about travels or whatever, it's only this… she's traumatized by her past and only the political stuff would get her totally upset. You know what was strange, when I met her first, was the idea that I am shaking the hand of a woman who had shaken hands with Hitler so many times. It's a bit absurd, but the idea came up in my mind, it's bizarre. This is just my personal opinion. I believe her when she says, 'I'm not interested in politics.' But of course she took advantage of the situation to a great deal. But only for her art. She is a possessed film-maker who would grab everything she can get to make a better film. Be it the money of Hitler, be it whatever – anything goes as soon as it's good for my work of art. And that, of course, is a totally irresponsible attitude, but she didn't see this, she just didn't care.

CH: At what point did you decide to show your arguments and the difficulty of filming with her?

RM: We had a shooting schedule and there were some days that we were shooting in her house at the editing table, etc… So this was when the political questions had to come out. I couldn't ask those questions somewhere else in the mountains, so the political stuff was more or less centred at her house because we had pictures, and also it was better because the atmosphere was more intimate. She felt secure.

CH: What about the archive material you use? There are photos of Riefenstahl with Goebbels and Hitler. How much material is there and did she have that material?

RM: I didn't get it from her. This is in the Bundesarchiv. She cut herself off but, on the other hand, she was always working within the circle of power. So she had to deal with Goebbels all the time. She was among the generals and, of course, being a personal protégé of Hitler, she could allow herself almost anything. The relationship between those two was quite special. I think they were two super-egos admiring each other. Hitler wanted to go to art school and he wasn't accepted, so she had the artistic talent he didn't have, the talent he lacked, and he had the power, which for her was very useful for her job. They were a type of synergetic pair.

CH: Is there any film footage of her with them?

RM: Well, the thing is, I don't know what is in her personal archive. She would not give me things that were detrimental to her, obviously. Let's say, I know what I needed – but maybe she had other reels that I was not aware of – she wouldn't mention that, of course.

There's a funny scene in the film, which underlines her sense of perfection. We were talking about *Triumph of the Will* on the staircase, and she made another film before that which was not so good (*Sieg des Glaubens/Victory of Faith*, 1933). And she was so angry that I mentioned that and I thought that it was because I mentioned that she made a second one – because normally in the public opinion, she only made one Party film – and I thought it annoyed her that I was aware of the second one at all, and that I mentioned it in public. But it wasn't that – it was that I dared to mention something that was not perfect, which is signed by her. That is an artistic thing, not a political thing.

CH: It's like the politics didn't come into it?

RM: No, it's like how can I mention a film by Riefenstahl which is not perfect? Because that does not exist.

CH: I think that is very telling. She constructed herself, and in constructing her image, she constructed a memory and she plays her part 'perfectly', to perfection: perfect image with perfect memories.

RM: She has even constructed a perfect truth for her. People always ask, 'Is she lying?' She is too proud to lie, so she has constructed her own truth to cover her trauma a little bit, and what she says, she actually believes. She is not lying, but this truth is not the real truth, it is her truth.

CH: It's really interesting about what you said earlier, about her personality, about her order and her control, because it is the sense you have when looking at her physically. For someone of her age, she obviously cared how she looked …

RM: But you as a woman, you see it differently anyway.

CH: How do you think she would have reacted to a woman director?

RM: Good question. I don't know. But what is interesting, and we have to bear in mind, is that movie-making is a man's job, even nowadays, and at that time even more so. So when she made her first film, long before she met Hitler, she was producing, the main star and directing, so impersonating three main jobs at the age of 29 in a male dominated business. So you can imagine what kind of power this woman had.

We heard that at the age of 98, she wanted to go to Africa to an area where civil war was going, to see her Nuba for the last time before she died. I just thought we'd go along with the camera because it sounds interesting. But it turned out to be an interesting film, although it was thwarted in the end – we had this helicopter crash and all that, but it reveals different parts of her character. I give you two examples. When the helicopter crashed, which we also survived by miracle, she was covered in blood, lying on a stretcher and I was sure she was dead, but after twenty minutes or so they moved her a little bit and I realized she had some movements, and then she opened her eyes and came to. Before I could say anything, she said, 'Well, did you film that properly, when you were tearing me out of the helicopter?' That is quite amazing. Another thing is very similar to that: we were going along in a jeep and we met some military, and she was getting into a discussion with those people. I don't know what about and all of a sudden she starts sobbing and crying or whatever, and we didn't want to interfere, and then she came over to me and started shouting at me: 'You know I just found out that two of my best Nuba friends are dead,' and we only filmed this with a small camera from afar. 'Why didn't you film this properly?' First of all, she is in grief and a second later she thinks whether this grief has been put on the screen in the right way. This is almost schizophrenic.

CH: Yes, it's an ability she had to divorce herself from her surroundings and the events that were happening in the moment. She was living in the Third Reich, so close to Hitler, Goebbels and the Nazi elite – she had to be conscious of what the regime was doing and intended and yet she had an ability to just cut it off?

RM: Totally. She is like a laser beam focusing on her job. She wouldn't see anything else. I think probably people would have asked her if she knew what was going on, but she would have said, 'No, I don't want to hear this kind of thing.'

CH: How do you see that? How is it seen in Germany – there were, after all, many other film-makers in the Reich and it is interesting that she tends to be focused upon…

RM: But that was her bad luck.

CH: Well, tell me a bit more about that…

RM: The Party rally film in Nuremburg. There was a Party rally every year, and it was filmed every year, and next year after her's was another one. Those films had really nasty commentary, they were very propaganda orientated. But she didn't use commentary and the problem was that it was such a masterpiece it has never been forgotten. All the other films are forgotten.

CH: They were like newsreel and she makes that distinction herself doesn't she?

RM: Exactly, so her bad luck was that the film was so good it has never been forgotten. It's been so popular, especially abroad, and it gave her that print of being an evil woman ever since. Of course, she dedicated her talent to the wrong man, but still, if it had been a bad film she would have been forgotten, the film would have been forgotten, so it's just unfortunate actually. Another thing about *Triumph of the Will* – and I'm not defending her, I'm just making a point that at that time – Hitler was not the demon yet. For example, the arch-enemy of Germany, the French, would never have given the gold medal to *Olympia* if it had been… But in retrospect, people tend to forget all that; it's just that this was evil and she was evil too and it is easy to say so.

There is a little scene in the film, when she is talking to her old cameramen, and she says, 'You know in '34,' when she made *Triumph of the Will*, 'even Churchill said we have to admire Germany for its big leader.'

CH: You can see at the time, in the early 1930s, how Hitler might have been seen as 'perfect' by other nations, in the sense of getting the country up on its feet; but the terror and the obscenity that was so fundamental with that leadership and regime, you have to reject, and Riefenstahl is a catalyst for that…

RM: The only thing you can really reproach her for is that she totally denies the responsibility of an artist. What the meaning of her work was. What can you do with a film like *Triumph of the Will*? She didn't care: 'I do a job, I do it as perfectly as I possibly can, the rest is nothing to do with me,' and this, of course, is absurd, because there are times when other things are more important than art. She would never agree to that. She said, 'I would have made a film for everybody, for Stalin, for Mao, I didn't care as long as I can make an interesting film.' She even says in my film, 'I would have made a film about vegetables….' It was marching troops, vegetables or whatever, it's the shot, the lighting that is important, not what is in front of the camera. Imagine this very revealing scene when she sits at the editing table and she runs a scene from *Triumph of the Will*, and you see these SS boots marching down the stairs, and she is still in love with the shot, saying, 'Don't you see how this is cut and the music comes in….' She doesn't see the SS boots at all. She just sees perfectly organized shots. This was hard to understand – the whole crew, we just looked at each other, but that's the way she is.

CH: It is really interesting how form completely subsumes content.

RM: Her concept of art was without any compromise. I mean you can discuss what is good art and bad art, but what she considered to be good art was not to be discussed. OK, you could discuss paintings with her, but in film, no. She was always convinced that what she did, she did it perfectly; nobody could have done it better.

CH: How would you sum up Riefenstahl's perfection?

RM: She was a control freak. She prepared everything meticulously. I mean she was like a general preparing for battle. And in this she was very good. Just imagine the task of preparing the Olympics with a hundred cameramen covering 130 sports. She studied the different sports beforehand intensively with the cameramen to see how you could best film horse riding or jumping or whatever, and then they developed the angles and they tried different techniques. I think she tested 23 different film materials only for *Olympia*. All this pre-production planning was unheard of at the time. Even for her first film [*The Blue Light*], which she directed and starred in, she wrote to Hollywood, to the cameraman who filmed Lilian Gish, because she wanted to find out how he gave her that special rim light and she got her answer, and at the age of 25, she went to Agfa and said, 'None of the stock in the market is good enough, I want to have a lot of nightscapes. Please develop something new for me.' So, she knew exactly what she wanted and always got it. She was perfect in organizing anything. She was a logisitic genius. But to my mind the main genius lies in editing. Having been a dancer, she had a feeling for rhythm, for images, for music and, of course, she controlled everything, but she had very good cameramen. So, part of the quality of her films is due to the cameramen, but the way in which she edited is outstanding. I think this is really her main gift, this rhythm and this feeling for an image in editing, although she also had a very keen eye. But I think editing was the gist of it.

CH: What were her thoughts on Sontag's statement that she had a 'fascist aesthetic'?

RM: I'll tell you a story about that. When my film premiered at the New York festival, it was the first film and everybody was very nervous because it was sponsored by rich Jews in New York, and the festival director was very nervous how the film would be received. In the beginning, he had already had telephone calls that he shouldn't show it, but it went very well. After we went for dinner with about ten intellectuals from the circle of the film society and we were discussing exactly the term 'fascist aesthetic' and as far as I recall, in the end after two hours of heavy drinking and heavy talking, they came to the conclusion that it doesn't exist. It's an interesting phrase, coined by a journalist, but then if you had this as a fascist aesthetic you should have it in music and all kinds of domains, which is very hard to prove. One guy said even the Lincoln Centre in New York looks like as if it was a fascist aesthetic to a certain degree, then all monuments under Stalin look exactly the same in the East, etc... So finally they abandoned the idea that it makes any sense. I mean, you can pick it in flagrant examples, but as a general term it was not accepted during that discussion.

CH: What about her construction of memory? What were your feelings through working with her on that level? How do you think she constructed herself and the past?

RM: In one moment I was very surprised. We were talking about the Goebbels diaries. I had them in front of me and I quoted something to her, and you know the scene when she jumps out and starts saying I am lying and whatever and we had to cut? I didn't get that. Why would she deny something that I can prove in a second? It was untypical of her. But then, in hindsight, she confused the dates because in the beginning she was on good terms with Goebbels and she was invited to parties, but then when the big quarrel started, she was never again invited. She probably thought I was quoting from afterwards, but I was quoting from before and in this tense situation, she may have confused the time. That's the only explanation I have.

CH: There is this need to deny any association, which is ridiculous.

RM: Well, she didn't deny that she admired Hitler. She even says, 'Even after the war I stick to that, but everybody says not me, only the neighbours. I always stick to that, that I admired Hitler,' and people didn't forgive her for that after the war. That is probably true also. So in that respect she was not lying at all. Of course she said that she was in good company for most of the time. Another thing is that people shouldn't forget is that when the war started she hadn't anything to do with the regime anymore. She made films, but they were totally unpolitical. This opera thing in Spain and her film company made a couple of films, documentaries on the famous sculptor, Arno Breker. But it was always art. As far as I know – my knowledge may not be total – she was not involved in anything political any more. I think she went to Poland, where they shot this famous photograph, and she was witnessing a massacre and she immediately complained to the general and went home. I think that was her last involvement with politics, and then she went fled to Spain and was shooting in the mountains in Tirol and Bavaria. Still, it does not take away the shadow from before.

CH: Was she playing a part? Did she have something rehearsed or was she spontaneous?

RM: I realized that with her being an actress that all the interviews were kind of staged. She always acts and delivers. I was getting bored with that and so we needed a second camera, because as soon as the camera was off she was normal. She was not so stiff. So we tried to get those moments – that's why we used a small camera, which we got interesting stuff with that that we would never have gotten otherwise. So that was the problem: how can you come close to people who are playing a part in a documentary? The part of a person being interviewed? She was a very good actress. Even when she was very angry, and she got angry with style, only when she exploded was she natural. She was well behaved mostly, because she is such a professional. Even in Nuremburg, on the staircase, she was getting into such a fit that I thought she was going to die, to get a heart attack and next day we would see a headline 'Young Director Kills Film Diva' or whatever in Nuremburg, but she came back two hours later, still white and shaking and said, 'For me no shooting day is called off because of me.' So she had iron discipline.

CH: The impression I have is that she decided a persona for the film and she was going to follow it through, which related to her perfectionism – she had to be seen as the perfect film-maker in the film and the perfect interviewee.

RM: You cannot imagine the discussions we had as to what she should wear for the interviews. I don't care, but then she would go to the wardrobe and ask, 'Do you think this red or this blue today? What light are we using?' This was of the upmost concern to her and I didn't care.

CH: Why does she keep coming up? In the 1970s there was a lot of discussion about her; you made the film in the 1990s, it was revisited as part of the symposium, 'On Perfection', in 2012. What is it about Riefenstahl?

RM: If she hadn't the political shadow, she would be an icon of women's lib because she was emancipated before the word existed.[7] So that's one thing, and secondly, of course, her fame is closely related to Hitler – being the most evil man in history or whatever, she is part of history somehow, because they go together. If she had only been a very good film-maker without Hitler she may not be so famous probably, and the controversy involved keeps her alive, because this controversy is still alive.

CH: But the moral responsibility and the relationship of art and politics is the key, isn't it? Where do you go as a film-maker in relation to the political entourage around you?

RM: You know, I wonder how long this will go on. How many students in film school in twenty years stills remember her name, I don't know. Those films are hard to watch now. I watched *Olympia* yesterday and they showed two parts as four hours, which is hard to bear as it's very boring, so who would want to see this if you are not a specialist? Even in film schools – not many students want to see the film probably. I think *Triumph of the Will* will be seen by more people study history or fascism – historians because I think it's stupid that it's not available in Germany – it should be shown at schools, because it is the perfect example of how fascism works, so why hide it?

When other people ask me, 'Do you think she was a fascist?' I say I don't know, but I point out the following: would a white woman at the age of 60 go to Africa and live eight months with a primitive tribe in their huts? Would a fascist do that? I don't know.

CH: Depends on how you define a fascist…

RM: What people forget when discussing this is that there was a zeitgeist. It is almost impossible nowadays to put yourself back into that spirit, and you can only understand if you were in the zeitgeist a little bit, or at least if you know a little bit about it. OK, that's a long story, but I give you another quotation: I asked what she would do if she met Hitler again. She was kind of surprised, then she thought and she said – I can almost quote: 'I would take a sword and I would stab him BUT, as a mother would kill her most beloved child.'

You know what she said once, that she could not get rid of that label of being a fascist, she said, 'Now I am only filming fish under water, but people certainly reproach me that I have shot more brown fish than any other colour!' Funnily enough, people always reproach her having this male body aesthetics, you know this beautiful strong body, but she would have been a precursor of fashion photography. Look at Adidas and Nike – they started this ten years ago – the same kind of photographs. Look at the Beckham photographs in his underwear! Now it's not a surprise anymore. She started the aesthetic, but for different motives of course. And I believed her when she said, 'Well, I am only inspired by something beautiful.' Because people reproached her in the Nubas, saying why didn't you photograph other stuff? Actually, she did, she showed me, it was not all beautiful bodies, but the publisher wanted only the beautiful bodies, but then she said, 'I am not inspired by someone ugly, other people can photograph beggars, but it is not my cup of tea, and you have to accept that.'

CH: She retreated through the underwater film into another world?

RM: From Germany, from people. From people who keep asking all those nasty questions all the time. She said the happiest time of her life was in Africa – this is amazing because in the Third Reich she was a superstar, so how can she say that? My personal interpretation was that she realized the difference between being admired and being loved. Her being a cool person... somehow this big admiration flattered her ego, but it may not have caressed her soul. Whereas in Africa, these simple people just liked her and so for the first time in her life she felt that difference.

CH: So when you finished the film and you knew it was going to be contentious and a challenge – how did you feel at the end of it and the process? Where did it take you personally?

RM: This is rare in our business – there were three producers and the film was twice as long as commissioned. I didn't have to change a single cut or a single word in the commentary. That's amazing isn't it? Very strange. Of course, she was sulking, she pretended not to have seen the film, which perhaps was even true – she didn't have a copy. I think they finally sent her a VHS, but she claimed she would never look at it and she didn't speak to any of us for a year at all, only when she heard that the film was so successful in the US. And that it put her back into the limelight and she was getting so many fan mails from America from the film, she sent me a photograph of her as a beautiful, young woman saying, 'This is to my director, who tortured me tremendously, but in the end he made a good film.' That was like a truce.

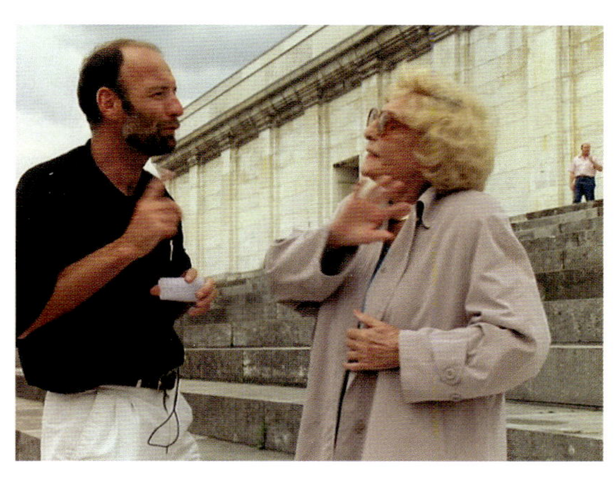

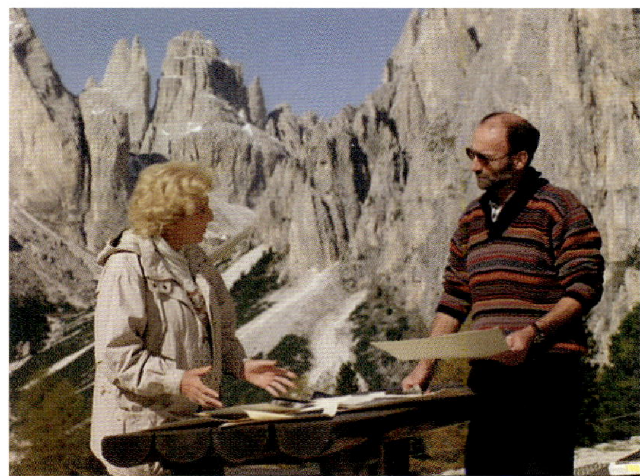

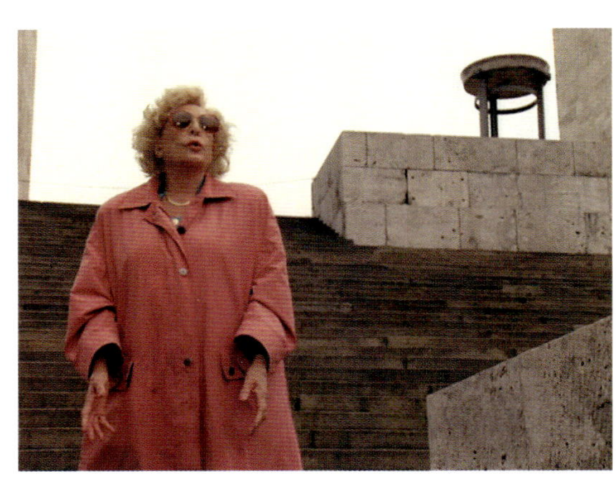

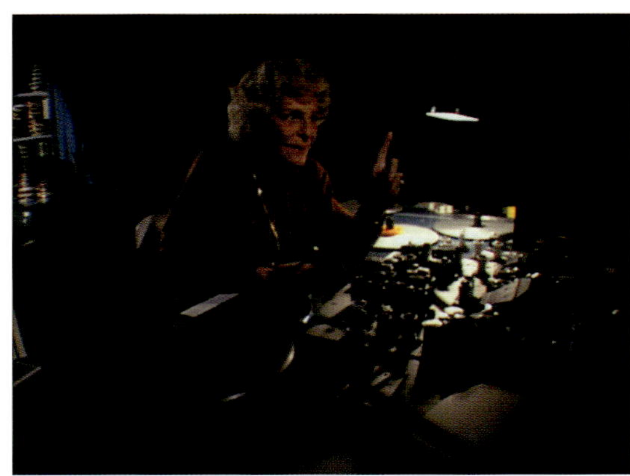

NOTES

1 Ray Müller quoted in Steven Bach, *Leni: The Life and Work of Leni Riefenstahl*, London: Little Brown, 2007, p. 285.
2 Susan Sontag, *Under the Sign of Saturn*, London: Writers and Readers Publishing Cooperative, 1972, p. 97.
3 Gitta Sereny, *The German Trauma: Experiences and Reflections 1938–2001*, London: Penguin, 2000, p. 245.
4 Bach (ibid. p. 91). In the film, Riefenstahl shows Müller her portrait as Junta, which she kept in her study. The same image is the cover of the English translation of her autobiography.
5 See Eric Rentschler, 'A Founding Myth and a Master Text: The Blue Light', in *Riefenstahl Screened: An Anthology of New Criticism*, New York: Continuum, 2008, pp. 151–78.
6 For a compelling critique of the film, see Wulf Kansteiner, 'Wonderful, Horrible Lies: Riefenstahl Memory and Riefenstahl History in Germany', in *Riefenstahl Screened: An Anthology of New Criticism*, New York: Continuum, 2008, pp. 98–129.
7 The argument that Riefenstahl was a feminist is convincingly contested by Eric Rentschler and Gisela von Wysocki, 'Leni Riefenstahl the Deceptive Myth', in *Sexual Strategems: The World of Women in Myth*, ed. Patricia Erens, New York: Horizon, 1975.

All film stills
The Wonderful Horrible Life of Leni Riefenstahl, 1993
Written and directed by Ray Müller
Executive producer: Hans-Jürgen Panitz, Omega Film GmbH
Co-producers: Jacques and Dimitri de Clercq, Nomad Film S.r.L

ERNST JÜNGER & POST-HUMAN PERFECTION

DAVID EVANS

INTRODUCTION

Perfection informs the perfect society that does not exist. Or rather, perfection and the perfect society only exist as imaginative constructs, most obviously in a well-established literary genre concerned with utopia or 'nowhere'. The perfect society may be 'nowhere', yet utopian literature often seeks to portray a society that readers can recognize as good and worth trying to attain, even though unattainable.[1] A modern example is *Der Arbeiter: Herrschaft und Gestalt/The Worker: Domination and Form* (1932) by Ernst Jünger (1895–1998), who hoped that his vision of a world revolutionized by the experience of mass mobilization in World War One would inspire a violent and nationalistic challenge to the perceived feebleness of the Weimar Republic.[2]

It must be stressed straightaway that Jünger's authoritarian Utopia is in part based on an acute understanding of the significance of World War One that would now be accepted by many professional historians: that is, the munitions crisis of 1915–16 caused the main belligerents to accept that the deadlock on the various fronts could not be broken by conventional military means, and that success depended on turning national economies into war machines. War subsequently became a *Materialschlacht* ('battle of materials') managed by teams of industrial, military and political leaders. A clear-cut distinction between soldier and civilian, or war front and home front, became untenable, and nations turned themselves into armed camps, servicing the front lines. Social recasting varied from country to country: Britain and France were able to draw on imperial reserves, but Germany had to rely more on its indigenous population, for example. Nevertheless, what was shared was an unprecedented militarization of civil society.[3]

In *Der Arbeiter*, World War One is presented as a process of accelerated modernization, and its heroes are the worker-soldiers who had most readily adapted themselves to technological innovation for the sake of the nation. Total war had initiated an age of the masses and machinery that was irreversible. Jünger emphasizes the profundity of war-fuelled transformation, but he is no technological determinist. Politics still has a role, but newly defined. Weimar parliamentarism is anachronistic, he claims, for only a new form of authoritarian leadership is capable of moulding the masses and their machines. Jünger respects Mussolini, but he is more impressed by Stalin. Stalin's First

Five Year Plan (1928–32) is presented as a concrete example of the positive results achieved by a strong leader unafraid of pursuing modernization as an urgent military campaign. Ostensibly, *Der Arbeiter* appears to be speculative contemporary history or political sociology. In fact, it is better understood as updated utopian literature that seeks to lend credence to the 'nowhere' it portrays with its supposed hard data and the front line experience of its author. Moreover, Jünger seeks to inspire action from his readers, for throughout the Weimar period he was associated with various organizations of the revolutionary right, regularly contributed to their publications, and was particularly close to Ernst Niekisch, advocate of a hybrid ideology that sought to reconcile Prussian traditions with Soviet communism called National Bolshevism.[4]

1

Der Arbeiter is one version of Jünger's reactionary Utopia of the mechanized body and the rearmed nation. A second version is *Die Veränderte Welt: Eine Bilderfibel unserer Zeit/The Transformed World: A Contemporary Picture Primer* (1933), a suavely-edited collection of agency photographs and captions that present the arguments of *Der Arbeiter* in the form of a 'picture primer'.[5] Overall, *Die Veränderte Welt* is underpinned by Jünger's assumption that his desired audience is more likely to regularly engage with the new illustrated press than conventional books and, in the process, he creates an oxymoron: a photographic utopia; or news from nowhere based on photographs that all contain traces of somewhere.

In the 1930s, photography's evidential reputation is still widespread and renders Jünger's image-text Utopia even more concrete than the literary version. But he is attracted to photography for a complex of reasons. He admires the camera's cold 'artificial eye' uninfluenced by human sentiment. He is fascinated by its role in World War One as an unflinching observer, but also as a participant, especially in aerial reconnaissance. 'Shooting' photographs is considered an inherently aggressive activity, comparable to using a gun. Hence his statement, 'At the moment when a city like Mecca can be photographed, it moves into the colonial sphere.'[6] Moreover, it is an accessible medium linked to his belief that 'the appeal to immediate appearances works more powerfully and incisively than the acuteness of ideas.' In other words, photography offers the chance to reach a mass audience generally untouched by a high, literate culture. He is keen to learn from the successes and failures of the cinema:

> One can see that very soon after the war, various unembarrassed uses were made of the photograph [...]. The very first really successful effort in this direction was that of the well-known film *Battleship Potemkin* – primarily because it fulfilled the most important condition of every propaganda effort, namely that it must not be boring [...]. In the same way – to cite another example – everything in the film *Metropolis* that has to do with the architecture or the machines is just as captivating as the attempt to develop a social message is tedious.[7]

Both *Battleship Potemkin* (Sergei Eisenstein, 1925) and *Metropolis* (Fritz Lang, 1926) intended to relay sociopolitical messages. However, according to Jünger, only Eisenstein succeeded because his message was presented as entertainment. His comments explain some of the main features of *Die Veränderte Welt*. It is compiled by a dexterous picture editor. Captions are short and snappy. The juxtaposition of images is often surprising. There is no pathos or moralizing. The end result is propaganda from the revolutionary right, disguised as a diverting guide to the contemporary world.

Section Three is called 'The Changed Face of the Individual' and includes a one-page layout that condenses many of Jünger's obsessions. The page contains two photographs of equal size (Figure 1). The top image (labelled 'The Bourgeois') shows a politician addressing an audience from a podium. The eagle on the podium signifies Germany and the banners behind the speaker confirm that the event is a conference of the Social Democratic Party. Below is a photograph of an aviator with the camera equipment used for aerial reconnaissance (captioned 'The Worker'). The pairing could be viewed as a straightforward visualization of the democratic politics of the Weimar Republic: above, the representative (Social Democratic politician); below, the represented (the skilled worker). Yet the titles render such an interpretation problematic. Drawing on the Marxist rhetoric officially professed by the Social Democratic Party (until 1959), the titles imply that the worker's nearest class enemy is to be found within the leadership of his own party. Thus, Jünger's juxtaposition is not about political representation, but about a political representation in crisis, and his aim is to challenge the continuing legitimacy of a party that claims to represent the interests of proletarian Germany.

The German Social Democratic Party was founded in 1875. Until it was banned by Hitler in 1933, it was the largest and best organized socialist party in Europe. With its huge network of educational, cultural and welfare organizations, the party formed a virtual state within a state, and provided a model for other socialist parties. But for Jünger, the party's national and international reputation was unfounded. The rhetoric was revolutionary, but the day-to-day practice involved a cautious reformism out of touch with the transformations of war. With this juxtaposition, then, Jünger wants us to note that the masked worker appears oblivious as the politician speaks. He wants us to observe, perhaps, that the Social Democratic leader appears as anachronistic as nineteenth-century statues of standing orators adopting classical poses. And as the politician makes a flamboyant manual gesture whilst giving his speech, the worker concentrates on work, using his hands to manipulate complex cameras.

The two images are intended to evoke different historical epochs, with the nineteenth and twentieth centuries confronting each other, separated by the Great War. And the bottom photograph introduces the new worker who cannot be represented by conventional party politics. The pilot-photographer is treated as an exemplary product of World War One, a modern hero who is able to defy gravity with an aeroplane and to supplement the limitation of human vision with the 'artificial eye' of the camera. Such a figure, Jünger implies, has earned the right to represent all of those worker-soldiers whose efforts have created a new world.

For Jünger, worker-soldiers are the advanced guard of the masses; an amorphous collectivity that is potentially capable of disciplined creativity and sacrifice in the pursuit of a goal. This new collectivity, created in conflict, is the subject of a chapter called 'The Transformed Face of the Masses'. How to present a collective 'face' that is more than an aggregate of individual physiognomies? One technique involves selecting images that show assertive group uniformity – a workers parade in the Soviet Union or a Brownshirt demonstration in Germany. In both cases, the ongoing militarization of civil society after World War One is evident. But Jünger also wants his audience to associate such images with other group portraits in which the theme of militarization appears more obliquely. A photograph of boxers training implies that sport is a form of displaced warfare. A neighbouring photograph is of a troupe of showgirls, implying affinities between their precise mathematical routines and the rationality of modern military industrial processes.

In addition, Jünger favours images taken from a high vantage point. The subject matter varies: mass mourning in New York in response to the death of Lenin; a crowd in London engaged in two minutes' silence to commemorate the war dead; a ticker-tape parade in New York to celebrate the aviators Post and Gatty who had flown around the world. Yet the shared birds-eye perspective has the effect of erasing the individual face to portray a collective 'face' in a public 'home' (Figure 2).

Mastering the masses is considered a central political problem of the post-war era, for which organizations like the Social Democratic Party are considered inadequate. World War One had demonstrated what could be achieved through a strong state, and in the post-war era, Jünger was hoping for a new type of authoritarian state that could direct the masses in equally ambitious projects. Stalin's First Five Year Plan is presented as an admirable example. A two-page layout is entitled 'Labour… as a Warlike Activity' and clearly identifies, with approval, the way in which Stalin's economic reforms were being pursued as a military campaign (Figure 3).

2

Jünger was not alone, of course, with his enthusiasm for the propagandistic possibilities of photography or for his musings on the significance of World War One. In 1912, the rotogravure process was perfected in Germany and was rapidly adopted throughout Europe. Henceforth, the illustrated press could be produced in large numbers with photographs of relatively high quality, and World War One was its first great theme. And post-1918, there is a proliferation of items incorporating photographic reproduction in which World War One and its legacy are explicitly or implicitly referenced.

Take the Soviet Union that fascinated Jünger so much. During World War One, Lenin led the first successful political challenge to capitalism, and roughly a decade later, Stalin initiated an economic programme that aimed to complement and complete Lenin's achievement. To service Stalin's First Five Year Plan, artists and intellectuals formed the October Association (1928–32), a name that consciously alluded to the October Revolution of 1917. The manifestoes and statements of the October Association are dominated by military terminology. Artists are urged to consider themselves as militants in struggle; their art is a weapon; their goal is mass mobilization on the cultural front. The bellicose rhetoric recalls the heroic years of the Russian Civil War, when counterrevolutionaries and foreign interventionists were successfully defeated. Additionally, it corresponds to Stalin's demand for a siege mentality, drawing on memories of the earlier period, but now to defeat supposed domestic and foreign wreckers. Finally, it facilitates an identity change with professional artists and intellectuals becoming the cultural equivalent of the shock troops of industry.

All cultural workers were urged to enter factories and collective farms as participant-observers, learning from workers and peasants as well as offering specialist skills which might be useful – the basics of journalism or photography, for instance, which could permit workers and peasants to create their own local newspapers. At the same time, cultural workers were required to gather the 'facts' of economic revolution, which would be given shape through editing or montage, and then released to a wider audience to encourage further effort at home and admiration abroad.[8]

By 1928, the technical preconditions existed in the Soviet Union to permit a new type of mass publicity incorporating still or moving photography with its well-established evidential reputation. Eisenstein's film *The General Line* (1929) was a product of this moment. Completed when he was a member of the film section of the October Association, it is his only released film which deals directly with contemporary events – the struggle for agricultural collectivization as a part of a project which aimed at nothing less than the creation of the world's first post-capitalist economy. Significantly, one 'hero' of the film is the tractor presented to the peasants who have recognized the advantages of collective endeavour, and it arrives with a driver whose leather helmet deliberately evokes the glamour of an aeroplane pilot (Figure 4).

Jünger observed, admired and sought to re-articulate aspects of the Soviet experience into a very different political vision.

3

Or take Le Corbusier. His most famous manifesto, *Vers une Architecture* (1923), is distinctive for its inventive use of mainly found photography, and in advanced publicity for the book, he specifically draws attention to this feature:

> This book draws its eloquence from new means: its magnificent illustrations present a powerful, parallel discourse alongside that of the written text. This new concept of

> the book with the explicit and revealing discourse of illustrations permits the author to avoid ineffective sentences and descriptions; things explode under the reader's eyes through the force of images [...].[9]

Photographs function like explosions, and World War One is the activating force in one of the most famous avant-garde page layouts of the 1920s, which pairs ancient Greek temples and modern sports cars (Figure 5). The left-hand page shows photographs of 'PAESTUM, 600-550 B.C.' (above) and 'HUMBER, 1907' (below); the right-hand page, 'THE PARTHENON, 447-434 B.C.' (above) and 'DELAGE, "GRAND SPORT," 1921' (below). The reader is encouraged to make vertical and horizontal comparisons, and Le Corbusier's main point is that the older temple and the Humber are prototypes, and the Parthenon and the Delage both represent perfection. Thus, the inter-page gutter functions as a temporal marker. For the temples, a century evolves between prototype and perfection; for the racing cars, one can assume that this process is telescoped into the four years of World War One.

'War was the hellish laboratory in which aviation became adult, and was shaped to flawless perfection.'[10] Le Corbusier's remark is made in the introduction to *Aircraft*, a book of aviation photographs, published in London in 1935 as part of a series called *New Vision*. It is a restatement of a position jointly propagated by Amedée Ozenfant and himself since 1918:

> The war has ended; all is organized; all is clear and purified; factories are built; nothing is just like it was before the War; the great Struggle tested everything, it destroyed senile methods and replaced them with those which the battle proved best.[11]

In short, the transformative dimensions of war are recognized, but there is no endorsement of Jünger's ideas. Rather, Le Corbusier urges a programme of post-war reconstruction that adapts war-driven innovation to peaceful purposes.

4

Ernst Friedrich was an anarchist and pacifist who ran an anti-war museum in Berlin in the Weimar years, and is now best known for a photo book, *Krieg dem Kriege/War against War* (1924), that can be considered his museum without walls. To transcend national boundaries, the book has written commentary in Dutch, English, French and German, but most prominence is given to what Friedrich assumes to be the universal language of photography. He wanted his book to stand as 'a picture of War, objectively true and faithful to nature' and was confident that this was the case since it was based on 'records obtained by the inexorable, incorruptible photographic lens.'[12] Friedrich's faith in the photograph as evidence was shared by Jünger, but in every other respect they were polar opposites.

Friedrich's book deliberately includes images of corpses, executions and human disfigurement that had been censored in wartime or ignored in the post-war period. In particular, he foregrounds a sequence of photographs of *gueules cassées* (roughly translatable as 'smashed-in mugs'), ex-servicemen from World War One who tended to suffer extreme social ostracism in the post-war era as a result of their severely disfigured faces. Often the captions for these portraits are factual and restrained: 'Railwayman. Mouth and right hand torn away. Lower jaw gone' or 'Many thousands have to be artificially fed, like this unhappy man.' But sometimes he was unable to hold back – next to one portrait he provides a quotation from General Hindenburg: 'War agrees with me like a stay at a health resort' (Figure 6). Hindenburg was the hero of the Eastern Front, who became joint leader of Germany's war effort in 1916, and his wartime reputation contributed to his successful campaign to become president of the Weimar Republic in 1925, shortly after the publication of Friedrich's book. In isolation, Hindenburg's statement displays a cool insouciance about the consequences of war. Next to a photograph of a *gueule cassée*, however, his words have an offensive, mocking ring.

Krieg dem Kriege is one of the most strident polemics against war and militarism ever produced. A simple argument is relentlessly repeated with words and images: the Kaiser may have gone, but his empire is basically intact, a world of privilege and privation renamed the Weimar Republic. In Germany and elsewhere, then, all the ingredients remain for a repeat of the proletarian tragedy acted out from 1914 to 1918. This can only be averted if workers of the world unite and take on their real enemy – the bourgeoisie. Since the profit motive had been the cause of all major conflicts in the modern era, Friedrich reasons, such a conflict would be the last war.

Friedrich wants a war to end all wars; Jünger is more interested in a war without end. Friedrich uses various techniques including irony, pathos and moral exhortation to inflect his photographic documents; Jünger prefers a calculated sobriety. Friedrich's worker-soldier victims are Jünger's modern heroes. And finally, Friedrich concentrates on the fragile human face that must be protected from the ravages of modern, industrialized warfare; Jünger takes it for granted that such views are anachronistic, failing to get to grips with a post-human civilization initiated by World War One.

5

Jünger's primer was published in 1933, predating by three years the Berlin Olympics which provided a perfect opportunity to present the Third Reich to many foreign visitors as some kind of model state. An elaborate 'Deutschland Ausstellung' (Germany Exhibition) was staged in Berlin, and former Bauhaus master Herbert Bayer was hired to design a tie-in brochure celebrating life in the Third Reich.[13] It is taken for granted that the portrait is of the Third Reich minus the warts. But what interests me more is its attempt to articulate a distinctive vision of Germany under Hitler, and how far this vision corresponds to the perspectives found in Jünger's picture book. Certainly there are designs that straightforwardly celebrate urban renewal, industrial might and the worker as hero – a hymn to modernization, composed by a graphic designer with an intimate understanding of Weimar modernism (Figure 7). Yet at the same time there is a hymn to the national heritage, and the Führer is presented as the strong leader who is able to reconcile the tensions between tendencies that historians have identified as 'ultra-modernism' and 'ultra-historicism'. Jünger would have appreciated the former, but would have had no time for an attempt to reconcile it with the latter. He didn't leave Nazi Germany, but he continuously refused to become a card-carrying National Socialist.

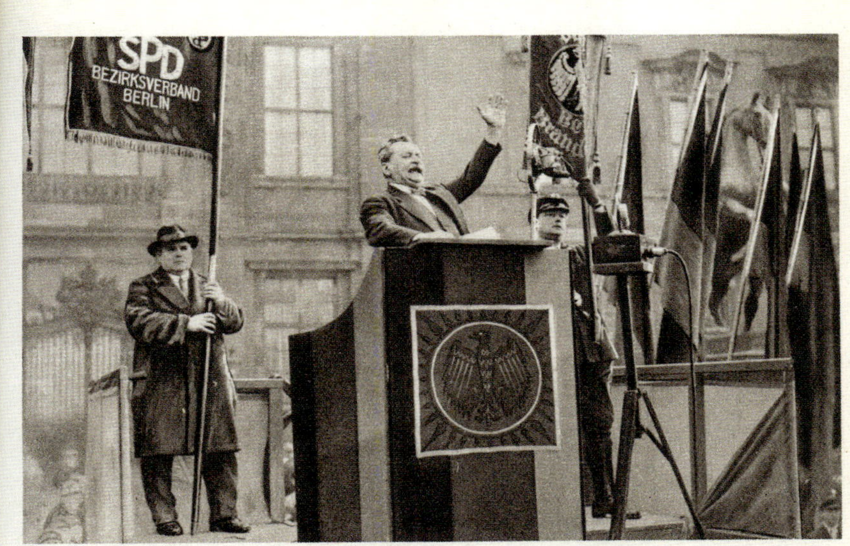

Der Bürger

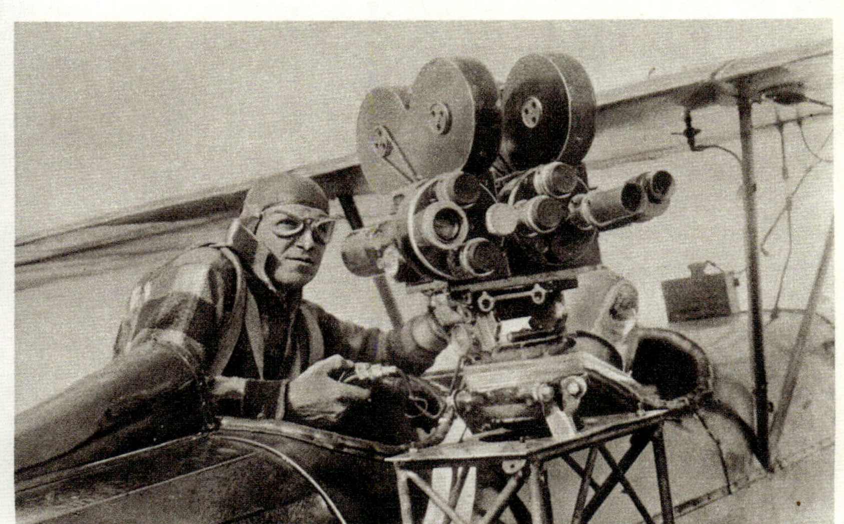

Der Arbeiter

45

Figure 1: 'The Bourgeois' and 'The Worker', Ernst Jünger, *Die Veränderte Welt*, 1933, p. 45.

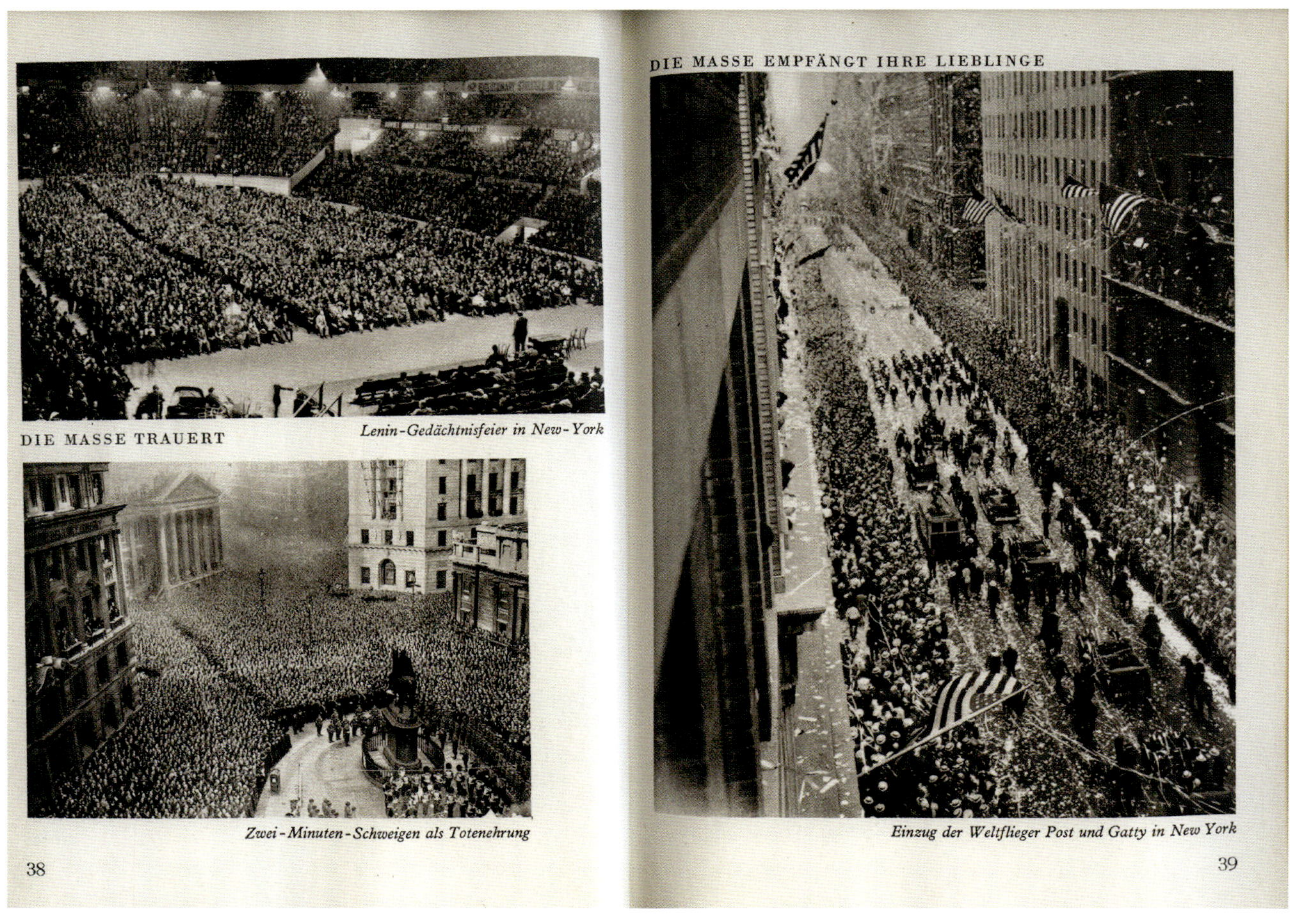

Figure 2: 'The Masses Mourn' and 'The Masses Receive Their Darlings', Ernst Jünger, *Die Veränderte Welt*, 1933, pp. 38–39.

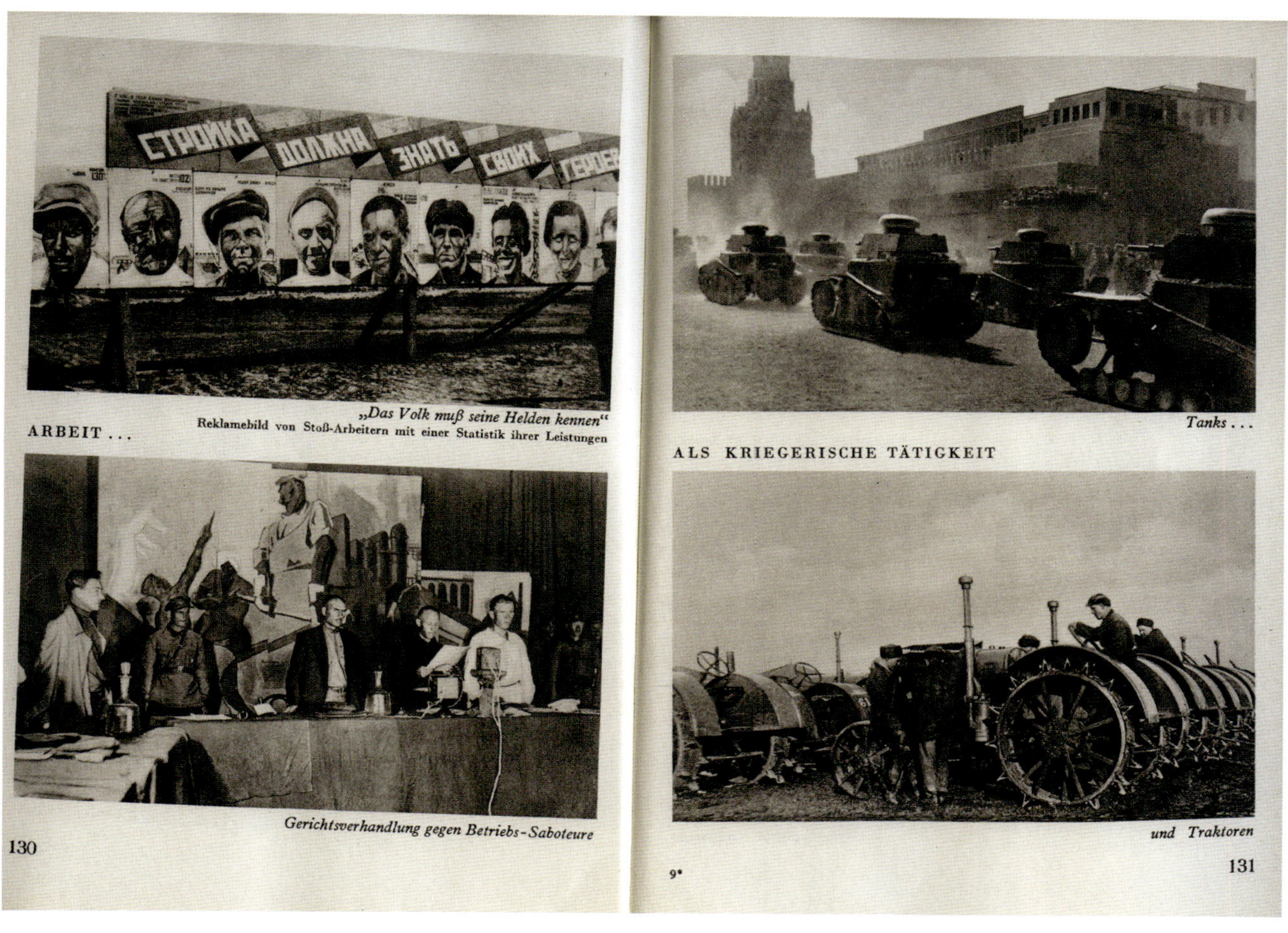

ARBEIT . . .

„Das Volk muß seine Helden kennen"
Reklamebild von Stoß-Arbeitern mit einer Statistik ihrer Leistungen

Gerichtsverhandlung gegen Betriebs-Saboteure

130

Tanks . . .

ALS KRIEGERISCHE TÄTIGKEIT

und Traktoren

9*

131

Figure 3: 'Labour… as a warlike activity', Ernst Jünger, *Die Veränderte Welt*, 1933, pp. 130–31.

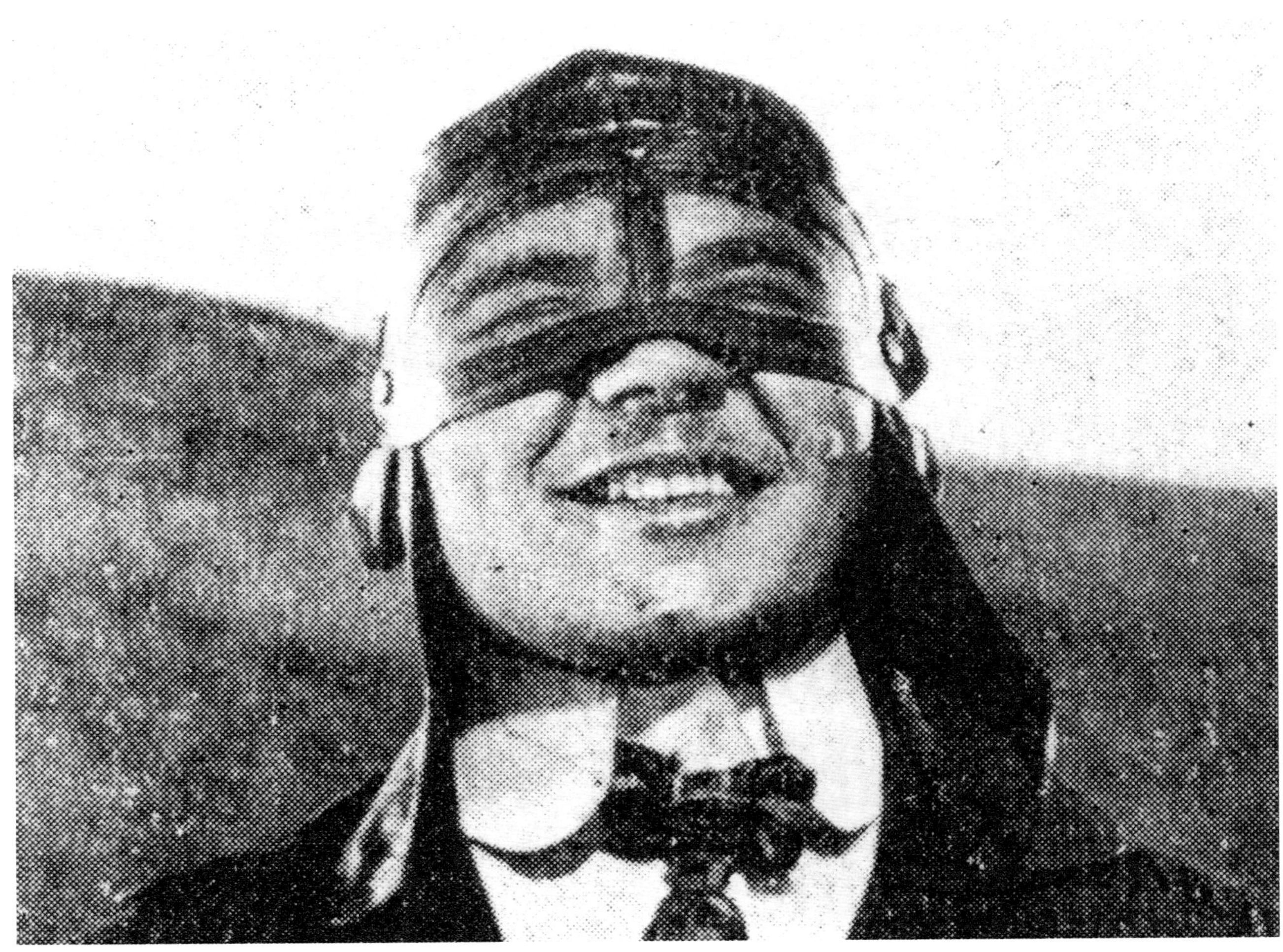

Figure 4: Film still from *The General Line* (Sergei Eisenstein, 1929) and *Documents 4* (1930), p. 219.

106 VERS UNE ARCHITECTURE

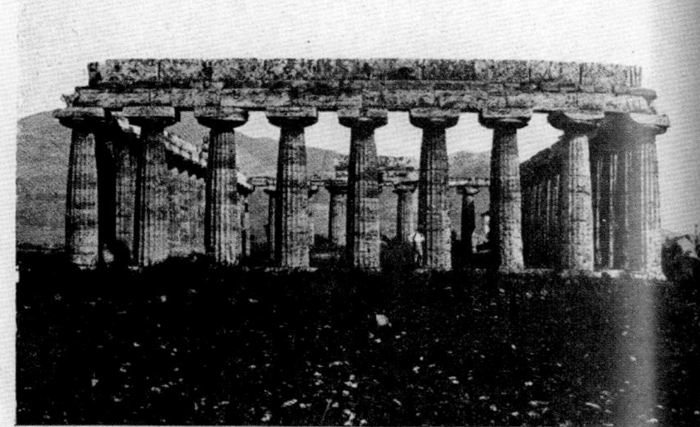

PAESTUM, de 600 à 550 av. J.-C.

Le Parthénon est un produit de sélection appliquée à un standart établi. Depuis un siècle déjà, le temple grec était organisé dans tous ses éléments.

Lorsqu'un standart est établi, le jeu de la concurrence immédiate et violente s'exerce. C'est le match; pour gagner, il faut

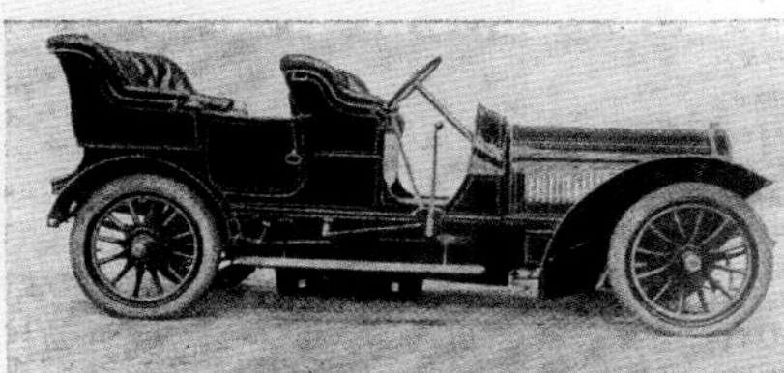

Cliché de *La Vie Automobile.* HUMBERT, 1907.

DES YEUX QUI NE VOIENT PAS... 107

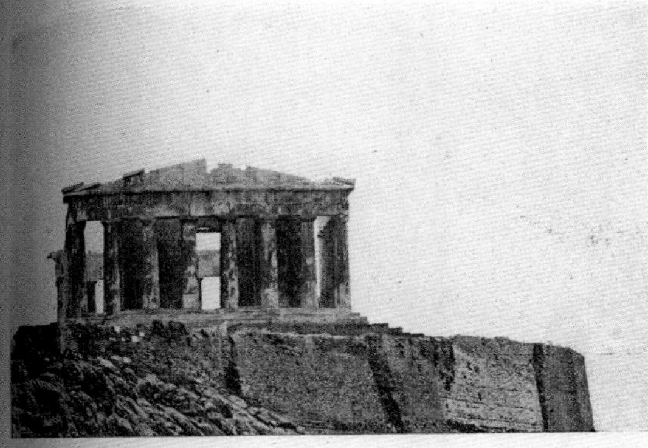

Cliché Albert Morancé. PARTHÉNON, de 447 à 434 av. J.-C.

faire mieux que l'adversaire *dans toutes les parties*, dans la ligne d'ensemble et dans tous les détails. C'est alors l'étude poussée des parties. Progrès.

Le standart est une nécessité d'ordre apporté dans le travail humain.

Le standart s'établit sur des bases certaines, non pas arbi-

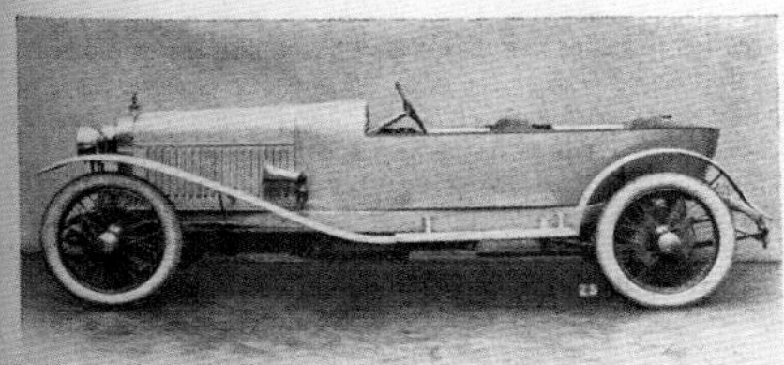

DELAGE, Grand-Sport 1921.

Figure 5: Le Corbusier, *Vers une Architecture*, 1923, pp. 106–07.

„De oorlog bekomt my als een kuur" (Hindenburg).

„War agrees with me like a stay at a health resort." (Hindenburg.)

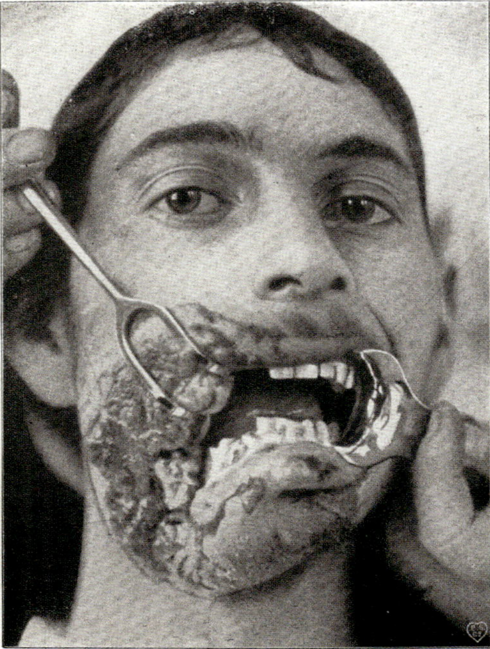

„Der Krieg bekommt mir wie eine Badekur". (Hindenburg.)

'La guerre est pour moi un traitement d'eaux minérales.' (Hindenburg.)

216

De kuur der proleten! Byna het heele gezicht weggeschoten.

The „health resort" of the proletarian. Almost the whole face blown away.

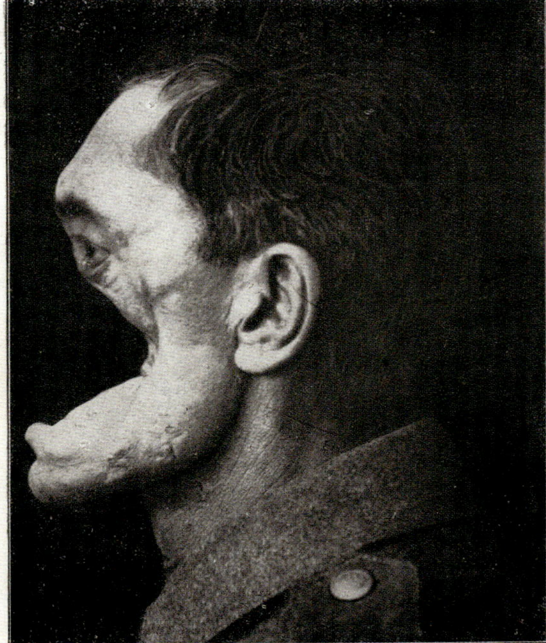

Die Badekur der Proleten: Fast das ganze Gesicht weggeschossen.

Le 'traitement d'eaux minérales' des prolétaires: presque la figure entière arrachée.

217

Figure 6: '"War agrees with me like a stay at a health resort." (Hindenburg)' and 'The "health resort" of the proletarian. Almost the whole face blown away', Ernst Friedrich, *Krieg dem Kriege*, 1924, pp. 216–17.

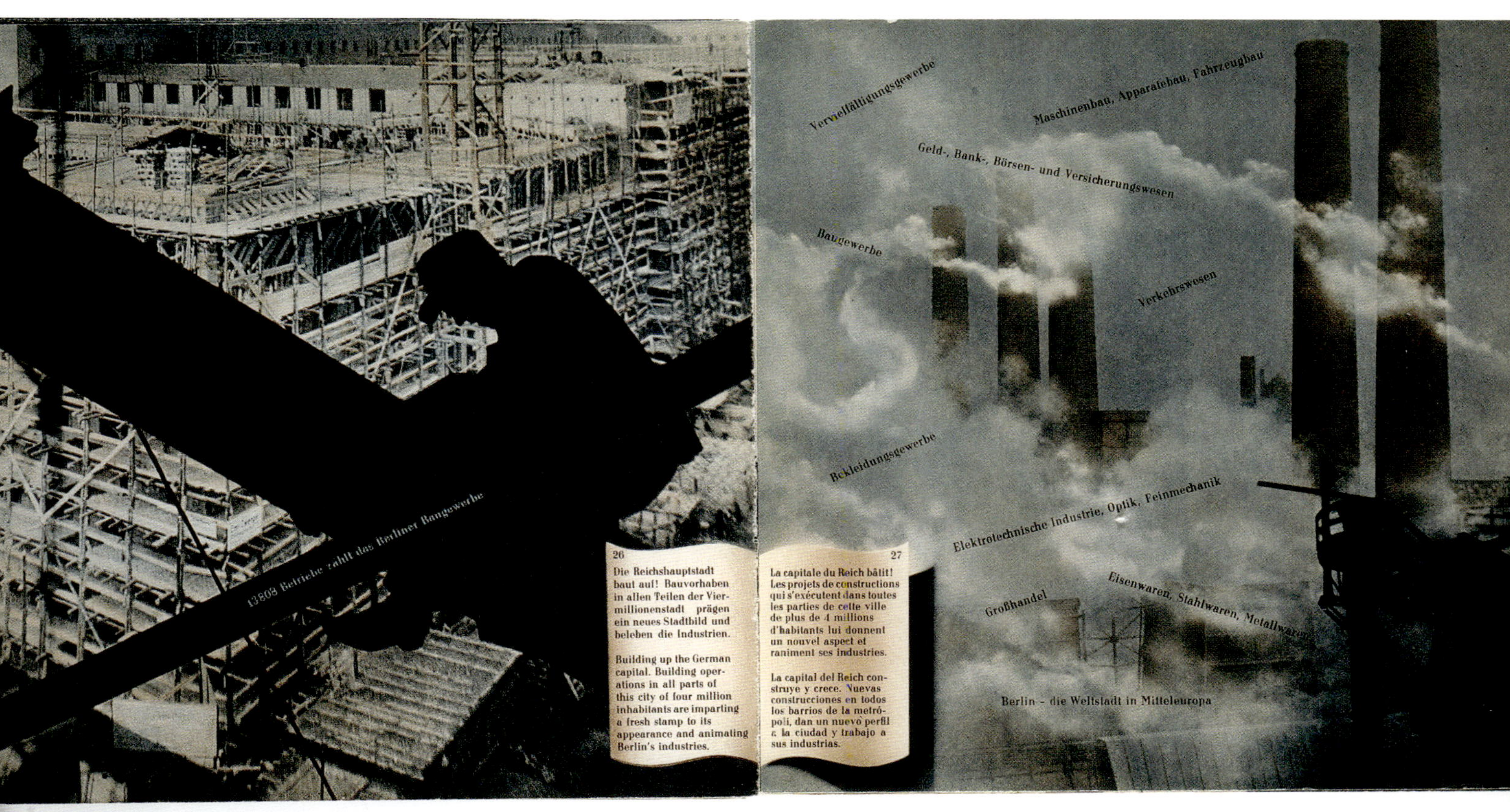

Figure 7: Herbert Bayer, *Deutschland Ausstellung*, 1936, pp. 26–27. Courtesy Bauhaus Archiv, Berlin / DACS, London.

NOTES

1 Krishan Kumar, *Utopia and Anti-Utopia in Modern Times*, Oxford: Basil Blackwell, 1987; *Utopianism*, Buckingham: Open University Press, 1991.

2 Issue 59 of *New German Critique* (Spring/Summer 1993) is a special issue devoted to Jünger and provides a stimulating introduction to the writer from multiple perspectives.

3 See, for example, Michael Geyer, 'The Militarization of Europe, 1914–1945', in John R. Gillis, *The Militarization of the Western World*, New Brunswick & London: Rutgers University Press, 1989, pp. 65–102.

4 See Jeffrey Herf, *Reactionary Modernism: Technology, Culture, and Politics in Weimar and the Third Reich*, Cambridge: Cambridge University Press, 1984, especially the chapter 'Ernst Jünger's magical realism', pp. 70–108.

5 The book was published in Breslau by W.G. Korn. An outstanding introduction to it is offered by Brigitte Werneburg, 'Ernst Jünger and the Transformed World', *October*, No. 62, Autumn 1992, pp. 42–64. *Die veränderte Welt* presents Edmund Schultz as its editor, and Jünger's role is merely as the author of an introductory essay. However, it is generally assumed that the picture editing and captioning are the work of Jünger. See Werneburg, p. 46, footnote 7.

6 Ernst Jünger, 'Photography and the "Second Consciousness"', in *Photography in the Modern Era: European Documents and Critical Writings, 1913–1940*, ed. Christopher Phillips, New York: The Metropolitan Museum of Art/Aperture, [1934] 1989, pp. 207–10.

7 Ernst Jünger, *Die Veränderte Welt*, Breslau, 1933, p. 6.

8 See, for example, 'Program of the October Photo Section', in Phillips, [1931] 1989, pp. 283–85.

9 Cited in Richard A. Etlin, *Frank Lloyd Wright and Le Corbusier: The Romantic Legacy*, Manchester: Manchester University Press, 1994, p. 186.

10 Le Corbusier, *Aircraft*, London: The Studio, 1935, p. 9.

11 Cited in Mary McLeod, '"Architecture or Revolution": Taylorism, Technocracy, and Social Change', *Art Journal*, Vol. 43, No. 2, Summer 1983, p. 134.

12 Ernst Friedrich, *Krieg dem Kriege*, Berlin, 1924, p. 7.

13 The brochure is analysed in David Evans, 'The Holiday of a Lifetime', *Eye*, No. 53, Autumn 2004, pp. 2–3.

SEEING THROUGH

FRANCETTE PACTEAU

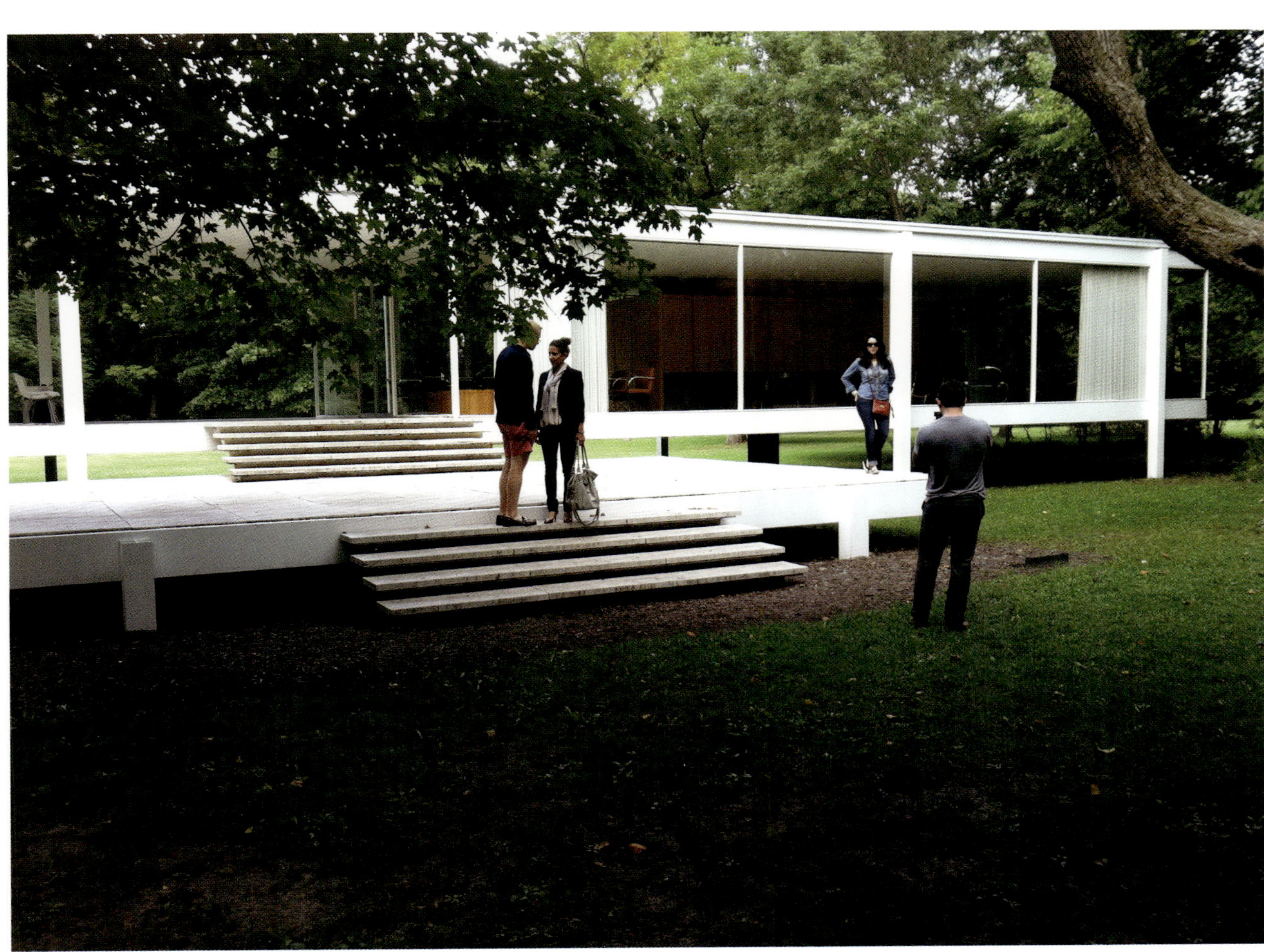

I do not recall when I first heard of the Farnsworth House, but I feel I have lived with the house for a very long time, living in a house of images and words. I can be sure I first saw it as a representation in a magazine or book – as a photograph, a pencil sketch, a plan or elevation drawing, or a picture of a scale model with its entourage of synthetic trees. Then I came to know it more intimately from written descriptions and narratives: from accounts of its realization between 1945 and 1951; from stories about its architect, German-born Mies van der Rohe, and his client, Dr Edith Farnsworth, and from the saga of their partnership and eventual estrangement; the law suits; the final painful settlement. When I first saw the house itself, in April 2009, it was after having travelled by train from Los Angeles to Chicago, reading, dozing and gazing out of the window at expanses of deserts, canyons and plains punctuated by scarce cities with nothing between them but occasional habitations in little clusters or alone. Memories of words read and images seen, mingled with such more recent impressions of isolation in limitlessness, to form the imaginary setting for my first visit to the Farnsworth House.

No other house built in the last century has been so much praised for its formal perfection. A writer for *Architectural Forum* in 1951 judged the house to be 'a concentration of pure beauty.' Other writers saw in it 'the realisation of a purity of form […] rarely achieved in architecture', the expression of 'spiritual rather than functional values', and 'a platonic perfection of order.' The architectural historian and critic Kenneth Frampton finds the house to be 'a work of metaphysical beauty', while the architectural theorist Reyner Banham concluded that the house 'left other architects little to do except to try and to make even more perfect that which was already perfected.'

Edith Farnsworth was 42 years old when she conceived the plan of building a weekend country retreat from her work in Chicago, where she was a highly esteemed researcher and consultant in diseases of the kidney. The architect she commissioned, Mies van der Rohe, was at that time relatively unknown. The house was built beside the Fox River, some 60 miles west of Chicago, in a meadow surrounded by deciduous woodlands. In the simplest formal terms, the house appears as a low longitudinal structure comprising two primary parallel horizontal planes intersected at regular intervals by eight vertical pillars delineating a volume of airy transparency – a single space enclosed in glass from floor to ceiling that transitions into a covered terrace or porch – from which a wide flight of steps leads down to a third horizontal plane, an open terrace, laterally displaced out of alignment with the main structure. A second, shorter flight of steps connects to the meadow over which the house and its terrace appear to hover (the floor of the house is raised one-and-a-half metres above the river floodplain). In winter, when the leaves are gone, the waters of the Fox River assert their own antecedent horizontal plane. On a winter day, as one stands on the southern bank of the river, it is easy to imagine that the house is silently floating, as if about to be towed away by its lower terrace.

Before the house there was the river, the meadow and the trees: organic life, the essential forms of which have anticipated those of the house; the air between the trunks and the branches now defined as open space between the floor and roof of the terrace, and further materialized in the almost nothing of the glass enclosure. While the slender stanchions suggest a weightless poise, the house is literally rooted in the land via its utilities stack, through which energy is brought into the house and rainwater drained from its roof into the ground. Painted matt black and barely visible in the gap between the floor and the ground, the base of the stack becomes a tree trunk and the roof of the house its canopy, an abstraction of the organic form of the great, black sugar maple that casts its cooling shade upon the house in the hot Illinois summer.

The house was praised, and the house was condemned, both by Edith Farnsworth herself and by sectors of the popular press. Elizabeth Gordon, writing in 1953 in the magazine *House Beautiful*, launched an assault on the Farnsworth House as 'nothing but a glass cage on stilts', denouncing an architecture that promotes 'a stripped-down emptiness […] and therefore lack of possessions' and that admits of 'nothing human that might disturb the architect's composition.' In the title of her article, Gordon judges the house to be 'The threat to the next America' – 'a social threat of regimentation and control.' Gordon's remarks here must be understood in the context of Cold War 'reds under the bed' paranoia, and the concurrent promotion of an ideal of American domestic life – implicitly assumed to be family life – premised on abundant and joyful material consumption. Gordon's attack was bolstered by Edith Farnsworth's own public expression of her disappointments with her house. In 1945, while leafing through the pages of books on modern architecture, she had told herself that 'it would be unbearably stupid of me to "put up" some contractor's cottage which could only ruin the site and remain as a token of empirical mediocrity.' Six years later, however, she will complain about the excessive condensation on the interior glass 'as though you are in a car in the rain with a windscreen wiper that doesn't work'; she complains about the fireplace, rendered ineffectual in winter by the necessity of opening the door and windows for ventilation; she complains about the house's vulnerability to the swarms of mosquitoes coming off the riverside meadow. Such shortcomings, however, may afflict even the most traditional house, and they have their technical solutions. One of Edith Farnsworth's criticisms was aimed straight at the very *raison d'être* of the house: its transparency; she writes:

> The truth is that in this house with its four walls of glass I feel like a prowling animal, always on the alert. I am always restless. Even in the evening. I feel like a sentinel on guard day and night. I can rarely stretch out and relax.

Entering the house, I pass from the open air – filled with the sounds and scents of woodland and meadow – to the muted enfolding of glass walls. But the passage between exterior and interior is almost indiscernible, as if inside and outside have simply exchanged places by some trick of reflection. Customary preconceptions of inside and outside are put in question by the ambiguities of this barely visible yet obdurate membrane; and the stirring presence of the living environment, for all that it is literally out of touch, envelops and suffuses interior space. This luminous volume has first been deployed with attention to the movement of the sun, and then apportioned according to functions – as an assembly of spaces not divided by walls but implied by the placing of furniture. These notional and interpenetrating functional areas are distributed around a solid volume, lined in primavera wood, that contains the bathrooms and the utilities stack, and which is flanked on its north side by a single galley kitchen, and on its south side by a fireplace. Another free-standing block clad in teak acts as a partition defining the sleeping area, providing storage for clothes and housing an audio cabinet. Only the utilities stack extends entirely from floor to ceiling, thereby connecting the ground below the house to the air above its roof. Bathroom enclosures, kitchen cabinets and the clothes cabinet stop short of the ceiling, their volumes visually disengaged from the main structure, with light intruding variegated slivers of foliage and sky into the resulting gaps. The pale travertine floor and the ceiling of white painted plaster appear to not quite touch the eight supporting columns of white painted steel. Lightness, transparency and impermanence define the interior space, while its opaque and immovable core affirms the most basic of life preserving functions – keeping warm, feeding, excreting. The 'platonic perfection of order' remains resolutely earthbound.

We are asked to remove our shoes before entering. We have stood together outside the house, our backs to the river, while our guide pointed out to us how the steel piers stop short of the planes of the lower terrace and roof – so that the ends of the piers not appear to break into the edges of the horizontal planes when these are viewed from a low angle. Inside the house, she will stand close against an all but invisible wall to show that – such is the transparency of the glass – there seems to be nothing between her and the outside (indeed I fear she may fall out). She explains that the two faces of the glass are ground perfectly parallel, to minimize the internal reflection of light passing through the glass, thus further reducing its material presence.

From our first assembly at the visitor centre, we have walked here through sparse woodlands, eyes fixed ahead for the first glimpse of the house we already know so well. It is not only the transparency of its simple and singular volume that will make the Farnsworth House appear to us so readily and wholly graspable, but our memories of the many images through which it is always already known. To enter it for the first time is to step into the already seen, already read – seen a few minutes ago as we stood outside, detained in details by our loquacious guide as we surreptitiously glanced into the house, and seen in carefully composed and uninhabited photographs, in colour, in black-and-white, photographs of the house in Edith Farnworth's time, its porch obscured by the mosquito screen, the original Shentung silk drapes, damaged in the 1954 flood, now replaced by roller blinds; photographs of the house after its purchase and restoration by Peter Palumbo in 1972, the bug screen and roller blinds gone, meadow cut down to a suburban lawn. And there are snapshots of Farnsworth conferring with Mies' assistant, Myron Goldsmiths, of Mies himself on-site supervising the laying of the travertine paving. And there are photographic portraits of Edith Farnsworth and Mies, both of them shown in early and later life, as if to suggest a common life trajectory where there was only a short-lived partnership, albeit some say a romance, that ended in feud over escalating costs and unpaid fees. And so this house, as I first see it, see through it, step into it, is already a palimpsest of memories of images of diagrammatic composure, enduring clichés, caught in the turmoil of imaginary lives. Standing before the house, I may have felt that none of what I was seeing was real. To the ghosts of Mies and Ms. Farnsworth, we visitors add our own ghosts as we linger and lag behind in the hope of being left alone, forgotten, so as to live even evanescently a dream of *being* in the house, of *having* the house.

No photographs of Edith Farnsworth 'at home' have been reproduced in the many publications I have consulted. The 2003 Phaidon monograph chooses to reproduce the two portraits of Farnsworth 'in early and later life' above those of Mies, but not even a photograph of the house at the time of her residency that lasted almost 21 years. It is their relationship as woman and man, as well as client and architect, that is foregrounded at the expense of her relationship, as a single woman, to her house. I have found only two inhabited photographs: one shows Mies van der Rohe sitting outside the house; the other shows the house's second owner, Peter Palumbo, sitting inside the house on Mies' Barcelona daybed. Both men adopt much the same pose: upper arms close against the body, forearms resting on thighs, hands folded together. In the absence of any corresponding representation of Mies' client, the house's first owner, we might suppose an unbroken line of descent from the older to the younger man, a simple history of filial inheritance from which Edith Farnsworth has disappeared.

In her 1992 essay titled 'Living in a Glass Prism' (presumably to suggest the near homonym 'prison'), Paulette Singley writes that 'while the opaque wall mimics the woman's body and her role as a protective enclave, the transparent wall consumes her in its reflection and distances her body as an erotic but untouchable object.' She approvingly cites Robin Evans' assessment of Mies' architecture as 'physical but bodiless' and Jorge Quetglas's finding that it is 'anti-sensory' to conclude that 'the body missing from [Mies'] residences is female.' Singley sees Edith Farnsworth as 'an object captured in glass', set in a 'display case'. The house, no longer the 'protective womb' of time-honoured metaphors for domestic space, is now conceived as an activator of the look. Dr Farnsworth herself said that her house was 'like an X-ray', evoking a technological gaze that transfixes the body and lays it bare. To make sense of Singley's poetically destructive image of a female body 'consumed' by light is to place Edith Farnsworth *inside* the house viewed from *outside*, perhaps by someone standing in the meadow or walking up the paved path (laid at Farnsworth's instruction and later removed by Peter Palumbo), or perhaps hidden in the trees. The house that one commentator tellingly describes as 'undressed' solicits the voyeuristic look and its attendant fantasies – fantasies that may then be called as witnesses in the investigation of the enigma of its inhabitant's sexuality, that of a single middle-aged woman, a sexuality that finds no accommodation in the normative familial settings of the *House Beautiful*. The lack of clearly demarcated spaces in the Farnsworth House may betray the unassignability of its owner's sexuality. Or its transparency may tell merely of the nothing to hide of an absence of sexual activity, or even of the owner's asexuality. In so many critical accounts of the Farnsworth House, transparency is presented as evicting sensuality in general and sexual intimacy in particular. Sight is assumed to overwhelm the other senses, particularly the eroticism of touch, which is denied by the glass wall. These accounts implicitly assume a sexuality expressed only under the covers and under cover of darkness.

Edith Farnsworth's weekend and summer retreat was to be a place abstracted from the continuum of working life; a parenthesis bracketing a non-hierarchical time regulated only by the rhythms of nature and personal inclination. Mies van der Rohe designed a house that is the projection into space of this brief – fluid, open, boundless – interpellating a body whose senses are intensified as its own boundaries soften. This all-seeing house dreams up a body released from the opacity of old walls, now bathed in light and endowed with an all-seeing skin. Far from negating the pleasure of touch, not least the touch that some feminist writers place on the side of the feminine, touch here is diffused throughout the house: most visibly in the touch of light that brings out the texture of stone, the grain of wood, the patina of painted steel, light casting ever-changing colours and shadows, inviting the caress of a gaze. Peter Palumbo speaks of the sound of branches lightly brushing against the glass.

As I walk across the main space to the sleeping area, I am aware that I never lose sight of the exterior. Unlike the picture window that frames a composition best viewed from a fixed position, the Farnsworth House invites and facilitates constant movement, as if walking along an ever-changing panoramic frieze. Edith Farnsworth said that she felt like 'a prowling animal, always on the alert', 'a sentinel on guard'; it is as if her pleasure in looking has given way to an apprehension of what the architectural historian Jonathan Hill has called, 'the excluded, the unknown, unclassified and inconsistent, to which the concept of home is a response.' Looking out of the glass house one reveals oneself as looking; consciousness awakened – seeing oneself being seen to be looking.

Visitors are told that photography is restricted to the outside of the house. The entrance is set slightly off-centre, a fact of which I am unaware as I enter – I shall read about it somewhere. I come to the house with assumptions of symmetry and alignment. But my gaze is nudged to the right, sliding over and past the solid wood-lined core, pulled by the luminous rhythm of the white steel columns, tracing a gentle curve forward to the end of the main space and out to the outside I have just left behind. The clothes cabinet that Mies had designed is gone. He designed it to be five-foot high, but Farnsworth insisted it should be six feet because, she said, 'I wanted to be able to change my clothes without my head looking like it was wandering over the top of the partition *without a body*.' The six-foot high cabinet was damaged in the flood of 2008 and is away being restored. Our guide expresses her preference that it should not be brought back, as she favours the uninterrupted views. As we stand in anticipation of being released into the space, she points to the almost invisible door to the first bathroom, and the doorknob which, she says ruefully, Farnsworth insisted should be fitted against Mies' own wish for a less conspicuous solution to opening a bathroom door. She directs our attention to one of the large panes of glass, inviting us to look through it to see how poorly it compares with the adjacent one, which is free from distortions. The flood waters broke through the glass in 1996, and new building codes dictated that the original pane be replaced by a sturdier mass-produced one. She opens one of the kitchen cabinets of blond primavera – her favourite moment in the tour, she says – to reveal the effect of the passage of time on the wood: the panel, once exposed to daylight, a darker, sanguine shade.

The house completed, the rift between client and architect widening, Edith Farnsworth moved in during the spring of 1951. Farnsworth and Mies had disagreed on issues of functionality, on the colour of the drapes, and she now cancelled her order for the furniture she had commissioned Mies to design. In the words of one writer, 'she filled the house with inappropriate articles – and prosaic furniture.' In one photograph, potted plants are aligned along the interior perimeter of the porch, now enclosed in the mosquito screen; in another, the pots have entered the house, similarly positioned along the glass wall, like so many sentinels keeping watch over the untrammelled meadow and woodland. In 1972, Peter Palumbo bought the house from Farnsworth, whose tranquil retreat was now within sight and earshot of the busy two lane road leading south to Plano that, in 1969, came to replace the former quiet country road much further away from her property. The story goes that Palumbo saved the house from the prosaic influence of Farnsworth's demand that her house be a home, and brought it back to Mies' original design concept. Gone are the wicker chairs, the potted plants and the Chinese lion sculptures. In their place are a few classic furniture pieces, positioned 'almost as sparingly and precisely as exhibits in an art gallery,' writes Maritz Vandenberg.

The story goes that Palumbo sold the house in 2003 because he was exhausted by the unending and costly fight against the destructive forces of the Fox River, which since Farnsworth's time have exponentially increased in extent and severity due to surface run-off from the runaway building developments of exurban Chicago along the river's formerly rural course. The Farnsworth House is repeatedly defined as compromised by human pragmatism and wounded by nature – albeit a nature perverted by the hand of man – so much so that as I stand in the house, with the awareness of its form around me and the knowledge that this embrace will not last, I sense the loss of the house. The house I have lost and shall lose again is not a material entity, but an unstable spectral projection of contradictory representations and fantasies to which the house has given rise. One of these is a fantasy of origin – as a foreign intruder, as a house that was not born and raised out of the Illinois soil, but bestowed on the earth in an immaculate conception. I find myself remembering the elevated floor planes and ubiquitous porches of the modest single-storey dwellings scattered throughout the emptiness I watched from the train, and of the cadences of vertical steel supports of a bridge as the train neared Chicago. Nevertheless, the Farnsworth House stubbornly elicits the fantasy of a perfection outside of this world, created in *vacuo* in a moment out of time before the compromises and affronts – a fantasy acted out in the repeated restorations that have all but erased any trace of its history and habitation. Standing in the house, remembering the house I too may be forever anticipating its perfection – a dream of the house finished and expectant on the spring meadow.

Mies van der Rohe in gallery with Edith Fransworth Residence model, Retrospective Exhibition, Museum of Modern Art, New York City, NY, 1947. William Leftwich, photographer. Edward A. Duckett Collection, Ryerson and Burnham Archives © The Art Institute of Chicago.

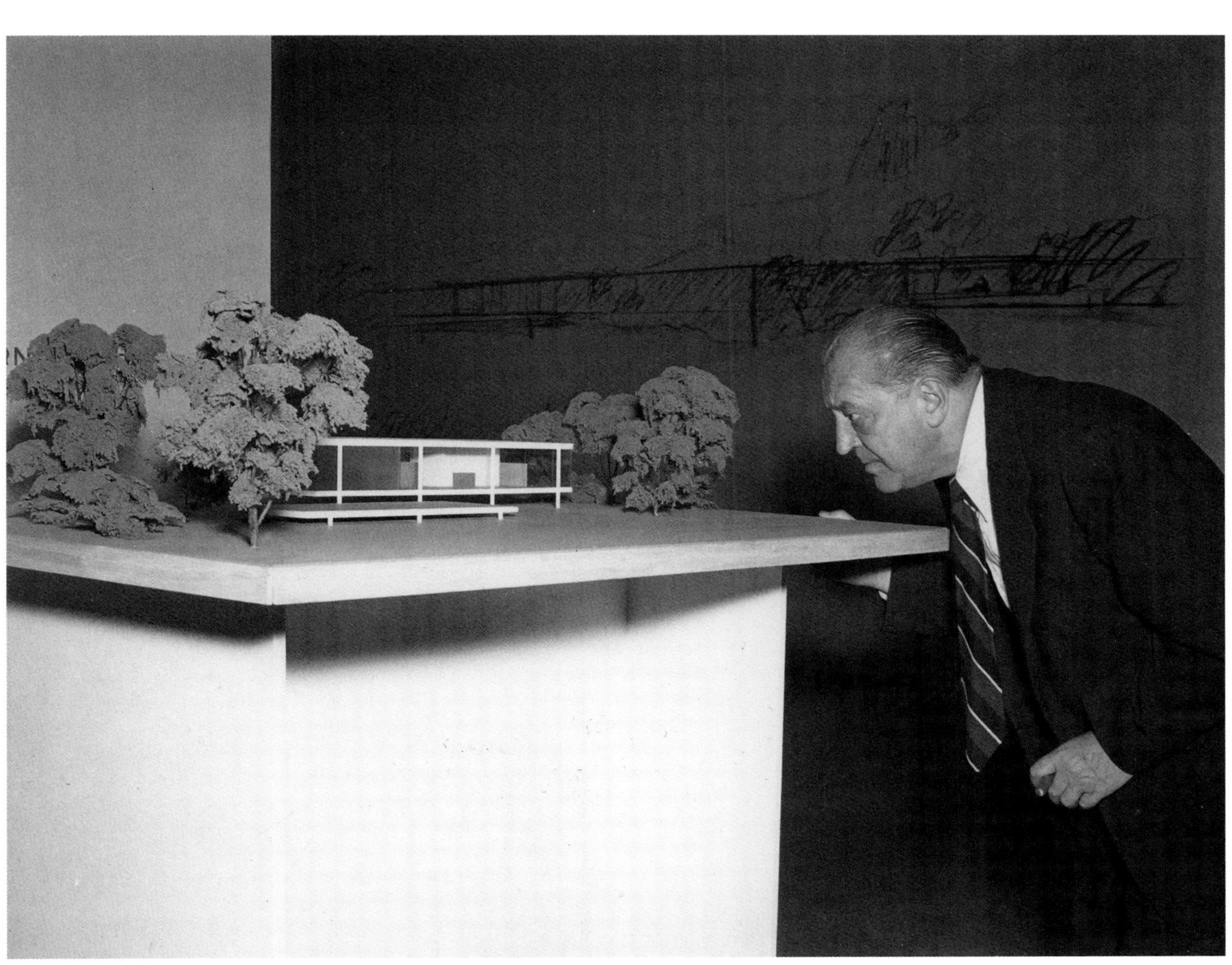

BOUNDARY LINES

LESLIE DICK, WITH AUDREY WOLLEN

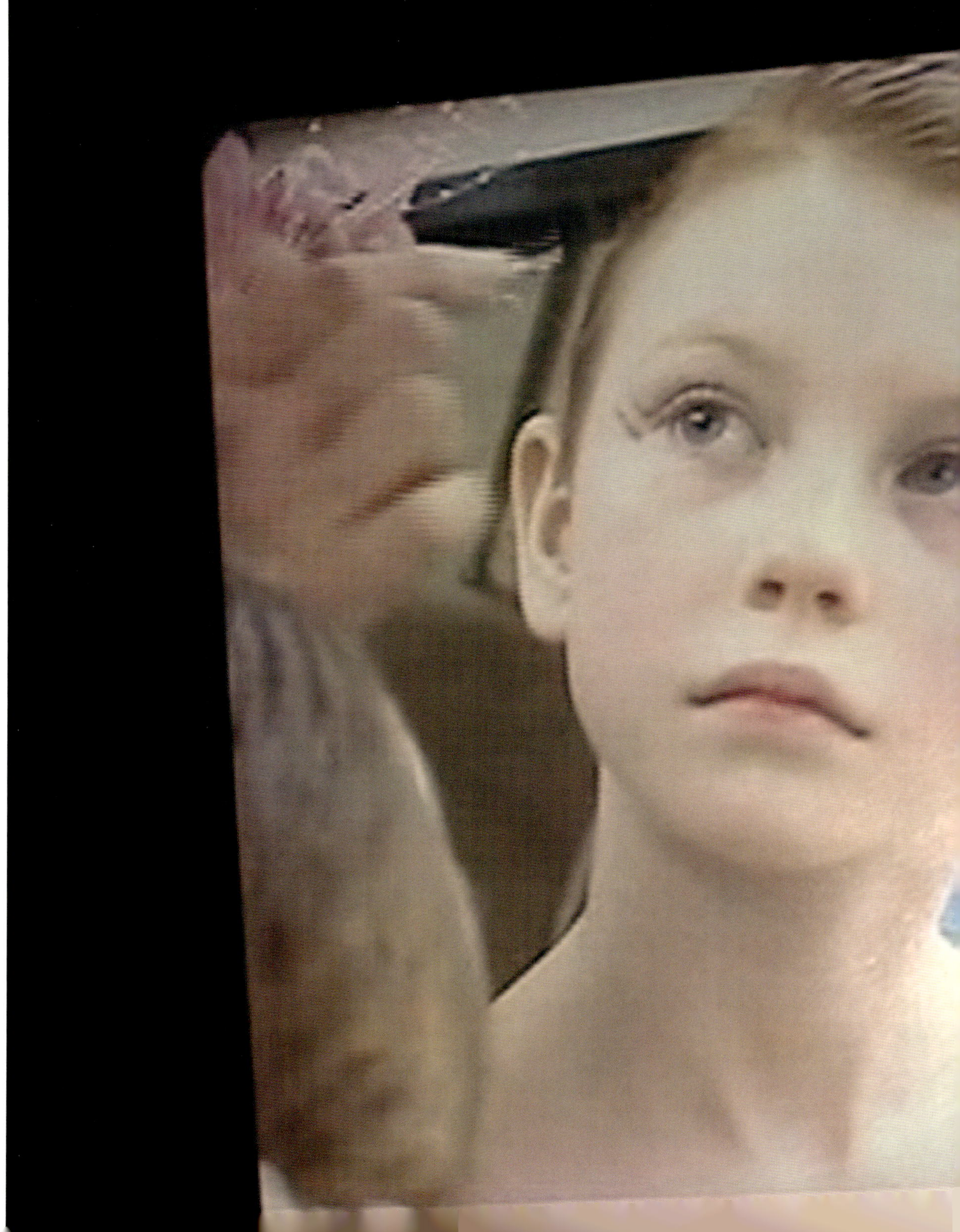

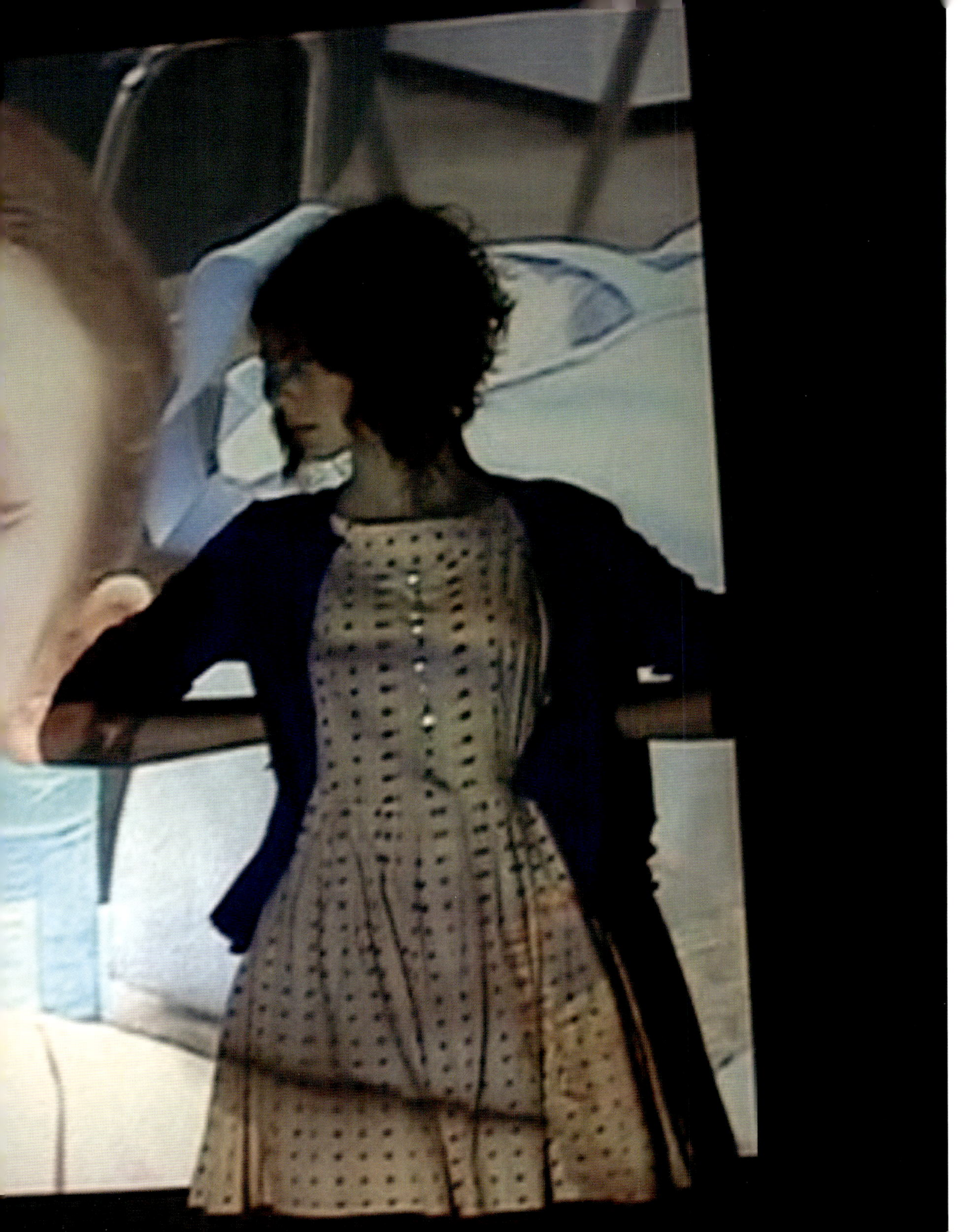

'I'm sick, you're tired. Let's dance.' Metric

1

When my daughter Audrey was 14, it was the middle of August 2006, one evening we were sitting on the sofa together in Los Angeles watching TV, and she said, 'My lump hurts.' And everything changed.

She had been aware of this thing, this thing she called 'my lump', for a long time, and she insisted she'd told me about it; in July, she'd had a sore throat, and she'd said, 'I have a lump under my arm,' and for some reason, I didn't say, 'What kind of lump? Show me.' I couldn't even remember the conversation, though I did recall the sore throat... So what ensued was an almost comic exchange, with me asking, 'Lump? *What* lump?' And Audrey saying, 'I told you about it, I *told* you.'

Eventually I said, 'OK, show me this lump.' And she lifted up her T-shirt, to present a large lump; and it wasn't under her arm, it was on her side, on her ribcage, bulging out, just where the band of her bra went around her torso. The bulge was the size of my hand, maybe six inches long.

I was so frightened that my immediate priority was to hide from her how frightened I was.

The next morning I made an appointment with the doctor, and the day after that she saw us. She presented a list of possibilities: TB, mononucleosis, thyroid, anaemia; she took blood (the first blood test), and spoke of possibly doing a biopsy at some point. I was really resistant to the idea of a biopsy. I didn't want anybody cutting into Audrey's body.

Over the weekend, while waiting for the results of the tests, I found myself in the strange state of hoping Audrey had TB. But she didn't, so the following week we went to the hospital for an ultrasound, and the doctor was told it was nothing to worry about: it was something called 'extra-mammary tissue'. Something that sometimes happens when breast tissue grows outside the breast. It was perfectly normal.

After maybe a day-and-a-half of feeling reassured, I went into free fall. I needed more information, and decided to take her to a breast doctor. Another week passed, and then we went to see Dr Kristi at the other hospital.

Probably because she's a breast specialist, and therefore rather matter of fact, Kristi was the first person to ask Audrey simply to sit on the examination table, naked to the waist, so she could look at her. She asked her to put her arms over her head; she asked her some questions about the pain; she told us it was most definitely not extra-mammary tissue. She pointed out how distorted Audrey's chest was, how her shoulder had moved out to the right, so her right arm did not hang next to her body, as if to make space for the lump. And Audrey's collarbones were asymmetrical, one concave, one convex. Another doctor came in and together they decided Audrey should have a CT scan to figure out what it was. They were talking about consulting an orthopaedic doctor, and I was sitting there, thinking: 'alignment, yoga, physiotherapy.' Reversible.

A few days later, there was the evidence: an image of a cross-section of Audrey's chest, a view from above showing a large tumour, intersected by her ribs, with most of it inside the chest cavity, but about a third of it pressing against and beyond the ribs to make the lump and cause the pain.

2

One of the strangest aspects of being a mother is the intensity of one's adoration of and identification with the body of the child. The child appears physically perfect, no matter what configuration of features it may have. It's as if the beauty that belongs to the baby is the only beauty that is outside cultural norms – the mother finds everything about the baby unspeakably beautiful, no matter what, and spends many hours marvelling at her every aspect.

There's a deep, unconscious gratification in the more or less acknowledged fact that she made this perfect thing; it's inexplicable, almost miraculous, but undeniable nevertheless, and it makes her deeply happy. Especially at this post-partum moment, when the maternal body feels like a train wreck, flabby, leaky and large, when total exhaustion prevails. Especially now, the image of the bodily perfection of the baby is terribly important.

It's not only that the baby's beauty compensates for the loss of control, for the maternal body exceeding its boundaries, the excess, the flow, the brutality of childbirth and after. A profound shift takes place, where the baby's wellbeing takes precedence over her own. D.W. Winnicott calls this 'primary maternal preoccupation', a form of temporary psychosis that is required for the mother to make the initial relationship with the baby, and vice versa, upon which the baby's later relationships will be based.

It's not that the mother sacrifices herself entirely – that's actually not such a good idea – it's more that the mother identifies with the baby, so that meeting the baby's needs feels right, feels like meeting her own. As if the baby's perfect body has, in her imagination, taken the place of her own damaged one, it's replaced it. Sometimes this is called bonding.

This intensity can't go on forever, needless to say. Eventually she returns to something like her own life, and the baby manages with what Winnicott calls the 'good enough mother', as the primary state of 'maternal preoccupation' fades. Still, that profound idealization of the child's body – experienced as perfectly beautiful, perfect and beautiful – and the mother's identification with the child as her better self, as something somehow belonging to her, these remain, to shape the landscape of their relationship for years to come.

3

Before I saw any scans, Kristi called me at home and said, 'Your daughter has a large mass on her right ribcage, involving both muscle and bone.' And I went into shock. I hesitated, then I said, 'This is so strange, I mean, I watch *House*, I watch *Grey's Anatomy*, and they're always talking about things like a large mass, how weird... What could cause such a thing?' I don't know if the doctor was perplexed by me talking about TV programmes, but that was when she said, 'It's definitely cancer; it's just a question of which kind.' And I fell down howling.

Then I said, 'I'm sorry, I'm so sorry, hang on,' and I took the phone outside, I stood on the empty pavement across the street, asking questions. There was a possibility, she said, that it could be Ewing's sarcoma, which, she said, kills 50 per cent of the people who get it, no matter what treatment they receive. It was hard for me to understand what she was saying. I asked her to say it again: 'It's definitely cancer; it's just a question of which kind.'

I felt a physical dread of going back into the house, because I would have to tell Audrey something; blankly, I told her she had to have more tests, that it wasn't clear what was wrong with her. She looked at me, she was 14, she looked me in the eye and she said, 'I heard you crying, you have to tell me what the doctor said. You have to tell me the truth.' Looking down, I said, 'The doctors think you might have cancer.' She pressed me further, and I remember saying, 'They think it's quite likely.' And then she laughed out loud; she couldn't believe it.

4

The mother idealizes the child, and she identifies with the child, so that all those nappies, the baths, the feeding and wiping and all the endless attention the baby requires become doable. Otherwise it's impossible. And this so-called 'adjustment' is predicated on the mother identifying with the baby at the deepest level. If for some reason that identification doesn't take place, then it's sheer hell, the hardest work in the world.

And the child grows, and thrives, and leaves for day care, school, leaves to hang out with her friends, she ventures out into the world, and then she comes back to the mother, who is imagined as a constant force, a reality. No matter if the mother works, or has other kids, or has other things to do, somehow that sense of the mother's unconscious identification with the child remains, and the child relies on it, she leans back against it: it's huge, immoveable, always.

Until the kid doesn't want it any more, and she kicks the mother out.

5

Eventually it was determined that Audrey had a large, slow-growing tumour, which would not metastasize; that is, it would not travel to her liver or her lungs or her brain, and transform into another, more lethal form of cancer. We were supposed to be really glad about this. It was a very rare condition, with a strong tendency to reoccur; the doctors said it came back 60 per cent of the time, or 80 per cent of the time. One said, 'Oh, it *always* comes back.' It was locally aggressive, which means it destroys whatever it's growing around. Because her tumour was so unusual, the doctors weren't clear what treatment to try, raising yet more questions. Crucially, it was not Ewing's sarcoma, and because it was slow-growing, there was time, and yet more doctors to consult.

In the end, Audrey had four months of chemotherapy, which was delivered as a weekly infusion through a port that was surgically implanted in her chest. I am unable to tell you about that time; it is too painful to describe. The chemo did not shrink the tumour, which was the intention, although it stopped it growing larger, and it made Audrey very sick.

Then the doctors decided on surgery to remove the tumour, and the destroyed ribs it was growing around. This involved permanently removing six ribs, and replacing them with a rigid patch so her chest wall wouldn't collapse. The hardest part was intensive care, and the ventilator, this machine that sounded like Darth Vader, which breathed for her. No one told her, no one told me, that she would be on a ventilator after the surgery. It was shocking, and I thought it was something they would unplug right away. In fact, she needed it for almost three days, she couldn't breathe without it. And she couldn't talk or eat during this time, the breathing tube taped over her mouth, so she would write notes to communicate. There's a notebook, which I kept, with notes to me, and notes to the nurse saying, 'Do you know when my mother is coming back?'

6

At a certain point, the child takes possession of her body; she takes her body back. The idea of her mother once upon a time changing her nappy, wiping her vomit, giving her a bath becomes if not horrifying, then merely disgusting, and almost impossible to imagine. Out come the mascara, the eyeliner, all the equipment, as if to say, I'm really not your little girl any more.

Quite frequently, this taking back of the body is aggressive. Hair is dyed bright unnatural colours, tattoos and piercings appear, permanent markers that the baby's body has been irrevocably lost. Sometimes it's darker: the refusal to eat, compulsive, can be an attempt on the part of the child to draw a line, a boundary around her body. Cutting lets the child know that only she can write on her body, indelibly marking the ecstatic pain of separation, the anguish of being one.

And the mother is returned to her aging body, deteriorating with each passing year. She learns to accept, gracefully or not, that the displacement of her own narcissism onto the body of the child was inevitable, necessary, yet now it has to change, to detach, making room for the kid... and her tattoos.

We've all seen those scary TV programmes about little kids in beauty contests and their insane mothers. I think all mothers are a little bit insane like that, as if the child's triumphs belong to the mother, the child's loveliness makes up for her aging, the child's power – her unlimited potential – compensates for everything the mother has given up.

Until the child kicks the mother out.

7

It took a long time for Audrey to recover from the surgery. She got better, slowly, and a whole year after the surgery, her energy returned in a way that I hadn't seen since she was maybe 11 years old. She's doing really well, now. She's 20 years old. She has chronic pain as a result of the surgery; she has a scar that travels from the side of her right breast around to her shoulder blade in back. She has quite a dent in her right side, and although her body has straightened out remarkably well, some of the changes, the odd distortions, are permanent. She has to have an MRI scan every six months, and so far the cancer hasn't come back. So far she's OK.

Audrey never kicked me out. The illness intervened and disrupted the process of physical separation that's supposed to take place, violently or gently, as the case may be. Instead of the deep pleasure of maternal identification with a more perfect body, I identified, deeply, with a body in pain: a body distorted by a growing, malevolent tumour; a body pierced by needles and chemo ports and biopsies and surgery; a body scanned and rescanned; a body marked by cuts made by doctors, scars that no one intended. And the horror of handing my daughter's body over to doctors and surgeons and nurses, to pierce and cut into and apparently to repair, is indescribable.

I've taken it on, as if to carry it for her, so that she can go out into the world, meds in her handbag, and have her adventures. I have internalized the damaged ideal; something perfect's been ruined; I couldn't prevent it, I couldn't protect her, and I couldn't fix it. My narcissism has suffered a double blow, and I must, in some sense, be responsible for all this.

Guilt is a very useful thing: it makes incomprehensible things make sense. There must be a reason (my wild thinking insists) for this illness; there must be a logic that I can understand.

I thought: Audrey got the tumour on her ribcage because I put her in a Maclaren stroller before she could sit up by herself. Or because I microwaved her baby food in plastic bowls. Because I sent her to day care in the Valley, right under the flight path to Burbank Airport. Because I didn't insist on a chest X-ray when she was 13, and had so many persistent coughs that wouldn't go away. At least then we might have caught it sooner, though the tumour itself wouldn't show up on an X-ray, maybe the weirdly distorted ribs would have been visible, maybe someone would have noticed, before it was so big that the surgery to cut it out of her body would change that body irrevocably.

I thought: Audrey is tall; she's six foot one-and-three-quarter inches tall. It's very tall for a girl. When she was born, she was enormous – eleven pounds three-and-a-half ounces – and she'd been squashed inside my body, so her right foot, ankle, knee, hip were rotated, her foot twisted sideways and turned up. The tumour was on the right side too, on her ribs. Maybe it was initiated by the confinement of my body. She was just too big. So maybe it couldn't have been avoided – unless she'd somehow been smaller; maybe if I'd eaten bad food, if I'd gone in for cigarettes and coke. Actually I did drink red wine through most of the pregnancy. Maybe that was it. Or if I hadn't had this baby with Peter, there was something bad about our combination of genes – but then it wouldn't have been this baby, this perfect girl.

It seems impossible to accept that it was random: a combination of genetics, and maybe some or all of those things, but none of it my fault, exactly. I would like to know what caused it, I really would. But they don't know, the doctors can't tell me. So I go on coming up with stories to tell, that somehow tie Audrey's illness in to my actions, to make it make sense. Because otherwise it's meaningless, it's random, and apparently that's the hardest thing of all.

8

The child idealizes the mother, too. The small child regards the mother as one might regard a goddess: all-powerful, exquisitely beautiful, lacking nothing. The child learns how to be in the world through a process of idealization and identification; the mother mirrors the child, repeating the baby's sounds and facial expressions, so the baby can, so to speak, know what it looks like, how it appears, and how it sounds. The mother's responses and reactions construct a world for the baby; the mother's ability to swoop in and sweep the baby up in her arms proves her power and her loving kindness. The mother's anger is like a thunderstorm: the sky darkens, there's distant rumbling and the occasional terrifying burst of light.

The child finds the mother perfect, as no one ever has, before or since, and when the kid grows up a bit, and kicks her out, what is lost is not only the child's loveliness, but also the idealization of the mother. Seen with new eyes, the mother is suddenly older, odder; it's horrible when she laughs out loud. She's no longer funny, more funny-looking. It's a real tragedy, a story of lost love.

The mother's power dissolves, deflating like a balloon, as the kid looks elsewhere for something to love. This has to happen, it's right on time, but there's no question that it leaves the mother reeling.

It played out differently with me. Before Audrey even had a chance to start thinking about tattoos, the tumour, and the treatment, had messed with her body, leaving their own indelible marks. She was so young; she bounced back (as they say). She chose to be optimistic. She said, 'I missed out on a year of high school, I'm never going to miss out on anything ever again.'

In my imagination, I hold the horror for her. I carry the imprint of the grotesque distortion and destruction of her ribcage, the surgical demolition and reconstruction of her chest wall, the memory of the two holes where the chest tubes, the fat drainage tubes, came out, like a huge vampire bite on her side, the sheer pain of the harm that came to her perfect body. She's beautiful now, she stays up late, dancing, working hard, having her adventures. And I carry the imprint of her wounds, like a coat made out of lead. I grieve and rage for the child that exists no longer, for the look in her eyes and the idealized body of that child that in some sense of the word was mine.

9

And then I thought, is this really what it comes to? I imagine myself somehow taking on the pain for her, so she doesn't have to carry it? What a truly bonkers idea.

I talked to Audrey about it a while ago, acknowledging how insanely presumptuous it was on my part to imagine I could somehow transfer her suffering onto myself so that she could be happy. She looked down, and she said, 'Well of course I've thought the same thing about you.'

In the midst of catastrophe, we both wanted the other, at least, to be OK. We wanted to imagine the other one able to leave this strange land, this place where you find yourself, as if pushed through swing doors into another world, into cancer land, a world where once you've entered it, you never really leave. We imagined taking it all on ourselves so the other one could be OK.

Idealization, regarding the other as embodied perfection, is an illusion, probably a necessary illusion, the foundation of love, untouched by reality. The ill body is a fact: it's non-negotiable, it's stubborn, it's ugly, it won't budge. Most of all, it won't make sense, won't fit into a story with cause and effect and a conclusion. It's random, this particular illness, and therefore meaningless; it's likely to come back, and there's horror in that, real horror. But it's dialectical, maybe; it's not either/or, but both, and as I'm bouncing back and forth from perfection to horror, maybe I can find a way to move towards a third position, towards something more like truth.

In this way I pick up the pieces, retrieve the disparate parts of myself; no longer reflected in the eyes of the child, no longer losing myself in her idealization.

When she was 16, Audrey took a summer art class at UCLA and made this video. The title is 'You Are Nothing (Without Her)'. It shows Audrey, aged 7 or maybe 8, being made up backstage before a ballet performance. And Audrey, aged 16, recovered from the chemo, the surgery, the illness, standing, watching herself as a child, before. The teenage girl contemplates the lovely child, as if to ask: 'Who is that? What happened?'

Needless to say, it was me, the mother, who shot the home movie footage of Audrey aged 7 backstage; it's me she's looking at when she makes that wry, amused expression. And Audrey made the set-up where the video was projected big, so she could stand next to it, walk up to it, walk in front of it.

For me, what's interesting about it is sometimes it's like Audrey the teenager is getting in the way, impeding our view of the child. And other times the child is superimposed on top of 16-year-old Audrey, so we can't see her because she's almost obliterated by the child. Looking at her, we can't tell what she's thinking, all we can tell is it's some kind of before and after. Some kind of after and before.

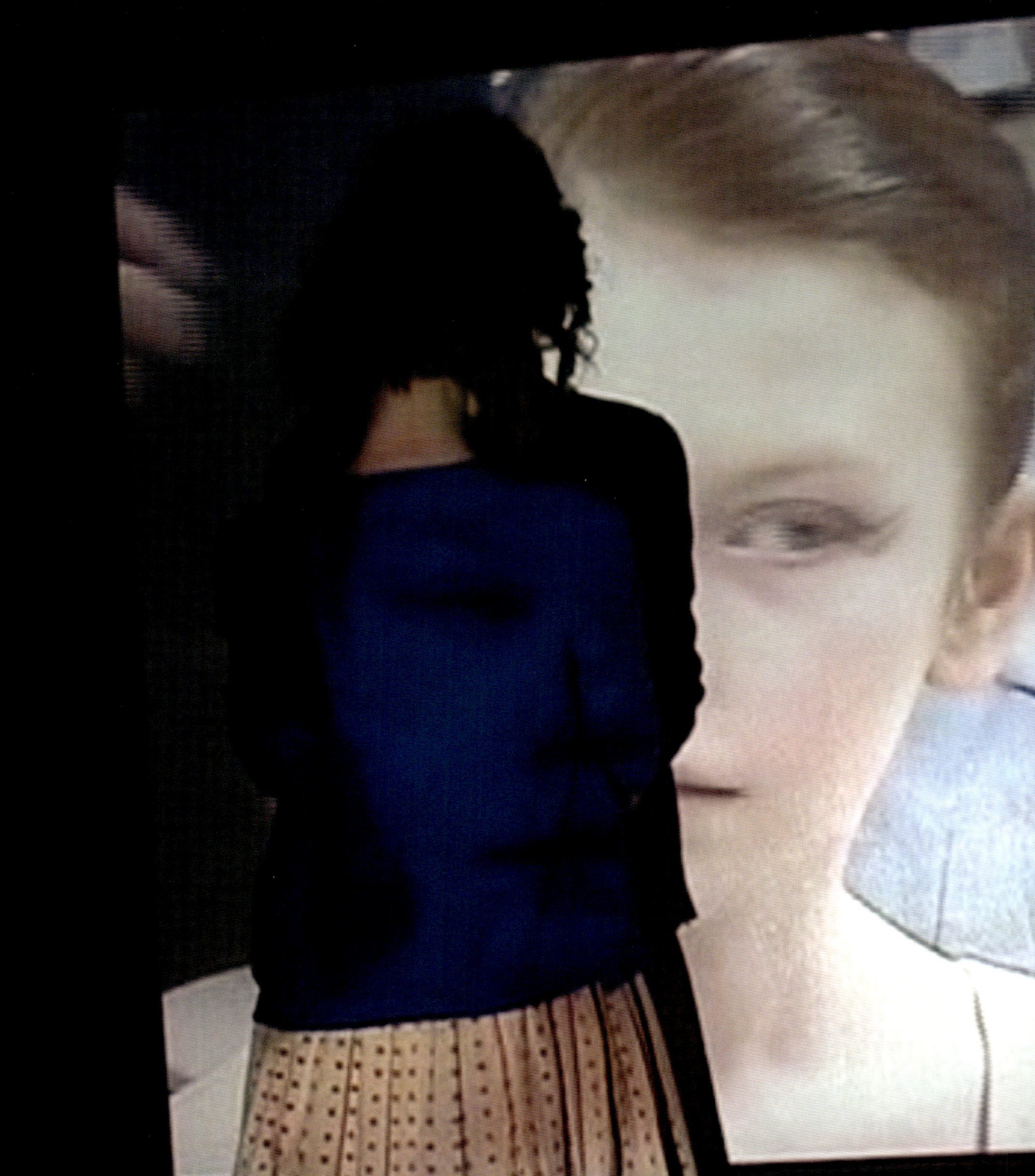

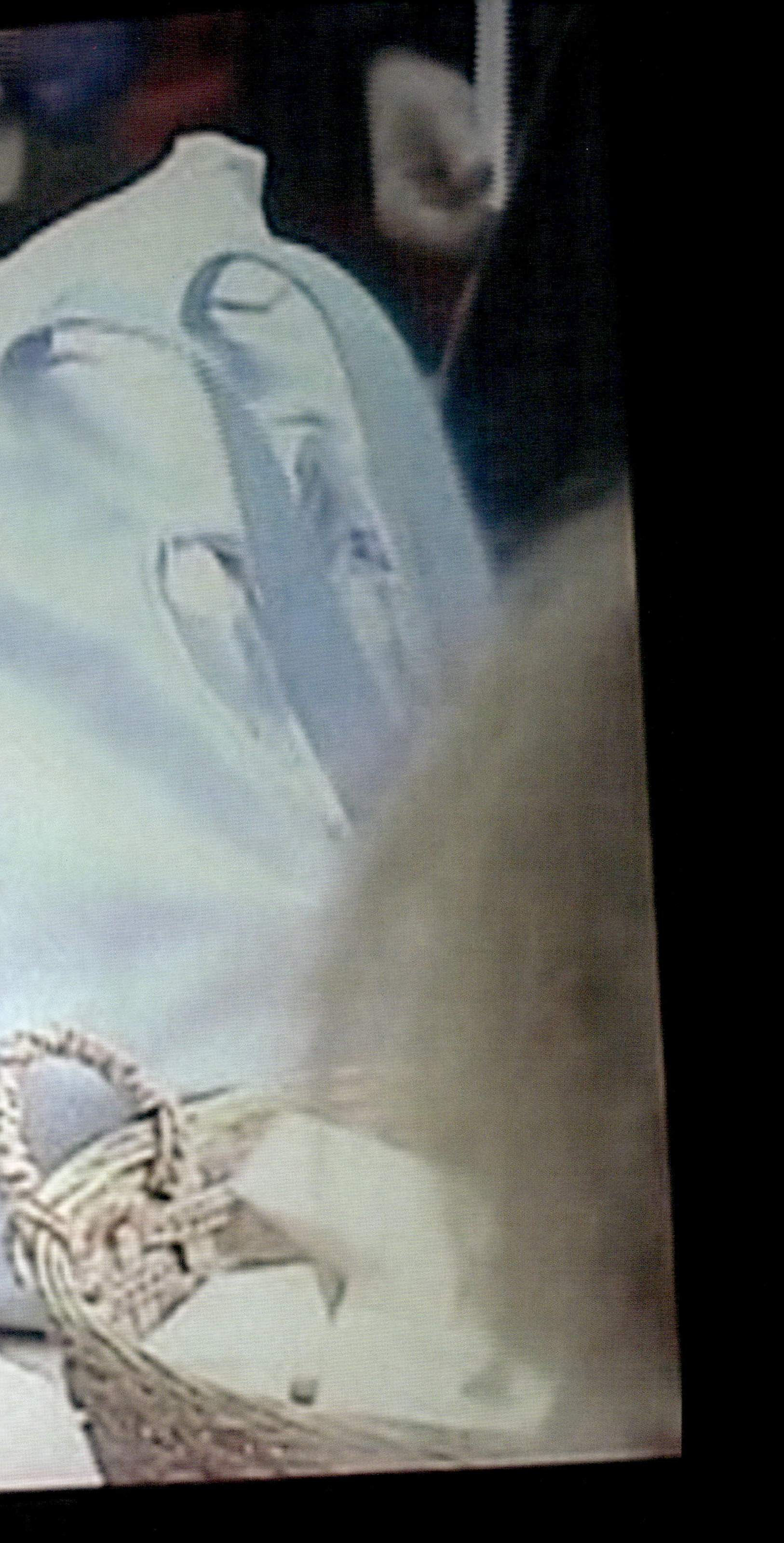

PERFECTING DESIRE

RECONCILING MEMORY

JONATHAN WHITEHALL

The way in which my work relates to ideas of perfection is most evident in its search for a transcendence of boundaries, or an overcoming of separation. These themes became central to a series of video works made from around 2003–08. Frequently evoked through the narrative of a love affair or emotional relationship, the search for symbiosis was formally rendered through the relationship of voice and image. For me, in the spaces between the voice and images, a certain 'lack' occurred – which carried a sense that neither image nor voice was enough, or was capable of carrying the full meaning of events – and this lack seemed to be suggestive of desire.

Desire often seems to be caught up with notions of perfection: perfection is something many of us desire, whether it is in relation to happiness, love or artistic creation. It is, of course, something that is rarely, if ever, attained. Is it ever possible to perfect anything, or to reach a state of perfection? The fantasy of perfection can provoke a longing which, even if we consciously choose to reject or supress, forms a powerful and structuring fantasy, one that may underlie many areas of our conscious and unconscious lives.

Last autumn, I was searching through my belongings in storage, looking for my old computer and external hard drive. I finally found the box that contained my computer and lifted out its heavy bulk. After setting up and a moment of hesitation, the computer whirred into life. As the screen lit up, I was confronted with a desktop from another time, a 'time capsule' of a life long since gone. Looking through the video files, I found footage I had forgotten about, that I had pushed to the back of my memory: a work in progress that I had never been happy with, that had never found a place, which I had never finished or shown.

As I watched the footage on the computer screen, my eye (and camera) stared at broken Greek and Etruscan vases, shadowy interiors, and scanned the crumbling surfaces of dirtied oil paintings. Slowly a sense of loss overtook me, and with it a desperate fight for memory, while simultaneously a sense that certain memories must be excluded or repressed to make this reviewing acceptable.

Shot on a now virtually defunct format, Digital8, the footage, taken in the failing light of a rainy day at the end of January or beginning of February years ago – I do not know the exact date – was of conventionally poor quality. Many of the shots were badly lit, and the resulting footage was extremely grainy. The images were taken in a house that was being dismantled, its contents packed away after a death. I filmed in one afternoon, aware that I would never be able to reshoot this footage, and that the house would never look the same again. I was also aware, in a sense, of looking at the remains of a life, a life of someone I did not really know. Likewise, I was not that familiar with the house, having only visited once before.

The video was unusual amongst the works I made of this period in that I allowed myself to do things which I usually would not: the use of fades, gestural camerawork, shifting focus and perhaps, most strikingly, the use of music; a short extract from the opening recitative of the aria 'When I am laid in Earth' from Purcell's opera *Dido and Aeneas* and the Prelude from Bach's Cello suite no. 2 in D minor. I was wary of the use of music, and still am, as it so easily unifies and smoothes over so much in a moving-image piece. Alongside the iconic pieces of music, and to add further to this borrowing from the cultural canon, the text used in the video was Shakespeare's 'Sonnet 104'. (Usually I wrote the texts for video works at this time, so again the working method was atypical.)

'Sonnet 104' tells of a lover who finds their beloved's beauty unchanged by time:

To me, fair friend, you never can be old,
For as you were when first your eye I eyed,
Such seems your beauty still.

Like the beloved's beauty, untarnished by the passing of the seasons, the lover's desire remains undiminished. Expressed in the context of physical and erotic attraction, desire in the sonnet is in a sense 'perfected' by the holding or denying of time. The desire for someone is held or sustained in the very intensity of its originary moment, something that so often in reality is impossible; for as we no doubt all know, sexual desire and erotic attraction can be all too fleeting. The speaker goes on, however, to say his eye might be deceived, and that change to his beloved's beauty may be occurring:

Ah, yet doth beauty, like a dial-hand,
Steal from his figure and no pace perceived;
So your sweet hue, which methinks still doth stand,
Hath motion and mine eye may be deceived:

Yet, he concludes, even if this is the case, the beauty of his beloved is such that beauty will never exist again:

> For fear of which, hear this, thou age unbred;
> Ere you were born was beauty's summer dead

The beloved's beauty, then, is an idealized or perfected beauty, one that surpasses any other. In a way, this vision of beauty is annihilating in that it prevents any other vision of beauty from existing. It is a perfect image of beauty that will endure, mocking any attempt by others to be beautiful.

The idea of an image of unsurpassable beauty in turn leads to the idea of a perfect image, and to a question raised by the flawed images of the footage: at a time when the drive is continually for 'sharper', 'brighter', 'higher resolution'; when images *have to be* 3D to be their most affecting; what is the 'value' of, or rather, what is the *affect* of, images that are 'flawed' or 'diminished'? Can their lack of clarity, at times, give the sense they are almost 'stand-ins' for the images one cannot represent? Do these flawed or diminished images evoke, or allude to, an imaginary perfection or plenitude, a fantasy of perfection evoked by lack? An absence that points to what is missing? To what is lost? To the processes of time and the erosion of memory itself?

Memory, Roland Barthes writes in *Le Neutre*, is not free from the passing of time. He writes: 'I believe, since memory is not an act of pure recollection of the past, as if it were external to time the better to grasp it: memory is itself submitted to time, to its injustices [...].'[1] For Barthes, memory paradoxically prevents the preserving of events. Altered by time and its injustices, and by rewritings, retellings, recallings and reconstructions, the past is gradually worn away; or, as W.G. Sebald puts it in his book *The Emigrants*, 'and the last remnants memory destroys.'[2]

Memory submits not only to time, but also to the workings of desire. Desire, it seems, is always present in memory, present in the way memory restructures events to make those events conform to our need for continuity and coherence. The need to construct a past to which we can reconcile ourselves occurs not only through the constant change and (re)organization of memory, but also through the repression and forgetting of memories that perhaps we cannot reconcile to ourselves or signify. Maybe this forgetting and repressing takes place in an attempt to preserve, or create, a notion of 'perfect love' or the 'perfect event' – something that can perhaps only exist in fantasy?

The recounting of the past leads to a questioning of how we remember our past, and how we represent or retell the past. In a well-known quote from his book *The Political Unconscious*, Frederic Jameson writes: 'History is what hurts. It is what refuses desire and sets inexorable limits to individual as well as collective praxis [...].'[3] Yet does history resist desire? If history relies on memory, then in that sense no, I think not. No personal or collective history can be immune to the drive to reconstruct, or from the desires, conscious and unconscious, which are present in that reconstruction.

On watching the video footage that autumn for the first time in years, I was shocked that it was not the piece I had remembered; images seemed to appear in places I had not expected them, the music and sounds did not occur when I had expected. Yet apart from this general sense that the footage was not as I thought it should be – was the process that had happened here a misremembering in order to create the piece as I felt it should be now? – something else struck me: what the piece had seemed to have become was, in a sense, a 'perfecting' of desire.

A perfecting of desire in that what was now in my mind was the love for someone I myself had lost; a memory of desire which, for the moments of viewing, disavowed much of the past. The footage, shot with little more intention than the preservation of a memory of a house now seemed an attempt to articulate something about the overcoming of separation; a separation, at the time implicit, which would later become explicit. In the missed regards of the portraits, in the few frames where a hand writes out the lines of the sonnet seen earlier in its completeness, it felt there was an attempt to evoke something of that moment where the subject/object distinction is lost, as in deepest fantasy; or rather, perhaps more precisely, an attempt to evoke the desire for the dissolving of that distinction. When I had finally finished watching, as it seemed to take a long time despite the footage being little more than eight minutes in length, I realized that what the piece was, in many ways, was a love letter: a declaration of love to someone now lost to me, but an idealized version of that desire, a 'perfected' version or vision, even if rendered imperfectly.

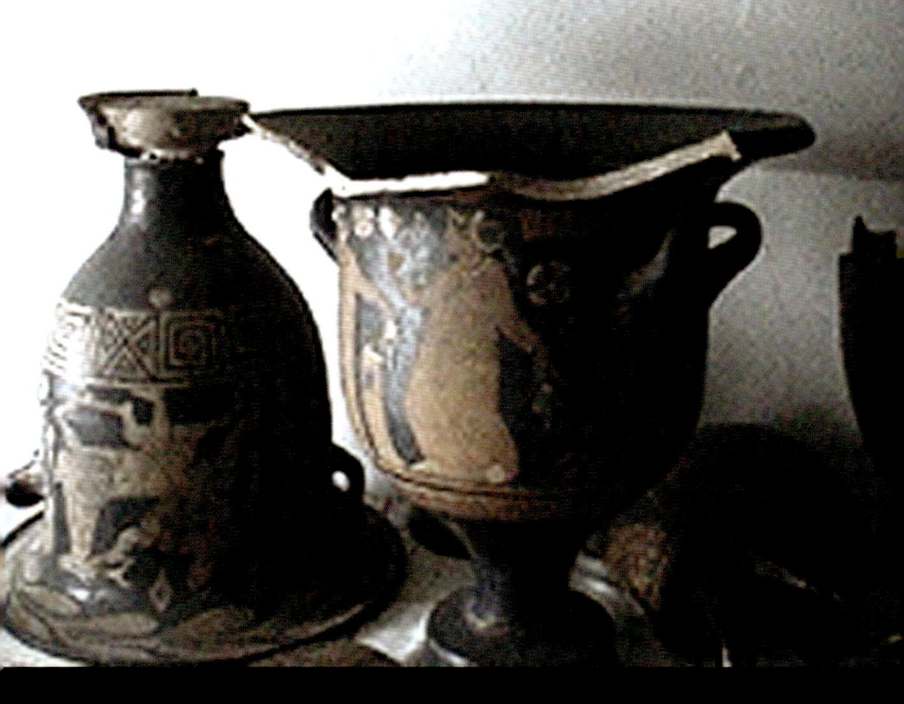

Music: Extract from the opening recitative of the aria
'When I am laid in Earth' from *Dido and Aeneas*, by Henri Purcell

To me, fair friend, you never can be old,
For as you were when first your eye I eyed,
Such seems your beauty still.

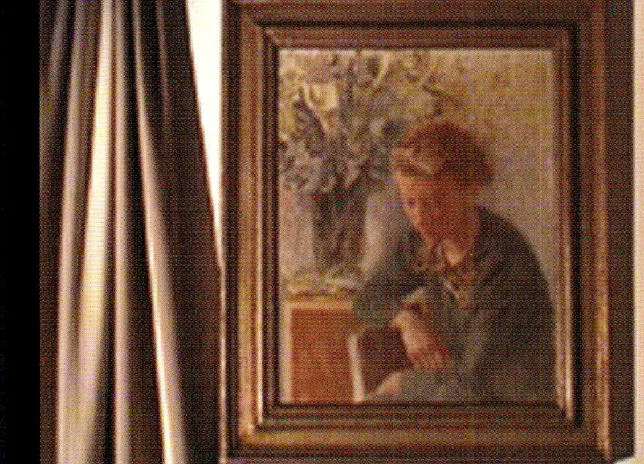

Three winters' cold
Have from the forests shook three summers' pri
Three beauteous springs to yellow autumn turn'd
In process of the seasons have I seen;
Three April perfumes in three hot Junes burn'd
Since first I saw you fresh, which yet are green.

Ah! yet doth beauty, like a dial-hand,
Steal from his figure, and no pace perceiv'd;
So your sweet hue, which methinks still doth stand,
Hath motion, and mine eye may be deceiv'd.

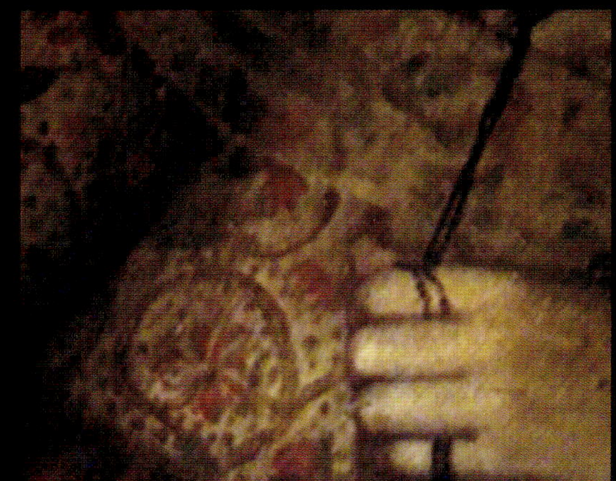

For fear of which, hear this, thou age unbred
Ere you were born, was beauty's summer dead

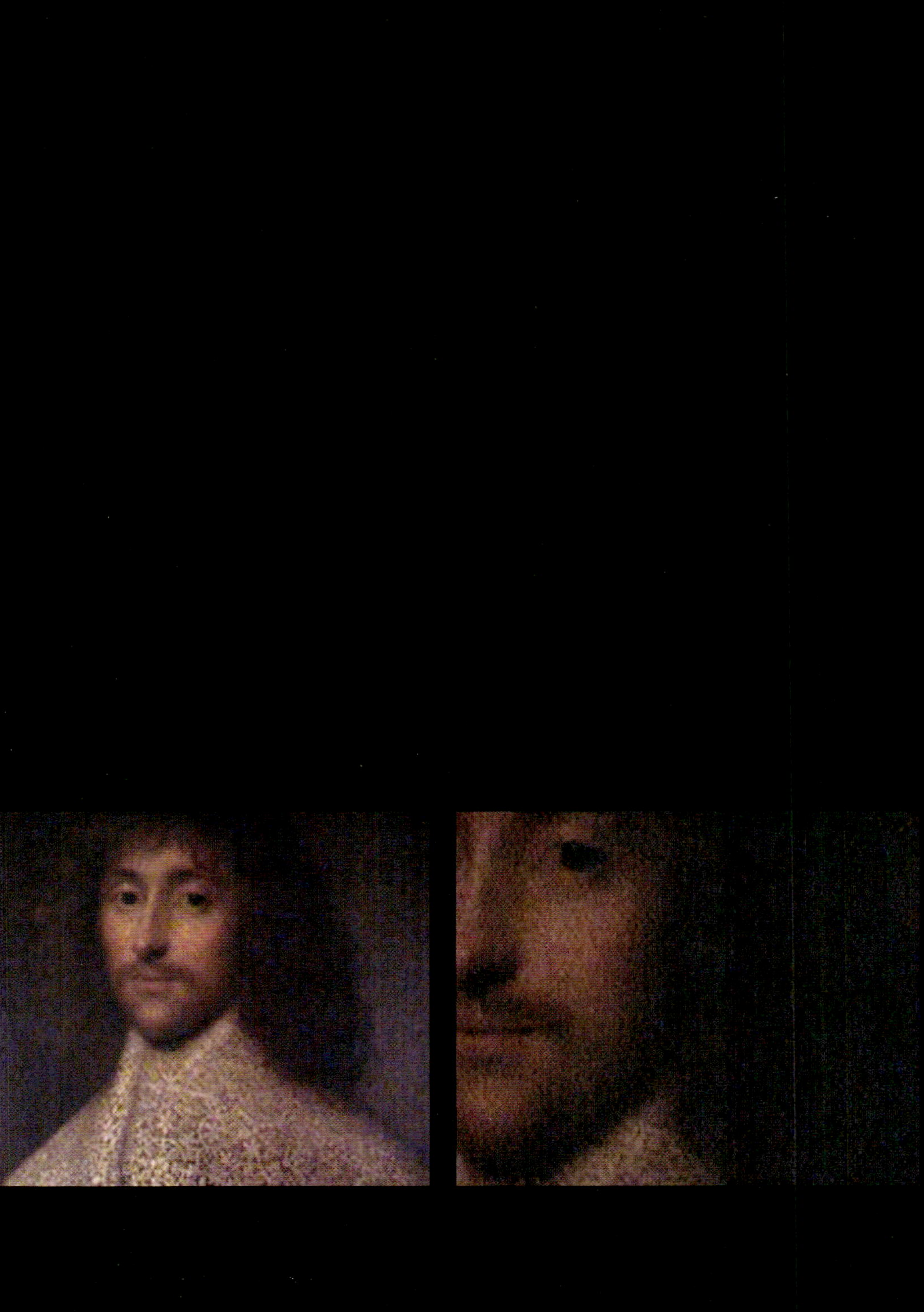

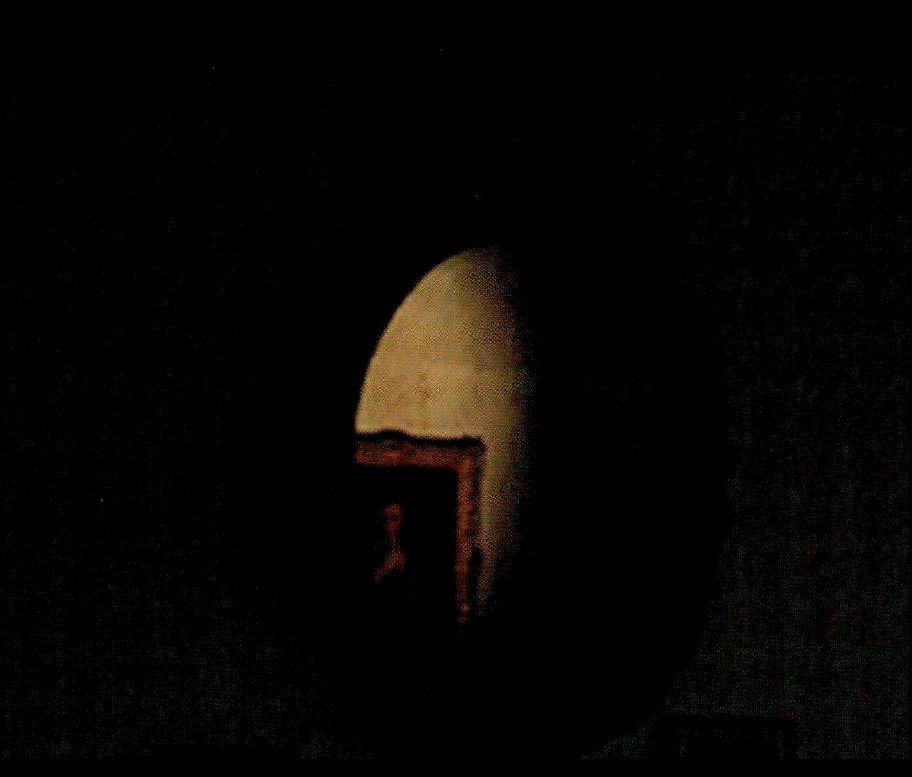

Music: Prelude from Bach's Cello Suite No. 2 in D minor

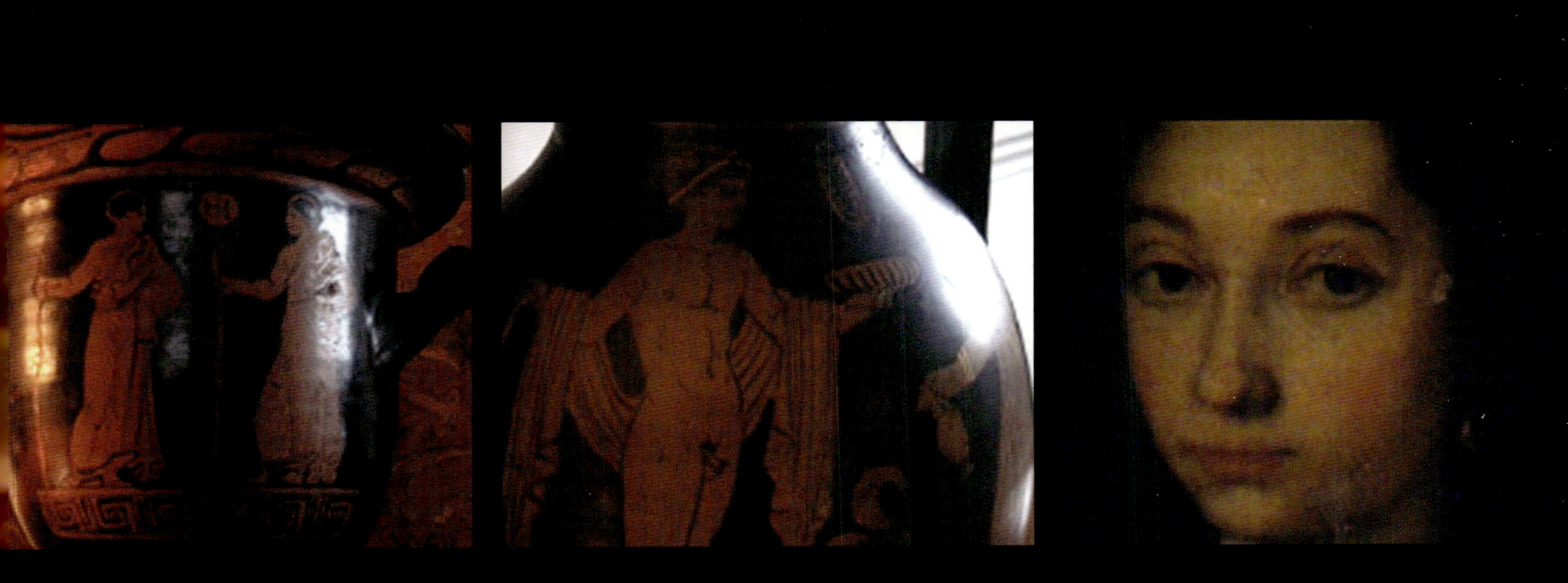

fair friend, you never
were when first
your

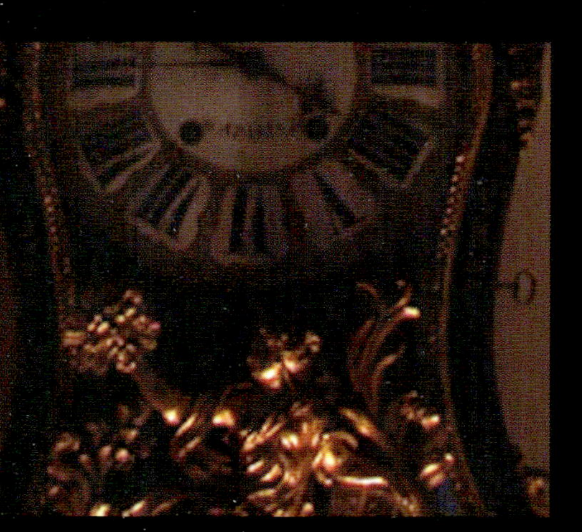

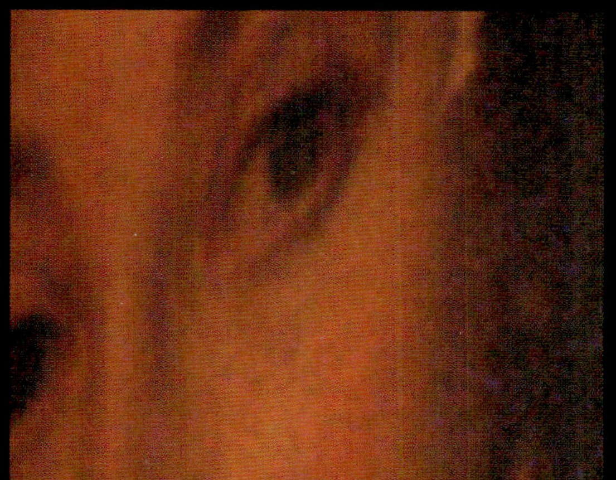

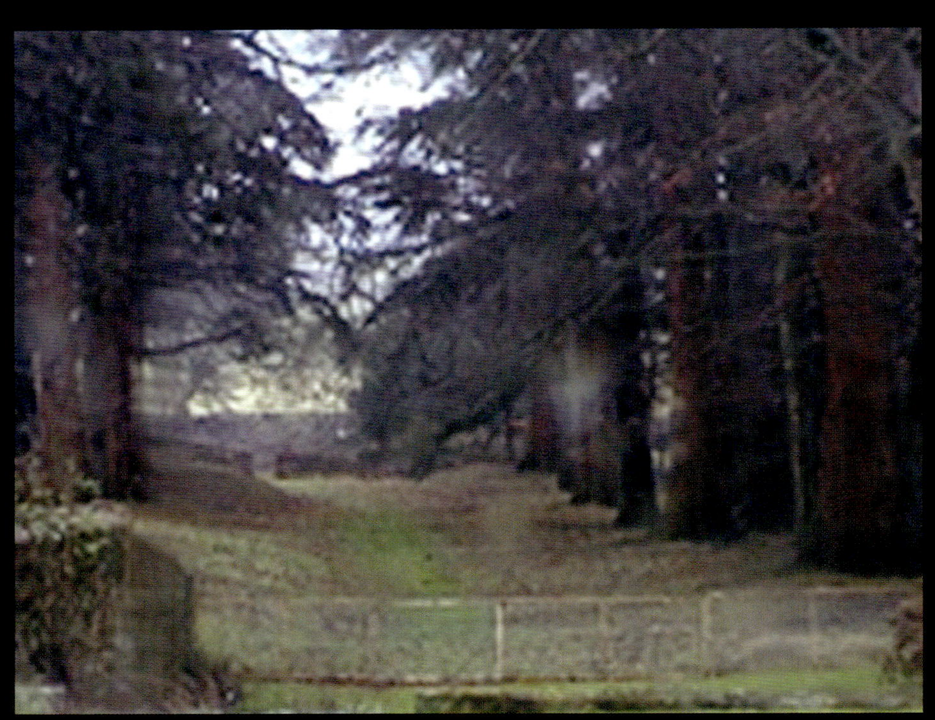

NOTES

1 Roland Barthes, *The Neutral*, trans. Rosalind E. Krauss and Denis Hollier, New York: Columbia University Press, 2005, p. 39.

2 W.G. Sebald, *The Emigrants*, trans. Michael Hulse, London: The Harvill Press, 1997, p. 2.

3 Frederic Jameson, *The Political Unconscious*, London: Routledge Classics, 2002, p. 88.

A PERFECT STRIKE

DOUBLE STANDARDS & ATTACKS ON PERFECTION

MICHAL HEIMAN

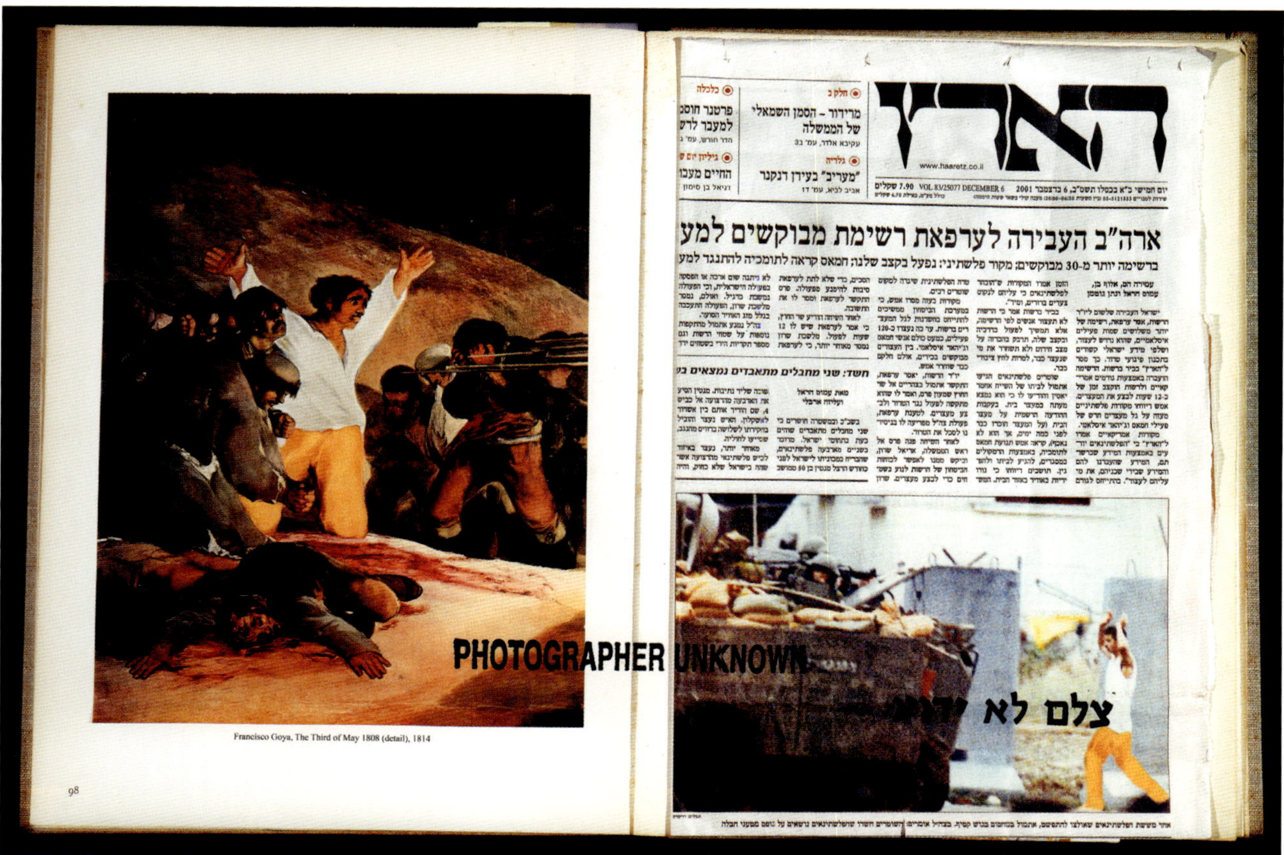

‘This truth, in its delayed appearance and its belated address, cannot be linked only to what is known, but also to what remains unknown in our very actions and our language.’
Cathy Caruth, *Unclaimed Experience: Trauma, Narrative, and History*, 1996[1]

Figure 1: Michal Heiman, *Do-Mino No. 1: Francisco Goya, The Third of May 1808 (1814)/ Photographer Unknown (Reuters, Haaretz), Gush Katif (6 Dec. 2001)*, 2008.

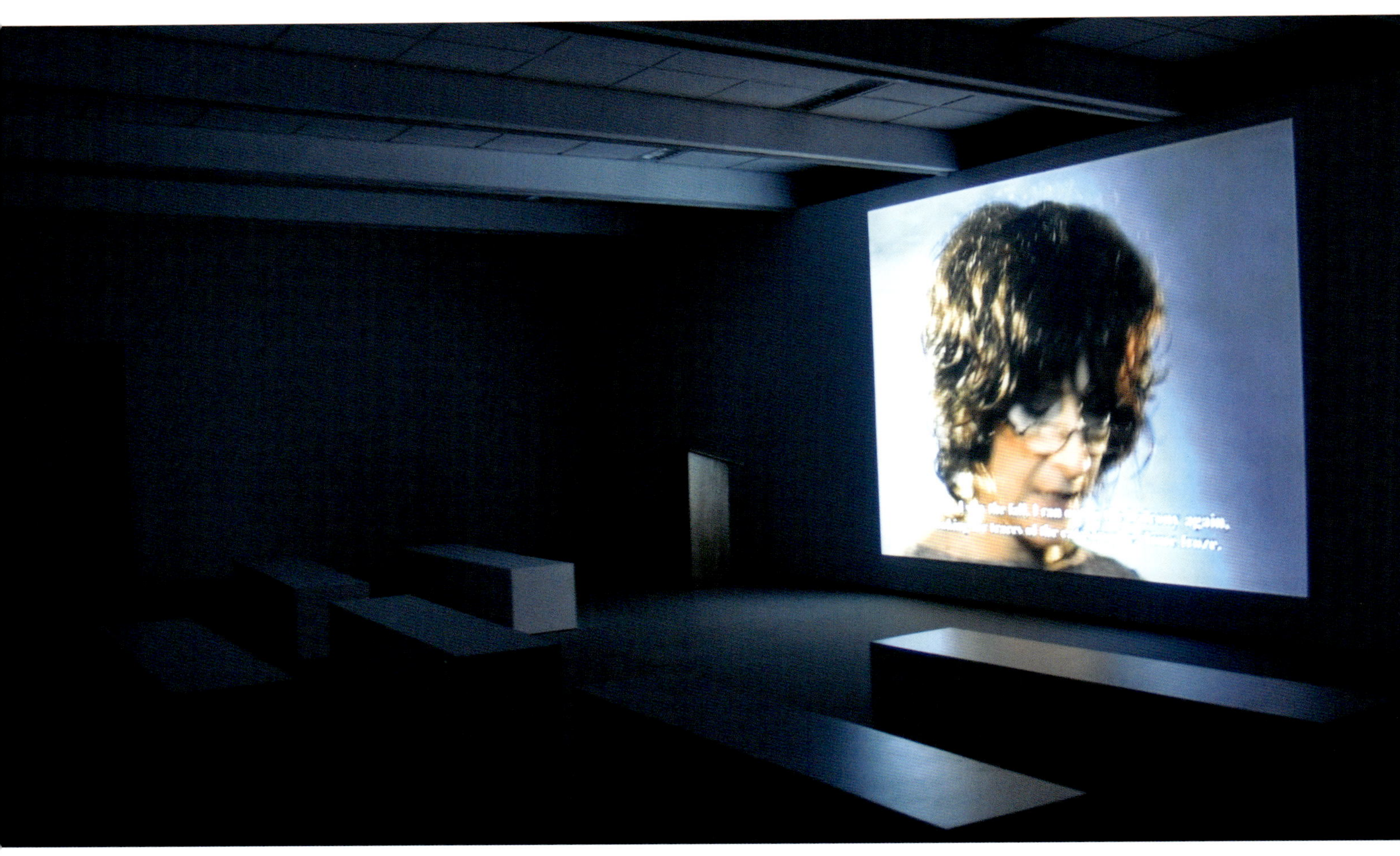

Figure 2: Michal Heiman's lecture/film *Through the Visual: A Tale of Art that Attacks Linking, 1917–2008*, 2008, exhibition view from 'Attacks on Linking', Tel Aviv Museum.

PREFACE

In a paper from 1985, Margaret I. Little, a British psychoanalyst (1901–94) describes her first acquaintance with British psychoanalyst D.W. Winnicott (1896–1971):

> The first scientific meeting of the British Psycho-Analytical Society that I attended was a noisy evening with bombs dropping every few minutes and people ducking as each crash came. In the middle of the discussion someone I later came to know as D. W. stood up and said, 'I should like to point out that there is an air raid going on,' and sat down. No notice was taken, and the meeting went on as before![2]

Was Winnicott's strike on perfection from within a refusal to allow a continuation of dissociation and double standards? I am interested in instances of resistance to simulated perfection, gleaning these voices for my archive. Throughout my work, I have been developing a new discipline that inhabits a field between art and therapy, photography and diagnosis, theory and praxis. This new discipline makes possible novel acts, such as a shared reading and discussion of mute photographs, films and events, jointly conducted by examiners (acting on my behalf) and viewers in public and *muséal* spaces in the Michal Heiman Tests (MHTs). Experiencing photography and trauma as bound together led me to a new understanding of the potential weight of double standards, inevitably manifest in whatever medium or vessel they are imprinted on.

One's first reaction to the surface of a photograph may be of intense attraction or repulsion, akin to love at first sight, sexual attraction or recognition of incestuous affinities; a site imbued with libidinal exchange and consisting of primal reactions and responses. It is an encounter that is often dangerous, inescapable and immediate – and therefore demands close attention and responsibility. I look for attacks on links, inseparable connections, voices and non-voices in 'spaces without witnesses' – sensitive, difficult spaces from which the (supposedly common) 'third' is taken as testimony into the public sphere, almost always by the same participant: the one who

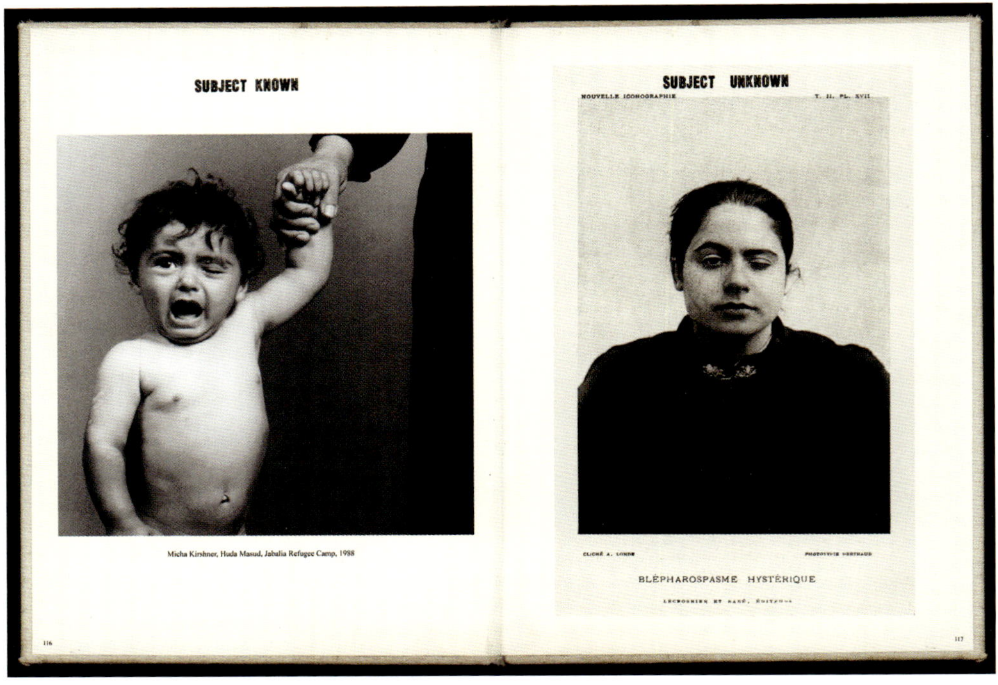

Figure 3: Michal Heiman, *Do-mino No. 10 (Micha Kirshner, Huda Masud, Jabalia Refugee Camp, 1988/ Albert Londe, The Hysterical Wink, 1889)*, 2008.

Opposite page: Figure 4: Michal Heiman, *Archive (detail)*, 2006, exhibition view, Petach Tikva Museum of Art (photography: Oded Löbl).

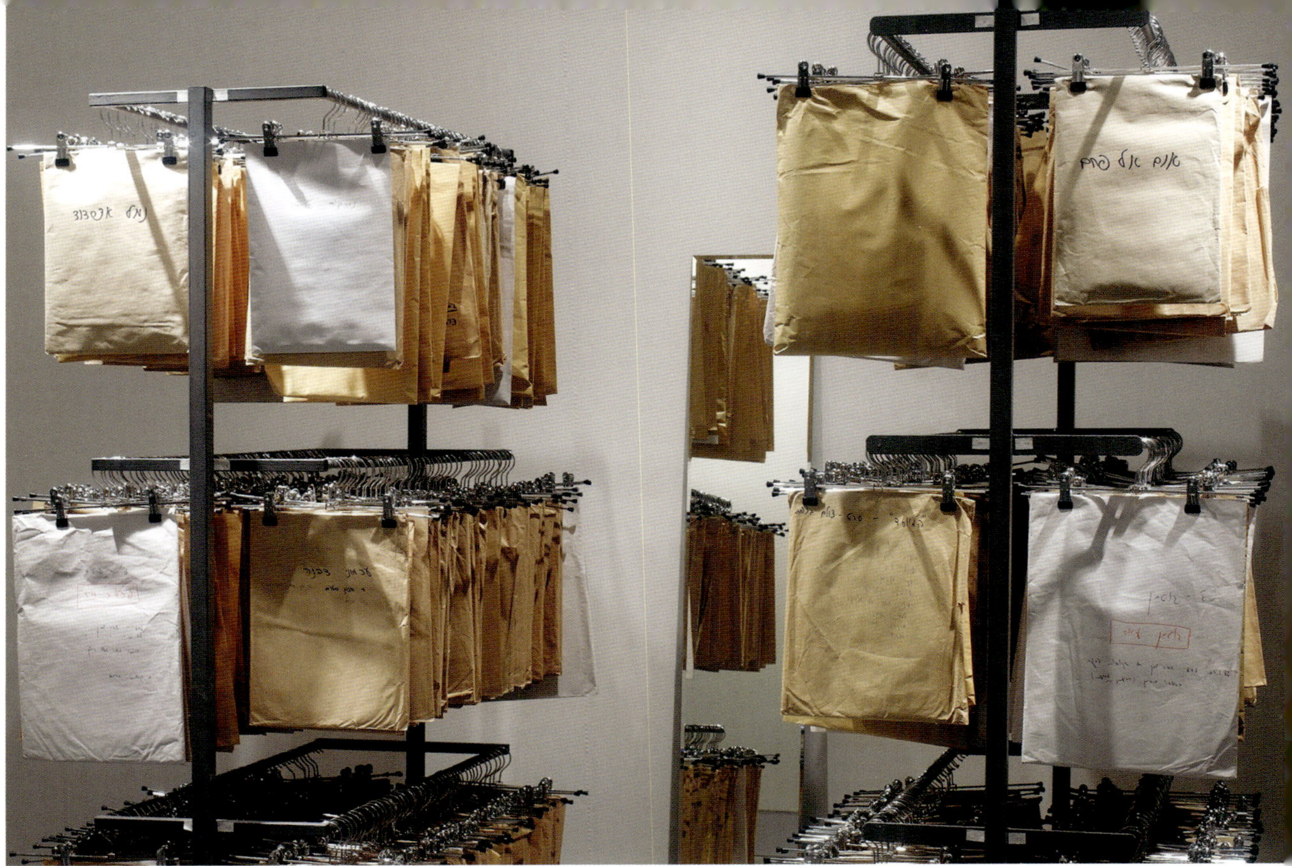

has the tools and ability to express himself, who has the capacity to create for himself a space in which to voice or show his findings.

By juxtaposing three situations – the psychoanalytic, the diagnostic and the *muséal* –while activating the structures of different therapeutic situations in a museum through the mode of the MHTs, polarized notions and inseparable connections are made visible. Nevertheless, both the apparatus of the museum and that of psychology, identified with perfection, order and hierarchical relations they seek to preserve, are disrupted.

Pointing to their fluidity, both the therapeutic (psychoanalytic and diagnostic) setting and the *muséal* setting are divested of their characteristic power relations, enabling the emergence of new relationships, narratives, occurrences, voices, images, biographies and questions of authorship. This also makes possible a regeneration of emotions, likes/dislikes, wounds and traumas, transference and countertransference, and questions that had been trapped in restricted spaces and confined moments.

A PERFECT STRIKE: MICHAL HEIMAN TESTS (MHTS)

In a museum exhibition, the image – any image – puts its viewers to the test, a test of their aesthetic and ethical judgment. Following my encounter with the Thematic Apperception Test (TAT) in 1985, I started considering the diagnostic situation and the enactment in space of the psychoanalytic practice, as well as its preoccupation with gaps, loss and destruction, and its complex relation to the visual which is open to infinite meanings. I began exploring the TAT box's origin and design. The TAT is a visually-based diagnostic tool developed in the 1930s by Dr. Henry A. Murray, together with Christiana Morgan and the staff of the Harvard University Psychological Clinic, whose aim is to reveal the dominant drives, emotions and conflicts of the subject's personality. The TAT cards include evocative illustrations and photographs taken from magazines and other sources, some of which were then redrawn by Christiana Morgan herself, possibly for the purpose of creating a uniform aesthetic style and avoiding copyright issues. Christiana Morgan (1897–1967), co-author of the TAT, was a lay psychoanalyst, artist and writer. Early versions of the TAT listed Morgan as the first author, but her name was dropped from later versions.

In 1994, I presented the exhibition 'Michal Heiman Test: Endopsychic Press' at the University of Melbourne Museum of Art, Australia. The installation deconstructed the TAT manual, undermining its authority and instructive role by excerpting test manual passages, giving them spatial form, and juxtaposing them with my own work.

Since 1997, I have been developing a series of test boxes and enactments, through which I continue to trace and critique the ways images – drawings, photographs, paintings, questionnaire forms, diagrams and so forth – have been used and appropriated throughout the history of psychology. I have called attention to visual materials that have not been considered in aesthetic terms previously: neither produced nor regarded as art, these materials were hidden away under designations such as 'case studies', 'therapeutic tools', 'diagnostic tools', 'scientific evidence', as well as practices of journalistic investigation and reportage, or curatorial practices. I have turned these materials into my analysand, performing various acts with them and thereby raising questions about responsibility, accountability and abandonment. These are all issues that, I argue, are inherent in photography and in both the apparatus of the museum and that of psychology.

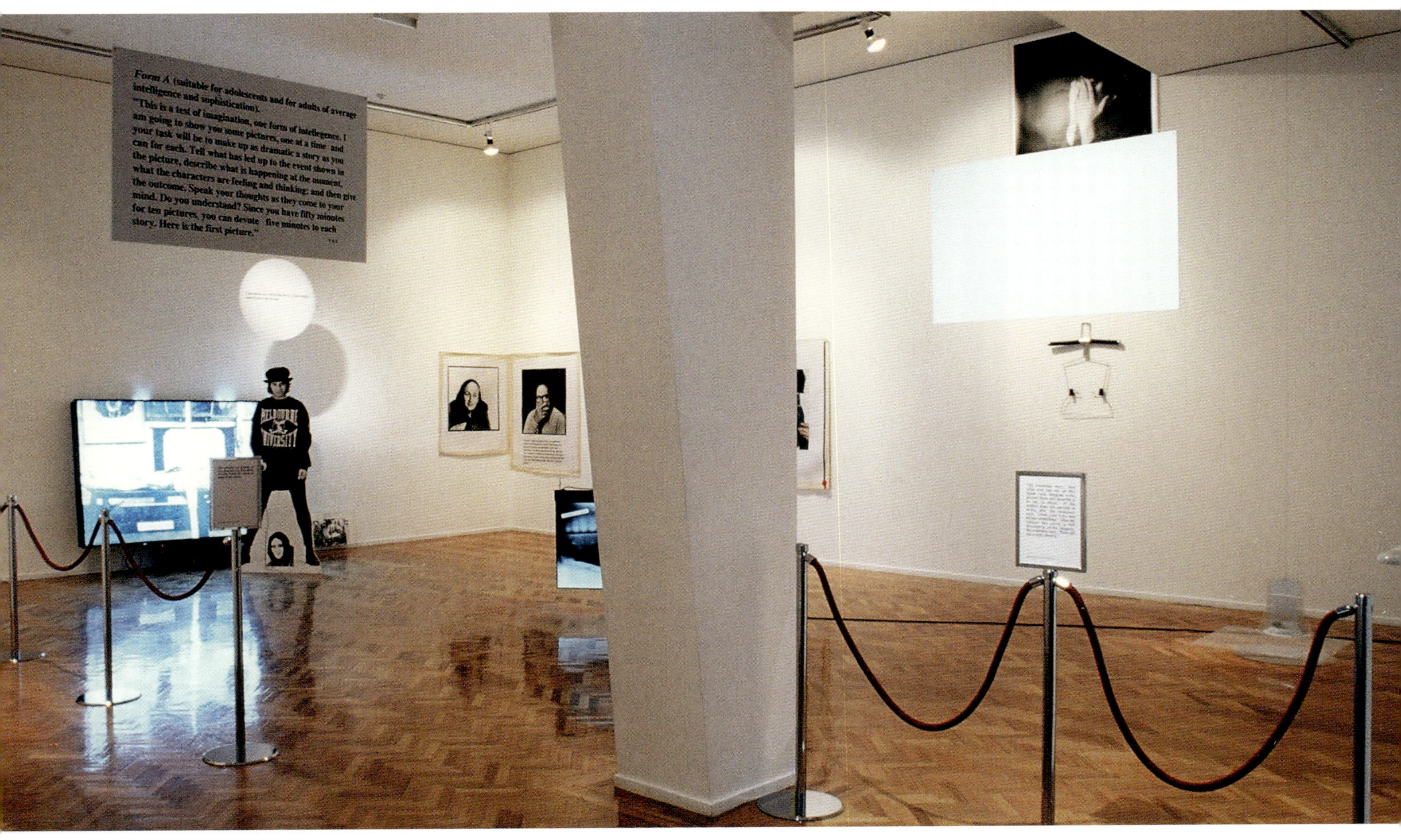

Figure 5: 'Michal Heiman Test: Endopsychic Press', 1994, exhibition view, University of Melbourne Museum of Art, Australia.

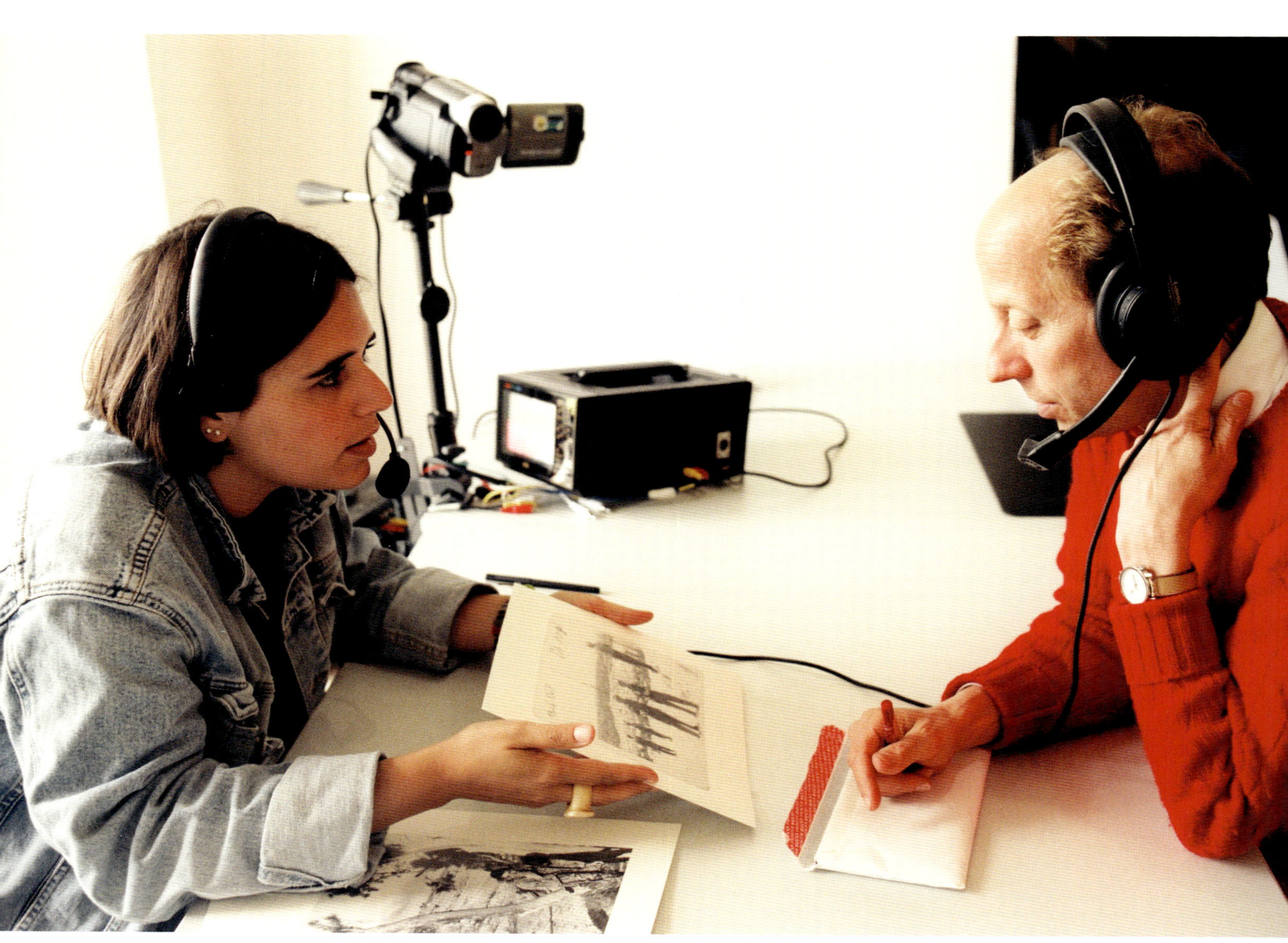

Figure 6: *Michal Heiman Test (MHT) No. 1* enactment, 1997, 'Documenta X', Kassel, Germany (photography: Miki Kratsman).

I have created the conditions for art viewers to act in venues such as museums, galleries or the theatre as they would in a diagnostic or psychoanalytic situation, examining the power structures set in motion in these venues by means of the MHTs. Thus the Michal Heiman Tests, based on methods of psychological diagnoses, on therapeutic settings and on models of observation in both diagnostic and *muséal* settings, problematize the relationship between image and language, as well as the conventions of the *muséal* order. The tests offer a new approach to reading images: a shared reading of photographs and events, conducted jointly by viewer and examiner. Both are consciously participate in acting out the situation, and are aware that this is a simulation of the test; as in any exhibitory setting, the suspension of disbelief is tenuous. Together, they discuss and analyse images while considering the power structures embedded in the photographs and implicit in their production process. By abandoning the diagnostic postulate, I call attention to the singular encounter that this test situation brings about. Channelled through the visual and mediated through speech, the encounter I summon straddles the line between the aesthetic and the diagnostic situation, also shedding light on the potential sense of abandonment and trauma that is inherent in the relationship between artists and viewers. Both the *muséal*, psychoanalytic and diagnostic settings, I suggest, are based on a unique encounter in which responsibility remains undefined.

The MHTs are devices, objects, proposals, events and an opportunity to re-examine the exchanges between people by means of images and narratives, and the ways in which they coalesce. At the same time, they call attention to problematic aspects of diagnostic tests. Kept hidden from the general public and made available only to professionals, the tests are designed to be administered in private and meant to map the psyches of subjects. Thus, they are dangerous tools in the hands of governments, militaries, medical and educational institutions, police forces, courts, universities, psychologists and others.

The first MHT blue box and procedure was created in 1997, for 'Documenta X' in Kassel, Germany. It was developed along the lines of the TAT, replacing it's visual materials and manual with my own materials – including traumatic images of Israeli wars and military occupation, as well as personal biography. *MHT No. 1* is enacted in a museum or a gallery space, at a 'testing station' consisting of an L-shaped table at which the subject and examiner sit the test box and questionnaires, headphones and

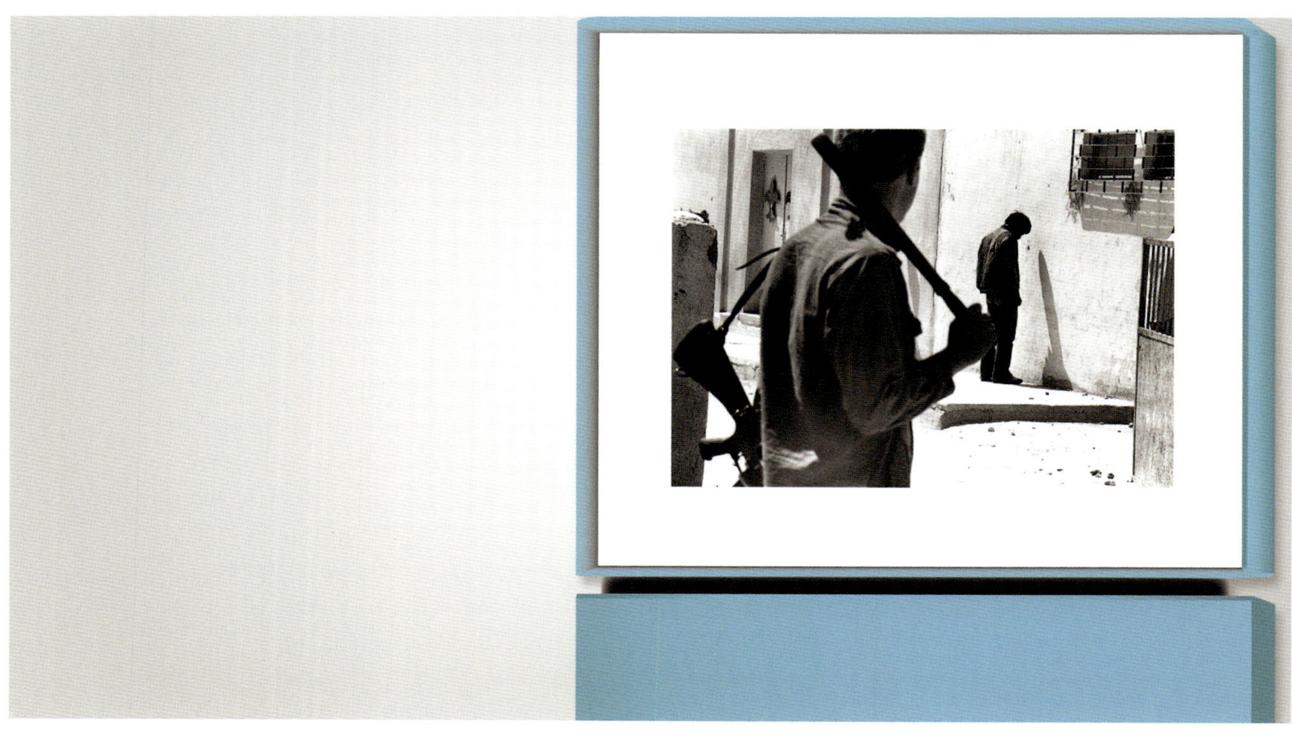

Figure 7: Plate No. 9 in the *Michal Heiman Test (MHT) No. 1: Kalandia refugee camp*, 1985 (photography: Anat Saragusti).

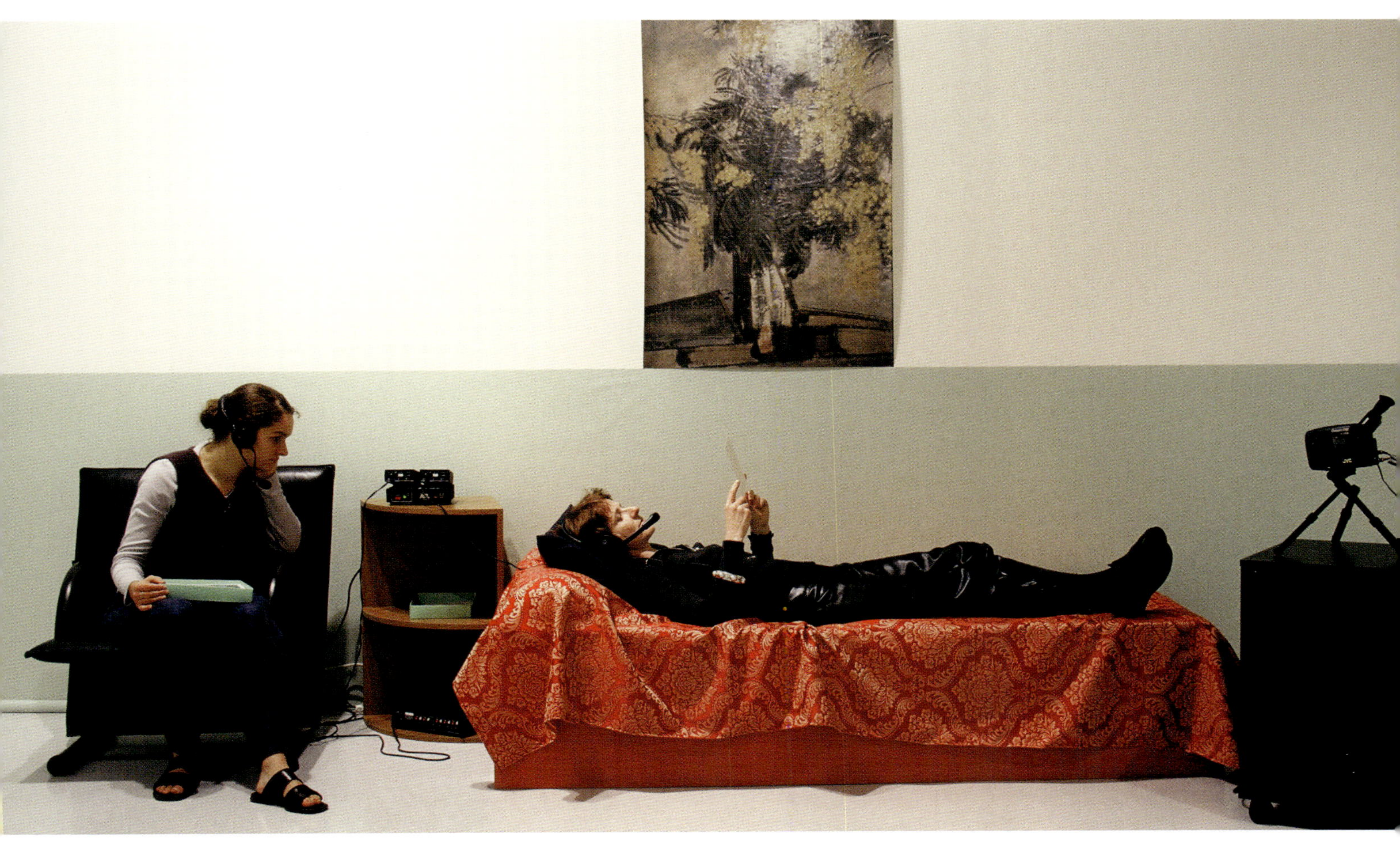

Figure 8: *Michal Heiman Test (MHT) No. 2: My Mother-in-Law – Test for Women* enactment, 1998, Quimper, France.

microphones, and a video camera.

The *Michal Heiman Test (MHT) No. 2: My Mother-in-Law – Test for Women* was administered for the first time at Le Quartier Center for Contemporary Art in Quimper, France, in 1998. The test is intended for women only. The test comprises a green box that includes the test and procedures for enactment and, like the *MHT No. 1*, was conceived along the lines of the TAT. The *MHT No. 2* contains 72 plates, consisting of black-and-white and colour photographs of women and one blank plate. Although the procedures of the *MHT No. 2* draw on those of the *MHT No. 1*, the test introduces new elements and a new setting for a joint reading of photographs. The test takes place while the subject reclines on a couch, with the examiner out of view, as in Freud's traditional prescription for psychoanalysis.

The *Michal Heiman Test (MHT) No. 3: What's on Your Mind?* was presented in a theatre rather than a museum, and accordingly sought to challenge and subvert conventions of viewership specific to the theatrical setting. The third Michal Heiman Test was presented during the 'Acre Fringe Theatre Festival' in 2004, and was based on the interpretation of short videos. The test procedure requested that the six volunteers, along with a mediator, attempt to reach a unanimous description of a film they viewed, while the audience observed this attempt, themselves partaking in the discussion generated, reminiscent of 'fish bowl' observation models used in medical training.

My latest test, *(MHT) No. 4*, offering a new diagnostic device and method called *The Heiman Test – Experimental Diagnostics of Affinities*, is based on the Szondi Test, a visually-based diagnostic tool developed by the Jewish Hungarian psychiatrist Léopold (Lipot) Szondi, first published in 1947. The Szondi Test operates essentially through affinity-directed choice-reactions, its stimuli consisting of 48 cut-out photographs of mental patients and criminals divided into six sets. Each set contains eight pictures of conditions defined as mental disorders by the psychiatric community at the time. Szondi's test procedures, most notably its demand of the subjects to declare attraction or repulsion (like/dislike) towards cut-out portraits of individuals defined as mentally disturbed, led me to search deeper into questions of traumatic encounters, transference and countertransference, ambivalence and photography's inherent ('genetic') double standards. Despite its unique visual stimuli and enactment, the Szondi Test has all but disappeared, forgotten, from the public sphere. This is an important point of my research and writing for the Shpilman International Prize for Excellence in Photography.

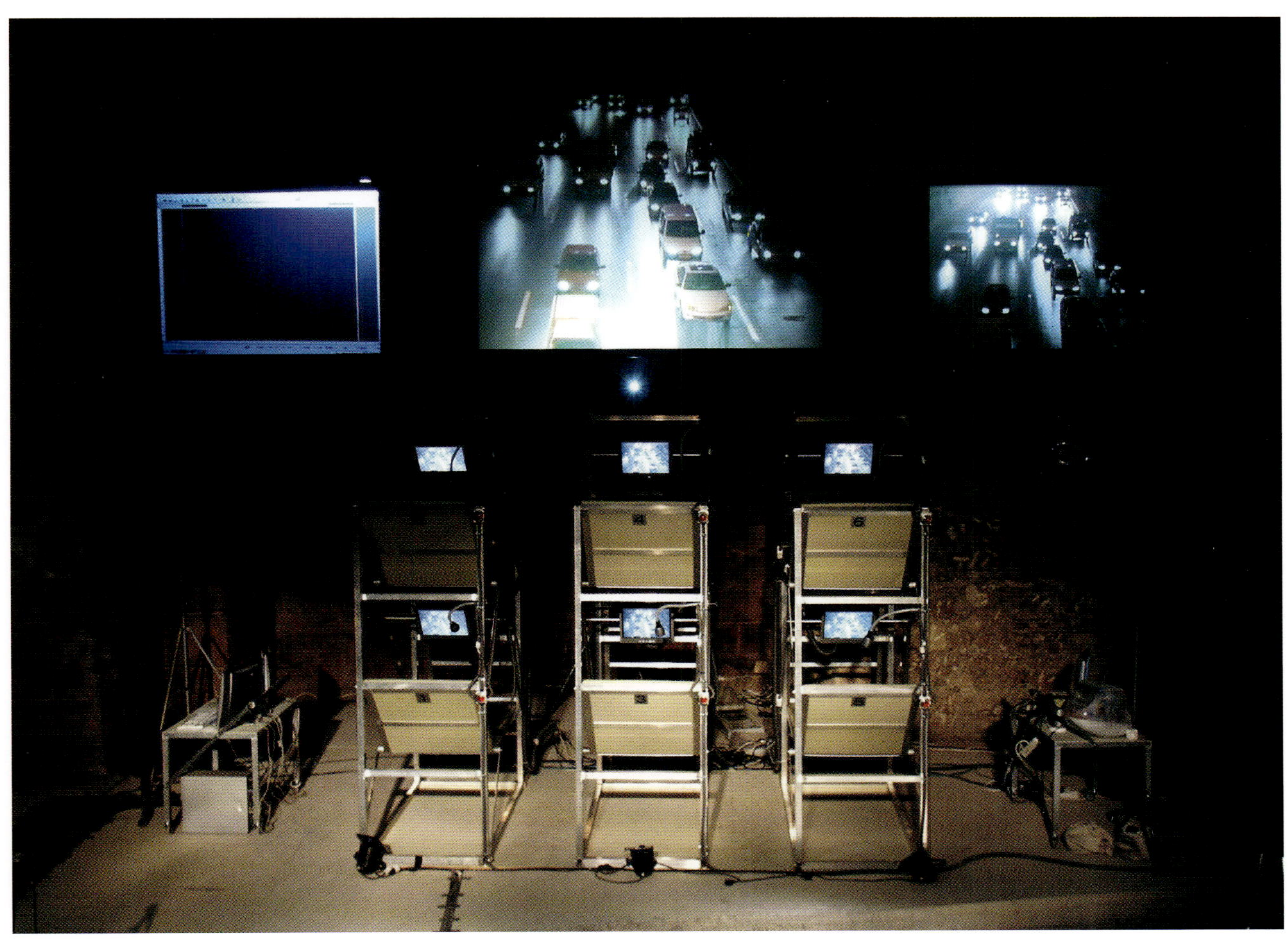

Figure 9: *Michal Heiman Test (MHT) No. 3: What's on Your Mind?* enactment, 2004, 'Israeli Fringe Theatre Festival', Acre (photography: Oren Sagiv).

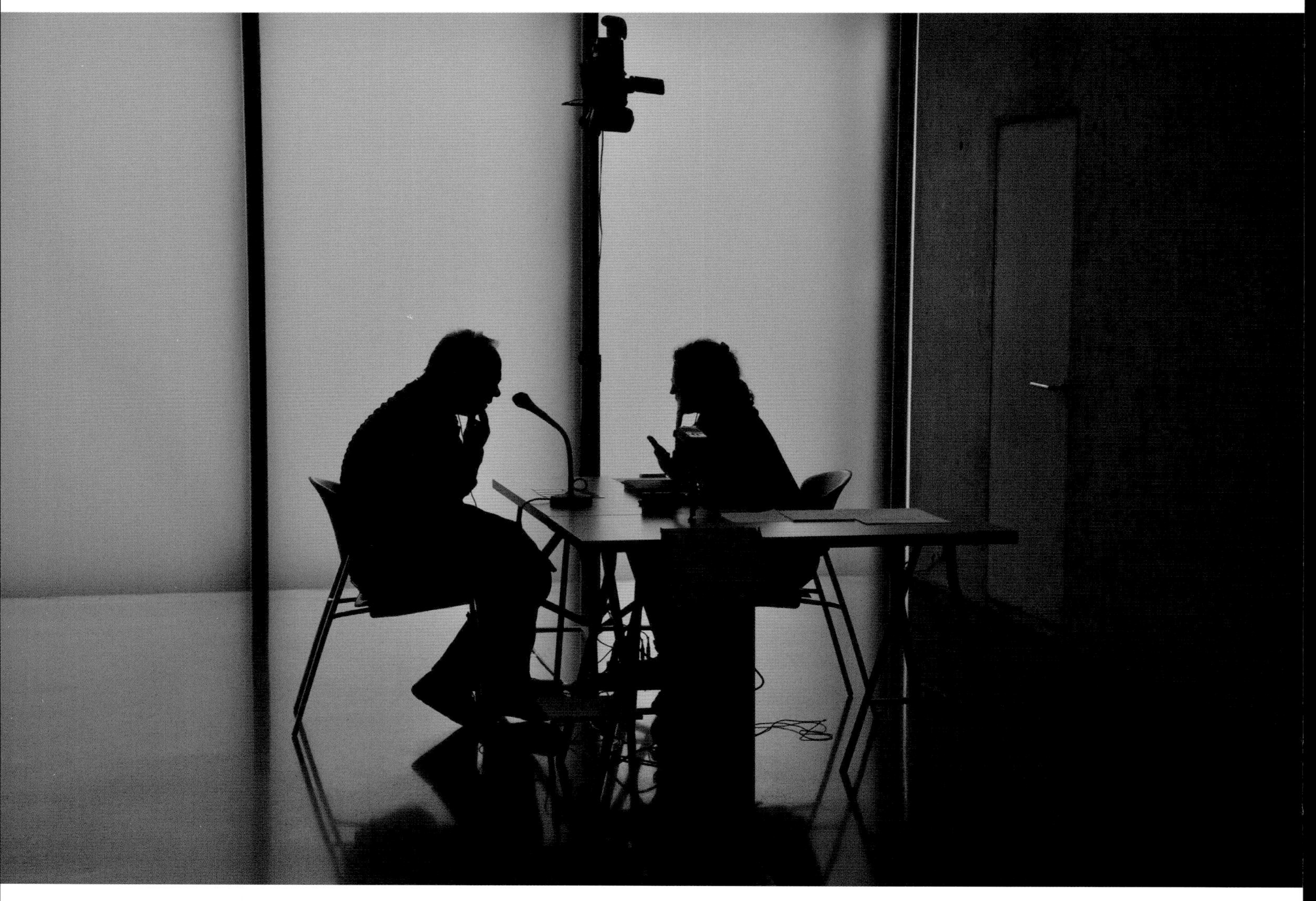

Figure 10: *Michal Heiman Test (MHT) No. 4: Experimental Diagnostics of Affinities*, 2011, Kuntshaus, Bregenz.

The 60 plates of the *Experimental Diagnostics of Affinities* are classified into five categories and ten subcategories according to the nature of the photographic portraits that serve as the test's materials. The classifications refer to different relationships the plates have to my work, my biography, and the connections and affinities to the political, the familial and visual culture. The test was administrated for the first time at the Van Abbemuseum, Eindhoven, Holland, in 2010.

MHT No. 4 replaces language and duration with judgment, immediacy and urgency, denying an extended reading, calling attention instead to the moment of initial encounter with the photograph.

'ATTACKS ON LINKING'

In museums, galleries, curatorial studies, human-rights writings, political science and philosophical texts, attackers are usually unaware of the attacks they perform, creating for themselves a perfect 'third' – an intermediate space which, in this case, hosts both attacker and saviour, who are in fact a single attacker-saviour figure. The attackers, once they are done attacking, return to saving, boastingly presenting that which was saved. In the wake of an attack, rescuers often appear out of the fog like saviours, running with those they saved in their arms. Nobody saw and nobody heard that a moment ago, in a space without witnesses, they themselves were the attackers. It is extremely hard to see in such faint frequencies, it is nearly impossible to be concerned addressees. Saving is a leitmotif in my work: attacking and saving. The saviour-attacker is immortalized in the press, in images of Israeli wars and military occupation; in imagery conveying Zionism's myth-building efforts; in the space of the family photo album; in the museum; in the annals of art history; as well as in the pages of psychoanalysis in dozens of case studies. I am interested in attacks perpetrated by intriguing potential thirds, and trace them in various contexts, including my own works.

The notion of 'attacks on linking', is after the title of a 1959 essay by British psychiatrist and psychoanalyst Wilfred Bion (1897–1979) that deals with the destruction of, and attack on, 'links', such as thought processes, language and emotional development.[3]

Born in India in 1897, Bion was sent to school in England when he was 8 years old. In World War One he served in France as a tank commander, and was awarded the Distinguished Service Order. He was 18 years old when he enlisted in the army. After the war, he studied history and medicine, and became more and more attracted to

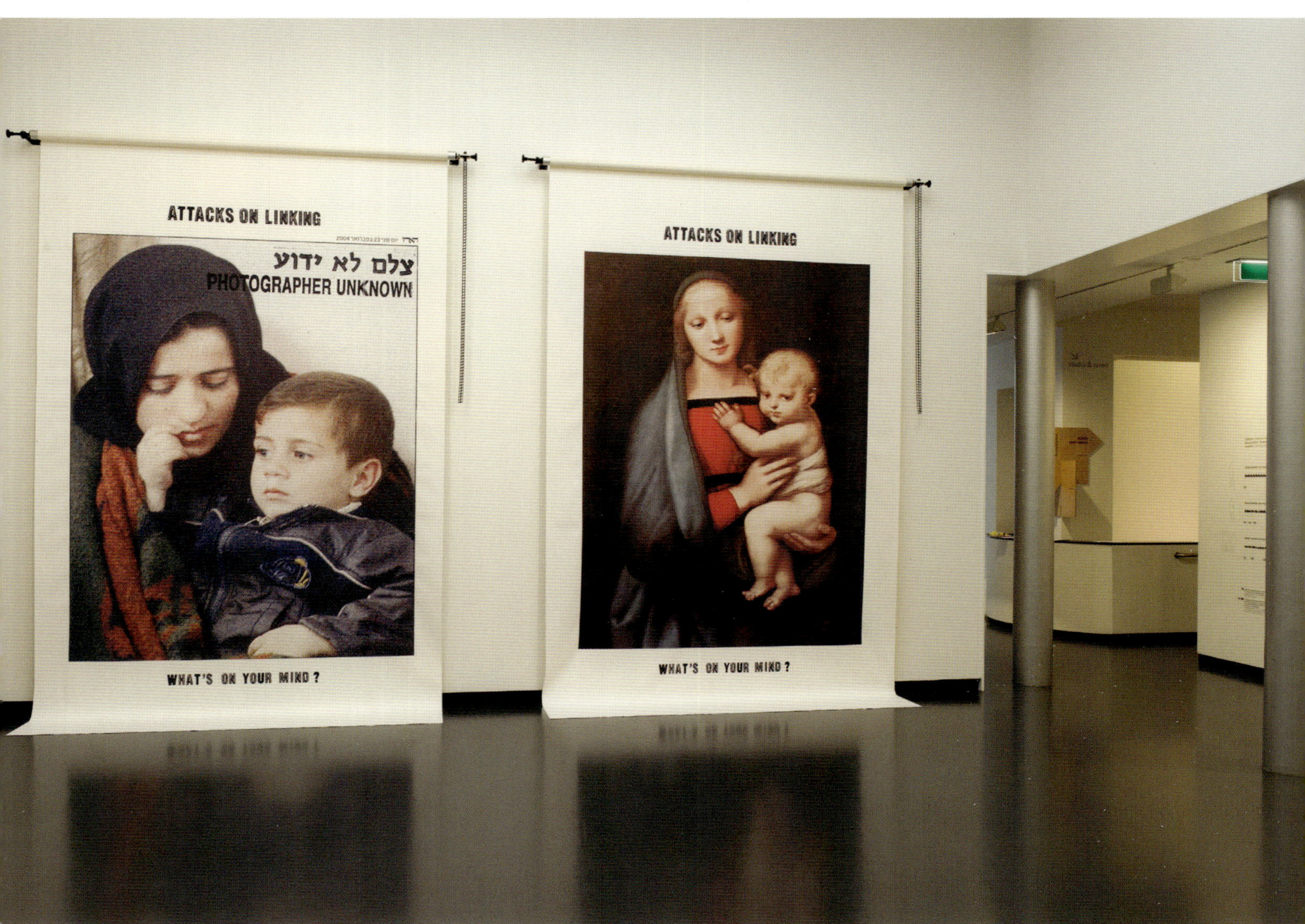

Figure 11: Michal Heiman, *Scrolls*, 2001, exhibition view from 'Attacks on Linking', Van Abbemuseum, (photography: Peter Cox).

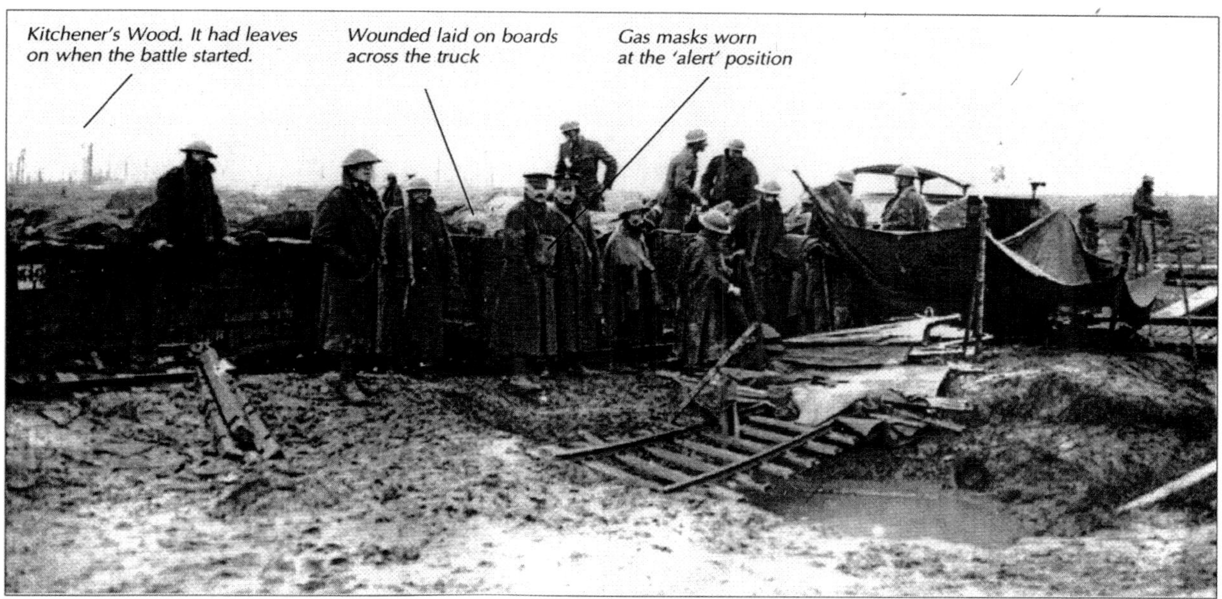

Figure 7

A light railway at Ypres. It brings up shells and takes back wounded. They are put in the hammock and then laid on the train. Note the isolation typical of whole Flandres battle. Note that although it is only about September 20th, men are all wearing heavy coats and that the shell-hole in the foreground is half full of water. All have got their helmets handy or are wearing them, as this is within a mile of the front line and light railways were frequently shelled.

Figure 12: A light railway at Ypres (photograph: Wilfred Bion's *War Memoirs 1917–1919*).

psychoanalysis. He underwent training analysis with John Rickman, and later (from 1945) with Melanie Klein. In 1967, when he wrote his *Second Thoughts*, his war memoir hadn't been published yet. It was only published in 1997, eighteen years after his death, in the book *War Memoirs 1917–1919*, 4 edited by his widow, Francesca Bion. The book comprises the 'reconstructed' war diary and two additional articles written in hindsight about the war and its effect on him. Francesca Bion wrote an introduction, and Bion's daughter added an epilogue. All of these were compounded by Bion's drawings, and by photos he collected during and after the war. Young Bion had experienced the horrible chaos and violence of World War One. During the war, he felt unable to write to his parents, which he found difficult to explain to them when he returned home. Only after studying history in Oxford did he write to them (and especially to his mother) that 'late diary', to which he added drawings and photos. The diary was presented to his parents in three hardcover notebooks.

I arrived at Bion's writings through the aforementioned article by Bennett Simon. I first saw drawings and photographs by Bion in his book *War Memoirs 1917–1919*, several years ago at the Bookworm bookshop in Tel Aviv. I was surprised at how many drawings and photographs were included in the book. The combination of visual elements and descriptions of war in this book were linked in my mind to thoughts and feelings elicited by years of reading Bion. His 'Attacks on Linking' and other articles gained meaning. Reading in the beginning of the book that Bion lost the original diary written during the war, and then wrote a 'late diary' for his mother, ideas and thoughts that he included in the foreword to his book *Second Thoughts* were endowed with meaning; I quote:

> It is usual to think that a report written within an hour or so of the events it is supposed to describe has a special 'built-in' validity and superiority over the account written many months or even years later. I shall suppose simply that they are two different accounts of the same event without any implication that one is superior to the other.

Bion's attempt to invalidate the importance given to the immediate testimony not only reminds me of the loss of his diary and his efforts to reconstruct a new one, but was

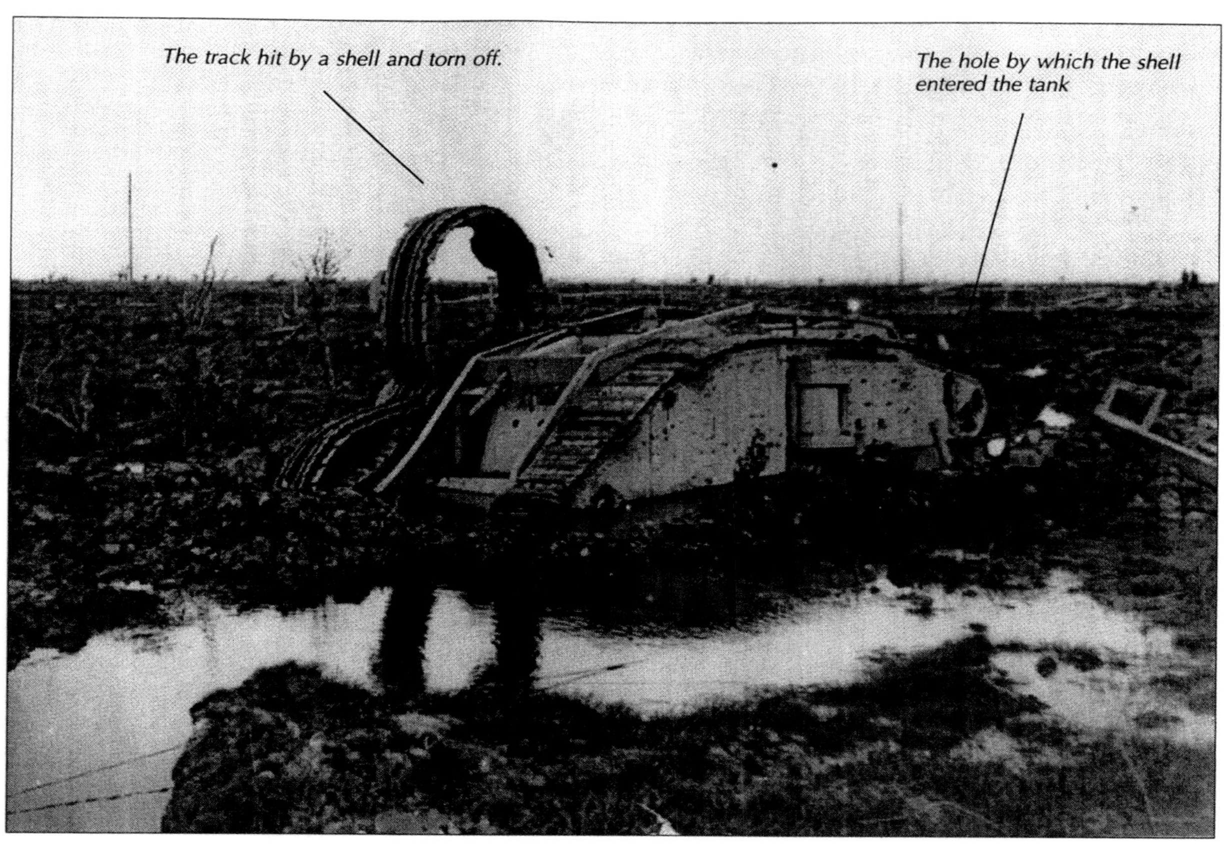

Figure 13: Tank after direct hit (photograph: Wilfred Bion's *War Memoirs 1917–1919*).

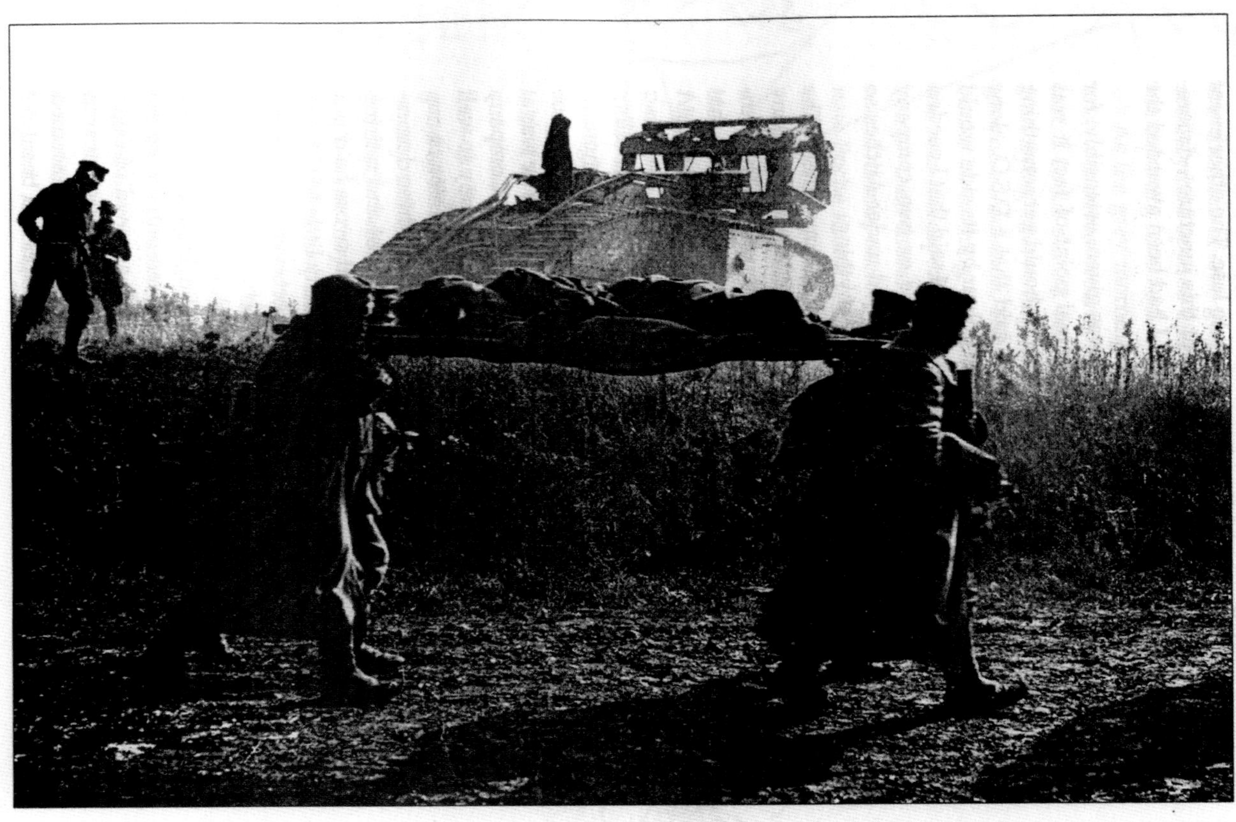

Figure 14: Moving forward for action: 'A photo of the 5th Battalion tanks moving forward in the mist of the morning on Sept. 29th' (photograph: Wilfred Bion's *War Memoirs 1917–1919*).

important to my thoughts on trauma and photographs. In choosing the position of the spectator looking at photographs and drawings accompanied by his descriptions, as well as transparencies he placed on top of photographs, I found myself turning Bion into my analysand, as well as the visual materials he attached to his war notebooks, containing Bion's trauma as part of my visual-psychoanalytic strategy.

It is hard to describe this significantly detailed diary. Bion is powerless, abandoned, bombarded, frightened and violent; he attacks and links, all the while brilliantly depicting his environment, his tank-mates, his impotence. His descriptions are incredibly sensitive to details, to landscapes, to the metal weapons surrounding him, to the sounds of war, to the stillness, the silences. Bion encircles the battle, round and round, remaining far, far away from conceptualizing himself as suffering from post-traumatic stress disorder (or shell shock, as it was called in World War One, since it was associated with the sound of exploding artillery shells). Bion – in his diary and in his entire theoretical work, both early and late – acts in the space of combative thought, the space of shell shock, like one under attack. His drawings to his mother, attached to his *War Memoirs* are delicate, broken lines like fragmented necklaces – drawings full of arrows and compasses, depictions of battles, attacks and war strategies – alongside harsh, sad black-and-white photos taken by Bion or by one of his friends. Often, the drawings originate in the photos. The Grid structure that Bion was to develop in the 1960s as part of his psychoanalytic theory, reverberates his diary drawings: letters, weapon types, names of fellow soldiers, tank details – male tank, female tank, taking great care to specify gender – and links, and a huge number of attacks on links.

DOUBLE STANDARDS: THE PSYCHOLOGY OF THE CAMERA

In 1988, American psychoanalyst Bennett Simon published his paper 'The Imaginary Twins: The Case of Beckett and Bion',[5] a study of the intriguing relationship between two unusual men: the playwright Samuel Beckett and the psychoanalyst Bion. Their paths crossed during the years 1934–35, when Beckett was in treatment with Bion in his Tavistock clinic. There appears to have been no contact between the two men subsequent to the interruption of the analysis, writes Simon, nor did they mention each other in their writings. Simon argues that in regard to certain themes, the works

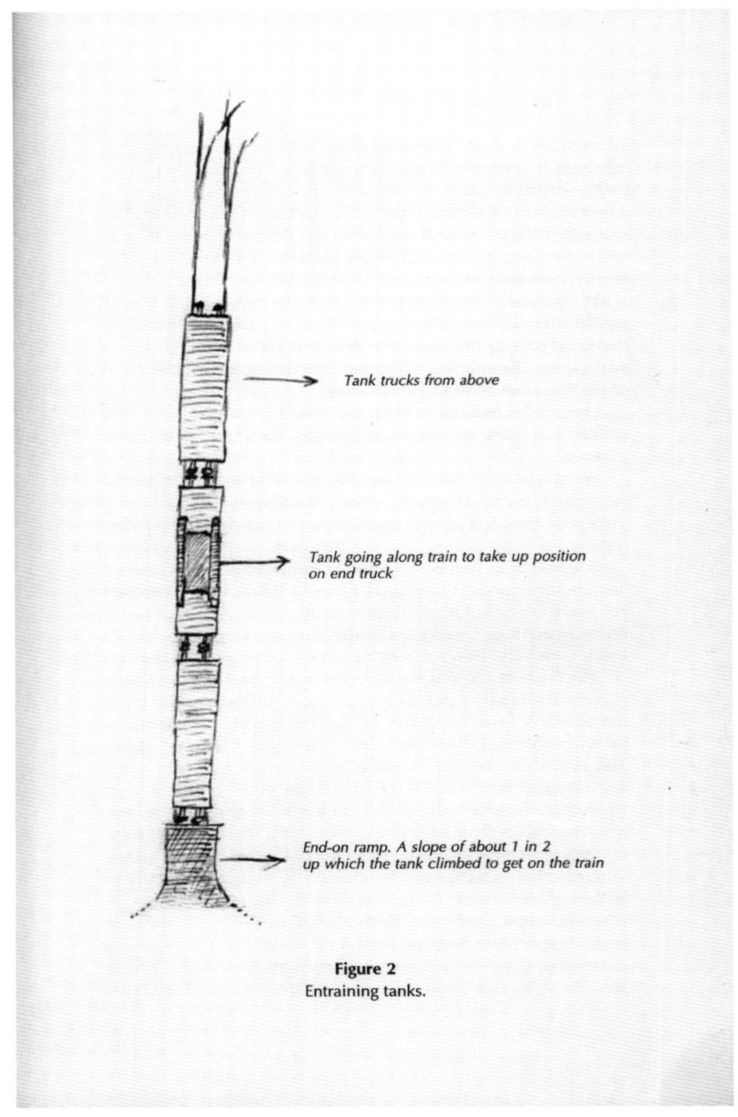

Figure 15: Entraining tanks (drawing: Wilfred Bion's *War Memoirs 1917–1919*).

of Beckett and Bion can be shown to run in parallel courses. Both, he writes, struggle to maintain interpersonal and logical connections in the face of the catastrophic modern breakdown of meaningful connections. Against this backdrop, he hypothesizes that a certain sort of 'imaginary twinning relationship' developed between the two, and that each used that brief actual contact with the other to help sustain his effort at exploring the pain of non-meaning and non-connecting.

Walking onto my fifth-floor balcony one morning, I immediately noticed an act of painting – action painting – taking place between the fourth floor and the fifth-floor roof just opposite, at the front of a neighbouring building. I watched two Arab labourers, dressed in red and green (like the Palestinian flag) tied in a strange, disturbing tangle of ropes, both to each other and to the room on the roof. Another rope was attached to a bucket, and the bucket ascended and descended, was filled and emptied. I walked back indoors, disturbed, and kept watching them through a window in a different part of my apartment, peeping. Years after last reading it, the Simon paper came to my mind. I thought about twinship, about control and catastrophe, and about the red and green that are considered complementary colours. I also watched the unprotected legs of the whitewashing labourer as he stood on an air-conditioning unit, and the other labourer, standing on the roof, leaning forward like a grasshopper, watching the painter at work. I walked stealthily onto the balcony again. Leaving a video camera on a tripod between the railings; I left home, going about my daily business. I will show you a shortened version of what I watched on my video camera screen when I came back home that day.

I would like to screen my film *Attacks on Linking No. 2: The Double, Case Study, B+B Link, 2003–06*, dedicated to Beckett, Bion and catastrophe.

When I came back home I went to the balcony. The labourers were no longer there. All that remained was a white strip of paint, shaped like an inverted U, around the window frame. I had a strange feeling, similar to that which had initially prompted me to leave the camera out there. The video camera, on its tripod, waited for me, lying in wait between the grey metal railings. Wishing to see the images the camera took for me, I rewound the video. When I saw the fall, I ran out to the balcony again, looking for traces of the catastrophe. Time froze.

Tel Aviv, January 2012

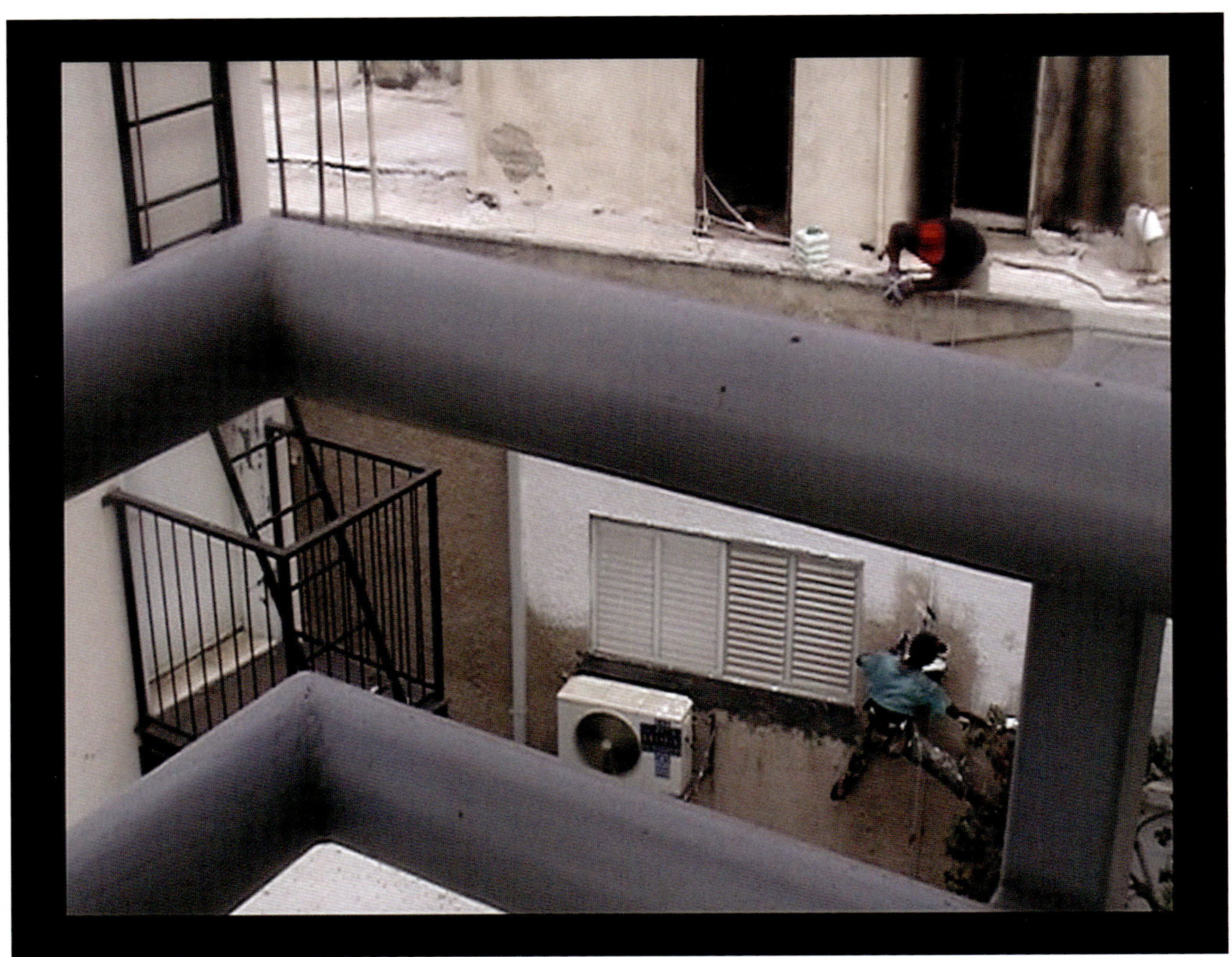

Figure 16: Michal Heiman, *Attacks on Linking No. 2: The Double, Case Study, B+B Link, 2003–06*, video still.

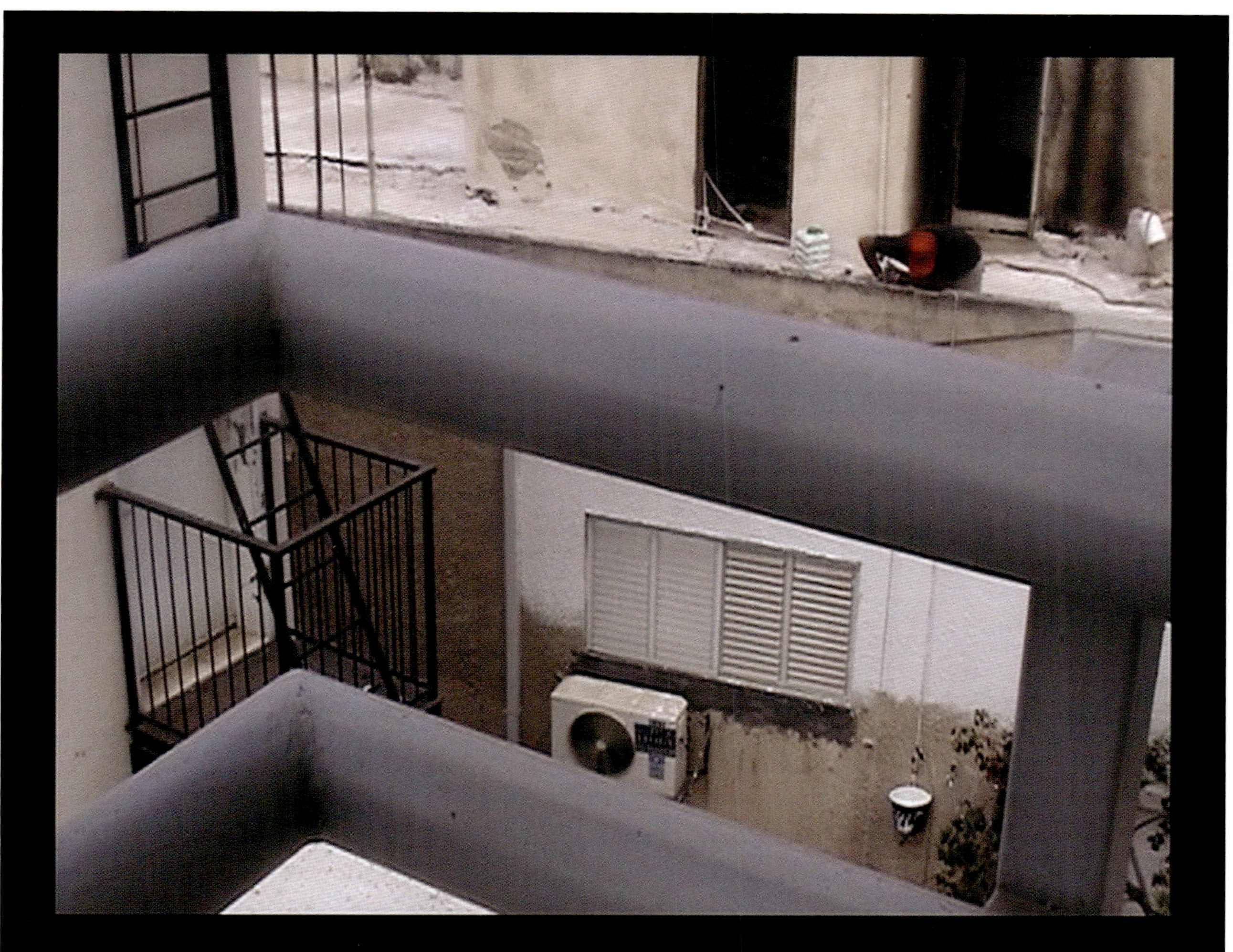

Figure 17: Michal Heiman, *Attacks on Linking No. 2: The Double, Case Study, 2003–06*, video still.

NOTES

1 Cathy Caruth, *Unclaimed Experience: Trauma, Narrative, and History*, Baltimore: John Hopkins University Press, 1996, p. 4.
2 Margaret I. Little, 'Winnicott Working in Areas where Psychotic Anxieties Predominate', *Free Associations*, Vol. 1, Nos. 9–42, 1985.
3 Wilfred Bion, 'Attacks on Linking', in *Second Thoughts*, London: Karnac Books, [1967] 1990.
4 Wilfred Bion, *War Memoirs 1917-1919*, ed. Francesca Bion, London: Karnac Books, 1997.
5 Bennett Simon, 'The Imaginary Twins: The Case of Beckett and Bion', International Review of Psycho-Analysis, No. 15, 1988, pp. 331–52.

JONATHAN WHITEHALL & MICHAL HEIMAN

DISCUSSION, CHAIRED BY **LIAM DEVLIN**

Liam Devlin: I want to thank you both for two really fantastic presentations. The struggle for perfection in an imperfect world, provoking two very different responses: desire and attack.

Michal Heiman: Attack is also desire.

LD: Michal, it was interesting that you ended on Beckett, that you dedicated your paper to Beckett. Your search between memory and desire reminded me of Beckett's *Krapp's Last Tape*, on a superficial level, let's say, although not quite so depressing. There is something that you said that I want to quote that is 'Beckett-esque' in that sense. You say that in the spaces between voice and images, a certain lack occurred which carried a sense that neither image nor voice was enough to carrying the full meaning of the events depicted. This lack, or failure, seemed to suggest a desire. The relationship between a sense of failure and desire brings me to your work Jonathan. Can we say that with your film, you're beginning from failure? Considering, as you said yourself, it is an unfinished or imperfect piece of work. I want to ask how conscious were you of the choice of imagery you used in relation to your notion of a perfect desire and a perfect beauty?

Jonathan Whitehall: As I say, I don't really see that as a piece of work, it's more of a document that I found for this symposium; I've never seen it projected before, so it was a bit shocking to see it. The footage of the interiors of the house was shot the day the contents of the house were being packed away. I thought, 'I've got to get as much footage as I can on this really dark day with this very bad old camera,' but then later I looked at it and thought, 'I can to do something with this.' I wanted to make something but was never really happy with it. I mean the footage was too bad, I couldn't actually resolve it into a finished piece. It was only going back to it later that I realized that what this filming was really about was desire, which at the time, I perhaps, could not acknowledge.

LD: The choice of Greek urns was interesting because they refer to the classical origins of our notion of beauty. They put me in mind of the Platonic idea of perfect forms.

JW: Yes, and that was something else I noticed when I watched it back last autumn.

Given that I knew at that point I was going to discuss perfection, I noticed there were allusions to perfection and imperfection; at the beginning the vases are broken, incomplete, later you see ones that are whole, complete. So in response to your original question in terms of intention, how much were ideas of desire and beauty a guiding force in my choice of imagery, really that only happened when I was trying to edit something from it. At the stage when I shot it, I was just getting footage.

LD: So it was more of a personal connection?

JW: Yes, yes.

LD: That's interesting. Plato writes about Socrates talking about the definition of love, romantic love known as Eros. He argues that if we can detach Eros from the desire to physically possess, it can help us contemplate beauty as an ideal, a notion of perfect beauty. But is that what you think you were doing?

JW: I'm not sure desire's necessarily about beauty. I mean, I think we use beauty to talk about desire. But I'm not actually sure desire is really about beauty.

LD: Is it about the trauma of loss?

JW: I think it is, yes. I actually think it is. It's more about the sense of lack or separation that provokes a desire to overcome that. Which is, therefore, of course never actually overcome in a way. I think perhaps going back to the Imaginary and the Lacanian sense of identification at that stage where there's a relationship which is symbiotic. I think it comes back to that.

LD: It's a process as opposed to destination.

JW: Yes.

LD: The notion of trauma brings me to Michal. Quite similarly, actually, in terms of the distrust of language, you talk about the pain of non-meaning. You very much specifically set your practice up within a therapeutic and diagnostic environment to establish meaning. You set up situations both aesthetic and diagnostic, and I want to come back to that distinction. The question is, as mediated through images specifically, are you attempting to build a consensus or the opposite?

MH: What do you mean by building a consensus?

LD: Are you attempting to build an agreed, established meaning to a particular picture?

MH: No, I don't think so. I think my work is a lot about being between knowing and not knowing. So you can never build a real grid if you're always there. And I think I'm coming from a place where knowing and non-knowing exist all the time, living in an environment of contested society. And I think a part of my work is to do with the questions that are thrown out there by this: through aesthetics you can maybe try and enter the place of trauma. There are lots of questions: Do you want to come to the place of trauma beforehand? Do you want to come at the moment of trauma? Are you going to come after the trauma? It's changing history; a challenge to history. There are lots of ways that it might work, but I think that I mainly wanted to try and do it with a shared reading. And this I take from my diagnosis and from psychoanalysis. First, it is important to break the silence at museums. People talking. I think about a thousand people came to my work in the museum. I didn't know if any would come, or how many, yet a thousand people took part, and each spoke for about one hour. Some people came again and this was the process: talking about images of war, about images of occupation. And now, when you look at it, thirteen years later, it's very meaningful and I think this is part of what I want.

LD: In that diagnostic frame, you mention that it's dangerous in the hands of governments when it gets appropriated. It becomes a tool of oppression.

MH: Yes, and I want to say it's the same between the viewer and the artist as well. The diagnostic situation is very strange. First I have to say that, in Israel, they do a lot of diagnostic tests if someone does not want to go to the army. So I encountered the test personally, twice. And what I found out is something fascinating: someone is showing me images and we are talking together about images, images which informed my work thirty years later – work about how fascinating it is to sit with someone else and discuss images. At the time I looked at the psychologist and I thought to myself, what he is doing with this image? But I also felt there was no one responsible there showing me the images, although some of them were very disturbing. After the army's test, the psychiatrist left; he left with the results and I was left without the results, only the experience, which no one knew about, or was responsible for, so I took it to the museums and galleries.

LD: I have a thought in relation to the construction of the framework you created for the people to sit in: there is a certain sort of authority that you have to step into within that diagnostic situation that can be oppressive, which I think is replicated in your structure, in that there's a cage that you have to get into.

MH: I built the big construction there with six beds for gallery visitors to lie in. There was an operator there playing videos to each person who had their own screen. There was a stenographer recording comments. There were 30 sessions with 100 people. They all saw a short movie that they were later asked to comment on. I asked a mediator to operate between them to try to reach an agreement, for everyone to agree on what they saw. And there is a documentation of thirteen failures.

LD: Which perhaps reaffirms your point Jonathan, about the impossibility of reaching some sort of conclusion. Do you see a therapeutic process in what you did? What you encountered?

JW: Ooh. Well no, I think it is more like Leslie said, 'I'm displaying my symptoms'… so perhaps in that sense… It's not therapeutic… I don't see the work as therapeutic when I'm making it, but perhaps that can happen later. I think rather, it is symptomatic.

LD: Personally, I'm attracted to the idea that loss and vulnerability is something that we all share.

JW: Yes – going back to the psychoanalytical thing – it's trauma, and Freud sees trauma as inherent to everyone. It's not like the trauma is external. It happens, it's part of human development. Freud distinguishes different levels or ideas of trauma, but it's systemic, in a way. It is part of every subject's becoming in a sense.

LD: Michal, let's go back to your image series, 'Photographer Unknown', that consists of news images that you collect documenting traumatic events. I was really struck by your intervention, stamping the pictures, 'photographer unknown'. There are two different means to play off that use of text. There's the idea that we think about these images as perfect windows onto the world, and we don't have to consider them as being mediated necessarily. The photographer is unknown, as we don't need to know. On the other hand, the definition of trauma is that you cannot understand it, it's beyond comprehension, it's beyond mediation. And therefore, even as the photographer's documenting the event, they cannot actually understand or see what is happening, the photographer is unknowing. But you do something else to it: you cut into the shadows. I wasn't sure what was happening. Can you talk about that?

MH: It's because it's a traumatic space in Israel, which belongs to the unthinkable. I take from Winnicott again, from the unthinkable space. And they're hiding there and they're waiting. Now when there is a photograph for which I don't know the name of the photographer – and family albums are spaces where no one thinks they should have their name – then they become mine. And I give the unknown photographer a credit. I sign the photograph 'photographer unknown' and then I'm able to talk about it. This photograph was published in an Israeli newspaper, and usually in an Israeli newspaper they're signed AP or Reuters. Most of the photographs of occupation or war are missing the name of the photographer. I'm also collecting the reasons why. Is it because the army took them? Is it because the Palestinians didn't want anyone to know that they were there? Or is it an amateur who didn't think he's entitled to have his name published? And, of course, the word unknown is important for me.

Catherine Grant: I have a question for Jonathan. I really enjoyed your paper and thinking about perfection in relation to memory and history, and I think this probably a Proustian or Barthezian comment or question. I was wondering whether you thought that, in terms of emotion, perfection is very rare in the present. You don't experience emotions as perfect. They can be, intense, painful, exciting, but it's only in retrospect that they can be perfect and whether that's something that is important to consider when looking at this old footage, and somehow it takes on a different quality, a wholeness with a passage of time.

JW: Yes, I think it's absolutely right. I think you don't experience anything as perfect when it happens. It's only when you look back and then perhaps you might – it's like happiness, almost. Contentment maybe, but happiness sort of happens in retrospect. I think perfection, of course, is the same. I think the notion of desire can be uncomfortable – it's predicating a lack, the idea of perfecting that is quite perverse in a way. And yet I think, perhaps, we do that very well in our lives. Certainly for this footage when I looked back at it, it's not been made whole and it's not been perfected in any way, but I felt that it did seem to have a resonance now that at the time of making, it just didn't have for me.

THE PERFECT STUDENT

ORIANA FOX

Oriana Fox cried her way through her MA in Fine Art. She didn't really know what she was getting herself into when she decided to move to New Cross and attend Goldsmiths. Her undergraduate experience had been full of encouragement; she was a straight-A student. The feedback she got on her paintings was that more was more, so she was prolific. But despite the fact that a portfolio of paintings earned her acceptance at Goldsmiths, she was quickly discouraged from doing any more of it and moved on to making sculpture, eager, as she had always been, to please.

Oriana had been suffering from low self-esteem since puberty. Throughout her adolescence and early adulthood, she attempted to overcompensate for her diminished sense of self-worth by overachieving in her artistic and academic pursuits. Despite her successes in these areas, she had always been plagued by self-doubt. She felt like an impostor whenever her accomplishments were lauded, and therefore she gleaned little satisfaction from her gifts.

Perhaps ironically, the subject that Oriana was passionate to address was female desire – ironic because her desire to please others seemed to regularly eclipse all other longings she might have had, so much so that most of the time she didn't know what *she* wanted at all.[1] Be that as it may, she tried a number of ways to challenge the active male/passive female binary that reading Laura Mulvey essays had taught her to recognize and despise.[2] She made womb-like, breast-like forms out of lush fabrics, wanting to envelope the viewer in an oceanic state where self and other would be merged.[3] However, when her tutors walked into her studio and encountered these works, they immediately compared them to a certain kind of '70s feminist art. Much to Oriana's dismay, they also made it clear that they disliked them. They explained, not only were these sculptures derivative, but they were also derivative of work that was bad.[4]

Oriana didn't know what to do. She felt misunderstood and depressed. So she did what many people do in those circumstances – she read a self-help book. John-Roger and Peter McWilliams, authors of *Do It! The Guide to Living Your Dreams*, suggested Oriana consult what they called her 'Master Teacher'. Your 'Master Teacher' is 'your ideal teacher, the being with whom you are the perfect student.'[5] Wanting very much to be the perfect student and escape the reality of her 'unsatisfactory' marks at Goldsmiths, she tried very hard to visualize who this person might be. That's when she had what she called a 'eureka moment'. She realized her Master Teacher was probably half-Judy Chicago, half-Carrie Bradshaw and boom! She knew what she had to make…

For her very first foray into video art, Oriana decided to embody her ideal giver of guidance: a woman with the relationship problems of today and the feminist principles of the 1970s. The protagonist of that first film, *Our Bodies, Ourselves* (2003) is sewing a Judy Chicago-esque vaginal quilt while bemoaning the fact that her boyfriend hasn't called. As Carrie's voice-over explains, '[She] needed to keep [her] mind from obsessing and [her] hands from dialling his number.' The soundtrack is lifted from *Sex and the City*, while the video's décor, costumes and props are all evocative of 1970s kitsch.[6]

With this two minutes-twenty seconds film not only had Oriana found a way to make a connection between her outdated sculptures and the contemporary representation of female desire, she also managed to please her tutors. But our story doesn't end there; there were more lessons to be learned. As explained earlier, Oriana had never been very good at incorporating praise into her self-image, so despite her achievement she still felt very unsure of herself. Luckily for Oriana, in the film she had made there was the seed of an idea that, once implanted in her mind and given some time to flourish, would change all that once and for all.

In the episode that *Our Bodies, Ourselves* takes its dialogue from, Carrie is afraid her boyfriend will leave her because she's not perfect. The fact that she isn't perfect was literally leaked by her body, as Carrie explains, she 'should never have farted.' She fears he will marry 'a perfect little woman who never passes gas.' The use of the word 'perfect' in that scene, in true Bradshaw style, got Oriana thinking… Why did she feel such pressure to be perfect all the time?

Explanations from feminist theorists, anti-neo-liberalists and pop psychologists abounded in Oriana's head.[7] Somehow she got the inkling that the key to her true liberation was to get to the point where she no longer craved the approval of others, when she would no longer feel she had to prove herself perfect. That's when Oriana happened to come across a man whose way of being in the world seemed to give voice to that very sentiment. 'Embrace Failare! [sic]' was his clarion call, and it resonated in her eardrums and reverberated in her soul. The moment she saw John Kilduff (aka Mr Let's Paint) igniting his canvas with oils, blending healthful drinks and taking calls – all whilst jogging on a treadmill going four miles per hour – Oriana knew she had found another Master Teacher.[8] (This makes perfect sense, because according to the *Do It!* Book, the 'MT knows all you need to learn, the perfect timing for your learning it, and the ideal way of teaching it.')[9]

In homage to her multitasking guru, Oriana bounced on a mini trampoline, flipped pancakes, painted portraits of a male burlesque dancer (as he stripped) and analysed the dreams of onlookers.[10] This was the first of many risks Oriana took to prove to herself that she could act imperfectly, make bad paintings and cook inedible food and still feel ok. Doing something badly wasn't as awful as she thought it would be.[11] What's more, she realized she was more than the sum total of all of her actions; her totality couldn't be rated, she was far more complicated than that.[12]

At around that time, Oriana came across the ideas of the psychologist Dr Albert Ellis, inventor of rational emotive behaviour therapy (REBT) and author of *How to Be a Perfect Non-Perfectionist*.[13] His ideas helped Oriana make sense of why she had been so drawn to Kilduff's work and why she felt compelled to follow in his footsteps. According to Ellis, the key to wellbeing is to unconditionally accept yourself as a fallible human being, and to challenge and act against your self-inhibiting irrational beliefs. If Carrie had been unconditionally self-accepting, sure she would have been embarrassed when she farted, but she would have accepted that as a human being it was inevitable that she would act imperfectly every once in a while.

As for Oriana, now that she has learned to embrace failare, who knows what creative risks she has yet to take…

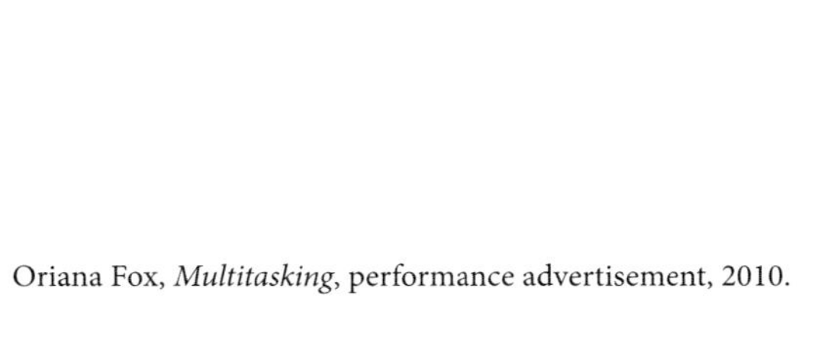

Oriana Fox, *Multitasking*, performance advertisement, 2010.

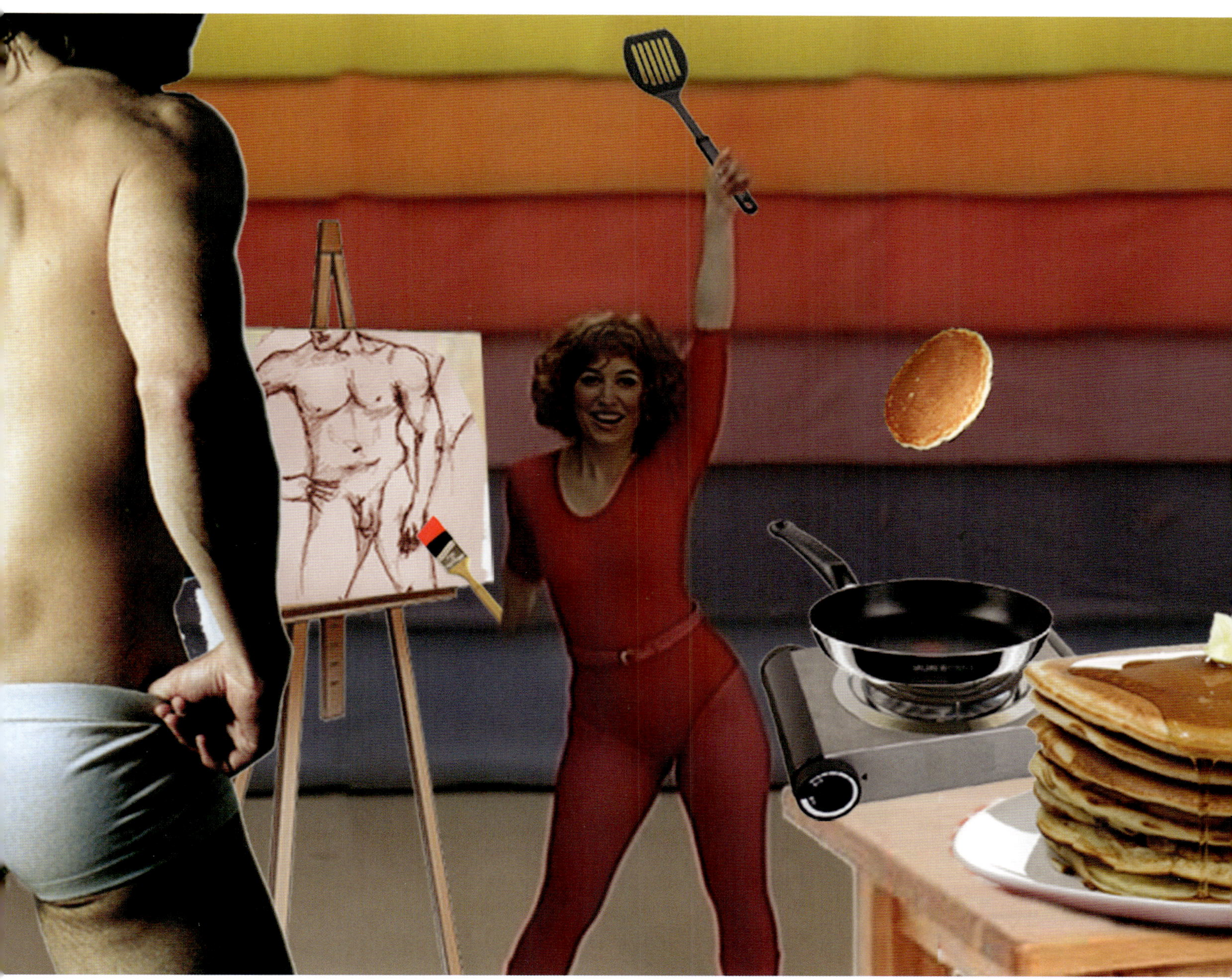

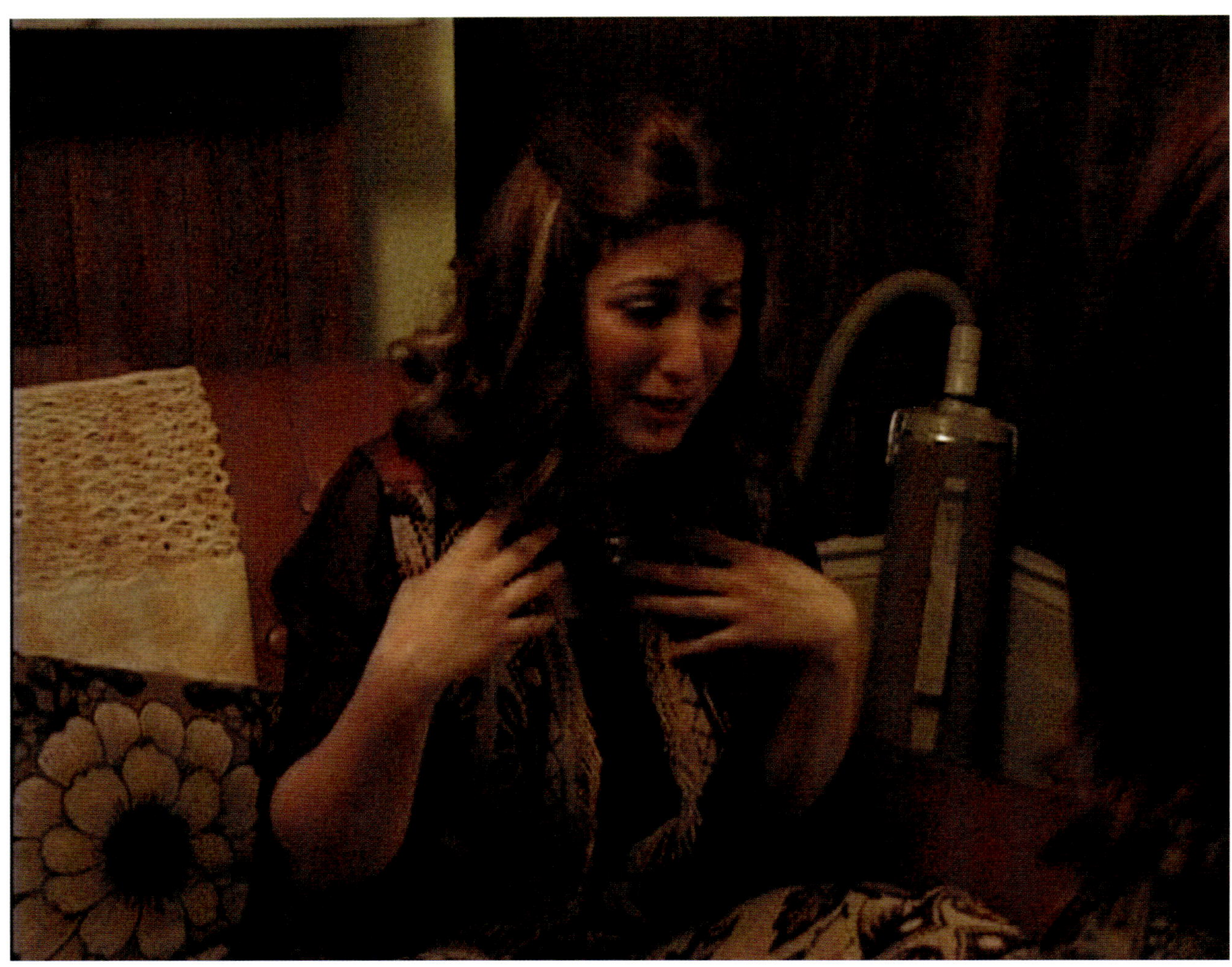

This page and opposite: Oriana Fox, *Our Bodies, Ourselves*, video stills, 2003.

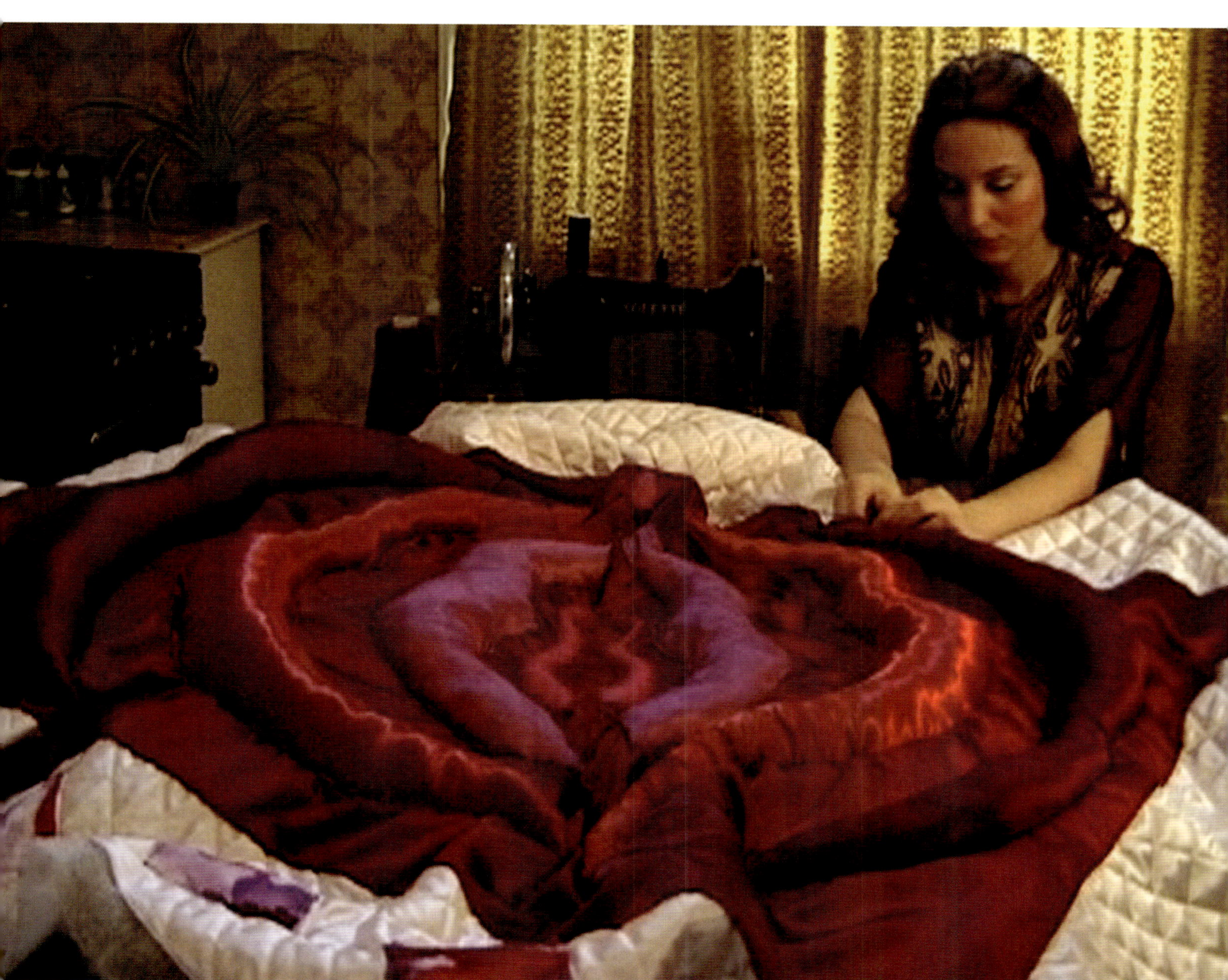

NOTES

1 This affliction is not particular to Oriana alone: for Sigmund Freud, the great mystery remained, 'What does woman want?'; see Ernest Jones, *Das Leben und Werk von Sigmund Freud*, Vol. 2, Bern & Stuttgart: Hans Huber, 1962, p. 493. Furthermore, while the portrayal of women as the object of heterosexual male desire is ubiquitous in western visual culture, images made for the female gaze seem strangely absent. Robert Doisneau's photograph *Le regard oblique/The Sidelong Glance* (1948), in which a couple peer into a shop window displaying paintings, illustrates this phenomenon perfectly; the man's eyes peer at a canvas of a nude woman, while the picture that the woman regards is hidden – we see only the back of the frame. Representations of women as active desiring subjects and the objects of their desire are missing throughout much of art history; however, in the mainstream media, woman's desire as consumer is all around us. It is as if everyone with something to sell has been clamouring to fill up the blank blackness of the picture frame in Doisneau's photograph. That frame is constantly filled with aspirational images of what she can have, experience and be. As the journalist and academic Rosalind Coward puts it: 'Female desire is courted with the promise of future perfection': in Rosalind Coward, *Female Desire: Women's Sexuality Today*, London: Paladin, 1984, p. 13.

2 Laura Mulvey's seminal essay 'Visual Pleasure and Narrative Cinema' – required reading for students of lens-based media – explains that desire is gendered within representation in that it is classically depicted as a subject/object dichotomy: 'In a world ordered by sexual imbalance, pleasure in looking has been split between active/male and passive/female. The determining male gaze projects its fantasy on to the female figure, which is styled accordingly. In their traditional exhibitionist role women are simultaneously looked at and displayed, with their appearance coded for strong visual and erotic impact so that they can be said to connote to-be-looked-at-ness': in Laura Mulvey, 'Visual Pleasure and Narrative Cinema', in *Film Theory and Criticism*, eds Gerald Mast et al., New York: Oxford University Press, 1992, p. 747.

3 It seemed that one way to get around the subject/object binary was to try to manifest in the viewer an experience of what Freud describes as 'the oceanic state', which

precedes the differentiation of the ego. The idea of a pre-lingual desiring subject is key within developmental theories by Melanie Klein and the object relations theorists, as well as Jacques Lacan (pre-mirror stage). It also plays a part in the theorizations of the French feminists Luce Irigaray and Julia Kristeva. Hence the enveloping womb/breast/vagina imagery became Oriana's tactic, albeit perhaps a bit too literal in its illustration of these complex ideas, which are summarized too simplistically here.

4 For example, Judy Chicago's 'central core' imagery (and her attempt to find it in the work of other women artists) was besieged with criticism because it implied that there is a fundamental connection between all women. When Oriana began creating vulva-like soft sculptures (albeit in response to theory that takes into account the social construction of femininity), her tutors thought she was being a naïve essentialist. As art historian Peggy Phelan explains, the rise of psychoanalytically-based critical theory (of which Mulvey's essay is a key example) fuelled the debunking of feminist projects by Chicago and other artists working in the 1970s. She goes on to point out that the 'vehemence of the denunciation of this work' should however be considered carefully, because it might be misogynist or 'a symptomatic repression of something threatening.' Indeed, during the 1990s, writers like Linda Cottingham began to re-explore this work; but it wasn't until the late 2000s that the art world and academia had a resurgence of interest in feminism and feminist art from the '70s, with shows like 'Wack! Art and the Feminist Revolution' at The Museum of Contemporary Art in Los Angeles (2007). However, when Oriana was sewing away at Goldsmiths in the early 2000s, her tutors for the most part failed to recognize that there might be something worth exploring in those old forms. See Peggy Phelan, 'Survey', in *Art and Feminism*, eds Helena Reckitt et al, London: Phaidon, 2001, pp. 36–39.

5 John-Roger and Peter McWilliams, *Do It! The Guide to Living Your Dreams*, London: Thorsons, 1992, p. 125.

6 Oriana based her video on this particular episode of *Sex and the City* (Season 1, Episode 11: 'The Drought') partly because the dialogue enabled her Carrie to be making something (the vaginal quilt) since the original Carrie is 'keeping her hands busy' by painting her kitchen, about which Miranda remarks 'nice colour'. But equally important to this choice of episode is the fact that it culminates with all four

characters gaping at the next-door neighbours having sex. The scopophillic gaze of contemporary woman is literalized, as if in response to Mulvey's observations cited above (footnote 2), asserting that women too can be active subjects with desires. Furthermore, it's worth noting that these protagonists have it all – pleasure in looking and 'to-be-looked-at-ness', completing this picture-perfect, contemporary fantasy of female heterosexuality. To juxtapose imagery from the mass-mediated cultural imaginary with work by artists like Judy Chicago and Hannah Wilke, to name two whose iconography Oriana references directly, is both apt and puzzling. The collision of representations past and present pose more questions about the state of female sexuality and feminist heredity than it answers. It is not to say that one is authentic and the other mediated, one sincere and the other artificial, despite Chicago's claim, for example, that she was 'symbolizing [her] true sexual nature.' In an essay which is critical of the type of work Chicago and Wilke were making (for being too easily recuperated by the dominant ideology), Griselda Pollock points out that there is an important difference between 'woman as image' – that is, as a 'signifier in an ideological discourse' – and images of women. I would argue that in trying to embody her Master Teacher, Oriana gets a little lost in a collage of signifiers from feminist-influenced ideologies. See Judy Chicago, *Through the Flower: My Struggle as a Woman Artist*, New York: Doubleday, 1979, p. 52; Griselda Pollock, 'What's Wrong with images of "Women"?', in *Framing Feminism: Art and the Women's Movement, 1970–85*, eds Rozsika Parker and Pollock, London: Pandora, 1987, p. 133.

7 The Coward quote in footnote 1 bears repeating here: did 'the promise of future perfection' hold Oriana under its sway? As theorist Rosalind Gill argues, 'the autonomous, calculating, self-regulating subject of neoliberalism bears a strong resemblance to the active, freely choosing, self-reinventing subject of postfeminism.' She goes on to add: 'to a much greater extent than men, women are required to work on and transform the self, to regulate every aspect of their conduct': in Rosalind Gill, 'Culture and Subjectivity in Neoliberal and Postfeminist Times', Subjectivity, No. 25, 2008, p. 443.

8 John Kilduff's show *Let's Paint TV* ran from 2002–08 on public access in Los Angeles, and many of the episodes have been later distributed and viewed by millions worldwide on YouTube. Kilduff continues to stream daily on stickam.

com. The early episodes can be analysed as examples of postmodern parody; using absurdity and irony, Kilduff critiques the values of perfectionism and consumerism espoused within US daytime TV programming. On one level, *Let's Paint TV* repeats the conventions of the infomercial except that the balding, out-of-breath Kilduff replaces the coherent, attractive and aspirational figure of the salesperson. On another level, the show places itself in the lineage of hobbyist, how-to painting programmes, with the distinction between John Kilduff and Bob Ross being that Ross demonstrates a certain level of skill that can be copied – a fact made all the more poignant because the main message of *Let's Paint TV* is to be yourself. Critic Doug Harvey describes it aptly: 'Boisterous, irreverent and surreal, *Let's Paint TV* is nevertheless utterly sincere in its espousal of painting as a path of creative liberation,' although I would substitute the word 'painting' for 'multitasking', or maybe even 'play'. See Doug Harvey, 'The Joy of Painting Saddam', *LA Weekly*, 2nd September 2004.

9 John-Roger and McWilliams, 1992, p. 125.

10 This was a performance for 'I'm with you' at MKII space in London on 27th February 2010.

11 This process is what rational emotive behaviour therapists call 'shame attacking', or what cognitive behaviour therapists call 'exposure and response prevention'; you gain confidence by getting used to the shame of acting imperfectly or doing something you fear or that is absurd (such as walking a banana on a leash, to give one of Albert Ellis' examples). For more on this therapeutic method, see Albert Ellis and Catherine Maclaren, *Rational Emotive Behavior Therapy: A Therapist's Guide*, Atascadero, CA: Impact Publishers, 2004, p. 95. Alternatively, watch 'The Therapeutic Process and Performance', an episode of Oriana's chat show *The O Show*, in which she discusses shame-attacking with her therapist: http://orianafox.com/2012/10/can-performance-cure/.

12 This idea is the foundational premise of Albert Ellis' philosophy which states that we are all works in progress and therefore our only option to maintain optimal psychological wellbeing in light of our fallibility as human beings is to unconditionally accept ourselves and others. See Albert Ellis, *The Myth of Self-Esteem: How Rational Emotive Behavior Therapy Can Change Your Life Forever*, New York: Prometheus Books, 2005.

13 Albert Ellis' *How To Be A Perfect Non-Perfectionist* is actually an out-of-print audio CD sold by the Ellis Institute in New York. Ellis is outspoken on the subject of perfectionism as a cause of emotional disturbances including anxiety and depression. See, for example, Albert Ellis, 'The role of irrational beliefs in perfectionism', in *Perfectionism: Theory, research, and treatment*, eds Gordon L. Flett et al, Washington, DC: American Psychological Association, 2002, pp. 217–29.

ZIDANE: A 21ST CENTURY PORTRAIT

A FILM BY DOUGLAS GORDON & PHILIPPE PARRENO

DAN HILL

This is an utterly overwhelming piece. The ultimate time and motion study, it's been described many times since its debut at Cannes last year, but for those unfamiliar with the idea, Douglas Gordon and Philippe Parreno set up seventeen cameras to follow Real Madrid 'galáctico' footballer Zinedine Zidane through the course of an average La Liga game. That's it. They follow Zidane the player, not the match. The idea, in Parreno's words, was to 'make a feature film which follows the main protagonist of a story, without telling the story.'

It's certainly not a traditional documentary: there is no exposition of the enigmatic Zidane's life amidst the celebrity culture of Madrid, or of his French-Algerian heritage, growing up in the mean streets of Marseilles. There are merely a few superimposed fragments of text, apparently from Zidane, which add little in the way of context or explanation. Without this, the film has only Zidane, and his movements, to portray. While the careful editing of image and sound is certainly an aesthetic intervention, it is otherwise the purest possible depiction of football.

Given Gordon's previous work are studies of 'time, movement, image and sound', football is an alluring subject. But this is also about portraiture, very clearly, and perhaps narrative too. So these seventeen cameras – including the first commercial use of two Panavision HD cameras with specially modified zoom, courtesy of the US Department of Defence – in the hands of the best camera operators in US and Europe – essentially Scorsese and Almodovar's crews – follow this player, for around 90 minutes, through a fairly average La Liga game against Villareal. And it's fascinating, both as a study of portraiture, movement, yes, but also as a study of football.

Zidane has the ball for about, oh, two to three minutes in total. It's fairly extraordinary how little he sees of the ball, and yet how creative he is within those constraints. Of Zidane the player, more later, but this paucity of ball possession also illustrates the overwhelming sensation derived from watching him. The solitude. The sheer loneliness of the player, particularly in the number 10 position – yes, he wears '5' on his shirt, but Zidane is formally a classic number 10 – the pivot through which play is articulated. Zidane has the ball at his feet for a few minutes, yet spends every other microsecond focused on it. His eyes rarely leave it, or the space around it, or the potential space that could be extrapolated from the perceived trajectories of ball and players. His focus is extraordinary, the saturated light of the football stadium at night reducing his eye sockets to deep pools of blackness, his face wearing a mask of intense concentration. Where other players look at each other, the crowd, the referee, Zidane only has eyes for the ball. The combination of zooms and pans swirl and dart around him, and only occasionally leave him to sweep out to reveal the immense scale of football, the fan's-eye view and the televisual view through which we usually see the game. Yet principally, the cameras are so tight that he's often alone in the frame, their gaze lingering over his hands, his feet, the famous bald profile dripping with sweat, the microphones picking up his pants, grunts, snorts, occasional cries.

Spanish football is perfect for this view. Close control, rapid interplay – all matador twirls and stiletto flicks. With the more expansive English game, you'd need a couple of cameras mounted in the roof; with the more studious Italian game, some kind of time-lapse, perhaps. And Zidane himself, the centre around which everything revolves, is perfect as a subject. Paul Myerscough in the *London Review of Books* writes:

> Zidane. His cropped hair, his leanness, give an impression of asceticism. His features are still, his eyes shadowed under heavy brows. There are flickers of consternation, of irritation, of concern, impatience and contempt; he smiles only once, sharing a joke with Roberto Carlos. But for the most part he is impassive. Even after his finest moment, in the 70th minute of the game, when he glides through the Villarreal defence, spins on his right foot and loops a perfect cross with his left for Ronaldo to score at the far post, his expression barely changes. It has always been the convention in Hollywood cinematography that the close-up guarantees intimacy with its subject; in this, it shares with one important tradition of portraiture, the notion that the image should express interiority. In Zidane, the relentless scrutiny of his face yields little in the way of an inner self, still less anything that would help us to account for his sublime skill. We feel for him, but do not identify with him; he is alone, lonely even, and distant, other.[2]

As Parreno notes, Zidane's reclusive nature also reinforces this sense of distance, that as a person, compared to his then compatriots of Beckham, Figo, Ronaldo et al., 'he only exists after the first kick, and before the last kick – he is the Total Footballer, after Cruyff [...].

Gordon notes that the entire thing – Zidane, his performance and the artwork – is really 'an exercise in solitude.' Fragility, too. It seems odd to describe such a commanding physical presence as fragile, but that's what comes across. His dark concentration exists purely for the ball, the game, and given Zidane's utter mastery of his particular subject – the ball – what it reveals most of all is the humbling impotence of the sportsman within the wider game; how even this greatest of players is incapable of controlling the result, even though he apparently effortlessly controls every ball pinged towards him, no matter the pace or direction. Hence his frustration, perhaps, and his apparent fragility. Zidane himself notes, watching the film, that it shows the intensity and focus of concentration in a way you never see with TV coverage. It also shows that, although he wanted to 'play the game of his life' given the presence of the cameras, you can't control that, no matter how intense the focus.

Gordon and Parreno didn't take football films as inspiration, thankfully, but rather Andy Warhol's *The 13 Most Beautiful Women* (1964). But more than this, they draw from the history of portraiture. Given that the production of the film was entirely unpredictable – no one knew what would happen in the match, whether Zidane would limp off after five minutes or play the game of his life – it was impossible to storyboard, or provide direction cues for the camera crew. So the 'Making Of' documentary reveals a live improvisation by Parreno, Gordon and the camera crew, directing on the fly. They have no control over the 'actors' in this particular drama. Intriguingly, in lieu of a storyboard, the only preparation the artists did with the crew was to take them to the Prado on the day of the game.

Having secured exclusive access to the gallery, Parreno and Gordon led the crew through a rapid yet extraordinary history of art, with particular emphasis on both the portraiture and reproductions of historical scenes in the art of Goya and Velázquez. Velázquez, in particular, resonates. As the movie becomes near ambient in its impassive singular vision – almost like a visual version of an aural drone, or raga – Velázquez, as an artist who repeatedly endeavoured to capture the point between sleeping and waking, seems entirely apposite for this dreamlike, hypnotic trance. Also, Goya's portraiture, most famously in the *Maja* pictures, clothed and naked, exploring different facets of portraiture of personality. Additionally, the crew paused in front of Hieronymous Bosch's *Garden of Earthly Delights*, presumably to explore depiction of narrative of multiple parts, stretched over a physical space.

Despite this art history lesson, the thing itself is pitched halfway between film and art. In the accompanying documentary, a contributor notes that Zidane in close-up has a 'darkness, density – reminiscent of Bresson', yet at other times it's 'epic, like a John Ford western.' Gordon and Parreno clearly like the idea of this playing in both galleries and cinemas (although whether it would've achieved a cinema release without Zidane's extraordinary contributions to the last World Cup, both creative and destructive, is a moot point). Gordon notes that it would 'take people from the white cube into the black box, or the black box into the white cube.'

The use of sound, as you'd expect from Gordon, is particularly strong. Not so much the musical soundtrack, composed for the film by fellow Glaswegians, Mogwai, although their languorous drones and dramatic dynamics work very well over the long distance of a football match. But the sound of the football match, from the close zooms of Zidane – his occasional polyglot shouts, his deep breathing, the soft crunch of his studs on grass – panning up to the incredible noise of the Madrilénos and their endless barrage of horns, a drone echoed in Mogwai's organs and guitars. The 'Making Of' documentary pauses on this process briefly. Unfortunately, it fails to introduce the participants, but what I assume to be the principal sound engineer notes that they were so 'dependent on sound – we're almost defining the images by using sound.' This is spot on: with the absence of traditional dialogue of any kind, the narrative is only perceived through a variety of flashpoints – goals, near misses, a sending off – leaving the rest of the match to be articulated in movement and sound. At one moment, the soundtrack appears to cut to another time and place altogether, layering the sound of kids playing football and dogs barking over that of the match. At other times it cross-cuts rapidly from the compressed sound of TV coverage to the rich detail of the sound at the middle of the pitch. At other times, the soundtrack and then silence: 'the silence of portraiture is very important.'[3]

It's a beautiful piece, to be absorbed carefully. It requires concentration from the viewer too, as the repeated image of Zidane searching for the ball, for space and not finding it become almost entirely abstract interwoven patterns of white shirt, dark skin and green grass. Warhol's *Empire* (1964) or Brian Eno's *Mistaken Memories of Medieval Manhattan* (1981) are precursors rather more than *Escape to Victory* (John Huston, 1981).

As a result, I can see why one user at the movie website IMDb posted the comment: 'The film is excruciatingly boring; it is a pain to watch, and it is better to watch paint dry.' I can only totally disagree; but those expecting something like a documentary or traditional coverage of a football match should indeed beware. This is a quite beautiful, challenging portrait, in sound and image.

And for the football fans amongst you, what of the player himself? Richard Williams, one of the foremost writers on the kind of player Zidane exemplifies, wrote:

> Virtually devoid of context, the economy of his movement and the sheer absence of fuss as he goes about his work are strikingly apparent, rendering the delicacy of his footwork even more moving.[4]

It is entirely moving. That's exactly the right word. To a player, a player of almost any standard, watching Zidane is extraordinary. While all the above context indicates that even non-football fans will get something out of this, perhaps those who love and play the game will be even more fascinated in the detail.

In his book *The Perfect 10*, Richard Williams describes the appeal of watching Zidane, of how his transformation when in possession of the ball perhaps explains the passion of his endless pursuit of it:

> Zidane is a big man, 1.85 metres tall and weighing 78 kg. He has a slightly ponderous gait and shoulders that tend to stoop, giving the illusion of ungainliness. He does not have lightning-fast feet or much of a sprint. But when the ball comes to him he suddenly reveals the lightness of a ballet dancer and the footwork of a fencer. Gracefulness falls upon him. Then he can do anything he wants with the ball, from the impossible delicacy of a running spin through 360°, his famous *roulette*, to the shattering violence of a waist-high volley fired from a range of more than twenty yards with his notionally weaker left foot. And when he does something like that, no one in the stadium envisages any other outcome.[5]

Even given that few minutes possession of the ball, he so rarely gives the ball away. He's always progressive, always trying to create. It's one of the purest acts of complete creativity I've ever seen. Nothing is mundane or regressive – every flick, every move, every dribble is trying to create, to lift the team, to shift the play upfield towards the opposition's goal, to keep the ball moving into interesting spaces. His first touch isn't just immaculate, to use a well-worn football cliché; it's an immaculate conception, as it inherently contains the logic and purpose of the next few moves. He traps the ball, body forming a triangle, as one should, no matter what angle and pace it arrives at, and in trapping it, he's also moving it forward, away from the defender, into space. There are details you've never seen before. The cameras and edits pause several times on Zidane's habit of tapping his toes into the grass, scuffing and pawing the ground like a thoroughbred in the stalls, or as Williams has it, 'a reflexive gesture like a trumpeter emptying his spit-valve between phrases.'

Even given the tight angles of Spanish football, and 21 other men sharing the pitch, he appears alone, so often, throughout. This is exaggerated by his complete concentration. His face betrays little emotion; even when Madrid score twice, one goal his own making, there is no smile – his face remains the same granite-hewn angles. In fact, he smiles only once, when sharing a joke with fellow left-sided player, the Brazilian Roberto Carlos.

And then within minutes, right at the end of the game, he suddenly loses it, and is attacking one of the opposition in a melee which is frankly nothing to do with him. It's shocking, out of nothing, apparently. And yet had his frustration been unconsciously and invisibly growing throughout an hour of pushes, kicks, shoves by Villareal's markers; of his teammates' inability; of his own inability to direct the game as he saw it in his mind's eye; perhaps even the lapse of concentration when he allowed himself to smile; maybe just the endless uncertainty of football itself? Or maybe none of those things. It's a curious and dramatic reflection of how he ended his career at the World Cup in 2006, which everyone knows by now. There's little point attempting to connect these events into a coherent explanation – there is none. There is only the recording of the event itself.

Gordon 'didn't want to make a heroic portrait, actually it's the portrait of an anti-hero.' We expect too much of people we want to be heroes, and Zidane's career constantly reminded us of this, even as perhaps the greatest player ever. Just because someone plays like an angel, doesn't mean they are an angel (cf. Miles Davis and a million other artists). It doesn't excuse it. It just *is*. Myerscough in the *London Review of Books* writes:

> Searching his face for 90 minutes brings us no closer to understanding his actions at the end of this game, just as no account of his interaction with Materazzi can account for his final self-immolation. If that's what it was.[6]

I adored this movie, or artwork, whatever it is. I pored over every aspect of the DVD extras. DVD is a satisfying way of experiencing it, given the intensity of focus it allows through proximity. Yet I suspect it will work very well installed in a dark gallery space, with a pin-sharp projection from floor to ceiling and bathed in surround sound – as per a Christian Marclay piece.

Last words go to Zidane: 'Magic is sometimes very close to nothing at all.'

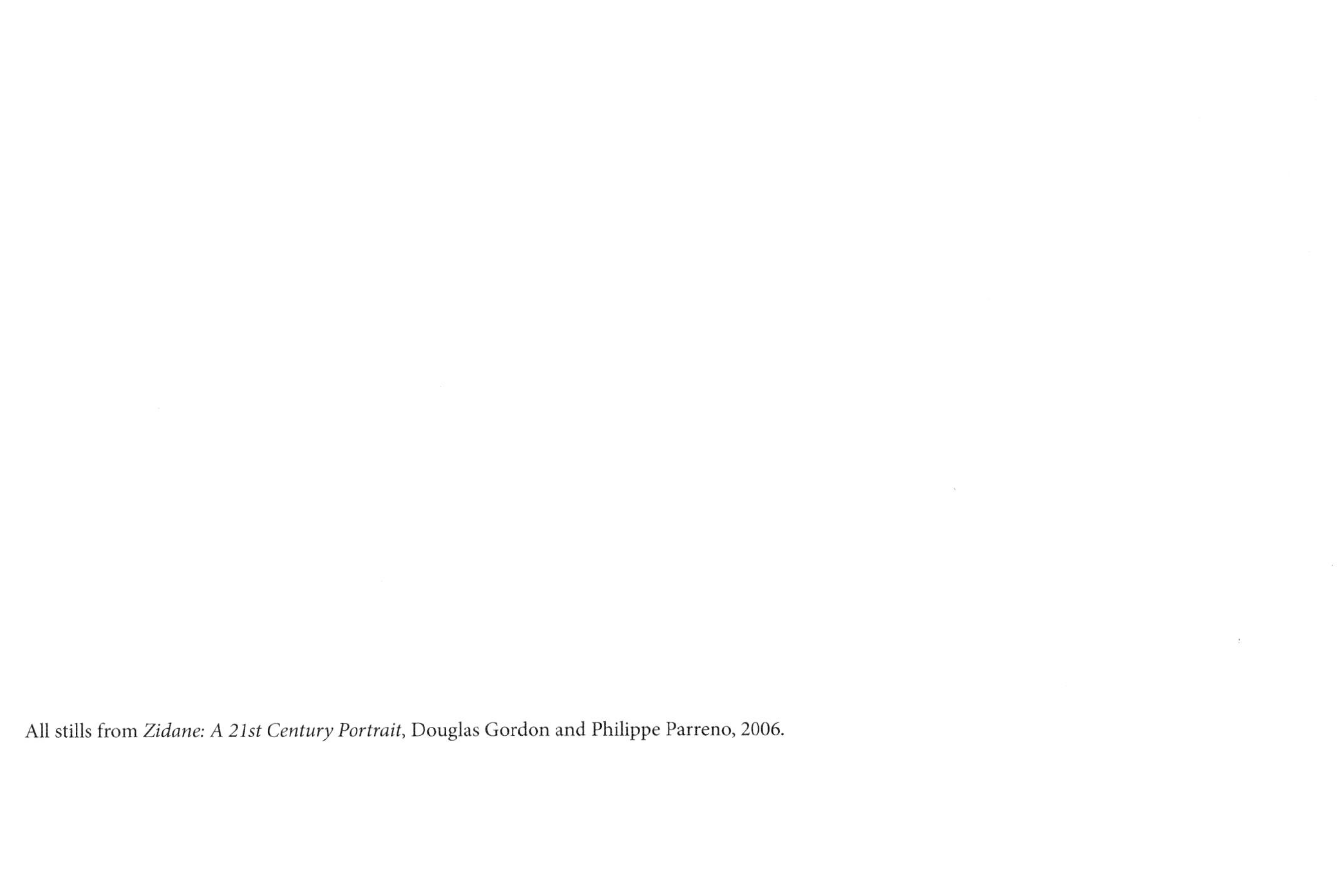

All stills from *Zidane: A 21st Century Portrait*, Douglas Gordon and Philippe Parreno, 2006.

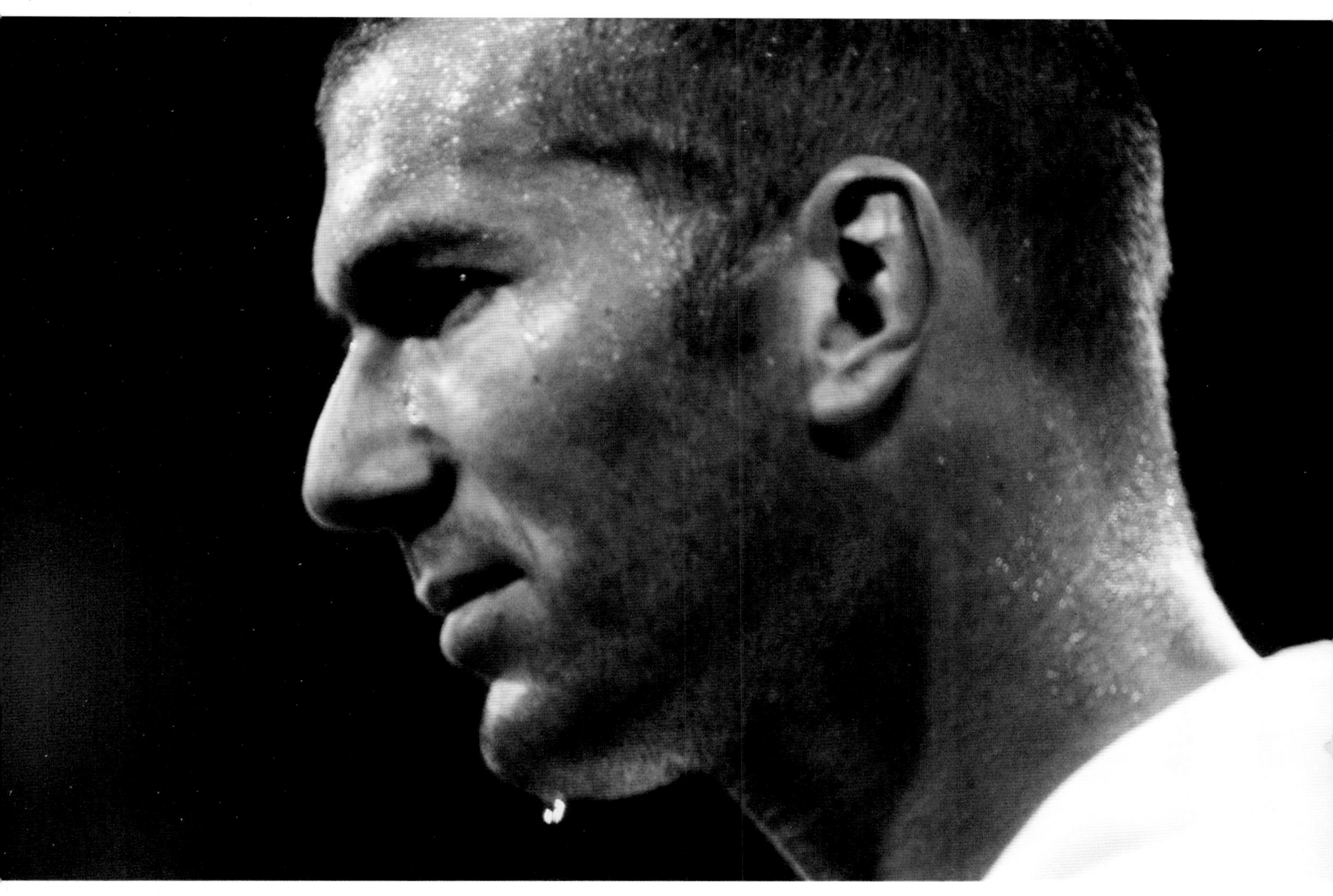

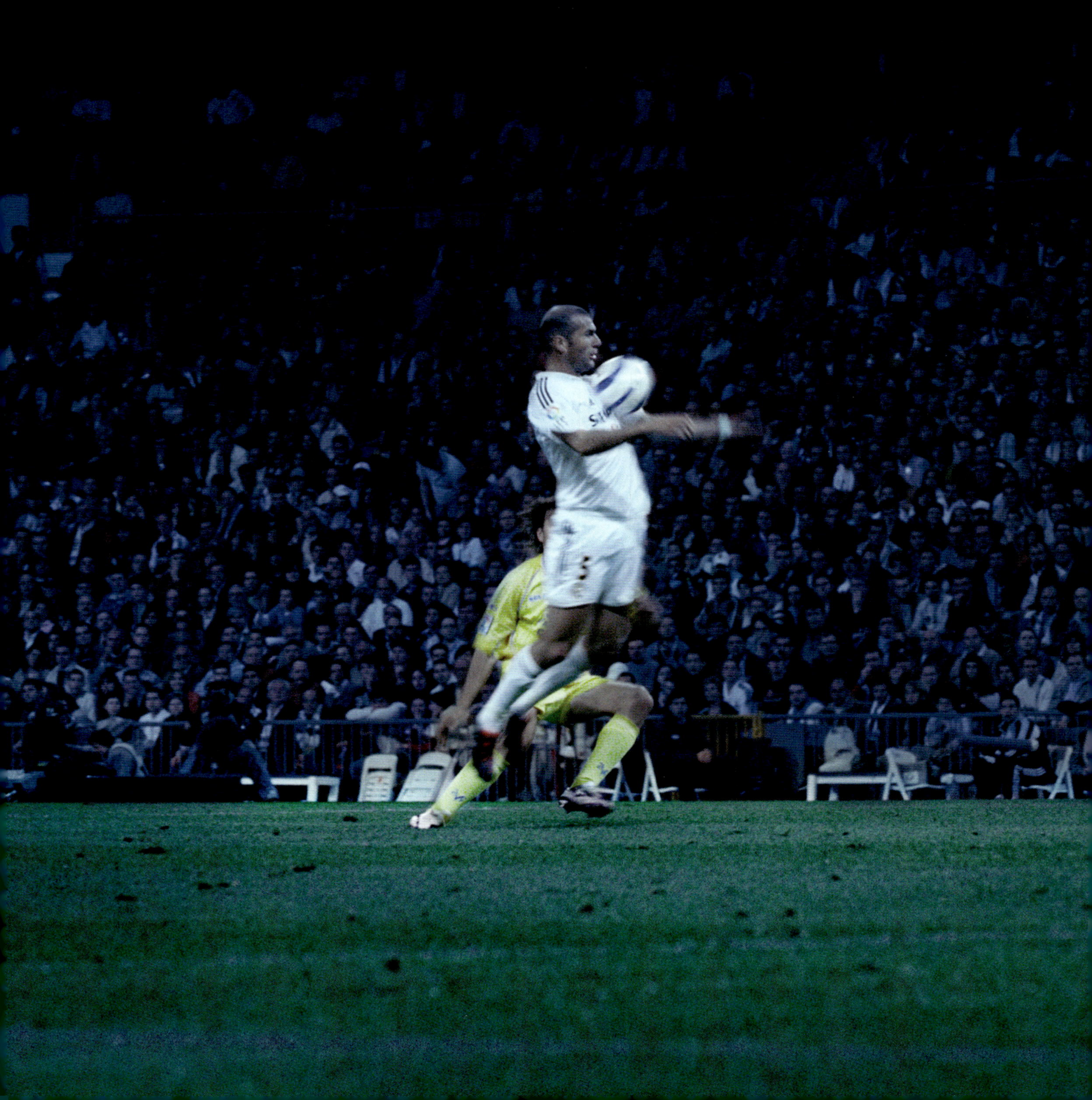

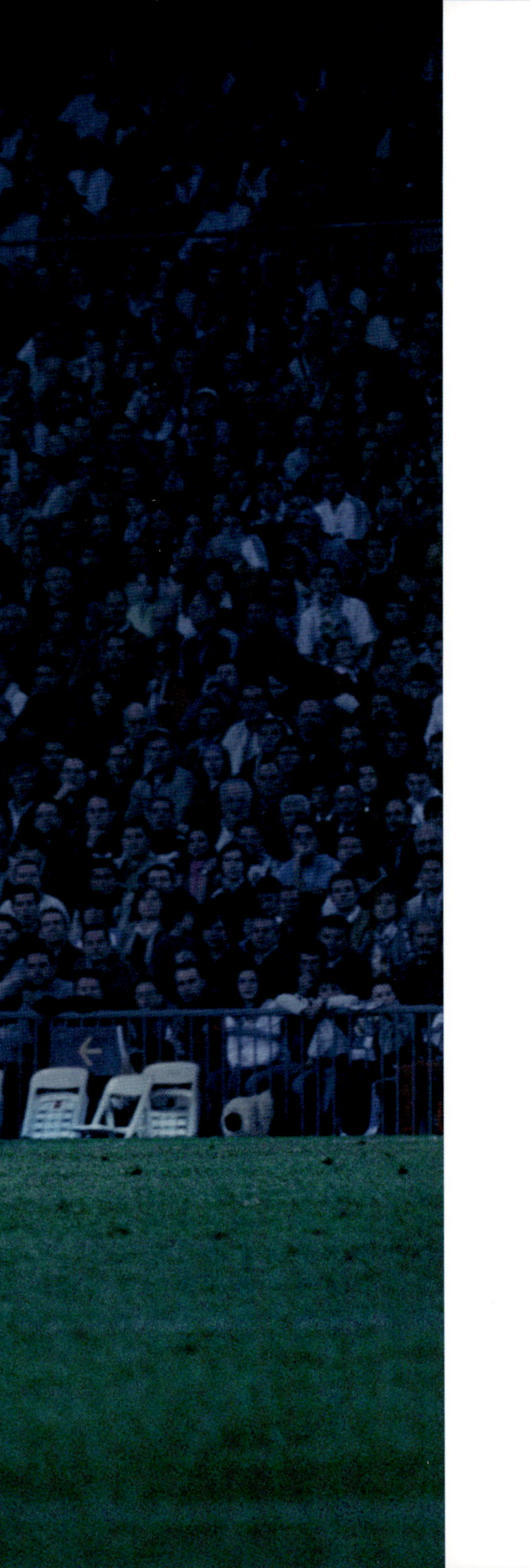

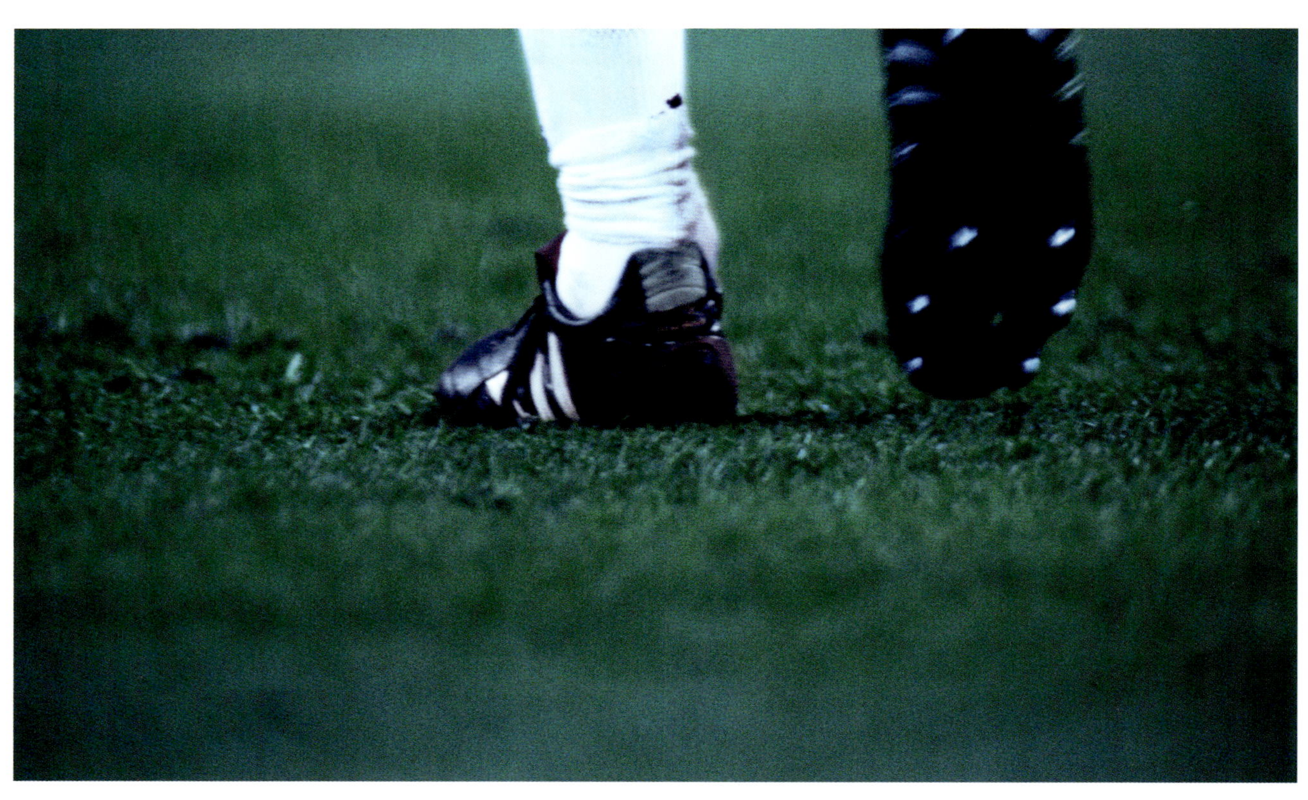

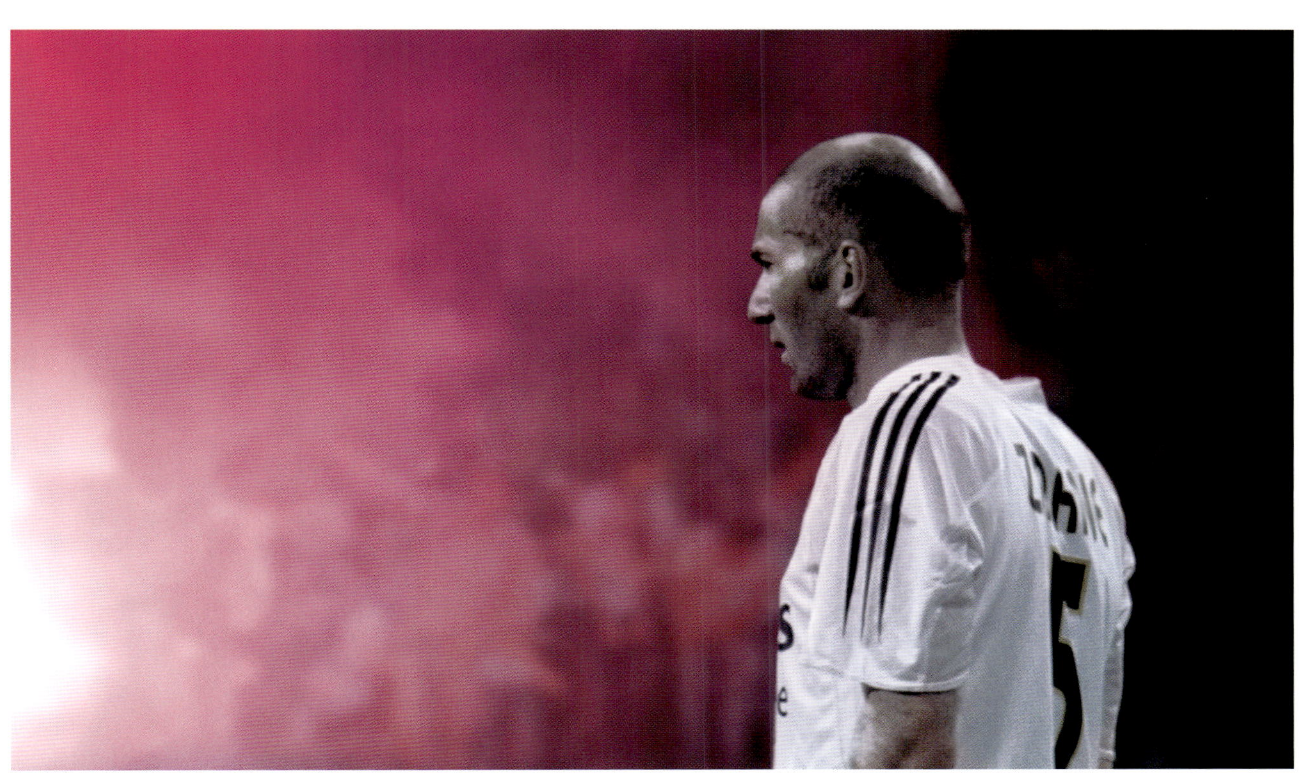

NOTES

1 This is an edited version of Dan's review: '"Zidane: A 21st Century Portrait", by Douglas Gordon and Philippe Parreno', on *City of Sound* blog, 4th March 2007, http://www.cityofsound.com/blog/2007/03/zidane_a_21st_c.html (accessed 1st October 2011).

2 Paul Myerscough, 'Short Cuts', *London Review of Books*, 5th October 2006, http://www.lrb.co.uk/v28/n19/paul-myerscough/short-cuts (accessed 4th March 2007).

3 Ibid.

4 Richard Williams, 'Pitch Invasion', *The Guardian*, 22nd September 2006, http://www.guardian.co.uk/film/2006/sep/22/1 (accessed 4th March 2007).

5 Richard Williams, *The Perfect 10: Football's dreamers, schemers, playmakers and playboys:* London, Faber and Faber, 2007.

6 Myerscough, 2006.

EREWHON

JANE AND LOUISE WILSON

This is a transcript of Jane and Louise Wilson's presentation, which was introduced by Mark Durden. The final reading was followed by a screening of the film work.

Mark Durden: Jane and Louise Wilson began working together in 1989. I'm sure many of you are familiar with their work. They work with video projections, photographs, sculptures and have had a succession of international exhibitions. They were nominated for the Turner Prize in 1999, and are going to talk about an installation from 2004 called *Erewhon*, which is based upon a novel by Samuel Butler. I'm really looking forward to see what the work looks like. I'm sure it will fit the theme of perfection in an interesting way, because these artists have consistently explored areas and sites that are charged historically, concerned with questions of Utopia and failed Utopia. And I think maybe it's in terms of Utopia, pre-empting their talk, that we may have a connection with perfection. Anyway, welcome, the stage is yours.

Jane Wilson: I'm Jane.

Louise Wilson: And I'm Louise. As Mark mentioned, Jane and I were invited in 2004 to do a residency with the Sofa Gallery in Christchurch on the South Island of New Zealand. And whilst we were there we were struck by this overwhelming, incredible landscape. Perhaps we went through similar thoughts about the place, or the same sense of how overwhelming the place was, as Samuel Butler obviously felt when he arrived in New Zealand in 1871 – he eventually wrote a book called *Erewhon* about his experiences. Well, not necessarily about his experiences, but he went ostensibly to become a successful, wealthy sheep farmer and then realized that he was very outnumbered by sheep and got a little freaked out about it, and actually ended up writing this amazing book, *Erewhon*, which is a play on 'nowhere' backwards.

JW: It's interesting you mentioned Utopia, as part of the conceit of *Erewhon* is that people who are not healthy and fit literally get put into jail. There's this idea that you can't live in normal society if there's something that is defective in terms of how you are. And so, in a way, it's a play on this notion of what this wonderful island is, and a questioning of this utopian idea of society And I think, for us, coming to New Zealand, what was very interesting, as Louise said, was the landscape, but also it was also interesting to see the amount of abandoned mental health institutions which were actually still there, on the South Island specifically. This is a piece called *Blue Skin Bay*: it's a photo-work that's 180 centimetres x 180 centimetres, so it's quite large-scale, very physical. Again, this is one of the images from the South Island. It's not quite of the sanatorium that Jane was talking about; this is actually Hanmer Springs. We went to a place where there are several buildings that comprised the sanatorium there. One was a shell-shock hospital built in 1914; there was another ward that was extended in the 1930s called Chisholm Ward. There was also Rutherford Ward, and we actually documented various buildings. The sanatorium had been recently decommissioned, and what was interesting, I suppose, was that the genesis of the site explained a lot about more recent New Zealand history: it started off as a hospital for First World War shell-shock victims, then it was used again in the Thirties, post-Second World War, and then it suddenly became a mental health institution in the Fifties. So they incorporated all the buildings. This is an image from Chisholm Ward.

LW: We were struck by the fact that there were two buildings that were built around the architecture of a panopticon. These buildings were built from the early 1920s and they were built, as Jane mentioned, to rehabilitate veterans from the First and Second World Wars and, of course, the extraordinary thing about New Zealand was that they probably suffered the most proportionate per head casualties in the First and Second World Wars than any of the other allies. So the wars had a devastating effect, but, as a consequence, there was this discrete government-sanctioned eugenics policy that came about in the early part of the twentieth century, post-First World War, to encourage fitness and health amongst young women and a drive to produce healthy citizens to populate this new country. And so we became intrigued by the fact there were, in terms of population, a profusion of sanatoriums in New Zealand. Which sounds like a very odd statement to make, but, actually, this had been a policy that had been introduced in the early and mid-twentieth century. And in the end, by the 1950s, some of these buildings were used to house young, unmarried mothers. The policy was basically to give the semblance of the ideal, if you like. The ideal of what the population should become; and young, unmarried mothers were something that they didn't want to be too visible.

JW: I think we felt there was some sort of parallel with what happened in *Erewhon*, in Samuel Butler's book, where the people who were ill and sick were basically punished by being put in prison. I mean, there's some sort of parallel with that text and, obviously, with the work we were trying to do. Obviously there's a lot of these institutions. Sunnyside's probably one that's very famous in a lot of people's minds because it's where Janet Frayn was incarcerated, but there isn't much left of that site. We actually visited there and most of it's been dismantled. So there wouldn't be much to actually see but, interestingly enough, there are other sites that we looked at around the South Island and most of them are not being used. I mean, they've been decommissioned, and it's interesting how people have co-opted them and taken them over and incorporated them into farming, or they have become part of various shops that sell their own goods and homemade stuff. So it's quite weird that these places are still used but, obviously, they're not the same in terms of what they were when they were mental health institutions.

LW: These pictures are all taken from the sanatorium that Jane mentioned, which was in a place called Hanmer Springs. It had just recently come up for auction, so the building and all the contents were being auctioned off. And we managed to time it correctly – when we were there, a lot of the contents were still there, and the place hadn't been pulled down, and these panopticon structures were very much still visible, and the architecture was still pretty much intact. This is in the Rutherford Ward that Jane mentioned earlier.

JW: We're talking a lot about the site itself and not so much about the work – we will show you the work that we made – but interestingly enough, this space is actually Maori-owned, so when it was decommissioned it was basically a prime piece of real estate handed back to Maori control. In New Zealand there's a very different balance in terms of how things happen. It's very different to what happened in Australia. This is up in Denniston Mine, and again that was a big part of the South Island, in these communities where you'd be living up on the top of a hill in the middle of nowhere and it was a mining town. And when the mist descended you couldn't even walk down the hill. It was perilous to even leave the town itself because you could fall and you wouldn't be able to survive. So, in a sense, to progress, there is an epic kind of battling with the landscape and the elements, which you become very conscious of when at these abandoned architectural sites from the last century – sites where existence was very tough.

LW: This is again inside the Chisolm Ward. This is an installation view of how we first showed *Erewhon*. It was actually a five-screen video installation and it was shown, for the first time in 303 Gallery in New York, in 2004. What you can see here is a floor-based screen that is roughly 4:3, and suspended above that is a 16:9 screen. And there's a mirror above the 16:9 to get the projection. Then there were two 16:9 screens that were suspended, that met in the corner, and above them is yet another 16:9 image. So you really feel like you could walk inside the work, in a sense, and be in that space. But also step outside of it. We wanted to try and disrupt that process of seeing the work just as a linear narrative film. We wanted it to be much more a physical encounter with the architecture as well. So the work is about eight-and-a-half minutes long, and what you are seeing here is images of the film that we shot in the South Island. But when we came back to the UK, to London in 2004, we started looking at the archival imagery which we'd seen in New Zealand. It was fascinating. Black-and-white documentation through news reports and other records of this health and fitness culture, the idea of the lovely ankle competition – things like that. It was made in a way that it was meant to engender positivity around the body and around physical health and such like, but there's something quite curious about these records, too. They're quite strange images. So we were very keen to incorporate something of the physical body with the actual physical buildings and the sites that we'd been documenting; to make that link in terms of a space. And so we actually reconstructed some of those images with some gymnasts at Heathrow. It's a gymnasium club and we actually dressed them and made them up, and did various things to simulate some of these images that we'd collected from New Zealand.

JW: Here's another installation view. So you can see this is how the other side – the two 16:9 screens and the overhead screen – work.

LW: It's interesting because it was based on a photograph from 1910. The gymnasts had to hold the positions for twenty to thirty seconds, so in a way the way the film sort of simulates some of that early photography. Again, this is 180 centimetres by 290 centimetres, it's actually not far off this dimension here in the projection, really.

JW: This image is called *The New Brutalist*.

LW: It's called *The New Brutalist*, exactly, and it was a recreation of an image that we found of lady gymnasts in 1910. We just thought this was an incredible title.

JW: It's very utopian as well, I suppose, in terms of the idea of community, and even in terms of representing women. I knew it was positive image. But it was strange to parallel that with the actual buildings from Hammer Springs, knowing the history there; knowing that there had been a lot of young mothers who'd gone there with children and who had been basically whisked out of society and kept hidden away. So there were a lot of things that went on there, which weren't particularly progressive, which were quite draconian. There was some sort of parallel there that we were trying to draw.

LW: I just wanted to say, as Jane mentioned earlier, that the gymnasts were filmed at a later date in a Heathrow gymnasium, after we'd done the filming in the South Island. And although they are obviously contemporary, their hair, make-up and clothing is made to look from a certain period. We wanted to get them to pose, if you like, to hold these quite strenuous poses, but to hold them for thirty or forty seconds to simulate the duration that would have been necessary for early photography from the turn of the last century. You know, that kind of thing where they would have had to have held their position, in a sense, to capture the image. We were aiming to simulate that in real time with the film. You can see it in the film, of course, that they were holding these poses for about thirty or forty seconds. This duration also references the time of the tracking shots in the film, which describe some of the interiors of these abandoned sites.

JW: Yes, we were actually on a very tight budget, so we counted each tracking shot to thirty seconds. Which meant that when we had a ratio of processing the film, it's pretty much a one to one ratio, which is good – we could use everything that we'd shot. I'm going to read a short text to set the scene for the film:

'The gymnasts were filmed in a Heathrow Gymnasium and are contemporary, yet disquieting in their poses for a series of tableaux vivants. Because of the duration there's a suggested ponderousness to their exercises. The women gymnasts climb ropes, exercise and hold poses. They employ a kind of visual rhythm through their uniformed bodies and through their repetitious movements, all of which become reflected in the studio mirrors behind them and in the patterns of the gym equipment's bars and cables. The effect is one of a constant surveillance as subjects. They become aware of being observed and employ their own kind of self-surveillance. They monitor themselves, assuming the poses that outside structures impose upon them. All of this is filmed against a backdrop of an abandoned landscape and architecture. So that all of the sites embody temporal self-contradictions because they are all recent ruins juxtaposed with the antiquated poses of the gymnasts. They evoke that sense of still living memories, of progress that came to an end. So that if modernist programmes fast-forwarding us to the future are unrealized, then what remains of them in the present are like spectres. *Erewhon* becomes a time that exists only in the imagination. A past future world allowing no present moment for coherent occupation.'

Following double page spread: Jane and Louise Wilson, *The New Brutalism II* (detail), 2004.

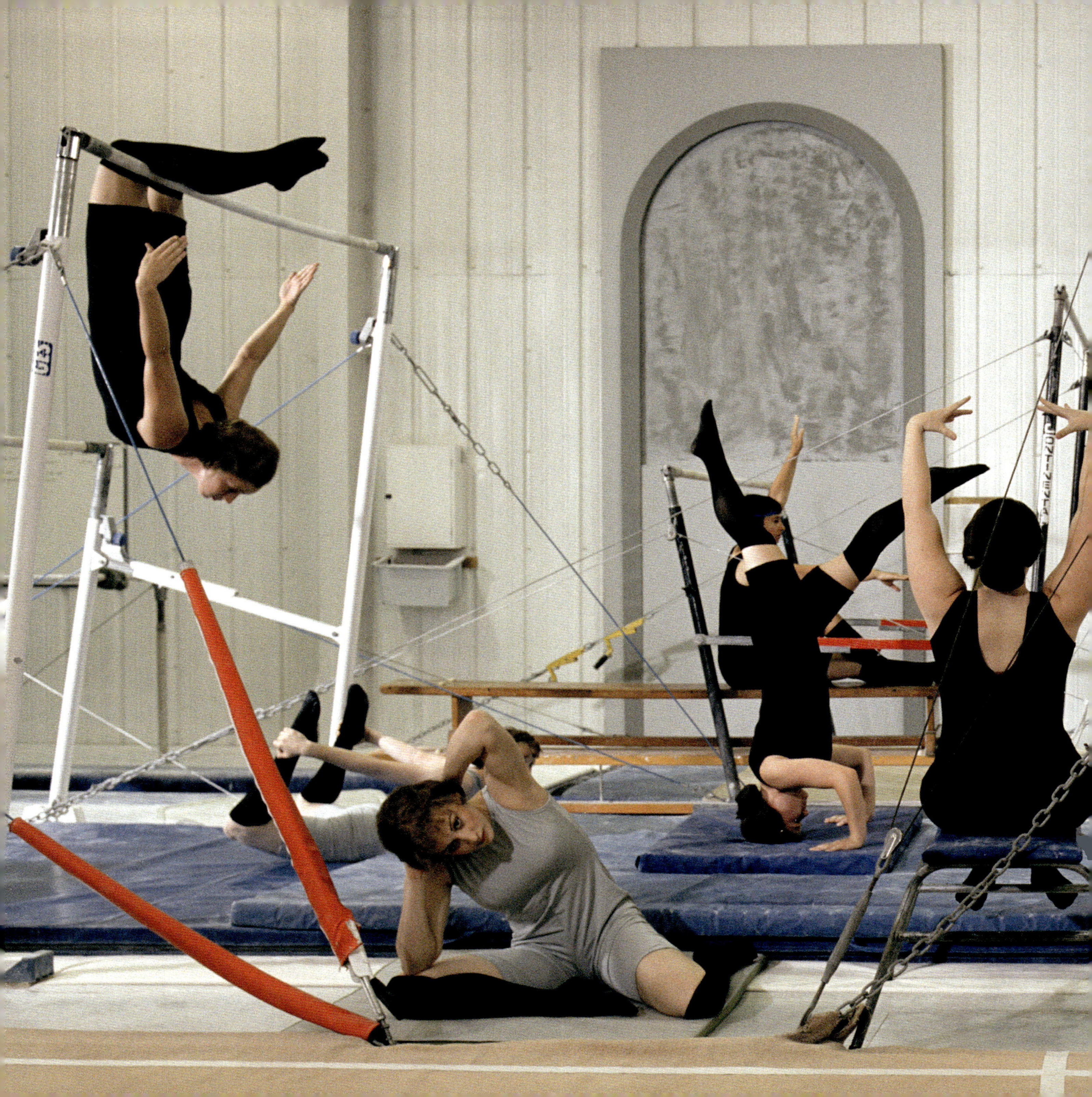

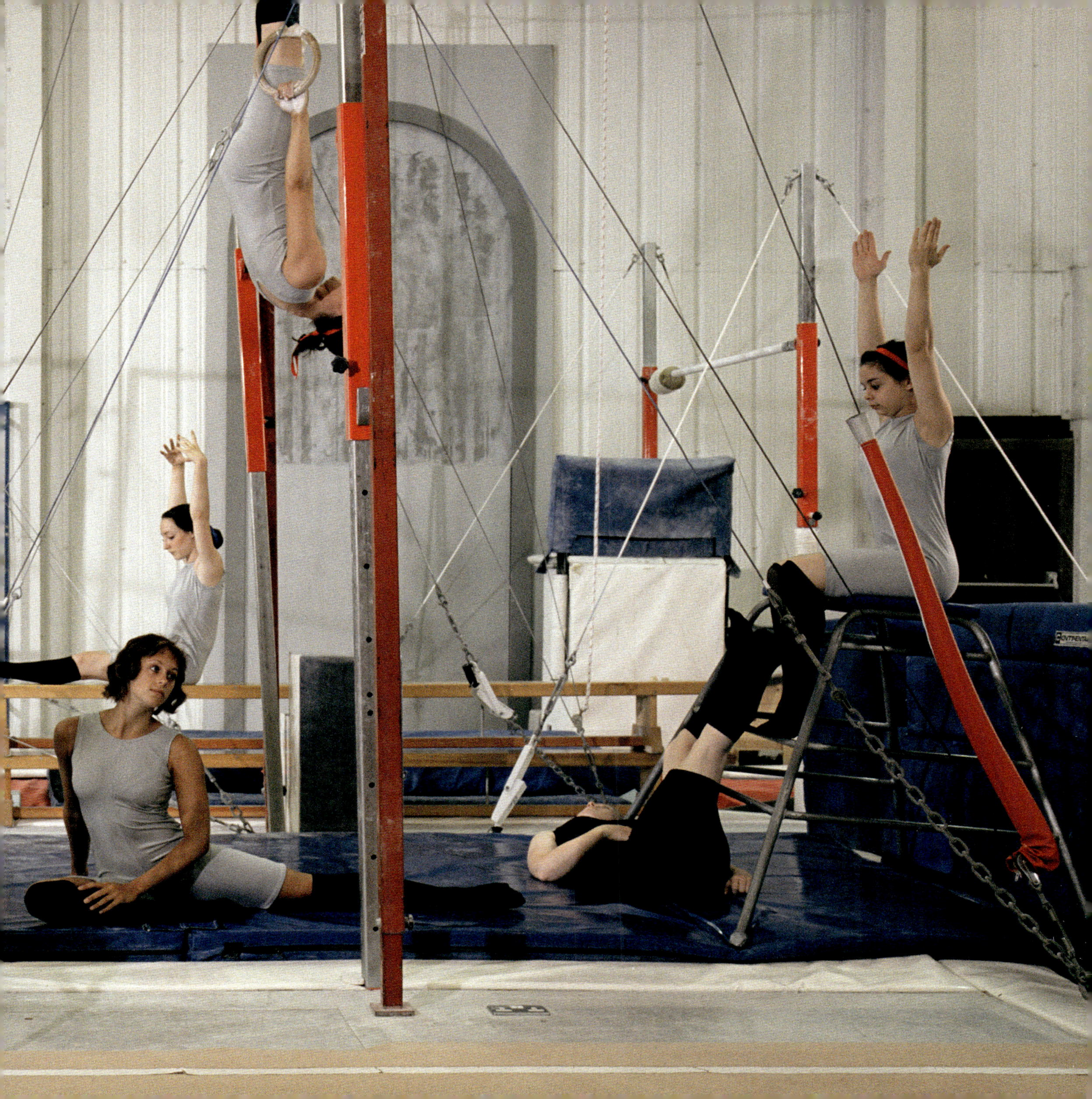

Jane and Louise Wilson, *Erewhon* (*Blue Skin Bay*), 2004.

Jane and Louise Wilson, *Erewhon* (*Shell Shock Hospital*), 2004.

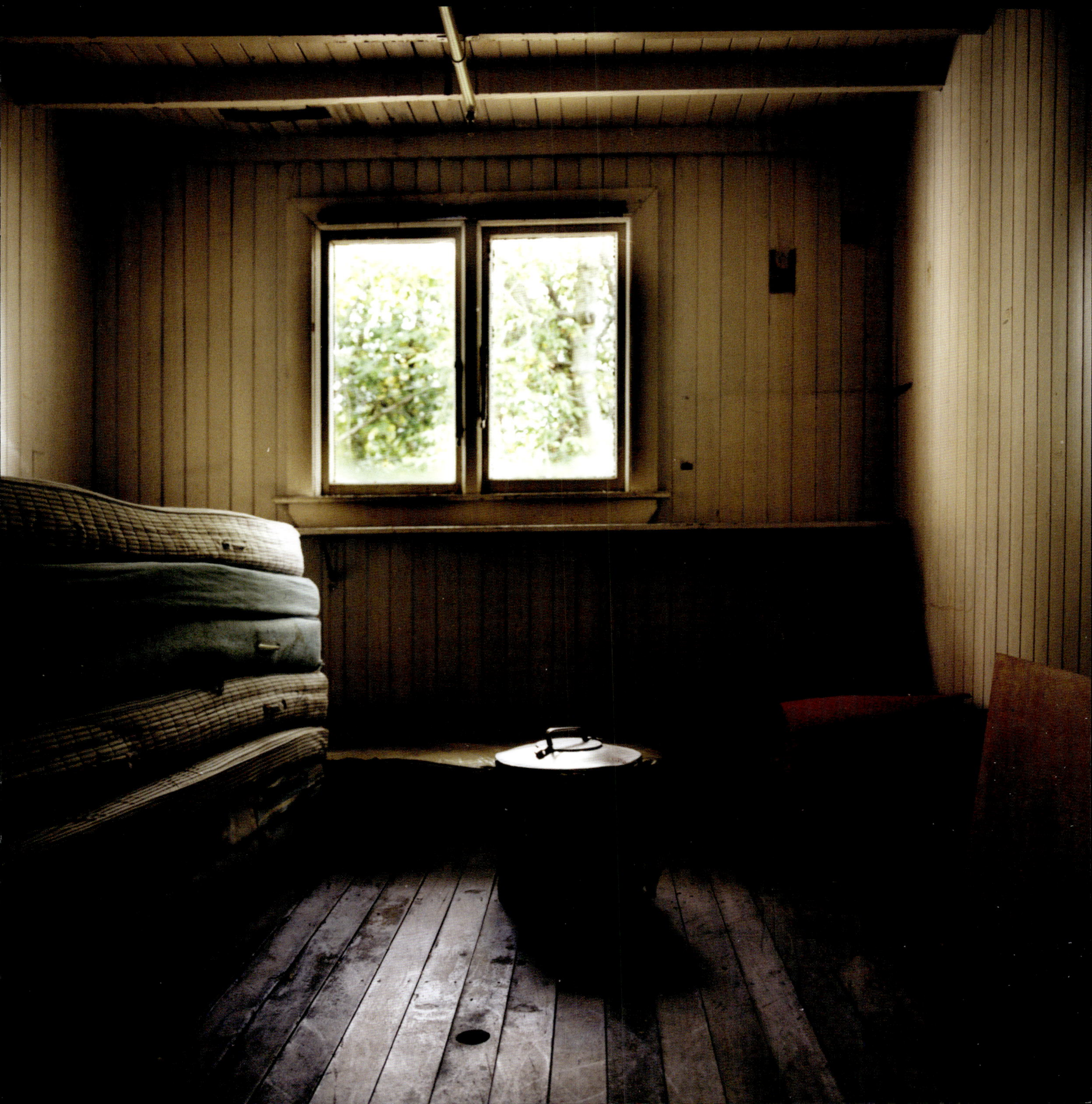

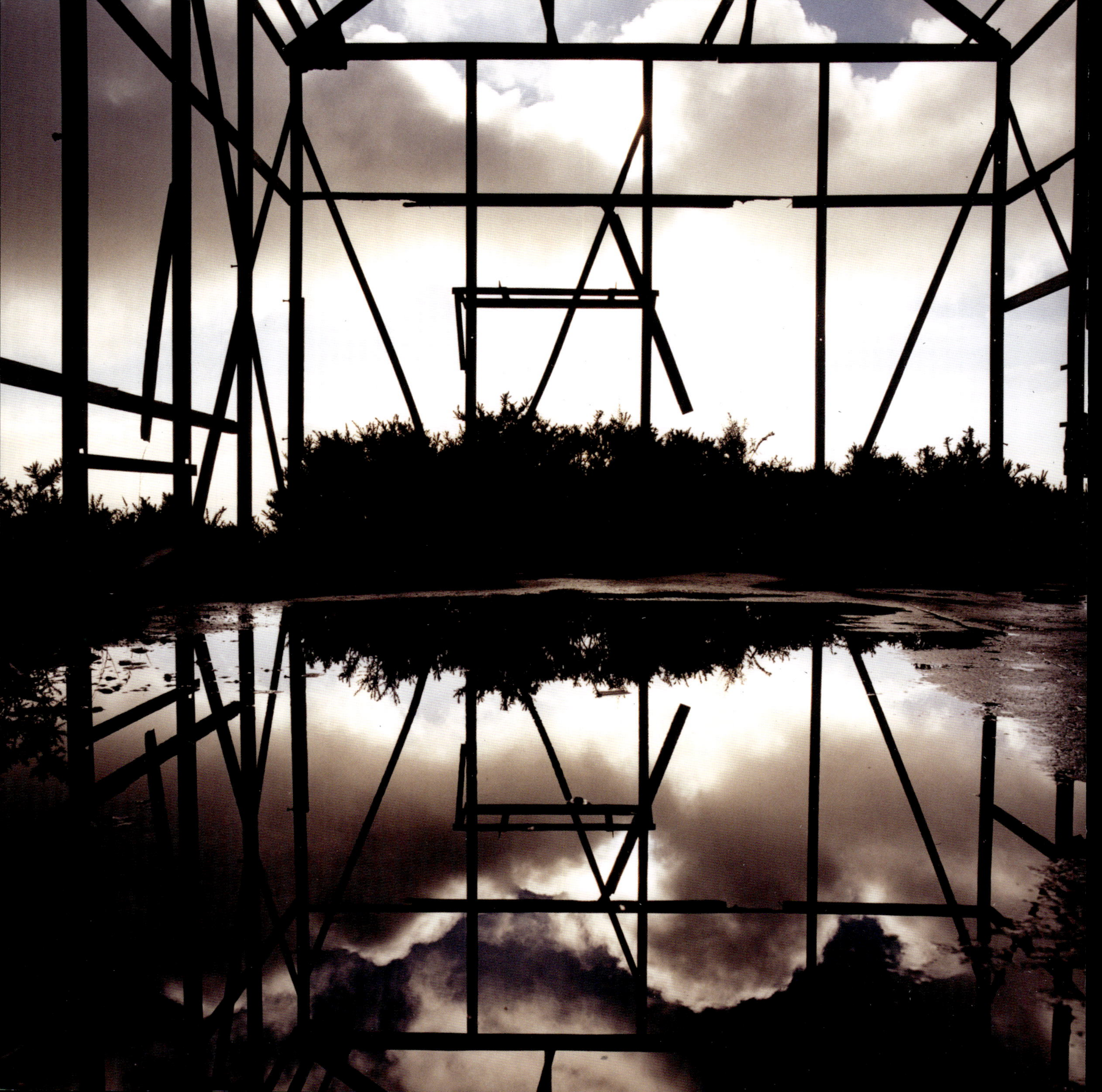

Jane and Louise Wilson, *Erewhon* (*Denniston*), 2004.

Jane and Louise Wilson, *Erewhon* (*Rutherford Ward*), 2004.

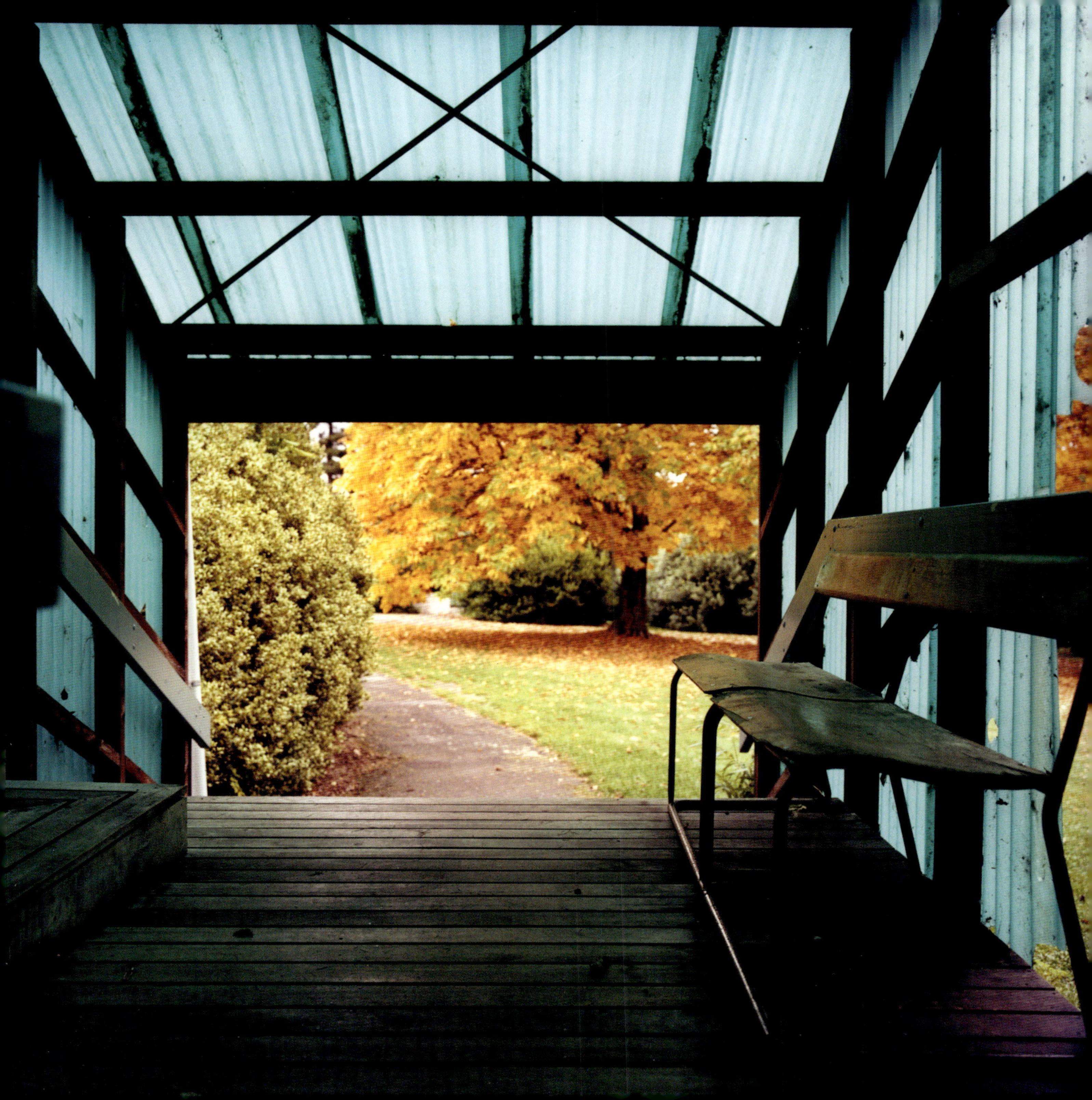

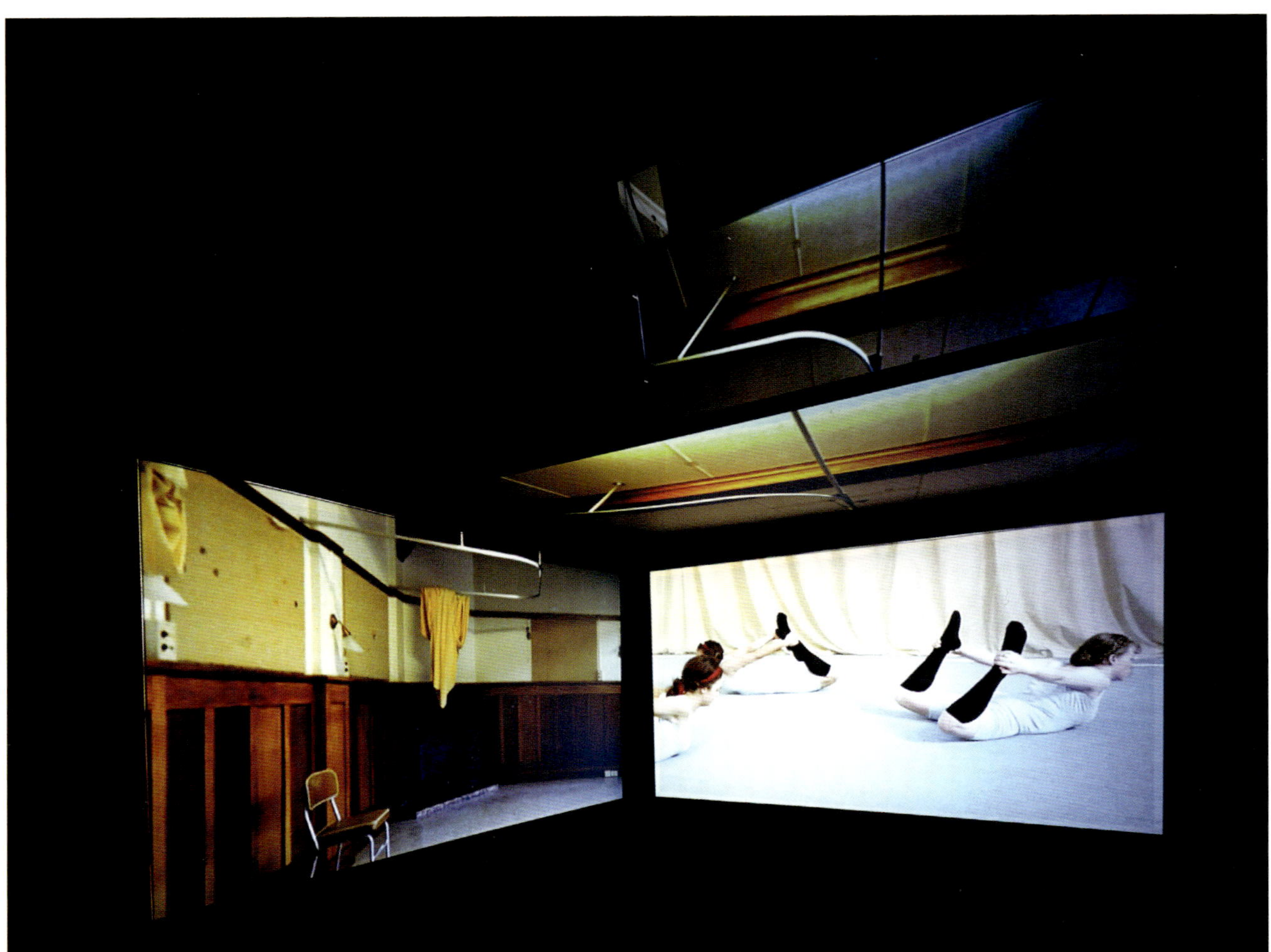

Erewhon (installation)

Jane and Louise Wilson, 2004. 5 channel/screen video installation. Dimensions variable.

DECONSTRUCTING GENDER IDENTITY & NON-PERFECTION

IN THE PHOTOGRAPHS OF YURIE NAGASHIMA

MARCO BOHR

In this chapter I analyse the work of Yurie Nagashima in relation to an aesthetic paradigm that embraces technical faults, motion blurriness, out-of-focusness, exaggerated contrast of colours, as well as other signifiers that can be associated with non-perfection. My analysis of Nagashima's work focuses on two specific movements in the history of Japanese photography in which a non-perfect, or even a self-consciously anti-perfect form of photographic practice emerged. During the 1990s, a group of young female photographers spearheaded by Nagashima became known for producing snapshot-style photographs that stood in sharp contrast to a type of photography, popular in the 1980s, in which image-making was considered a technical craft. These female photographers, although they never considered themselves as part of a group or a movement, were called 'girl photographers' by the Japanese media. In reviews of their work, as I will point out, critics continuously emphasized the perceived technical deficiencies and shortcomings in the photographs.

My analysis will contrast the emergence of an apparently non-perfect photography in the 1990s with a group of photographers who similarly embraced a technically flawed type of photography in the late 1960s. In parallel to protests against the Vietnam War, growing student unrest and the government's crackdown on social dissent, the late 1960s produced a style of photography generally referred to as *are, bure, boke*, or 'rough, blurred, out-of-focus'. Examples of this photography could be a found in the avant-garde photography magazine *Provoke*. In the history of Japanese photography, this important political, social and aesthetic shift in photographic practice is referred to as the 'Provoke era'.

While the work of the female photographers of the 1990s was generally criticized for lacking the technical detail of a previous generation of image-makers, those photographers associated with *Provoke*, on the other hand, were applauded for breaking boundaries and subverting codes of representation. Rather than assuming that these differences in perception are solely related to the gender of the photographers, in this chapter I analyse how these differences are largely related to the political context in which the photographs were produced. In other words, this paper investigates whether the photography of the late 1960s was an accepted form of non-perfection, while the non-perfect photography of the 1990s appears to have been perceived as technical and artistic weakness or even inability. While these differences in perception are related to the political context of the time, these differences also point to a culturally specific dimension in which non-perfection is either embraced or rejected.

A DEFINITION OF PERFECTION

Before I analyse the discourse of non-perfection in relation to the work of Yurie Nagashima, it is important to consider how the notion of 'perfection' relates to aesthetics in a Japanese cultural context. In his classic essay *In Praise of Shadows*, Junichiro Tanizaki argued that the subtle and subdued forms of Asian culture represent an appreciation of shadows and ambiguity.[1] In examples ranging from architecture to kitchenware, Tanizaki contrasts this appreciation of subdued tones, worn surfaces and darkness in Japanese culture with the search for light and clarity in the West. In other words, perfection is not found in the shiny surfaces of glass and metal, nor is it found in the dazzling clarity of crystal, for instance; but rather, Tanizaki argued, perfection can be found in rust, aging wood, even in dirt. In his 1933 essay, Tanizaki sets out the binary opposition between 'traditional' and 'modern', a shorthand for a crude distinction between 'Japan' and the 'West' that has long dominated the study of contemporary Japanese art in general and Japanese photography in particular.

In contrast to Tanizaki's self-orientalizing model of a unique Japanese aesthetics, the etymology for the Japanese word for perfect, *kanpeki*, alludes to a more universal definition of aesthetics. Derived from two Chinese ideographs which can be translated as 'completion' and 'sphere', as well as referring to a visually perfect dimension, *kanpeki* also refers to a mathematical perfection: the perfectly shaped circle or ball. The notion of perfection thus alludes to the 'perfect' axiomatic shape of a completed sphere symmetrical from whichever side it is viewed.

This emphasis on geometrical symmetry is indeed perceptible in the work of a number of Japanese photographers, such as Toshio Shibata and Naoya Hatakeyama. Emerging during a time of unprecedented economic growth in the 1980s, both photographers work with technically advanced photographic equipment to produce images that investigate the effects of the booming economy on the countryside and the city. In order to emphasize the encroachment of industry and technology, their photographs emphasize man-made structures, buildings and waterways. Man's desire to control the flow of nature is partially signified by producing technically extremely controlled images. For the contemporary artist Yasumasa Morimura, on the other hand, perfection lies in the act of referencing iconic images from western art history in digitally-manipulated photographic self-portraits. In his well-known project *Daughter of Art*

History, Morimura assumes various roles (Van Gogh, Rembrandt, the Mona Lisa, etc.) in photographs that closely resemble the original artwork. The emphasis on symmetry in perfection is thus also visible in Morimura's body of work as his photomontages are a near symmetrical visual response to iconic images from western art history.

THE PHOTOGRAPHS OF YURIE NAGASHIMA

Against this backdrop of perfection in visual, conceptual, even geometrical symmetry, a new generation of female photographers emerging in the 1990s appear to subvert these aesthetic paradigms. At the forefront of this shift was the photographer Yurie Nagashima (born 1973), who came to national fame after being awarded the prestigious Urbanart award in 1993. Nagashima's rapid popularity consequently led to her first photo book publication in 1995. In the book, self-referentially titled *Yurie Nagashima* (published by Fuga), Nagashima photographs herself as she changes her appearance in various photographic sequences of about six images each.

As a reference to her own increasing popularity at the forefront of a new generation of female photographers, in the first sequence of the book Nagashima photographs herself in the clichéd style of beauty photography: wearing bright-red lipstick, she looks straight into the camera as she smiles (Figure 1). The position of her arm on her shoulders suggests that she is trying to cover her naked body. With a few, very carefully selected signifiers (or lack thereof), Nagashima immediately positions herself as *gravure idol:* derived from the term Rotogravure, so-called *gravure idols* are girls who model primarily for men's magazines or photo books. As the etymology of the term *gravure idol* suggests, the perceived beauty of the subject is not necessarily in relation to her looks, but rather, it is in relation to her looks as perceived in an image; in this case, a photographic image. This is an important distinction which Nagashima's self-portrait is openly referencing: the photograph is the medium with which Nagashima seeks to project and protect the perfection of her youthful looks. This perfection is partially signified in the way the image was taken: the focus is crisp; the colours are saturated; the contrast covers the full gamut from the whites of her eyes to the shadows in her hair.[2]

Yet as the viewer progresses through the book, it quickly becomes apparent that Nagashima is acting out these various personas – she constructs the image so that she looks like a *gravure idol*. In another image, Nagashima photographs herself in a

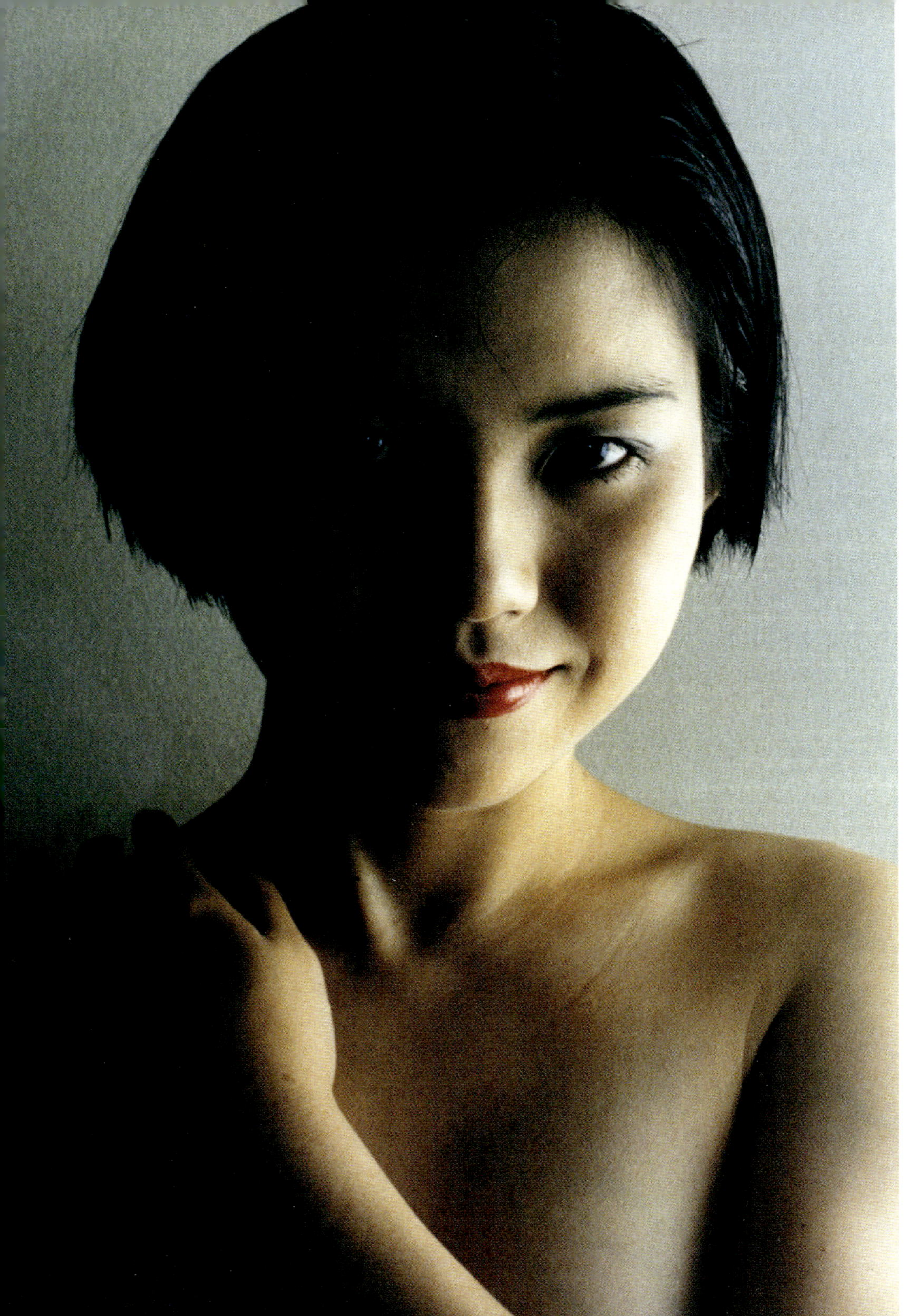

Figure 1: Yurie Nagashima, untitled, 1995 (©Yurie Nagashima; Courtesy of SCAI the Bathhouse, Tokyo).

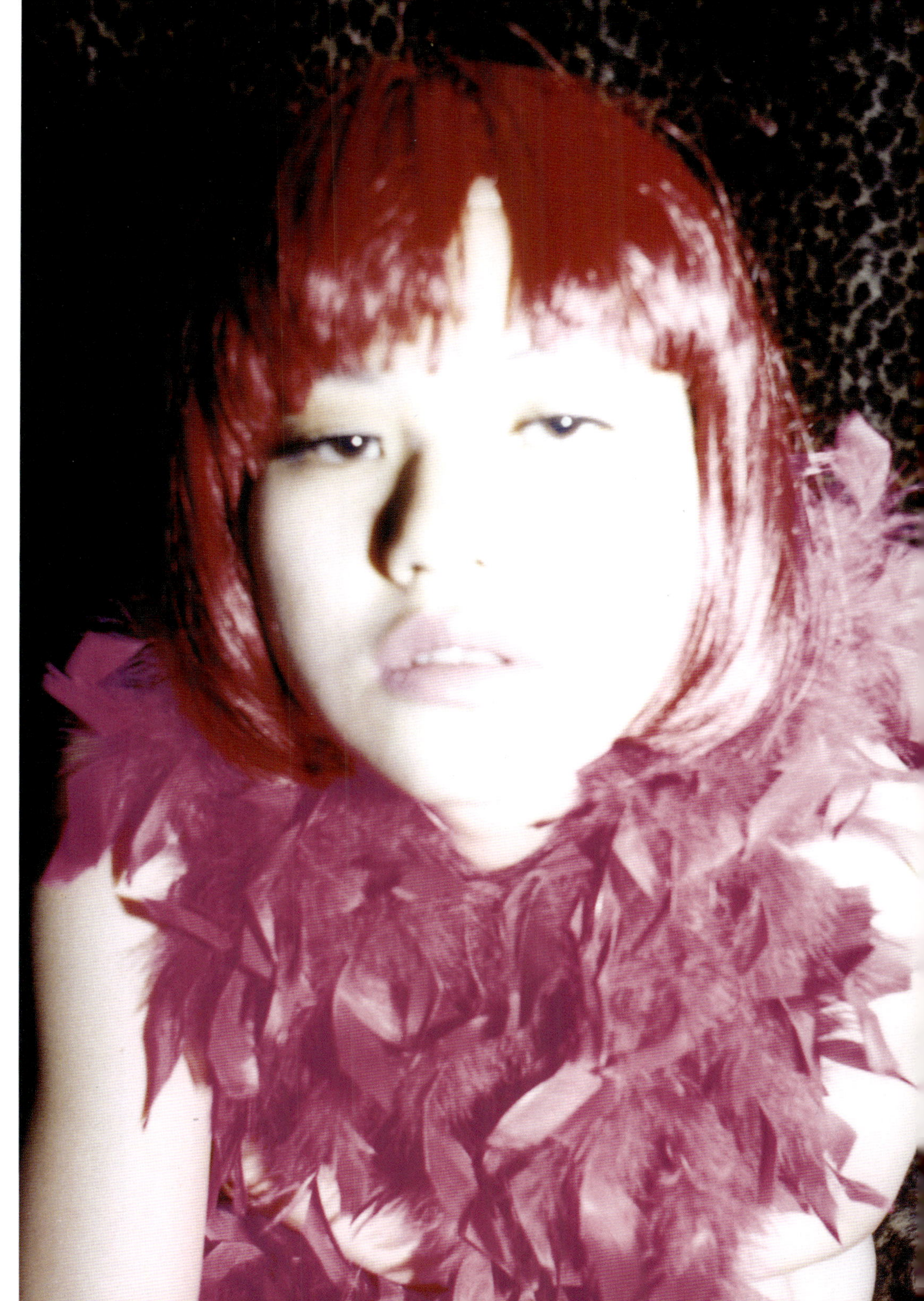

Figure 2: Yurie Nagashima, untitled, 1995 (©Yurie Nagashima; Courtesy of SCAI the Bathhouse, Tokyo).

pink wig, wearing boa feathers around her neck (Figure 2). While in the first image Nagashima looked more demure, in this sequence Nagashima's eyes are half-open, looking seductively into the camera. The image has similarly sexual undertones, yet here, Nagashima embraces the technical faults of the photographic apparatus to create an all-together more imperfect representation of herself: her face is out of focus and her skin is overexposed. Rather than accurately representing herself, Nagashima seems more interested in distorting this representation. In other words, similar to the pink wig, the technical attributes of the camera, such as the overexposure and the lack of focus, support Nagashima's agenda of distorting a representation of herself.

As the viewer flicks through the book, the photographs that represent Nagashima's shifting personas increasingly allude to sexual connotations. In one photograph, Nagashima appears to contort her body so that it assumes the reverse position on an exercise bike (Figure 3). Wearing nothing other than shoes, knee-high socks and knickers, Nagashima continues to deconstruct well-known stereotypes of representation in this image: a woman 'riding' a bicycle, a motorcycle or a horse has long been a favourite subject for the phallocentric representation of the female subject in both Japan and the West. Importantly, however, it is clear that Nagashima seeks to inverse this stereotypical representation in a number of ways. By cropping out her head, Nagashima underlines the fact that this clichéd representation solely focuses on the body as sexual object. The face, and therefore the individual character of the subject, is represented as irrelevant. Secondly, the various imperfections in the photograph, even the grime and dirt stains on the sliding doors, undermine the usually high print quality of advertising or glamour photography. Lastly, and perhaps most obviously, by riding the exercise bike in reverse, the photograph also seeks to reverse the assumption that to be photographed, the female body needs to be perfected through continuous exercise. Ultimately, Nagashima puts into question the complex dynamic between the female body, the perfect body and the photographic representation of the body. Nagashima effectively attacks a hegemony of images that equate the female body with perfection and sexual availability using the very tool (the photographic apparatus) with which this hegemony is sustained and promoted in the first place.

In another photograph in the book, Nagashima photographed herself sitting on the bathroom floor, her body inconsistently wrapped in bandages and her left eye covered

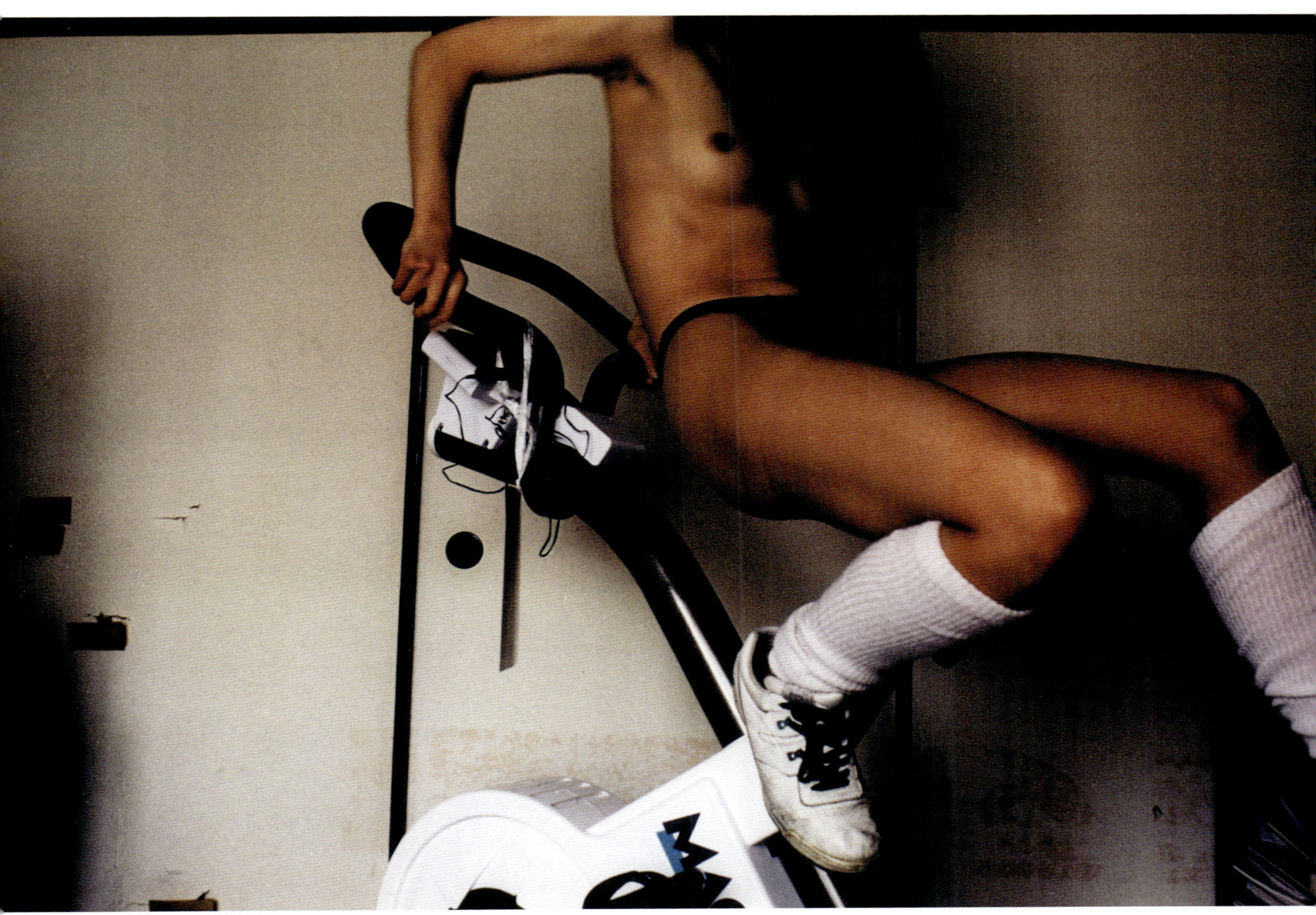

Figure 3: Yurie Nagashima, untitled, 1995 (©Yurie Nagashima; Courtesy of SCAI the Bathhouse, Tokyo).

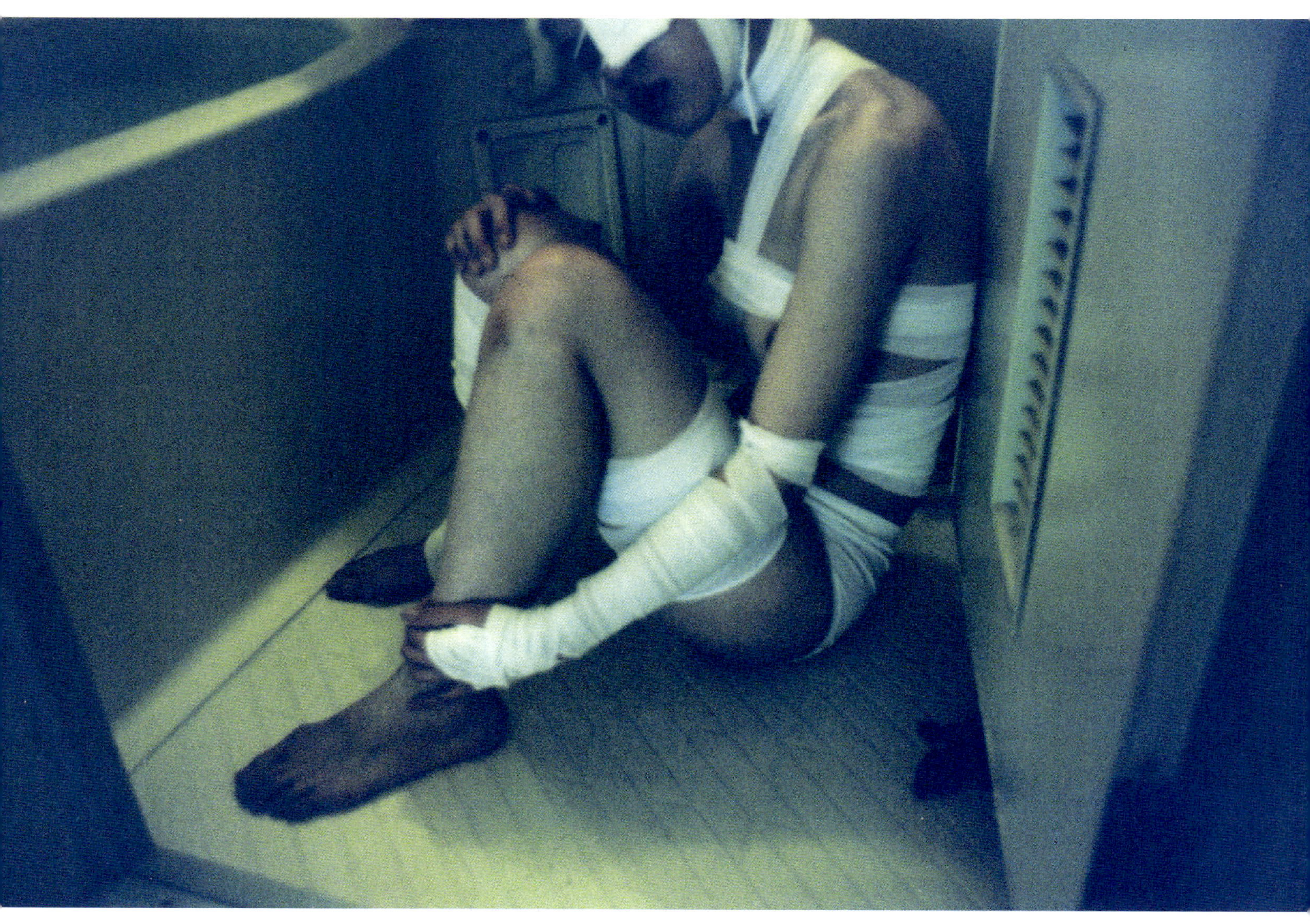

Figure 4: Yurie Nagashima, untitled, 1995 (©Yurie Nagashima; Courtesy of SCAI the Bathhouse, Tokyo).

by a white patch (Figure 4). Far from the perfect body, the perfect smile and the perfect glance into the camera as portrayed in the first photograph, here Nagashima represents herself as a heavily injured person. Her frailty is further emphasized by crouching on the floor of the bathroom and looking up towards the camera. The imperfections of representing her body as injured are underlined in the technical attributes of the photograph: the image is heavily underexposed, the camera is awkwardly tilted towards the ground and the print has a blue tinge. What appears to be a toy crocodile on the floor is perhaps a hidden reference to the work of Nobuyoshi Araki, who frequently incorporates plastic Godzilla and dinosaur toys in his photographs. Like a number of Araki's many female subjects, Nagashima represents herself as a *kegadoru* (injured doll) – the fetishistic representation of the female subject as apparently injured or physically hurt. While the origins of this fetish can be traced to a genre of *manga*, Nagashima's self-portrait is a reference to the encroachment of such fetishistic, and perhaps also pornographic, depictions in visual culture. The image emphasizes the fact that Nagashima purposefully applies the technical limitations of photography in order to emphasize the liminal state of her body withdrawn from society.

By becoming the subject of her own photographs, deconstructing gender identities and subverting cultural stereotypes, Nagashima established an important visual and conceptual platform that would have a major impact on female photographers of her generation. Her photo book signalled the possibility of women artists using photography in order to critique photography. Like Nagashima, photographers such as Hiromix, Sakiko Nomura and Mika Ninagawa embraced the technical limitations of photography to create a visual, as well as a conceptual, contrast to the work of previous generations. In parallel to that, the use of metaphors, hidden references, role-play and tongue-in-cheek humour are all aspects that female photographers increasingly applied in their practice in order to critique and deconstruct the representation of gender.

THE DISCOURSE OF LACK

Ever since the emergence of Yurie Nagashima in 1993, photography critics, curators and fellow photographers began to describe the so-called 'girl photographers' as lacking certain abilities or knowledge. There are numerous examples for what I call a discourse of lack: in 1995, the established artist and aforementioned photographer, Yasumasa

Morimura, argues that the up-and-coming photographers Yurie Nagashima and Sakiko Nomura 'casually use their cameras like toys and don't care whether or not they are breaking any traditional rules [*jūdai no ruru*].'[3] In reference to the rising star Hiromix and 'girls' in general, the photographer Nobuyoshi Araki comments: 'Without thinking too much, they let their feelings rule their actions.'[4] It is a perception that had a long-lasting effect on how the female photographers discussed in this chapter were, and still are, perceived in Japan. Even as recently as 2005, the respected art historian Midori Matsui argues that 'girl photographers' are 'artists without special training or theoretical equipment.'[5] The marketing analyst Atsushi Miura confirms the direction in which this discourse was inevitably heading, as he points out the following: 'When my daughter was three she took pictures with a disposable camera, which look like Hiromix's work, no sense of composition, light coming from weird directions or without any good framing.'[6]

In regards to the perceived technical faults in the work of Yurie Nagashima and the photographers of her generation, a historical parallel can be drawn with the photographer Daidō Moriyama (born 1938), whose photographs are closely associated with a photographic 'style' referred to as *are, bure, boke* (rough, blurry, out-of-focus), which emerged out of the chaotic days of student uprisings in the late 1960s. Shōji Yamagishi, a well-regarded editor of *Camera Mainichi* and a key figure in photography until his death in 1979, once wrote that Daidō Moriyama 'has come to be called "a standard bearer of the blurred image."'[7] While the 'girl photographers' of the 1990s are collectively critiqued for their technical weaknesses and their perceived amateurism, the blurriness in the work of Moriyama was, on the contrary, received with critical acclaim.

Apart from the crude modernist pretensions of associating a single person, a man, with this 'style', what does not seem to figure in the formula 'Daidō Moriyama equals blurred image' is that *are, bure, boke* was born out of the necessity of student protestors clashing with the police, and photographers working under rapidly changing situations and low light conditions.[8] While on one hand Moriyama is lauded as the 'bearer of the blurred image', the 'girl photographers', on the other hand, are said to 'casually use their cameras like toys.' The blurriness in the work of Moriyama was perceived as intentional, while in the work of the 'girl photographers' it was perceived as accidental. Underlying this cultural emphasis on regarding Moriyama as the 'bearer' of the blurred image is that it perhaps feeds into the perceived uniqueness of Japanese aesthetics as described by Junichiro Tanizaki. Moriyama's blurry images are the photographic equivalent of the rusty kitchenware so poetically described by Tanizaki.

Within the many commentaries regarding 'girl photographers' several patterns began to emerge concerned with the photographers' instinctive use of the camera, an emphasis on their feelings and their alleged amateurism. One aspect in the growing 'girl photography' discourse seems particularly important and that is the constant reiteration of a lack on the 'girls' part: their lack of care for the rules, their lack of rationale, their lack of training and, most crudely, their lack of skill. In other words, instead of focusing on what they might possess, the emphasis falls on what the 'girls' do not possess. In that sense, the term 'girl photography' is always tied to a perception of the female photographers not quite complete, missing certain attributes, not understanding the world, and so forth. In the case of Yurie Nagashima, for example, this emphasis on a lack of 'training and theoretical equipment' seems particularly unjustified considering that she studied at Musashino University, one of Japan's most renowned art schools, and at the California Institute of the Arts under the tutelage of the American photographer Catherine Opie, with whom she had a two-person show at the Parco Gallery in 1995. Evidently, there is a disjuncture between who the 'girl photographers' are and what they are supposed to represent. In a recorded conversation with the German photographer Wolfgang Tillmans, Nagashima addresses this disjuncture between perception and actuality: 'The reason why I couldn't explain my work properly, was not because I didn't have any ideas how to explain it, but because of the gap between my intentions and how critics perceived my work.'[9]

At the heart of this misperception described by Nagashima was the discourse of lack attached to her practice almost from the moment her work entered the public domain. The discourse of lack is not as much a distinction of skill, talent or style, but rather a distinction between the sexes. In psychoanalytical discourse, sexual difference is based on the visibility of difference, whereas the feminine is perceived as lacking from the masculine norm. As the psychoanalyst Jacqueline Rose pointed out:

> In so far as it is the order of language which structures sexuality around the male term, or the privileging of that term which shows sexuality to be constructed within

> language, so this raises the issue of women's relationship to that language and that sexuality simultaneously.[10]

Based on this psychoanalytical framework of lack, which hinges on the phallus as universal signifier, the male is the norm whereas the female is understood as a deviation from that norm. As Sean Homer points out, the French feminist Luce Irigaray used the framework to make a point, which also relates to the case of the 'girl photographers'. Homer writes: 'Irigaray is suggesting not that women are irrational but rather that rationality itself has been historically constructed in such a way that the feminine is inevitably repressed.'[11] The very name 'girl photography' alludes to such a repressed status: apart from creating a misleading category, it also points to the very fixity of 'girl' as a social construct. In that sense, to point out that photographers are using 'their cameras like toys' or that they lack 'training and theoretical equipment' is much less related to their photographic practice than it is to a culturally, historically, ideologically and socially constructed perception of femininity.

It would be too simple to argue that the differing perceptions of non-perfect photography is solely related to the sex of the photographer. The political climate of the late 1960s has had a major effect on the way *are, bure, boke* has been so favourably received by historians: the radicalism of the era was conveniently also represented in the photography coming out of that era. That is not to say however that the mid-1990s were in any ways less radical. The battleground for a new generation of artists was not the street or a confrontation with the state, but rather, for photographers such as Yurie Nagashima, the battleground was demarcated by their own private space and their bodies within this space. The confrontation was not an ideological clash with the state, but it was a political clash with the various media that construct female identity. From the sexualized representations of the glamour idol to the highly fetishized representation of a *kegadoru*, Nagashima establishes this clash with the very medium that reinforces a stereotypical representation of gender. Photography becomes the tool, the device and the methodology to articulate, visualize and problematize the positionality of the subject in relation to her social condition. In a sense, similar to the postcolonial critic Homi Bhabha 'mastering' the English language, the language of the colonizer, Nagashima masters photography in defiance of photography colonizing the female body. Here, by using photography and by photographing herself, Nagashima essentially mimics the cult of youth as consumed and reinforced by the photographic medium. The postcolonial application of the concept of mimicry also concerns this analysis, as Bill Ashcroft points out:

> When colonial discourse encourages the colonial subject to 'mimic' the colonizer, by adopting the colonizer's cultural habits, assumptions, institutions and values, the result is never a simple reproduction of those traits. Rather, the result is a 'blurred copy' of the colonizer that can be quite threatening.[12]

The threat, so aptly described by Ashcroft, is similarly discernable in the critical response to Nagashima and the photographers of her generation. In order to quell this threat, cultural gatekeepers (both male and female) got consistently trapped in the discourse of lack. The threat issued by Nagashima and the photographers of her generation mainly lies in the suspicion that the images that they produce (including the technical inaccuracies) are part of a tantalizing visual game that they are in full control of.

CONCLUSION

Yurie Nagashima was at the forefront of a major shift in the history of Japanese photography. Her work, particularly in her first photo book, functions as a visual precedent in deconstructing gender identity via the medium of photography in the context of contemporary Japanese culture. Far from seeking to avoid technical inaccuracies (a habit most photographers are obsessed about), Nagashima utilized the various characteristics of the camera and the photographic print not only to deconstruct her identity vis-à-vis photography, but also to deconstruct the photographic image, the way it is produced, consumed and disseminated. Her aim was not to create an accurate or a natural representation of herself, but, rather, she sought to distort this representation with the technical attributes of the camera. The radicalism of her photography is compounded by the act of mimicking – an act that was meant to provoke, disturb and certainly also to threaten a hegemony of images that historically situates the female body as the object of sexual desire.

NOTES

1 Junichiro Tanizaki, *In Praise of Shadows*, London: Vintage Classics, [1933] 2001.
2 The 'perfect' black-and-white print is said to incorporate the whole tonal spectrum from white to black.
3 Yasumasa Morimura, '*Gendai no shikaku hyōgen de hijyū takamatta shashin nihon no dentoubi to shinwa ni sanhiryouron*'/'Photographs grew in importance due to the present form of expression: the pros and cons of traditional Japanese art and its affinities', in *Asahi Yūkan*, 2nd February 1995, p. 11. (Translations from Japanese to English are by Tajana Wesley).
4 Nobuyoshi Araki and Fumio Nanjo, *New Cosmos of Photography: 10th Anniversary Commemoration*, Tokyo: Canon, 2002, p. 127.
5 Midori Matsui, 'Beyond the Pleasure Room to a Chaotic Street: Transformations of Cute Subculture in the Art of the Japanese Nineties', in Murakami Takashi (ed.), *Little Boy*, New Haven: Yale University Press, 2005, p. 225.
6 Atsushi Miura, 'How to grasp "Nippon?" Thinking about contemporary Japan and its photographers: Conversation between Atsushi Miura and Hiromi Tsuchida', in Guardian Garden (ed.), *Photo Documentary "Nippon" 2004–2006, Tokyo: Recruit*, 2006, p. 320.
7 Shōji Yamagishi, *A Hunter by Daido Moriyama*, Tokyo: Chūō-kōron-sha, 1972.
8 I have written about this extensively elsewhere: Marco Bohr, '*Are-Bure-Boke*: Distortions in late 1960s Japanese Cinema and Photography', *Dandelion Journal*, Vol. 2, No. 2, 2011.
9 Yurie Nagashima in conversation with Wolfgang Tillmans, *Switch*, December Issue, Vol. 22, No. 12, December 2004, p. 124.
10 Jacqueline Rose, 'Jacques Lacan and the École Freudienne', in Juliet Mitchell and Jacqueline Rose (eds), *Feminine Sexuality*, London: MacMillan, 1982, p. 54.
11 Sean Homer, *Jacques Lacan*, London: Routledge, 2005, p. 117.
12 Bill Ashcroft, *Post-Colonial Studies: The Key Concepts*, London: Routledge, 2000, pp. 124–25.

LOUISE WILSON
&
MARCO BOHR

DISCUSSION, CHAIRED BY **MARK DURDEN**

Mark Durden: Thanks to both speakers and it's quite a mix, actually, quite an interesting collision. I'm aware of the differences in Marco's reflection on Japanese photography, in particular the shift from the work of a male photographer, Daido Moriyama, to 'girl photography', and the different receptions the work has received. And then the presentation of Jane and Louise Wilson, two female artists making work that is dealing with questions of power, subjugation and gender. So, particularly because Marco used the word 'politics' a few times, I want to ask you Louise about the politics of *Erewhon* in terms of gender and agency and how important is that to the work?

Louise Wilson: Well, I think there's a mordant quality to the fact that you see these contemporary women dressing up in a way that looks as though it's from another period, and there's a playfulness around it as well. It's constructed and it's very much something where their agency is implicit – they're controlling their movements and how they look in the image. It's also shown in real time: we're not capturing that perfect moment or that idealized view of how they should be pictured. It implies a process, in a way. As for all those ideas, I'm not sure how that rests, how I can articulate the politics as such…

MD: Can I push it as authors in terms of that, I think it's integral to the film to have this awkward response to these women that are re-enacting and holding a pose. It's about posing and it's about photography as well as film. It's a static camera shot of women holding difficult poses.

LW: This image that we mentioned from 1910, *The New Brutalists*, is an extraordinary, protofeminist suffragette image. It's very powerful, especially considering the time that it was taken. I mean obviously we're referencing it over a hundred years later, but there is something about that that I think is important. I'm not sure if that's answering the question.

MD: I was interested in the control as two female authors, the control you have as film-makers in relationship to these extraordinary scenes – and I found it really powerful seeing it on a single screen, which cannot obviously do justice to experiencing *Erewhon* as an actual installation. So I want to know about the kind of control that you have and how important it is as two female artists making that kind of work.

LW: We work very much in a dialogue: we don't have a unilateral ego that's out there just making that decision. It's much more about the tension and the questioning that comes from dialogue. I don't really see it as being necessary that there be one name and one author and all of those things – we work through collaborative practices…

MD: Is it a bit more democratic? Less author-centric?

LW: Democratic; it's just not about that individual ego. Simple. We're not at all bothered by that or concerned with that.

MD: Unlike the Japanese photographers, perhaps? Is that about the question of authorship and the narcissism of 'girl photography'?

Marco Bohr: Yes, I think narcissistic is the right term to use. And it struck me that the work that I'm talking about here emerged in the mid '90s, but it's a type of photography that I, through Facebook and Twitter and celebrity culture, see more and more often. And it's weird because I'm talking about these photographs; they were photographed on film with a point-and-shoot camera, but actually it's much closer to photographs I see taken on an iPhone or taken on the cell phone through a mirror. So there is definitely a good portion of narcissism involved.

MD: It's a subtle shift. You say this is political work because it's deconstructing. It's miming, but mime of the kind of more misogynist aspects of Nobuyoshi Araki's work, for example, and you also said miming popular Japanese culture's representation of women. Is the mimesis enough to actually challenge those stereotypes? It's a subtle difference and it's quite a provocation.

MB: Yes. In fact you could argue it's just as provocative as the first Provoke group. So it's definitely a provocation, and if this symposium had been on provocation, I could have shown many more images on that theme. But I wanted to stick to perfection or anti-perfection. Well, is the work I have shown successful?

MD: I haven't got the answer. I'm just interested.

MB: I'm not sure either. But maybe the success is that we're talking about it now and here. And I met the photographer who is the main subject of my thesis a few times and she is very grateful that her work is looked at. She has had to go through a lot of trouble in her career as a photographer. She has rarely been exhibited in any public museum in Japan. I believe it's down to a sort of very old hierarchy. And I'm not even using the word male-dominated, because that's incorrect. The curator, the only curator I quoted from, is actually a woman. So I'm talking about an old system, which a few photographers – who were wrongly put together in the same pot – were not able to overcome. But, nevertheless, we're speaking about it now…

Leslie Dick: Marco, I'm really intrigued by these 'girl photographers' and I think it's a sign of the intensity of the obligation towards perfection in Japanese women that they are resisting in their quote/unquote 'imperfect' photographs. And every imperfection is a sign of resistance. And the fact that the institutions have not welcomed them and co-opted them is the sign of how powerful making a dirty photograph of yourself on your balcony or in your messy apartment is, because it transgresses against expectations and standards of how women should be. And I think that's true especially in Japan, but it's true everywhere.

MB: Yes, that's a very good point and, in fact, I wholeheartedly agree with you. This is certainly not specific to Japan. I mean in England just the other day there was a L'Oreal skin cream advertisement which depicted Rachel Weisz, and it was banned because what L'Oreal claims the cream could do was not true, or more accurately, it was impossible. The model was Photoshopped to such an extent that the image was just unreal. So it's not specific to Japan but, yes, it is a huge discourse in Japan and, in fact, in my research I came across a magazine for teenage girls and it gave specific instructions on how to be photographed. So instead of being photographed full frontally, it recommends you turn your body to the side so you look thinner. It suggests you ask the photographer to photograph from a higher vantage point so that you also look shorter. Tilt your head slightly to the side so that you're sort of coquetting with the camera. And finally – this was the best thing – the instruction was to stand behind an object – in this case it was a tree trunk – to make the subject look even more thin and small. I couldn't stop thinking about this big, huge phallic object there. But, you know, I'm sure if I go through a teen magazine in England or in the US or in Germany, you would find very similar promotions.

Charlotte Cotton: I wanted to add to Leslie and your views on where perfection fits within 'girl photography'. There's something else going on, maybe another explanation beyond the sexism of the art world as to why the 'girl photography' hasn't been particularly well represented in institutions in Japan. It's partly because of the way that photography is highly provocative within the discourses – the broader discourses of photography – in Japan, in a way that isn't quite as incendiary as it is in the West. To go right, right back, if you think that in the West, when photography is conceived, it lands right in the middle of the debate about what is or is not art. So, immediately, it's got a relationship with artistic practice – modern, contemporary artistic practice – whereas it's not the same in Japan. I mean, you've got traditional crafts which tend to be about reaching the archetype, the ideals, so perfection. And then there's photography. I mean, I might be wrong in this, but I've always thought of Provoke as a group which just proved how liberated photography was from always having to ultimately be validated as an art form. That actually the photographic discourses of Japan are just as much about *kawaii* – you know, books of cute rabbits – as they are about a 'girl photographer' producing a run of a hundred books. So I don't quite know where 'girl photography' would fit within institutional practice, which in Japan is either about photography in relation to the perfect and the archetypal as seen with traditional crafts, so an encyclopaedic museum; or Japan as a place that's looking at media, so technology. Or looking at modern and contemporary art, and again I think 'girl photography' has a difficulty fitting into those institutional narratives of photography.

MB: Yes, it does. I mean this could be another topic for another Ph.D. because I don't have the actual answer for that myself. In Japan it's partially also related to the way institutions are funded by the state. Of course institutions are also funded by the state here, but they go via a different avenue such as the Arts Council. Whereas in Japan the idea is actually that the museums are directly funded by the taxpayer. So institutions tend to be a bit more conservative with what they're going for, and usually the emphasis is on producing exhibitions with a lot of foot traffic. So a van Gogh exhibition or a Manet exhibition, they would be the popular exhibitions.

MD: I'm conscious about balance and I just wanted to ask Louise about the form of the presentation. Because you've chosen – and I know you've done that as well in the installation I saw at QUAD – a deliberate way of presenting video. It's not a monocular kind of video. It's multiple. And it's a multiple sensorial experience. You've got sound and you've got two different primary camera movements in *Erewhon*. You've got the static camera and the gymnasts' re-enactment performing, and you've got the video camera moving around the space. So there's this multi-sensory experience, and I think it recurs in a lot of your previous work. Is that really integral to an opposition to all the structures and the way in which they discipline the body in *Erewhon*, the panopticon, let's say, and the way the panopticon works?

LW: The panopticon is about surveillance and it puts the body at the centre, in a sense, so you can view that 360 perspective. But we were thinking much more about breaking down that space – so it's important that you can be outside of the work. You can be behind the work. You can't view it all at the same time, so you break down those screens and you break down that viewing experience that you normally have in a cinema. With the five screens, some are above and some are behind – so it breaks it down and it opens it out in a sense and, yes, that is a very conscious decision to not make it so centred.

MD: You're decentred in maybe a productive way.

LW: That's up to whoever the audience is, whoever comes to see it – it's up to them what they think. Personally, a lot of what was expressed came out of our frustration at seeing a very validated format of this experience in film. And only ever having that way of encountering it. What we were more interested in was creating something that was confrontational: a more bodily and more kinaesthetic experience; almost making it film and sculpture in a sense. All of those things we think about.

MD: It just seems integral to your work and I'm trying to make a link here with materiality. And I wondered if there's something about that in *Provoke* – I know they're very different works, but there's something about your account of the snapshot that's let in the light and the film becomes material. So there's something about the physicality of prints that maybe goes against this – I mean you're both dealing with big clichés like surveillance and the monocular perspective of the camera, the fetishizing camera. And I wondered if those 'girl photographers' are using the medium as a point of resistance as well? Different to *Provoke*, because the fact that if the light goes in the camera, and you said about mortality as well, didn't you, in that one image. And it's a beautiful light.

LW: About aging, wasn't it?

MB: Yes, aging.

MD: But there's also something about how it goes against – and their arguments about blur as well fit – about resisting the fetishizing of the camera.

MB: That's a good question.

MD: It's about these forms they're occupying because they're both against that kind of monocular, empowering situation.

MB: You know, I've never thought about that before, but the prime way to disseminate photographs in Japan is actually the photo book. Not necessarily the exhibition. So the Provoke group might have kicked that off a little bit with their fantastic publication. But the funny thing is that when you walk into a second-hand bookshop in Tokyo and you ask for a photo book or *shashinshu*, which is the word, you get shown a rather seedy corner of the bookshop which is just full of representations of naked women. And so the idea is actually the *shashinshu* is a photo book of naked girls. So there is this dominant idea that the photo book is necessarily girls taking off their clothes. And yet the 'girl photographers' are primarily disseminating their images with photo books. Their emergence must be seen in parallel to the photo book industry – a huge industry in Japan - which actually boomed in the 1990s as well.

LW: But do you think some of that came about because there's a tradition of women photographers as well. I mean traditionally there's a whole back catalogue of artists, like I can think of Cindy Sherman for example, whose later works were very much about the horror of the image. I was just thinking of that picture you showed us of a woman with Elastoplasts. You know, she's almost sporting open wounds. And yet, interestingly enough, it's about the multiplicity of self; it's not necessarily about taking a political stance by doing photography as such. I think that's important. We can't ignore that as well when we're talking about where this understanding of work lies in a bigger context.

MB: Yes, that's right, and that's something I struggle with. Because at the beginning of my research I thought I'm just looking at Japan. But then I realized that this emergence must also be seen in a global context: the emergence of celebrity culture, surveillance culture and the democratization of photography by digital media is something that we are all very aware of and it's not specific to one culture.

MD: I'm sorry, we're going to have to call a stop. A great discussion. Thank you.

ABSTRACTS & BIOGRAPHIES

DESPOILING THE IDEAL

Eva Stenram is a London-based visual artist who sees photography as a medium of inconstancy and transformation. Incorporating digitally-manipulated photographs, found photographs and images from the Internet, her work comments on our complex relationship with the photographic image, our relationship with surveillance culture and our relationship with privacy.

Since graduating from the Royal College of Art in 2003, Stenram has exhibited internationally, including shows at the V&A Museum (UK), Seoul Museum of Art (South Korea), Bhau Daji Lad Mumbai City Museum (India) and Zendai Museum of Modern Art (China). In 2012, she was nominated for the Les Rencontres d'Arles Discovery Award.

ON PERFECTION AND AFFIRMATION IN STREET PHOTOGRAPHY

Mark Durden considers the continued vitality of the street photography tradition, looking at the differing ways in which photographers have responded to Henri Cartier-Bresson's 'Decisive Moment'. The lyrical and life-affirmative aspect of the tradition is explored through a range of examples, from Garry Winogrand and Joel Meyerowitz to such contemporaries as Tom Wood.

Durden is Professor of Photography at University of Wales, Newport, UK. He has published extensively on contemporary art and photography. His books include *Face On: Photography as Social Exchange* (co-edited with Craig Richardson, 2002); *Dorothea Lange* (Phaidon, 2006); and (with David Campbell) *Variable Capital: Art and Consumer Culture* (2007). Durden is also an artist, and as part of the artist's group Common Culture, has exhibited regularly, both in the UK and worldwide.

LEADING PLATO INTO THE DARKROOM

Even though Plato's philosophy predates photography by over two millennia, there are at least four correspondences between it and photography, especially photography as something which invites or demands perfection: (1) perfection lies at the heart of Plato's metaphysics; (2) his philosophy is organized by images of sunlight and dark chambers; (3) according to his metaphysics, in order for the good life to prevail, visual representation must be banned; and (4) he also suggests that technology can assist human being in pursuit of the good life. Ultimately, his philosophy is a metaphysics of perfection inclined against the value of photography. However, it also offers concepts and claims that can be worked with and challenged respectively to arrive at a positive evaluation of the ontological value of photography, by which I mean the value of photography as a technological practice which can upset the stable distinctions of reality. I explain how Plato's concept of *technē* leads to a splitting of photography into at least four different photographies. This though is a prelude to photography's response. I argue that these four photographies are strongly intersecting and, as such, are evidence of photography's capacity to challenge Plato's metaphysics. With support from Heidegger's philosophy of technology, I show that the intersecting photographies lead to a concept of photography which rejects perfection in favour of seeing what is possible.

Clive Cazeaux is Professor of Aesthetics at Cardiff Metropolitan University. His research interests are the philosophies of metaphor, visual thinking, visual arts research, and art-science collaboration. He is the author of *Metaphor and Continental Philosophy: From Kant to Derrida* (Routledge, 2007) and the editor of *The Continental Aesthetics Reader* (Routledge, 2011). His recent articles have deconstructed and reconstructed artists with Ph.D.s, considered sensation as participation in visual art, and explored the notion of living metaphor.

FAILURE AND PERFECTION

FILM WORKS BY JULIAN ROSEFELDT

Julian Rosefeldt presents a series of production stills from his 'Trilogy of Failure': *The Soundmaker* ('Trilogy of Failure' / Part I), *Stunned Man* ('Trilogy of Failure' / Part II), and *The Perfectionist* ('Trilogy of Failure' / Part III).

Rosefeldt studied architecture in Munich and Barcelona. He has lived and worked in Berlin since 1999. He has participated in numerous group exhibitions, most recently: 'Video-Holes: I do not know what it is I am', Manege, Moscow, 2012; 'Montevideo Biennial', Uruguay, 2012; 'Beyond Time. International Video Art Today', Kulturhuset Stockholm, 2012; 'Gesamtkunstwerk: New Art from Germany', Saatchi Gallery, London, 2011; 'Star Voyager', ACMI Australian Centre for the Moving Image, 2011; 'The Order of Things', MuKHA – Museum of Contemporary Art, Antwerp, 2008; and 'The Cinema Effect – Illusion, Reality and the Moving Image. Part II: Realism', Smithsonian Institution – Hirshhorn Museum and Sculpture Garden, Washington, DC, 2008.

Solo exhibitions include: Young Projects, Los Angeles, 2012; Taipei Fine Arts Museum, 2012; Bayerische Akademie der Schönen Künste, Munich, 2012; Kunsthalle Wien project space, Karlsplatz, Vienna, 2012; Dirimart Garibaldi, Istanbul, 2012; ACMI Australian Centre for the Moving Image, 2011; DA2 Domus Artium Salamanca, 2010; British Film Institute, London, 2010; Berlinische Galerie Berlin, 2010; Kunstmuseum Bonn, 2009; Galería Helga de Alvear, Madrid, 2008; BALTIC Centre for Contemporary Art, Gateshead, 2004; KW Institute for Contemporary Art Berlin, 2004; Hamburger Bahnhof – Museum für Gegenwart Berlin, 2002; ZKM Karlsruhe, 1999; and Kunstsammlung NRW, Düsseldorf, 1998. He has exhibited his work several times at Arndt & Partner Berlin, and at Max Wigram Gallery, London.

CLIVE CAZEAUX AND JULIAN ROSEFELDT

DISCUSSION, CHAIRED BY LIAM DEVLIN

Liam Devlin is a writer and visiting lecturer at Goldsmiths, University of London, and the University of Wales, Newport. His research explores the use of documentary imagery in relation to art practices that explicitly operate in social and political realms, and he is interested in how antagonistic socially-engaged art practices are a vital force in democratic society. He is currently completing a Ph.D. at the University of Wales Newport, entitled 'Creating Kurdistan: The role of photography as discursive documents'. The thesis uses Susan Meiselas' ongoing project on Kurdistan as a case study to frame the discussion between politics, aesthetics and the documentary image.

THE EFFORT OF PERFECTION

PERFORMING ADOLESCENCE

Focusing on photographs of girls by contemporary artists such as Rineke Dijkstra and Katy Grannan, **Catherine Grant** considers how their images play with stereotypes of perfected femininity. She explores how these photographic portraits reveal the effort of performing an idea of perfection, with the figure of the adolescent focusing attention on this process; and the tension between the idea of perfection and the performance captured by the camera that characterizes the images and gestures of girlhood in contemporary photography.

Grant is a lecturer in the Visual Cultures Department at Goldsmiths, University of London. Her recent publications include the edited collections *Girls! Girls! Girls! in contemporary art* (Intellect, 2011) and *Creative Writing and Art History* (Wiley-Blackwell, 2012). She has published on a number of artists who photograph girls, including Anna Gaskell, Collier Schorr, Hellen van Meene and Sarah Jones.

OTHER SPACES

NEW WORKS WITH ELITE GYMNASTS

Gymnastics has a long social and political history, and one often entwined with an idea of aesthetic perfection. **Jo Longhurst** presents a new body of work, which explores the physical and emotional experiences of elite gymnasts through photography, video, performance and installation. Inspired by Plato's perfect solids and Liubov Popova and Aleksandr Rodchenko's revolutionary experiments with aesthetic forms, she works with a body of original photographic source material – sketches and studies made as visiting artist at Heathrow Gymnastic Club, and the World Artistic Gymnastics Championships – to create hybrid works, which reference earlier attempts to define and create perfect worlds.

Longhurst is best known for *The Refusal* – a study of perfect body form, human/animal relations and the British Whippet. She graduated from the Royal College of Art in 2008, and was Leverhulme Fellow at the University of Wales, Newport between 2008–12. *Other Spaces* was a solo exhibition at Mostyn, Llandudno, 2012, and Ffotogallery, Penarth, 2012–13. Selected works from this project were also exhibited at the Art Gallery of Ontario, Toronto, where Longhurst was awarded the Grange Prize for Contemporary Photography 2012. Other exhibitions include: 'The Worldly House', dOCUMENTA (13),

Kassel, 2012; 'Suspension', ICIA, Bath, 2012; 'Photography in Britain since 2000', Krakow, 2010; 'Cocker Spaniel and Other Tools for International Understanding', Kunsthalle zu Kiel and Ursula Blickle Foundation, 2009/10; 'Becoming Animal, Becoming Human', New Society for Visual Arts, Berlin, 2009; 'New Works: Pavilion Commissions', National Media Museum, Bradford, 2008/9; 'Bloomberg New Contemporaries', Liverpool Biennial of Contemporary Art and A Foundation, London, 2008/9; and 'The Refusal', Museum Folkwang, Essen, 2008.

A PERFECT MYTH

RAY MÜLLER, DIRECTOR OF THE WONDERFUL HORRIBLE LIFE OF LENI RIEFENSTAHL, IN CONVERSATION WITH CERI HIGGINS

German film-maker, writer and director **Ray Müller**'s three-hour portrait of the controversial film-maker, made in 1993 when Riefenstahl was in her nineties, presents a riveting and encyclopaedic biography of an extraordinary woman. But it also poses heavy questions. Can art ever be isolated from its political context? Müller grapples with the central controversy of Riefenstahl's career: was she a 'pure' film-maker whose political naiveté allowed her stunning visions to be harnessed by Hitler, or was she the key myth-maker of the Nazi propaganda machine? In this biography, Riefenstahl masterfully dissects her own *Triumph of the Will*, a chillingly brilliant work of demagoguery which she helped design and stage as well as film, and the poetic, technically breathtaking documentary *Olympia*, a record of the 1936 Berlin Olympics. Müller's dialectical approach allows him to expose many half-truths (and a few outright lies) by offering contrary evidence.

Müller agreed to take on this project after eighteen film-makers declined, concerned about being associated with the 'Nazi director'. The resulting Emmy-award-winning documentary received numerous international awards, and in 1999 was listed among the best documentaries of the century.

Ceri Higgins interviewed Ray Müller about his experience of working with Leni Riefenstahl – Hitler's infamous propagandist and the ultimate perfectionist.

Higgins is a film-maker and academic. Over the past 25 years she has worked for the BBC, Channel 4 and ITV in the UK, and as a production executive for Televisa in Mexico and the USA. She is currently developing independent projects and is a senior lecturer in screen-based media at the Bournemouth University Media School.

ERNST JÜNGER AND POST-HUMAN PERFECTION

David Evans introduces and assesses a rare but influential photo book from the early 1930s called *The Transformed World* by German writer Ernst Jünger. Deftly editing agency photographs and his own captions, Jünger describes and celebrates the post-human world supposedly emerging from the First World War. The book is of significance because Jünger is often cited as a major inspiration for the reactionary modernism that became a distinctive current of National Socialism, and which was manifest in the publicity for the 1936 Olympics in Berlin.

Evans is a senior lecturer in the history and theory of photography at The Arts University, Bournemouth, England. Recent edited publications include: *Appropriation* (Whitechapel Gallery and MIT Press, 2009); *Moholy-Nagy: 60 Fotos* (Errata Editions, 2010); *Critical Dictionary* (Black Dog Publishing, 2011); and *The Art of Walking: A Field Guide* (Black Dog Publishing, 2012).

SEEING THROUGH

Designed and built between 1946 and 1951 by German born architect Mies van der Rohe, the Farnsworth House is often described as 'exquisitely simple and beautiful'. It is commonly considered, in the words of the architect Peter Blake, 'as an abstract statement about structure, skin, and space [that] was meant to be, and succeeded in being, a clear and somewhat abstract expression of an architectural ideal – the ultimate in skin-and-bones architecture.' This small steel and glass house was built as a weekend retreat, on the outskirts of Chicago, for Edith Farnsworth, a single, professional woman. The issues addressed in this paper can be expressed in the form of a question posed to the house itself: 'What body does this house think I have?'

Francette Pacteau is research tutor in the photography department at the Royal College of Art, London. She is the author of *The Symptom of Beauty* (Reaktion Books and Harvard University Press, 1994).

BOUNDARY LINES

Leslie Dick presents a text and image work that explores the maternal idealization of the body of the child, interrogating that structure through a personal examination of the 'ideal' body and its relationship to illness. Incorporating a short video piece by her daughter, Audrey Wollen, the text outlines some of the pleasures, risks, and disappointments of the maternal position, as they unfold in the context of a private catastrophe.

Dick is the author of two novels, *Without Falling* (1987) and *Kicking* (1992), and a collection of short stories, *The Skull of Charlotte Corday and Other Stories* (1995). She has taught in the Art Program at CalArts in Los Angeles since 1992. Her writing has appeared in numerous magazines, art catalogues, and anthologies. She wrote on photography in *Real Allegories: Olivier Richon* (2006), and she writes regularly for *X-TRA*, a quarterly journal of contemporary art, whose editorial board she joined in 2011. She is currently Visiting Critic in Sculpture at Yale University.

PERFECTING DESIRE
RECONCILING MEMORY

Jonathan Whitehall is an artist who reflects upon desire and temporality, working across a range of media, including video and installation. In Whitehall's practice, ideas of perfection manifest themselves thematically in the desire to transcend boundaries or overcome separation, and the narratives of many of his works evoke a love affair or the search for an idealized relationship. Whitehall's contribution addresses his work's relation to ideas of perfection and how, in an attempt to preserve a notion of 'perfect love' or 'perfect desire' – something which can perhaps only exist in fantasy – memory is itself 'perfected'.

Whitehall completed his Ph.D. at the Royal College of Art in 2006, and has exhibited internationally. He currently teaches at the Sir John Cass School of Art, London Metropolitan University.

A PERFECT STRIKE
DOUBLE STANDARDS AND ATTACKS ON PERFECTION

Michal Heiman performs various 'attacks on linking' (Bion, 1959), confronting questions such as responsibility, accountability, double standards and abandonment, which she argues are inherent in photography, and in both the apparatus of the museum and that of psychology.

Heiman is an Israeli multidisciplinary artist, curator, theoretician, creator of the Michal Heiman Tests (MHTs), and the first winner of the Shpilman International Prize for Excellence in Photography, awarded jointly by the Shpilman Institute for Photography and the Israel Museum. Heiman teaches at the Bezalel Academy of Art and Design in Jerusalem, and the Tel Aviv University Faculty of Arts, and the Sackler Faculty of Medicine, Psychotherapy Program. For almost three decades she has been developing a new discipline that inhabits a field between art and therapy, photography and diagnosis, and theory and praxis. This new discipline makes possible novel acts such as a new approach to reading images: a shared reading of photographs and films conducted jointly by examiners (acting on her behalf) and viewers in public and muséal spaces in the Michal Heiman Tests (MHTs). Among her notable works are photographic installations such as *Photographer Unknown, Do-Mino, Attacks on Linking* (Bion, 1959), *Thirdly*, a lecture/film on British psychoanalyst Wilfred Bion, and video works based on case studies by psychoanalysts Sigmund Freud and W.D. Winnicott.

THE PERFECT STUDENT

Oriana Fox embraces feminist theory, psychoanalysis, self-help books and female desire as she struggles to be the perfect student. In *Our Bodies, Ourselves* she plays all four characters of the popular TV show *Sex and the City*, exchanging contemporary dress and interior design for that of the 1970s. The film begins with her protagonist sewing a Judy Chicago-esque vaginal quilt and hoping that her new boyfriend will call. The soundtrack, which is lip-synched, provides the continuity from which the juxtaposition of stereotypes from past and present are seen and understood.

Fox is an American artist based in London. After graduating with an MA in Fine Art from Goldsmiths, she has shown her work in galleries, festivals and art fairs worldwide, including the 'Liverpool Biennial', Tate Modern, Kunsthalle Wien, 'Dashanzi Festival' in Beijing, Solyanka State Gallery in Moscow and 'Photo Miami'. Currently she is pursuing an MPhil/Ph.D. in the visual cultures department at Goldsmiths, and teaches art at London Metropolitan University. Her research and art explore how to be a happy woman, looking to the self-help industry, pop psychology and the self-representation of feminist artists for ideals and norms to aspire to and/or defy.

ZIDANE: A 21ST CENTURY PORTRAIT, A FILM BY DOUGLAS GORDON AND PHILIPPE PARRENO

Seventeen cameras follow Zinedine Zidane, widely regarded as one of the greatest football players of all time, through the course of a Villareal vs. Real Madrid match. They follow the player, not the match, in an intimate portrait of the 'total footballer'.

Dan Hill is a designer and urbanist. Throughout a career focused on integrating design, technology, cities and people, Hill has been responsible for shaping many innovative, popular and critically-acclaimed services, spaces and strategies. He works for Sitra, the Finnish Innovation Fund, in their Strategic Design Unit in Helsinki, exploring how design might enable positive systemic change throughout society. Prior to Sitra, Dan was an associate at Arup, Web & Broadcast Director for Monocle, and Head of Interactive Technology & Design for the BBC.

Hill writes the well-known blog cityofsound.com, as well as being Interaction Design Editor for Domus magazine. His design work has featured in the AAA exhibition 'Remodelling Architecture: Architectural Places – Digital Spaces', Sydney, 2009; and 'Habitar: Bending the urban frame', Laboral, Gijon, 2010. His essays feature in *Sentient City: Ubiquitous Computing, Architecture, and the Future of Urban Space*, ed. Mark Shepard (Architectural League and MIT Press, 2011); *Best of Technology Writing 2009*, ed. Steven Berlin Johnson (Yale University Press, 2010); and *Actions: Playing, Gardening, Recycling and Walking*, ed. Mirko Zardini (Canadian Centre for Architecture, 2008).

EREWHON

Erewhon takes its name from the title of Samuel Butler's satirical novel of a young British man who goes to New Zealand to build a new life on the isolated continent – a classic colonial experience. **Jane and Louise Wilson** encounter the vast landscape, looking particularly at two sites in the South Island: the once functioning mining town of Denniston on the West Coast, and the recently vacated sanatorium of Queen Mary's hospital in Hammer on the East Coast. These expansive exterior spaces, coupled with the interiors of neglected hospital buildings dating from 1916, emphasize the physical and emotional seclusion of a particular time in New Zealand's history. After the First World War, the country suffered huge losses of its young male population. Their devastation, and a need to colonize a relatively new country, prompted a discreet government-sanctioned approach to implementing early eugenics policies. This resulted in a proliferation of state-run sanatoriums and asylums, where recovery and prevention were instilled on willing and unwilling patients. The level of commitment to the idea that every person should be physically fit became a national preoccupation.

Jane and Louise Wilson were born in Newcastle and studied respectively at Newcastle Polytechnic and Duncan of Jordanstone College of Art and Design, Dundee. They began working together in 1989, and the following year undertook an MA in Fine Art at Goldsmiths College, London. Their work utilizes video projections, photographs taken during the filming process, and three-dimensional sculptures. Underlying their work is an interest in issues of power, surveillance and paranoia. They have exhibited at major galleries internationally, and were nominated for the Turner Prize in 1999.

DECONSTRUCTING GENDER IDENTITY AND NON-PERFECTION IN THE PHOTOGRAPHS OF YURIE NAGASHIMA

This paper investigates the work of the Japanese photographer Yurie Nagashima in relation to a deconstruction of gender identity and notions of non-perfection. With reference to perfection in the context of Japanese culture, the paper investigates whether Nagashima's work can be regarded as a visual and conceptual antithesis to the work of a previous generation of photographers.

Marco Bohr is a photographer, academic and writer on visual culture, based at Loughborough University. His Ph.D. thesis, awarded by the University of Westminster in 2011, investigates the work of a new generation of female photographers emerging in Japan during the 1990s. While his main research lies in the histories, theories and practices of photography, Bohr's interests extend to cinema in periods of ideological shifts, the relationship between photography and cinema, and the globalization of photography via the Internet. Bohr has contributed to a number of edited volumes such as: *The Contemporary Visual Studies Reader* (Routledge); *Directory of World Cinema: Japan Vol. 2* (Intellect); and the series *World Film Locations* (Intellect). He has also contributed to the *Dandelion Journal* and the exhibition catalogue for 'Modernity Stripped Bare' held at the University of Maryland. Bohr uses a blog as a platform for emerging research interests, which can be found at visualcultureblog.com.

ACKNOWLEDGEMENTS

The 'On Perfection' symposium was curated by Jo Longhurst in collaboration with the European Centre for Photographic Research (eCPR), University of Wales, Newport, Whitechapel Gallery and The Photographers' Gallery, London. It would not have been realized without the generous support of the eCPR, Leverhulme Trust, Whitechapel Gallery, The Photographers' Gallery, Arts Council England and Anna Lena Films.

Jo Longhurst would like to thank the participating artists and writers for their commitment to this project: Marco Bohr, Clive Caseaux, Charlotte Cotton, Liam Devlin, Leslie Dick, Mark Durden, David Evans, Oriana Fox, Douglas Gordon, Catherine Grant, Michal Heiman, Ceri Higgins, Dan Hill, Sarah James, Ray Müller, Francette Pacteau, Philippe Parreno, Aaron Schuman, Eva Stenram, Jonathan Whitehall, and Jane and Louise Wilson.

She would also like to thank: Alfredo Cramerotti, Bethan Ball, Holly Rose, Stephanie Sarlos and the team at Intellect Books; Richard Johnson, Nicky Sim and Sofia Victorino at Whitechapel Gallery; and Robert Hiscox, Steve Langan and Whitney Hintz of Hiscox, whose generous and enthusiastic support has allowed us to produce this book as a lasting record of the event.

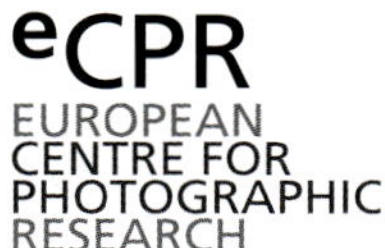

The Photographers' Gallery

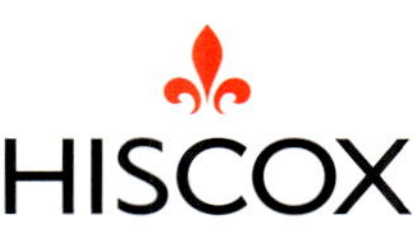

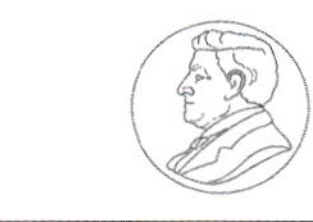

The Leverhulme Trust

Whitechapel Gallery

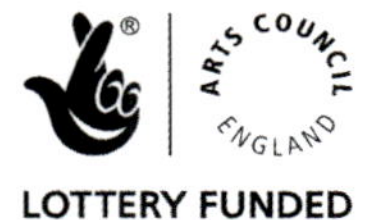